A CLOWN IS FUNNY IN THE CIRCUS RING, BUT WHAT WOULD BE THE NORMAL REACTION TO OPENING A DOOR AT MIDNIGHT AND FINDING THE SAME CLOWN STANDING THERE IN THE MOONLIGHT?
LON CHANEY

DEVIL'S CARNIVAL

THE GAFF, THE BALLYHOO, THE MIDWAY, THE FREAK SHOW, PICKLED PUNKS, LINGERING GHOSTS AND THE SECRET HISTORY OF AMERICAN CIRCUSES AND SIDESHOWS

TROY TAYLOR

AN AMERICAN HAUNTINGS INK BOOK

DEVIL'S CARNIVAL

THE GAFF, THE BALLYHOO, THE MIDWAY, THE FREAK SHOW, PICKLED PUNKS, LINGERING GHOSTS, & THE SECRET HISTORY OF AMERICAN CIRCUSES AND SIDESHOWS

© Copyright 2024 by Troy Taylor

All Rights Reserved.
ISBN: 978-1-958589-20-5
First Edition

Published by American Hauntings Ink
American Oddities Museum
301 East Broadway - Alton IL - 62002
www.americanhauntingsink.com

Publisher's Note:
No part of this publication may be reproduced, distributed, or transmitted In any form or by any means, including photocopying, recording, or other electronic or mechanical methods, without the prior written consent of the publisher, except in case of brief quotations embodied in critical reviews or other noncommercial uses permitted by copyright law.

Cover Design by April Slaughter
Interior Design by Troy Taylor

Printed in the United States of America

TABLE OF CONTENTS

INTRODUCTION - PAGE 7

1. LIONS, TIGERS, AND BEARS... OH, AND ELEPHANTS - PAGE 16

2. RUNNING AWAY TO JOIN THE CIRCUS - PAGE 46

3. AMERICA'S GREATEST SHOWMAN - PAGE 58

4. THE NAME THAT CAME AFTER "BARNUM" - PAGE 102

5. THE "GREATEST SHOW" BEGINS - PAGE 113

6. THE BROTHERS FROM BARABOO - PAGE 122

7. THE GREAT CIRCUS TRAIN WRECK OF 1918 - PAGE 142

8. THE MEETING OF EMPIRES - PAGE 183

9. THE ROARING TWENTIES - PAGE 192

10. "THE LAST ONE LEFT ON THE LOT" - PAGE 203

11. HELL CAME TO HARTFORD - PAGE 226

12. WHAT REMAINS FROM THE ASHES - PAGE 268

**PART TWO: STEP RIGHT UP!
THE AMERICAN SIDESHOW - PAGE 283**

13. BEFORE THE MIDWAY - PAGE 289

14. ALIVE! ALIVE! ALIVE! - PAGE 305

15. THE REST OF THE MIDWAY - PAGE 433

CARNY GLOSSARY - PAGE 526

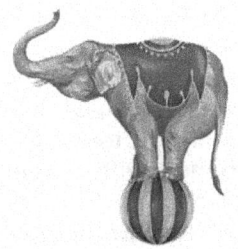

INTRODUCTION

"IT WAS LIKE YOU'D OPENED HELL'S DOORS."
UNNAMED CIRCUS ROUSTABOUT IN 1944

AMERICA WAS A DIFFERENT PLACE ON JULY 6, 1944.

Just a month before, Allied forces had landed on the beaches of Normandy in France, and people were hopeful that D-Day would be a turning point in a war that had already cost the lives of so many young men. Americans were tending their victory gardens to try and ease food shortages. Able-bodied men working on the Homefront were making about $50 a week if the job was a good one. Rent might take a week's pay, but a loaf of bread was just a dime, and gas, if you could get it, was 15 cents a gallon, and drivers could even put together a set of dishes if they saved enough coupons from filling up.

Hartford, Connecticut, was a typical American city at the time, larger than most but far from a metropolis, which is probably why the turnout was so great for the circus set up on the outskirts of town that week. But it was no ordinary circus – it was "The Greatest Show on Earth." The Ringling Bros. and Barnum & Bailey Circus had attracted about 7,000 paying customers on July 6 – mostly women and children – and they were packed inside the sawdust-strewn big top to have some fun and forget about the worries of daily life.

By the 1940s, the circus had changed with American life. In the past, only three days highlighted most people's lives – the Fourth of July, Christmas, and the day the circus came to town. Everything stopped on that day. Businesses closed, banks locked their doors, and schools were dismissed. And while the movies had caused the public's fascination with the circus to wane – and the war made everything difficult – this day was still a special event. With what seemed like everyone in town jammed side by side in a hot tent, the air thick with the smell of animals and wood shavings, it was impossible not to be excited about the circus coming to town.

The show that day opened with a spectacular parade around the three big rings – bespangled performers and exotic animals like majestic elephants, dancing bears, prancing horses, lumbering hippos, lions, tigers, and panthers in cages, and the steam-driven calliope that hooted and whistled like no other music-making contraption on earth. They were, of course, followed by a troupe of clowns that brought gales of laughter to the children and adults in the seats.

Because of a weather forecast that predicted thunderstorms, the circus managers, Fred Bradna and George Smith, quietly decided to shorten the program. As soon as the parade ended, the famed Wallenda high-wire performers started their act two slots ahead of schedule. There was no net to protect them from the circus floor. Instead, they performed above the runway cage through which Alfred Court's big cat menagerie – 40 lions, 30 tigers, 30 leopards, and two dozen bears – would soon travel from their cages outside the tent to the center ring.

The Wallendas had headlined the circus since John Ringling had seen them perform in Havana in 1927. By then, Ringling had been in business for nearly a half-century, and while he was always on the lookout for something new and exciting, he was not a man who was easily impressed. When he saw Karl Wallenda mount a chair balanced on a bar that spanned the shoulders of two men on bicycles riding across a thin wire 50 feet off the ground, only to have a young girl spring onto his shoulders to complete a three-level, four-person rolling pyramid, John had signed them on the spot.

The Wallendas were set to debut at Madison Square Garden in 1928 when roustabouts reported that the safety net had somehow been lost in shipping and the act would have to be canceled. The Wallendas refused. The show must go on, of course. They went on without a net and received a standing ovation that lasted for 15 minutes. They have performed without a net ever since.

It was during this dazzling performance that the fire began. Later, it was speculated that someone had dropped a cigarette into the sawdust spread over the ground. As it smoldered, the wood shavings caught, glowing orange and unseen, and slowly spread to the walls of the canvas tent.

Regrettably, the tent that had been raised that day by a crew reduced from its normal number due to the war was not the new flame-resistant model, which had turned out to leak badly during its first use. This was the old big top, pressed back into service – the one that was coated with paraffin wax dissolved in gasoline. This one, the old hands knew, never leaked.

Today, using a tent like that seems unimaginable, but in its 73-year history, no patron has ever died during a performance at John Ringling's Circus.

A photographer named Dick Miller had just finished taking pictures of clowns disappearing down the chute from Clown Alley when he turned and saw the flames sweeping up the tent walls. "Fire!" he cried, and scores of others soon echoed his warning.

Fanned by a breeze from the storm coming in from the west, the flames advanced at dizzying speed. As the Wallendas were sliding down lines not yet burning toward the chaos on the ground, ushers ran into the tent with water buckets to fight the fire. It was too late by then. As soon as the three men neared the flames, the intense heat caused their hair and clothing to smolder. They retreated, using the water in the buckets to douse themselves.

From outside, spectators saw a great burning glow push against the top of the tent with great speed before it finally erupted into flames. They could hear the screams of the audience inside and the roaring cacophony of the great cats trapped in their cages.

Inside, roaring sheets of flame rained down on the audience, who clambered and tumbled from the bleachers. The luckier ones would escape through the gaps in the bleachers to safety as the unlucky fought helplessly as the heavy canvas of the tent fell on top of them and burned them alive.

Others ran away from the advancing flames in a frenzy and found themselves cut off by the animal runway, which cut across the arena. Before they could turn back, they were trapped, then crushed and trampled by the hundreds who stampeded behind them.

One woman managed to drag herself out from under the bottom of the tent, her face blackened, and her clothing charred. She jerked to her feet and began running toward the entrance of the flaming tent before a policeman grabbed her. She thrashed in his grasp, shouting, "My God! My God! My kid's in there!"

Throughout this cataclysmic nightmare, the circus band, led by organist Pete Heaton, at the east end of the big top, blasted "Stars and Stripes Forever" – the traditional circus signal for disaster – right up to the moment that the main poles toppled over and the last remnants of the tent roof collapsed.

And then, as suddenly as it had begun, it was over. The entire big top was gone, the bleachers were reduced to ash, and the dead and dying were everywhere.

The survivors stared in disbelief at the ruins around them. Bodies were piled four and five deep – at least a dozen children were pulled from under the animal chute – and the animals were still wildly wailing and screeching. It seemed impossible that it happened, but it did.

Hell had come to Hartford, Connecticut – and it would leave lingering ghosts behind.

And that should not be a surprise. The worst circus fire in American history had started and ended in less than 15 minutes and claimed dozens of lives.

There seemed to be no question that this was the end of the Ringling Brothers empire, too – and likely the end of the American circus itself.

It seemed that would be the case, but it wasn't. Not only would the circus continue for another handful of decades, but the Ringling show wouldn't stop using the big top tent for another dozen years.

But the Hartford fire would change the circus, much like the Great Depression had done years before. It wouldn't die, but it would soon be struggling on life support as the movies, television, and cultural changes would put a stranglehold on the old and outdated concept of the American circus.

Eventually, the world would win, and the circus, as we'd once known it, was gone. The last Ringling show was in 2017, and the "Greatest Show on Earth" was no more – or would at least never be what it once was.

These days, a few small circuses still survive, a shadow of what they once were. Carnivals still travel from town to town in the summertime, bringing rides, games, and fried food to county fairs and local celebrations. There are even a few "oddities" shows out there, but like today's carnivals, they certainly aren't what they were in days gone by.

Those days are gone – but they're not forgotten.

They left their history, their legends, and even their ghosts behind.

I'VE BEEN WORKING ON THIS BOOK FOR MOST OF MY LIFE.

I have always been passionate about the circus, carnivals, sideshows, ballyhoos, baby shows, grind shows, illusions, mitt camps, and walk-throughs. I blame it on my childhood. I had family in the carnival business for years, so I was around to experience the waning days of the sideshows before the changing tastes of the American public finally killed them.

During what became the heyday of the carnival sideshows – the first half of the twentieth century – performers were usually people with physical abnormalities that made them unusual – "freaks," they were called. Many of them chose to put themselves on display, and most of the performers were enterprising, ingenious people who often made a very good living in the only way they could during the era in which they lived. To the close community of sideshow performers, it was the rest of us – the "rubes" and "marks" – who came to gawk at them, who were the real "freaks."

THE AUTHOR AROUND THE TIME WHEN HE WAS ABLE TO EXPERIENCE SOME OF THE LAST OF THE SIDESHOWS. THIS WAS TAKEN IN THE DESERT, WHERE HE WAS PROBABLY LOOKING FOR A JACKALOPE – WHICH HE STILL INSISTS ARE TOTALLY REAL.

If any of my uncles were looking for me, I could usually be found around the sideshow. I loved the two-headed cows, the five-legged calves, the sheep with three eyes, and, of course, the more exotic stuff like "the smallest woman in the world" (who wasn't), the "headless girl" (an illusion created with a mirror), the beautiful girl who turned into an ape "before your very eyes," the "spider girl," "the mermaid," and even the "missing link" preserved in ice.

Those were the best summers of my life, and being around the sideshows inspired my love for their history – a love clinched by seeing my first "pickled punk," as the carnies cheerfully called them.

A "pickled punk" is a term for a human fetus preserved in a jar of formaldehyde. It's a longtime staple of the sideshows, and most of those displayed had some anatomical abnormality like conjoined twins or enlarged heads, but the deformities wildly varied. It should be noted that there were a lot of fake pickled punks out there, too.

A ROW OF SIDESHOW "PICKLED PUNKS"

Carnies called them "bouncers" because they were made from rubber or wax and tended to bounce when dropped on the floor.

Wandering through the tent like one of the rubes, I remember the talker outside promising everything inside was "Alive! Alive! Alive!"

But most of it wasn't.

There were a few little people and a handful of animals with various deformities, but the rest had clearly come from a mad taxidermist's shop – like the jackalope.

And then there was the thing in the dark corner in the back. I couldn't see much around the heavy canvas curtain, but it looked like a big shelf filled with glass jars. As I edged around the curtain, I got my first glimpse of those backlit, eerily glowing jars, each containing objects designed to give a kid nightmares for weeks.

There were babies with extra limbs, babies with two heads, an additional set of arms, bug eyes, cleft palates -- the kind of stuff that you knew existed but never actually wanted to see.

But, of course, I couldn't look away.

By the time I experienced my first pickled punk display, I was already well on my way to the life that fate had in store for me. I've spent most of my life writing and researching stories of ghosts, weird history, and true crime, but my love for American circuses, carnivals, and sideshows has always been my secret joy.

Until I finally had the chance to own my own oddities museum in 2024, I had kept that love hidden behind a heavy canvas curtain in a dark back corner of my regular job.

But if you're ready, step right up, and we'll go behind the curtain and introduce you to a history you may not know.

AND IT'S ALL ALIVE, ALIVE, ALIVE!
TROY TAYLOR
SUMMER 2024

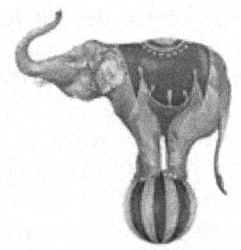

PART ONE: UNDER THE BIG TOP THE CIRCUS IN AMERICA

AMERICAN CIRCUS HISTORY BEGAN WITH A HORSE.

It wasn't a single horse, of course, but a group. In the 1700s, horse shows were the closest thing we had to what would later be considered a circus.

I realize that doesn't sound terribly exciting, but in those days, horses were still considered a luxury by many people. Horses weren't native to the New World and bringing them across the Atlantic Ocean was expensive. But given that there were no other practical ways to travel anywhere that wasn't on a river or a coast, it wasn't long before they started showing up on our shores. Horse breeding and training businesses began appearing throughout the colonies. So, by extension, anyone whose livelihood depended on travel – doctors, lawyers, judges, sheriffs, salespeople – became a horseman to some degree.

The ability to handle a horse or train one became a skill that could also entertain. Horse races, contests, and shows became wildly popular after the first organized exhibition was publicized in November 1771. More exhibitions followed, although they ran into some trouble in Boston, where officials still felt the effects of their Puritan heritage and were wary of "entertainments." Although the exhibitions didn't offer anything theatrical, all applications were denied.

By the mid-1770s, there wasn't much attention being paid to horse shows – there was that pesky Revolution to worry about – but by 1793, America was well on its way to hosting its very first circus.

The man who brought the concept to the newly formed country was John Bill Ricketts, a Scotsman cousin of George Washington. He had arrived the previous year to establish a riding academy in Philadelphia and began to realize he could attract attention to the school by offering exhibitions. On April 22, 1793, he opened the doors to his new 800-seat building on the academy grounds and presented a program described as the first true circus performance in America.

Ricketts – and his horse -- was the star attraction, along with his son, Francis, and another young man named Strobel. Also on the bill was rope walking by a Signor Spincuta, additional riding displays by Madame Spincuta, and comic riding and "miscellaneous foolery" by a Mr. McDonald, a clown. Among other things, Ricketts was said to have "rode around the ring with a boy on his shoulder in the attitude of Mercury and danced a hornpipe on the saddle while his horse galloped at full speed."

THE AMERICAN CIRCUS BEGAN AS HORSE SHOWS, WHERE TRICK RIDERS OFTEN PERFORMED.

The newspapers made certain to point out that none other than President Washington attended the show. He also allegedly attended other show performances, including the closing in July. But Ricketts didn't need his famous cousin to be successful. His show was a hit, and he went on to do shows in New York, Hartford, and even Boston. When Ricketts returned to Philadelphia, he opened a new, larger venue where he delighted audiences with additions to the program like the acrobatic "Polander Dwarf" and riding two horses at full gallop toward a stretched ribbon 12 feet high over which he would jump and land on his mounts again.

By 1797, Ricketts had added a second amphitheater on Greenwich Street in New York and was taking his troupe on occasional excursions to as far away as Albany.

But his luck didn't hold forever.

In 1799, his New York circus burned down. Worse, on December 6 of that same year, while the opera *Don Juan* was being performed on his stage in Philadelphia – and just at the point when the hero is descending into Hell to be punished for his sins – the flames being produced by the prop crew got out of control. In moments, the entire building was engulfed in flames. There were no fatalities, but the $20,000 loss forced Ricketts into bankruptcy.

And that wasn't all. The fire also destroyed the hotel next door to the theater, where Ricketts lived. Now broke and homeless, he struggled to survive. He leased some ground and advertised that his shows would become "open air, after the manner of the old amphitheaters of Rome," but he couldn't make a profit.

So, thinking maybe a circus could make some money in the West Indies, he outfitted a ship to transport himself and his horses to the islands.

JOHN BILL RICKETTS, A COUSIN OF GEORGE WASHINGTON AND OWNER OF THE FIRST AMERICAN CIRCUS.

And then things got even worse.

On the way, pirates boarded the ship, ran it aground, stole the horses, and seized all the lumber Ricketts had brought to construct his ring.

The next twist to the story was when the merchant who bought the lumber and horses from the pirates hired Ricketts as a partner to produce a circus. According to reports, Ricketts earned back his losses, but one of his riders got sick and died, and his son ended up in prison under murky circumstances.

That was the last straw for Ricketts, and he booked passage for England, hoping to find better luck there.

Believe it or not, though, there's one last twist.

The ship Ricketts was on went down in a storm and never reached England. Instead, it took the first American circus owner – and everyone else aboard – to his doom.

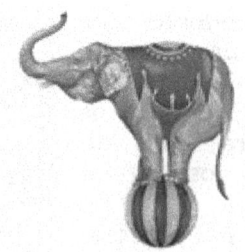

1. LIONS, TIGERS, AND BEARS... OH, AND ELEPHANTS

THE DEPARTURE OF J.B. RICKETTS FROM Philadelphia marked a milestone in America's circus history – because nothing happened for a long time after that. With Ricketts gone, no other individual seemed to want to step up and rekindle the interest that people were starting to show in the kind of spectacle he'd offered.

There were a few performances of European shows – Robertson and Franklin in New York and Pepin and Breschard's Circus in Boston –. However, it wasn't until 1812 that the American circus started to come into its own.

That year, you see, the elephant and the circus were combined for the first time. The rest, as they say, is history.

Years later, P.T. Barnum would say. "Clowns and elephants are the pegs upon which the circus is hung." The benefit of clowns can be debatable, but everyone loves elephants.

The first time an elephant was displayed in America was in 1796 when Captain Jacob Crowninshield brought a three-year-old specimen to New York aboard his ship. He had purchased it in Bengal for $450. The elephant toured the states for years. Adults paid a whopping 25 cents to view the beast, and children half that much. Handbills advertised the elephant as a creature who "in size surpasses all other terrestrial creatures" and whose "intelligence makes as near an approach to man."

He was also something of a drunk, with a fondness for "all kinds of spiritous liquors. Some days, he drank 30 bottles of port, drawing the corks with his trunk." And then, in 1812, the often-inebriated elephant joined the Italian troupe of Cayetano, Codet, Menial & Redon for a performance in New York City.

As fabled as that elephant has become in circus lore, the beast's place in the circus was truly cemented by the second elephant to come to America in 1805. This elephant's name was Old Bet, a female African elephant purchased by the sea captain brother of Hachaliah Bailey, a farmer from Stephentown in New York's Westchester County. Bailey's brother had bought Old Bet at auction in London for just $20, but Hachaliah was happy to hand over $1,000 for the animal. He quickly ferried the elephant up the Hudson to put her on display in barns and tavern yards.

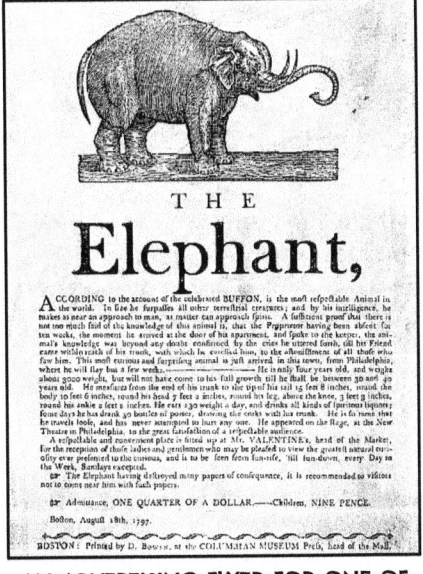

AN ADVERTISING FLYER FOR ONE OF THE FIRST ELEPHANTS ON DISPLAY IN AMERICA.

Old Bet was too big to be carted around on any kind of wagon or conveyance of the time, so she had to be led along the road from one venue to another. But Bailey cleverly traveled at night so that no one could get a free glimpse of what he was exhibiting at the next place for a fee.

Of course, some of the locals were just as clever as Bailey was, and they'd often pile stacks of brush along the roadsides and set them ablaze when Old Bet – and later, other circus menageries – so the beasts could be seen in the firelight.

In turn, circus promoters would send scouts out in advance of their processions, and if they spotted the makings of a bonfire, they'd warn the handlers of the elephants and other animals. The showmen would then blanket a horse and send him ahead, shouting "Mile up! Mile up!" a command often used by elephant trainers. When they heard this, the locals would light the bonfires, only to discover they'd been fooled when the horse approached. They'd be disappointed a short time later – after the fires had died out – to find the huge object of their curiosity passed by unseen in the darkness.

In any case, Old Bet proved to be such a sensation that by 1808, Bailey was renting the elephant out to a pair of neighbors – Andrew Brown and Benjamin Lent -- who owned an animal menagerie. They paid him $2,400 for the right to exhibit Old Bet for a year.

In 1816, Bailey partnered with a young man named Natan Howes, who made Old Bet part of a traveling animal menagerie. When Howes failed to turn over the agreed-upon split of profits, Bailey tracked him down in New Bedford, Massachusetts, and demanded his money. But Howes insisted there had been no profits. Bailey looked at the crowds flooding through the gates and told Howes that Old Bet's days with his menagerie were over.

But Howes shook his head. "I have a contract," he sniffed and walked away.

The next morning, Howes went to the barn he'd rented for the elephant, ready to move Old Bet to the next stop on the tour. But when he walked in, he found Bailey there, aiming a loaded musket at the elephant, ready to shoot her. Howes panicked. "Stop!" he cried out. "Half that elephant is mine!"

Bailey replied, "I'm aiming at my half."

This convinced Howe to offer up Bailey's share of the profits, and Old Bet's tour continued, but not for long. On a Sunday in late July 1816, Howe was taking the menagerie to Maine, and as Old Bet and her handler plodded down a narrow road, there was a rustling in the nearby brush. A series of gunshots rang out, and suddenly, Old Bet collapsed to her knees, then fell over, blood pouring from wounds to her head that turned out to be fatal.

A local man named Daniel Davis was later arrested for the crime. He told the authorities that he'd killed the beast to benefit his fellow citizens.

BAILEY HAD OLD BET'S REMAINS BURIED NEXT TO HIS ELEPHAN HOTEL, WHICH HE'D OPENED USING THE MONEY HE'D EARNED BY EXHIBITING HER FOR SO MANY YEARS. THE MONUMENT AT LEFT MARKED OLD BET'S GRAVE.

He claimed it was the same as stealing to charge hard-working farmers 25 cents to look at a giant, useless creature. Besides that, the menagerie was traveling on the Sabbath Day, which was a sin. Davis spent three days in jail before he was released.

Hachaliah Bailey had Old Bet's remains – all 7,000 pounds of her – brought back to Somers, New York, and buried next to his Elephant Hotel, which he'd built with the money he'd made by showing her all those years. The brick building still stands today as the Somers Town Hall, and a granite pillar with a statue of Old Bet on top stands on the lawn.

AS YOU'LL FIND WITHIN THESE PAGES, ELEPHANTS became a staple for American circuses. Every show wanted them; if they could afford it, they bought at least one. There is nothing that exemplifies the circus in the way an elephant does. Every red-blooded American loved them, and when promised – in person or on posters – the locals were guaranteed to fork over their hard-earned nickels and dimes to see them.

That was something that circus impresario P.T. Barnum knew well.

Despite his many successes – yes, his chapter is coming soon – he had long envied the London Zoo for its most prized possession – a giant African elephant named Jumbo. The beast had grown to nearly 12 feet by 1882, weighed nearly 13,000 pounds, and had become something of a British national treasure after carrying literally thousands of children around the zoo on its back.

African elephants, though, can be a bit on the cantankerous side, and even though Jumbo had stayed out of trouble for almost 20 years, one of Barnum's agents in Europe had gotten wind of rumors that Jumbo had been causing some trouble. With the zoo concerned about its liability, should anything happen to one of the children constantly under the elephant's large foot, the agent thought there might be a deal to be made. After some discreet inquiries, the agent sent a cable to Barnum and told him that an offer of $10,000 might snag him his own elephant. Barnum wired back immediately and said he'd gladly pay but didn't believe the zoo would sell. He was wrong. Two days later, the zoo accepted the offer, and Barnum put a man on a steamship with a check for $10,000 in hand.

Barnum was thrilled, but guess who wasn't? The people of London. They were enraged. The newspapers decried the sale, British children wrote pitiful letters to Barnum, and the Daily Telegraph sent the showman a telegram asking that he simply name his price for

which he'd cancel the contract and allow Jumbo to stay at the London Zoo.

Barnum wrote back and said that now that "Jumbo-mania" had overtaken the United States, he had no choice but to follow through with his purchase.

One of the zoo's principal stockholders filed a lawsuit to prevent the sale, but Barnum's lawyers managed to get it squashed. No pleas, letters, or threats would prevent him from bringing Jumbo to America.

But then Jumbo decided he had something to say about the situation.

When the gigantic cage constructed for his transport was wheeled into the zoo, he refused to enter it. Prodding by his long-time trainer, Matthew Scott, did no good. Jumbo just bellowed in protest and lay down. Eventually, he got up, but only to return to his old cage, leaving the humans to figure out what to do next.

The problem was eventually solved by bringing a cage to the door of Jumbo's quarters with sliding doors at either end. The cage acted as a hallway through which the elephant became accustomed to traveling whenever he wanted to go out. Then, one day, as he strolled along, the doors at both ends were closed, and Jumbo was moved to the docks to be loaded onto the ship to America. Matthew Scott came to work for Barnum and accompanied his old friend to New York.

The ship arrived on April 9, and Jumbo was immediately displayed in the menagerie of "Barnum's & London" at Madison Square Garden. Between the purchase of the elephant, the legal costs, the transportation, and the contract with Matthew Scott, Barnum had spent nearly $30,000, but the increase in receipt for just the next two weeks more than covered what he paid.

Over the next four years, Barnum continued to add to his shows, traveling about with a scaled-down version of his famous museum, a sideshow, and two menagerie tents through which audiences passed on the way into the big top. Under that vast canvas, they were seated in an immense oval surrounding his three-ring extravaganza. Separating the rings from the stands was a broad track that was used for the entry parade as well as for races of all kinds – chariot races, clowns-riding-ostrich races, races with camels, giraffes, and even ladies pulled from the crowd. This was also where the equestrian performers put on their acts. Horses were, of course, still an important part of every circus.

JUMBO, OF COURSE, ARRIVED IN THE UNITED STATES BUT IT WAS MANY YEARS BEFORE THE PEOPLE OF LONDON FORGAVE BARNUM FOR ABSCONDING WITH THEIR BELOVED ELEPHANT.

JUMBO IS SEEN HERE WITH HIS TRAINER, MATTHEW SCOTT. THE PAIR HAD A CLOSE RELATIONSHIP THAT ONCE LED TO JUMBO SAVING MATTHEW'S LIFE.

But still, even after three-and-a-half years, Jumbo the Elephant was still the biggest draw. He was the unquestioned star, and as his keeper Matthew Scott put it, "I have seen them by the thousands, when they couldn't find 50 cents to get into the show, ready to pay a quarter to just go inside and have a peep at Jumbo. 'It's all we want to see, and we won't look at anything else; we don't care about the balance, but oh! Let us see Jumbo!'"

Of course, Matthew's account might be slightly colored by the unquestioned bond between him and his elephant. Jumbo was said to bellow and stomp if Matthew was even a few minutes late for the accustomed feeding or exercise time and would tolerate the rattle and bumps of train travel only if Matthew slept in his car with him. He rarely got much chance to sleep, though. He often said that as soon as he'd doze off, he'd feel a trunk groping around in his bed, making sure he was there and was awake to talk to Jumbo and reassure him that everything was all right.

As annoying as that often was, there was one occasion when Jumbo undoubtedly made up for any trouble he caused his friend. During a stop in Ottumwa, Iowa, in 1883, after the tents were set up and the afternoon show was about to start, Matthew had just entered Jumbo's special tent when he heard a sound like a sudden rumble of thunder. He ran to pull the tent flap open only to find the rest of the show's elephants – all 30 of them – charging his way. Whatever had panicked them, they were out of control and had snapped their chains, which were now dragging behind them.

The herd rushed into the tent, but out of the mass of animals, Jumbo came to his rescue. His trunk twined around Matthew, and he lifted him up and then placed him out of harm's way between his legs. Jumbo stood firmly and stretched out his trunk, not allowing the other elephants to get past it. In just moments, Jumbo had halted the entire charge, leaving the herd to stomp and snort harmlessly until their keepers arrived to lead them away.

Tragically, though, Jumbo's days with the circus were numbered. On September 15, 1885, Barnum's circus arrived in St. Thomas, Ontario, by train. As usual, when the circus pulled into the Grand Trunk Railroad yards, their train was shunted onto a siding just south of the main line, separated by a few feet of gravel roadbed. On the main track's north side, a steep embankment dropped about six feet to the vacant field where the circus tents would be set up.

As the train came to a stop on the siding, workers began uncoupling the circus train in the middle, making a passageway so that the animals and equipment wouldn't have to be moved all the way to the ends of the train to cross over to the north side of the tracks.

Later that night, as the show was ending, 29 of the elephants completed their "military drill," and keepers herded them back to the train where they could be loaded and prepared to move on to the next town. According to the testimony that he later gave at a hearing, St. Thomas depot manager Fred R. Armes warned the animal handlers that a westbound express train was due to pass through that night and that they needed to plan to delay crossing back over the tracks with the elephants until 9:55 P.M. at the earliest. The crossing they were supposed to use would be attended by a railyard crew, and it would be close to the station, farther up the tracks from where the show tents were erected.

Whether these instructions were ever given to the elephant handlers remains a mystery. If they had been, what happened that night would have never occurred.

THE CIRCUS BIG TOP IN ST. THOMAS, ONTARIO, IN 1885

The elephants finished their work just after 8:00 P.M. that evening, and following their departure from the big top, the handlers marched the herd directly south toward the tracks. When they arrived, they dismantled the right-of-way fence and prodded the elephants up the steep embankment and across the main line to the circus cars waiting on the siding.

Meanwhile, back under the big top, the two remaining elephants – Jumbo and a comical dwarf elephant named Tom Thumb – were performing their popular closing routine. When they were finished, Jumbo's trainer, Matthew Scott, guided the pair out of the tent and toward the cross the other elephants had used.

Not far off, but unknown to Matthew, the westbound express train -- Grand Trunk Special Freight No. 151 – was approaching St. Thomas, but it would not stop there. In fact, there was a downgrade coming into St. Thomas from the east, and the train rapidly began picking up speed as it barreled closer to the railroad yards.

Engineer William Burnip was at the throttle of the express train, which was picking up speed as he neared St. Thomas. He couldn't see very far ahead on the line. The kerosene lamp mounted over the cowcatcher on the front of the engine provided little illumination – but even if it had been brighter, there would've been little he could do. An average freight train today, pulling 100 cars and traveling at 55 MPH, takes at least one mile to stop with modern air brakes. On Burnip's train, every car had its own brake wheel, which had to be turned individually by the brakeman.

By the time the engineer was sure of what he saw in front of him on the tracks – two elephants walking toward him in rural Ontario – all he could do was slam the engine into reverse and give three short blasts on the whistle, the signal for the brakeman to get to work quickly. Sparks flew as the wheels of the great locomotive fought to churn backward, and the locked wheels of the boxcars began to scream.

When Matthew, walking behind Jumbo and Tom Thumb, heard the whistle blast, he turned to a nearby flagman in alarm. "What line is that train on?" he called.

The flagman was shocked. "My God! It's on our track!" He ran toward the engine, waving his lantern with desperate fury.

Matthew stayed with the animals between the steep embankment on one side and the circus cars just a few feet away on the other and somehow managed to get the elephants turned around.

"Run, Jumbo, run!" he cried.

He tried to guide the huge animal down the steep slope to the right, but Jumbo refused to go. He kept the middle of the track as if he meant to outdistance the train rapidly approaching him from behind. He quickly outdistanced the diminutive Tom Thumb.

If they could reach the parked train beside them, Matthew thought there would be room to veer away from the tracks, but as the roaring sound of the train drew closer, he realized there was little hope. Still, that gap ahead was where the circus train had been uncoupled in the middle. If they could make it to that spot, he might be able to turn the elephants into that opening and allow the train to speed past harmlessly.

His heart filled with hope – it could be done. He knew it. "Run, Jumbo!" he screamed again. "Run!"

And then came a horrible sound behind him as the locomotive's cowcatcher rammed into Tom Thumb, breaking one of his legs and tossing him over the side of the embankment. Matthew turned back around and realized they'd reached the gap between the two sections of the circus train. He dodged off the main track and begged Jumbo to follow him.

"Jumbo! Jumbo!" he yelled, but the massive train and the huge animals were somehow alike. Jumbo's size and speed carried him two cars past the gap before he could stop.

And that was when the locomotive slammed into the huge elephant.

The impact dropped Jumbo to his knees and sent the locomotive hurtling off the tracks, the cars tipping and crashing over into the embankment. Jumbo was knocked off the tracks in the other direction and his head jammed violently under the wheel carriage of a circus car. One of his enormous tusks was driven backward into his brain, and as horrible as that was, at least it shortened his agony.

The stricken Matthew Scott, tears streaming down his face, ran to Jumbo, realizing he was still alive. He crawled under the wreckage of the car and worked his way through shattered wood and twisted metal to try and comfort his closest friend of more than 20 years. With his last breath, Jumbo wrapped his trunk around Matthew's hands, and then, while the man wept uncontrollably, the great elephant died.

THE BODY OF JUMBO THE ELEPHANT, STILL LYING NEXT TO THE RAILROAD TRACKS WHERE HE DIED, STRUCK BY AN ONCOMING TRAIN.

IT TOOK 160 MEN WITH ROPES, TIMBERS, AND PRY bars to remove Jumbo from beneath the train car and shift his corpse across the tracks to the side of the embankment.

Swarms of reporters and photographers rushed to the scene, pushing aside the curious crowds who came to gawk at the great beast's body. Worse were the souvenir hunters who mutilated the corpse, each wanting a piece of Jumbo's hide. A furious Matthew Scott chased them away, standing vigil over the body for as long as he could before eventually falling asleep while lying atop his old friend. When he awoke to find that someone had hacked away a piece of Jumbo's ear, he became enraged. Soon after, members of the St. Thomas police department arrived to mount a 24-hour watch over Jumbo's remains.

When word reached Barnum in New York about Jumbo's death, he was stunned. He sank into a chair and blurted, "The loss is tremendous." But Barnum, being who he was, quickly recovered and started looking for ways to make the best of the bad news.

Within three days, he had already contacted Harper Brothers, the well-known publisher, about a book to memorialize Jumbo. He also put his own spin on the last minutes of the famous elephant's life, writing on October 20:

It is proved beyond question that when the great noble beast first saw the deadly train approaching, he immediately seized the trick elephant Tom Thumb, threw him over the track to a place of safety, then instantly pushed Scott out of danger. It being too late to save himself, Jumbo then charged the locomotive and was crushed to death in three minutes by being pressed between a heavily loaded freight train standing still on a sidetrack and the incoming freight train.

Good grief.

And it gets better. Barnum saw to it that Jumbo's hide was removed and stuffed, and his skeleton was repaired and reassembled so that these items could be placed on display.

On a happier note, little Tom Thumb recovered from his injuries and carried on with the circus, featured as the little fellow for whom Jumbo gave his life. Barnum also acquired another elephant from the London Zoo named Alice, who, of course, he promoted as Jumbo's widowed mate. Alice was never as popular as Jumbo, but she traveled with the circus for two years, displayed next to Jumbo's stuffed body, as though she was still mourning her loss.

After Barnum's death – and until it was destroyed by fire in 1975 – Jumbo was displayed at the Barnum Museum at Tufts University, where the athletic teams eventually became known as the Jumbos. His impressive skeleton remains in the holdings of the Museum of Natural History in New York – while his legend lives on as one of the greatest circus elephants of all time.

WHILE AT TUFTS UNIVERSITY, PIECES OF JUMBO'S TUCKS WERE REMOVED FOR GOOD LUCK. HIS TAIL WAS ALSO PULLED FOR GOOD LUCK – AND YES, IT CAME OFF. WHEN THE HALL WHERE JUMBO WAS KEPT WAS GUTTED BY FIRE, HIS ASHES WERE GATHERED IN A JAR AND REMAIN AT TUFTS UNIVERSITY TO THIS DAY. STUDENTS STILL RUB THE JAR FOR – WHAT ELSE? – GOOD LUCK!

AS TRAGIC AND TERRIBLE AS JUMBO'S DEATH WAS, there's no question that it was an accident –

possibly negligent, too, but still an accident. Unfortunately, the same thing cannot be said about another famous circus elephant of the era.

Topsy's death can't be mistaken for anything other than being barbaric and cruel.

Topsy was born in Southeast Asia in 1875 and was captured soon after by elephant traders. Adam Forepaugh, the owner of the Forepaugh Circus, had the elephant smuggled into the United States, where he began advertising her as the first elephant born in this country. Forepaugh was in direct competition with P.T. Barnum's circus over who had the most elephants at the time. After Forepaugh started advertising his show, boasting the "the only baby elephant ever born on American soil" in 1877, the animal trader who'd sold Topsy to Forepaugh tipped off Barnum about the ruse. Barnum publicly exposed the hoax, and the advertising was quickly dropped.

Over the next decade, Topsy gained a reputation as a "bad" elephant – a troublesome animal that often refused to perform and even ignored and injured her handlers. Sadly, not all circus elephant trainers were of Matthew Scott's caliber.

And, frankly, not all elephants were Jumbo.

TOPSY BEGAN AS A STAR ATTRACTION FOR ADAM FOREPAUGH'S CIRCUS, BUT THAT DIDN'T LAST LONG. EVENTUALLY, HE EARNED A REPUTATION AS A "BAD ELEPHANT" AND BECAME PROBLEMATIC FOR THE CIRCUS.

In 1902, the most infamous event linked to Topsy was the killing of a spectator named James Blount at a performance of the Forepaugh & Sells Circus in Brooklyn. Accounts vary as to what happened, but it boils down to that, in my opinion, Blount probably deserved it.

On the morning of May 27, 1902, a likely inebriated Blount wandered into the menagerie tent where the elephants were tied up in a line. As he walked past, he began teasing them, offering them drinks from a bottle of whiskey. He also tossed sand in Topsy's face and then burned the tip of her trunk with a lit cigar.

Topsy was not happy. She threw Blount to the ground with her trunk and then crushed him with either her knees, foot, or some combination of the two. Ignoring what Blount had done, the newspapers outraged the public.

Stories were printed about Blount's death and printed wild accounts about Topsy's "man-killing past," claiming she'd killed as many as 12 men. She didn't. The stories repeatedly cited the claim that, during the 1900 season, she had killed two Forepaugh & Sells workers in Texas. She didn't do that either, although she did injure a handler named Mortimer Loudett in Paris, Texas – but he probably deserved it, too.

The publicity generated by the attack on Blount brought huge crowds to the circus to see the "dangerous" elephant -- and they couldn't resist trying to aggravate the creature again. In June, Topsy was being unloaded from a train in Kingston, New York, when a spectator named Louis Dondero used a sharp stick to "tickle" Topsy behind her ear. Startled, the elephant turned, seized Dondero around the waist with her trunk, lifted him into the air, and threw him onto the ground before her handler could stop her.

After this last incident, Forepaugh & Sells decided to sell her to Paul Boyton, owner of Coney Island's Sea Lion Park, and she was added to the menagerie he had on display there. Topsy's handler from Forepaugh & Sells, William "Whitey" Alt, came along with the elephant to work at the park. This, it turned out, was a mistake.

After a bad summer season in 1902 – and competition from the nearby Steeplechase Park – Boynton decided to get out of the amusement park business. That fall, he leased Sea Lion Park to Frederick Thompson and Elmer Dundy, who redeveloped the park into a much larger attraction, which he renamed Luna Park.

They used Topsy in all the publicity for the new park, photographing her moving timbers and even the fanciful airship Luna – part of the amusement ride A Trip to the Moon – from Steeplechase to the newly updated park. The media characterized this as Topsy doing "penance" for her bad behavior.

In October 1902, during the park renovations, handler Whitey Alt -- who was drunk at the time -- was trying to get Topsy to pull the amusement ride and stabbed her with a pitchfork to prod her along. A police officer was on hand and confronted Alt about his cruelty, which led to Alt freeing Topsy from her harness and allowing her to run free in the streets. Alt was arrested, and Topsy was eventually corralled. Newspapers, of course, reported the chaos, blaming the elephant for the incident.

WHEN LUNA PARK WAS UNDERGOING RENOVATIONS, THE OWNERS PUT TOPSY TO WORK, MOVING TIMBERS AND HAULING LARGE LOADS. TOPSY WASN'T HAPPY -- AND HIS DRUNK KEEPER, WHITEY ALT, MADE THINGS WORSE.

Two months later, in December, Alt was drunk again and rode Topsy away from Coney Island and tried to force her to enter the local police station. Accounts say Topsy tried to batter her way through the door and "set up a terrific trumpeting" that caused officers to take refuge in the cells. Alt was arrested again and, this time, was fired by the park's owners.

Although this was obviously an excuse based on the behavior of the trainer with the drinking problem, Luna Park owners Thompson and Dundy claimed that without Alt to handle Topsy, they could no longer handle her. They attempted to get rid of her, but no circus or zoo would take her, even when offered for free. The newspaper publicity had ruined her chances of finding a place to go.

That was when they decided to take a drastic step that would be unthinkable today. On December 13, 1902, Luna Park press agent Charles Murray released a statement to the newspapers that Topsy would be put to death in a few days by electrocution. It didn't happen right away, though, for one simple reason -- the park hadn't managed to generate enough publicity for the execution yet.

On January 1, 1903, a new plan was announced. Thompson and Dundy told the newspapers that they planned to hold a public hanging of the elephant on January 3 or 4 and would charge 25 cents per person to witness the spectacle. The hanging would be held on an island in the middle of the lagoon for the old Shoot the Chute ride. This was where they were building the centerpiece of their new park, the 200-foot Electric Tower. Charles Murray arranged media coverage, and word quickly spread.

The news reached John Peter Haines, President of the American Society for the Prevention of Cruelty to Animals, and he immediately stepped into the fray. He told Thomson and Dundy that the hanging was a "needlessly cruel means of killing Topsy" and demanded they cancel the public spectacle to which they were selling tickets. The newspapers picked up that story, too, and this time, the publicity had been turned against the park.

Thompson and Dundy discussed alternatives with Haines, going over methods used in previous attempts to euthanize elephants, like poison and execution. I'm not sure why, but there seems to be no record of Haines suggesting that Topsy should not be killed. The park owners tried to give the elephant to the ASPCA, but Haines refused.

After much negotiation, they devised a plan to not only strangle Topsy using large ropes and a steam-powered winch but to poison and electrocute her, too.

The date for Topsy's demise was set for Sunday, January 4, 1903. The press attention given to the event drew more than 1,500 spectators and 100 press photographers, as well as agents from the ASPCA, to oversee the proceedings. Thompson and Dundy allowed 100 spectators into the park, but hundreds of others slipped through the fences and paid admission to watch from balconies and rooftops of nearby buildings.

Ropes had been rigged on the Electric Tower that would be used to strangle the elephant, and details for the electrocution were handled by workers from the local power company, Edison Electric Illuminating Company of Brooklyn, under the supervision of chief electrician P.D. Sharkey. The workers spent the night of January 3 stringing power lines the nine blocks from the Coney Island electrical substation to the park. The alternating current was coming from the much larger plant in Bay Ridge.

Topsy was led from her pen into the unfinished park by Carl Goliath, an elephant veteran who had once worked for Carl Hagenbeck, but she refused to cross the bridge onto the island. She ignored Goliath's prodding as well as bribes of carrots and apples. The park owners even tried to get William Alt to help, offering him $25 to coax her to her death. Alt declined, saying he wouldn't lead Topsy across the bridge "even for $1,000."

Finally, they gave up and, as the newspapers reported, decided to "bring death to her." The steam engine, ropes, and electrical lines were re-rigged to where Topsy stood. The electricians attached copper-lined "shoes" connected to AC lines to her right forefoot and left hind foot so the charge would flow evenly through her body.

Chief electrician Sharkey ensured everyone was clear while press agent Charles Murray fed Topsy carrots laced with 460 grams of potassium cyanide. He quickly backed away, and at 2:45 P.M., Sharkey gave the signal, and an electrician on a telephone told the superintendent at the Coney Island station to close a switch. Luna Park chief electrician Hugh Thomas closed another switch at the park, and 6,600 volts tore through Topsy's body for the next 10 seconds.

As one account stated, she toppled to the ground without "a trumpet or a groan." After Topsy fell over, the steam-powered winch tightened two ropes that had been placed around her neck, cutting off her air for the next 10 minutes.

AFTER TOPSY WAS FED POISON-LACED CARROTS, HE WAS JOLTED WITH ELECTRICITY, AND THEN STRANGLED. VETERINARIANS DECIDED THAT THE ELECTRICITY HAD KILLED HIM. THE STRANGULATION WAS MERELY A BACKUP.

Finally, at 2:47 P.M., Topsy was pronounced dead.

An ASPCA official and two veterinarians employed by the park determined that the electric shock had killed Topsy. The ropes had been merely a backup.

There was one silver lining to this horrific event, in any case. During the murder, the superintendent of the Coney Island station, Joseph Johansen, became "mixed up in the apparatus" when he threw the switch sending power to the park and was nearly electrocuted. He was knocked unconscious and suffered burns on his right arm and left leg.

THOMAS EDISON.

DESPITE POPULAR OPINION, EDISON WAS NOT DIRECTLY INVOLVED IN TOPSY'S EXECUTION. ONE OF HIS FILM CREWS WAS THERE THAT DAY – AND THE ELECTRICITY CAME FROM AN EDISON PLANT – BUT EDISON HIMSELF HAD NOTHING TO DO WITH TOPY'S DEATH.

Unfortunately, though, unlike Topsy, he survived.

But that's not quite the end of the story. Among the press on the day Topsy was killed was a film crew from the Edison film company. They shot a 74-second film of Topsy's electrocution. Within a few weeks, it was added to the films available in Edison kinetoscopes in nickelodeons and amusement parlors nationwide. It could be found under the charming title of *Electrocuting an Elephant*.

Interestingly, it was an Edison film crew on hand that day – and the electricity used for the execution came from the Edison Illuminating Company. Even though Thomas Edison wasn't directly involved in the Topsy incident, he was at least partially to blame for the fact that the electrocution occurred at all. Many have called Topsy a casualty of what became known as the "War of the Currents" that was waged between Edison and his many rivals at the start of the twentieth century.

Edison is, of course, remembered today as the inventor of the first practical electric light bulb and the motion picture camera. However, many people don't remember that Edison electrocuted cats, dogs, horses, and an orangutan with alternating current (AC) electricity as part of a campaign to bolster support for his allegedly safer direct current (DC) method of electricity distribution. The electrocutions were carried out to show how dangerous the AC current promoted by his rivals was.

The "War of Currents" rivalry Edison had with George Westinghouse and Nikola Tesla, both AC proponents, began in the late 1880s when Edison launched a public campaign against alternating current. He explained that direct current was like a "river flowing peacefully to the sea," while alternating current was like a "torrent rushing violently over a precipice." Edison sent Professor Harold Brown on a tour to demonstrate the dangers of AC by electrocuting all those animals on stage in front of audiences that included schoolchildren.

However, the demonstrations backfired, and instead of scaring everyone away from AC currents, there were institutions -- like the state of New York -- that saw deadly currents as beneficial. Why hang condemned prisoners when you could electrocute them instead? So, on August 6, 1890, New York sent the first prisoner to the electric chair with help from Edison's engineers. Professor Brown obtained a Westinghouse generator and, with two surges of AC current, shocked killer William Kemmler to death.

Just over a decade later, electricity met its greatest challenge when Topsy the elephant was killed the same way. With the flip of those two switches, she became the largest victim to fall in the "War of the Currents."

THE SUCCESS ENJOYED BY HACHALIAH BAILEY with his elephant created a great demand in the region, spreading to the point that nine competing businesses – including one with Bailey as a principal – merged into one going concern that would exhibit such exotic animals as elephants, camels, bison, and antelope. The new traveling menagerie would be called the Zoological Institute, hoping to convey that a trip to the circus wasn't just a lark but an educational opportunity.

THE IDEA OF THE CIRCUS GATHERED STEAM WITH THE SUCCESS OF TRAVELING ANIMAL MENAGERIES.

The formation of the Institute created a center for circus-related activity in the region, so much so that the surrounding 20 square miles later came to be called the "Cradle of the American Circus."

The menagerie, thanks to Bailey's success with Old Bet, was the initial focus of the show. However, it wasn't long before the animal exhibition began incorporating jugglers, acrobats, and trick riders, bringing the elements of European-style circuses into the show. This finally combined the two distinct types of performances into something uniquely American and set the stage for the circus industry to truly develop in the years to come.

THE AMERICAN BIG TOP BEGAN WITH JOSHUA BROWN'S PAVILIONS, BUT IT WAS AARON TURNER WHO BEGAN USING A LARGE CANVAS TENT AND PUTTING ON HIS SHOWS BENEATH IT. OTHER SHOWMAN SOON COPIED THE IDEA.

At first, these shows were relatively modest, moving from town to town, rarely extending their stay, and when the nature of the show called for it, performing outdoors. A plank floor would be laid in a field, surrounded by a fence or canvas cover, and audiences would circle the exhibition or sometimes watch for a hillside or hastily built bleachers that were scrapped when the show moved on.

Over time, shows began carrying their own necessary equipment, and as the productions became more complex, a support industry grew around them. Animals were bred and trained, wagons and rolling cages were built, tents were sewn, movable bleachers were designed, and programs and posters were printed – all contributing to the region's thriving economy.

Though Joshua Brown was the first to stage a performance under a "pavilion," which was a wood-sided tent, in Delaware in 1825, credit is given to Aaron Turner, a former partner of Hachaliah Bailey, for adding another essential part of the American circus – the canvas tent.

To avoid the ever-present possibility of having to cancel the show because of bad weather and to create a pleasant space for audiences, animals, and performers alike, Turner designed a huge, round tent that could be hauled around in a wagon and erected for an exhibition in just a few hours. When he took his show on the road for the 1826 season, staging the performances in this marvelous new enclosure, the "big top" was born.

From that point on, the circus was free to travel in all its glory to just about any location, and there's little doubt that this innovation was responsible for the popularity of the circus across the country.

Shows like Turner's eventually mixed both animals and traditional circus acts, but it took quite a while before the two elements formed a seamless show. Generally, once a production arrived in town and the tent was set up, tickets were sold for an afternoon matinee so audiences could view the animals on display.

A separate nighttime performance – with a separate admission – featured riders, tumblers, and acrobats.

It seemed a bit clunky, but promoters used it to their advantage in conservative areas where it might be argued that although a circus performance might be outside of what was allowed on a Sunday, the exhibition of exotic animals – their pedigree traced back to Noah's Ark – was a godly enterprise and surely no one could protest against it being open on the Sabbath.

THIS ERA OF THE AMERICAN CIRCUS PREVAILED until about 1870, with a myriad of smaller shows that crisscrossed the nation, some more menagerie than circus, others the opposite. Some troupes were polished and professional, others, not so much. Many were backed financially by syndicate interests, while others were fiercely independent. The reputation of dubious business practices often associated with the circus began when the art of competition was honed to a fine and deadly point.

Among the most successful circus men of the time was George Bailey – nephew of Hachaliah Bailey – who married Aaron Turner's daughter and took over his operation. By 1858, George was in control of three separate traveling circuses and continued his success until 1880, when the rise of P.T. Barnum and James Bailey (no relation) made him a very rich man.

Bailey was also responsible for one of the many novelties and advancements during this period. He was credited with inventing a wheeled tank that was large and sturdy enough to transport a hippopotamus. Hippos were often billed as "the blood-sweating Behemoth of Holy Writ" for the bible-thumpers who came to shows, and the beasts made many men wealthy.

This was also when the famous circus archetype of the lion tamer made his debut. As early as 1833, a menagerie showman, Issac A. Van Amburgh had gone into a cage with a lion in New York City's Bowery,

even though big cage acts wouldn't become a staple in most shows until around 1910.

In 1850, Hemmings, Cooper & Whitby Circus advertised that the keeper of the lions would enter the cage at each show. Most acts remained just displays of bravery until Wilhelm Hagenbeck, a German trainer, invented the portable circular exhibition cage in 1888. Hagenbeck also invented the pedestals on which the animals sat. Karl Krone, another German menagerie and circus man, devised a tunnel-style runway that ran from the exhibition arena in the tent back to the cage wagons outside. This prevented the shows from being disrupted when the cages were dragged in and out of the tent.

Although even that was less disruptive than allowing the big cats to be brought in without a cage, right? In 1905, Dr. Ludwig Heck invented rope netting, placed over the top of the arena to keep cats from jumping out. This was undoubtedly seen as a welcome addition by audiences.

BUT IT WASN'T JUST BIG CATS AND ELEPHANTS that were thrilling audiences as the menagerie slowly became the circus.

Wilhelm Hagenbeck and his brother, Carl, became some of the most important animal exhibitors in the circus business in the 1880s. Before they arrived in America, they'd first made money exhibiting exotic people at European venues. Those earnings went into their passion for collecting and training wild animals, and Americans got their first look at the brothers' showmanship at the 1893 World's Columbian Exposition in Chicago.

The Hagenbeck's Arena and World's Museum was presented in a World's Fair building that could accommodate 40,000 daily visitors to their zoo and 6,000 seat spectators for every performance. Those shows were offered thrice daily and presented routines featuring elephants, trained pigs, Shetland ponies, lions, tigers, panthers, leopards, polar bears, sloths, and Tibetan bears.

THE MIDWAY AT THE 1893 WORLD'S FAIR IN CHICAGO BECAME IMPORTANT IN THE RISE OF THE AMERICAN CIRCUS AND ALSO WITH THE CARNIVAL MIDWAY AS AMERICA WOULD SOON COME TO KNOW IT.

From 1894 through 1903, Carl Hagenbeck and Frank Bostock – an English showman who also specialized in animal acts -- competed at Coney Island and for winter zoo locations. In 1903, Carl was averaging 8,000 visitors daily at Coney Island – about half the size of Bostock's crowd despite sensational newspaper stories about lion escapes from Bostock's show.

But in 1904, Carl took his show to St. Louis to play at the World's Fair and reported profits of $70,000. When the fair ended, he hired the Bothe Wagon Co. of Cincinnati to build 48 wagons to start a new railroad circus. When it opened in April 1905, the big top seated 7,500 people, and the show was presented in two rings, offering "15 of the most exciting and humorous acts ever performed by wild beasts."

Other circus showmen, like A.L. Barnes, quickly followed Carl's lead, and the era of the big wild animal circuses began. This is a little humorous since animals started the circus in the first place.

But those shows were nothing like these new ones.

Remember Frank Bostock, Carl Hagenbeck's fiercest competitor? Hagenbeck had trouble competing with him, even after an escaped lion story was plastered all over the newspapers – but Carl didn't know the story had been planted by Bostock's friend, Tody Hamilton, the best circus press agent in the business. Audiences didn't stay away from Bostock's show because of the lion escape – it was why they came!

(LEFT) FRANK BOSTOCK, WHO DUBBED HIMSELF THE "KING OF ANIMALS"

(RIGHT) WALLACE, BOSTOCK'S ESCAPING LION.

In October 1893, Bostock's lion, Wallace, escaped from his cage and killed a horse in a Brooklyn stable near the show. The next day, his trainer, after a long battle, got Wallace back into his cage, and East Coast residents were safe again. Their fears had been fanned by the newspaper stories – stories that claimed Wallace weighed over 900 pounds and had killed three men in England.

It turns out this was a promotion for an old trick used in the British circus, where the trainer entered the animal's cage, and the lion leaped around or over him, running past the bars on the side of the cage to frighten the audience. People flocked to the show after the newspaper stories – and kept returning when it seemed like Wallace might escape again.

The escaping lion act was copied and went into shows across the country. Various circuses still featured it into the 1950s, and it is still called a "Wallace Act" today.

Animal acts continued to bring huge success to the circus and provided a lucrative off-season show in dime museums and vaudeville theaters. The Ferari brothers – Joseph and Francis – offered Big Frank, a boxing kangaroo, and Fatima, the Hoochie-Coochie bear. In addition to Wallace, the lion, Bostock offered Rham-a-Sama, the Missing Link, and a lady animal hypnotist.

His greatest moneymaker was his "man chimp" Consul, who wore clothes and walked erect like a man. He also drank wine, smoked cigarettes, rode a bike, and was more well-mannered than most humans.

Consul was first presented in Europe in 1903 as the pampered companion of a rich Chicago pork merchant. He arrived by ship – in first-class accommodations, of course – and occupied a suite at the Paris Hotel Continental. The press had a field day with the ape, and his performances were hugely successful. After a summer season at Coney Island, Consul returned to Europe but became sick with bronchitis in Berlin. After three days of illness, he died. His body was embalmed and placed in a coffin, where he lay in state for a week.

Back in America, Bostock was already booking Consul II.

But he was not a hard-hearted man. His motto was always, "Kindness is the whip used to lead dumb animals to obey." He treated people the same way and was always free to give advice to those starting in the business. When showman George Rollins purchased an animal show, Bostock advised, "Don't fool away your money on deer, armadillos, bears, or alligators. While they're good, the public wants to see good, big animals with a mouth and teeth; those which will bellow with trainers that are not afraid to make their charges talk. If the public wanted to see a goat or sheep show, they would not have spent their money with a wild animal aggregation."

BOSTOCK'S "MAN CHIMP" CONSUL, WHO BECAME SO FAMOUS THAT HE EVEN HAD A BRAND OF CIGARETTES NAMED FOR HIM. WHEN HE DIED SUDDENLY, BOSTOCK REPLACED HIM WITH "CONSUL II"

According to his employees and other showmen, one of Bostock's traits was bravery, which came close to absolute fearlessness. He had been mauled and bitten many times over the years, mostly when rescuing trainers who worked for him.

One of the worst times he was mauled occurred when he saved the life of Gertrude Planka in Kansas City, after which Bostock spent four months in the hospital. In 1911, one of his trainers, Jack Genter – billed as Captain Jack Bonavita – lost a hand while presenting lions. The trainer was again attacked during a fundraising dinner held for Bonavita in the lion cage. True to form, Bostock came to his rescue.

Eventually, in partnership with the Ferari brothers, Bostock moved most of his shows onto the carnival midway, a different form of entertainment we'll return to later.

The two companies continued to offer animal acts, though, featuring lions who wrestled and rode horses, tigers, wolves, bears, boarhounds, and boxing kangaroos. They also added other attractions, including camel, elephant, and burro rides, a $50,000 Venetian gondola ride, Chiquita the Midget, a Streets of Cairo show that was lifted from the 1893 World's Fair, a Crystal Maze, Gypsy Village, a trip through Oriental opium dens, and several girl-oriented productions and illusion-based shows.

Bostock dropped out in 1903, and he died in England nine years later at the age of 46. The Ferari brothers operated together until 1905, then ran separate shows to the end of their careers. Francis died at the end of the 1914 season, and his wife continued the show until the decade's end. Joseph retired in 1920 to Staten Island, where the Ferari shows had their winter quarters. He made and repaired carousels, imported organs, and sold used show equipment until he died in 1953.

OTHER MIDWAY SHOWMEN LEARNED A LOT FROM the operations of Bostock and the Ferari brothers. One big lesson was that, in those early days, more publicity could be obtained with wild animal features than with any other attractions. Animals appealed to the young and old and combined fear and curiosity. One way to get free newspaper space and the wide-eyed attention of locals was to stage a wedding in the show's lion cage. The promoter would find a young couple who planned to get married and offer them money to do so in the cage with the lions, the trainer, and a brave minister – which was always the toughest part of the equation to find.

George Rollins once said that the key to a successful wild animal show was to keep it working whether there were 10 people or 1,000 people in the tent. If there was activity, the animals would respond, and their roars would attract more paying customers.

Other showmen agreed, and in fine carny fashion, they devised a way to create the sound of the big cats even if the real animals were quiet. They came up with what the carnies called a "groan box." The easiest way to make one was to get a pair of rawhide shoelaces, punch a hole in the bottom of a gallon can, tie a knot in one of the shoelaces, and shove the loose end of the shoelace through the hole and into the can. Then, they'd wet a hand and place the can under an arm. If they gripped the lace and pulled it, a deep roaring sound was produced.

Many of the Midway shows not only continued to use animals, but many of them skewed closer to a real circus than as part of a traveling carnival. Among them was the Great Patterson Show, which toured in the 1920s. It was performed under a big top and offered acts like a 12-pony drill, high-school horses, an unrideable mule, riding monkeys, three elephants, a five-lion act, plus musical groups, trapeze acts, and acrobats.

In the 1940s, famous wild animal trainers appeared with carnival animal acts, including Clyde Beaty, who spent the 1942 season with the Johnny J. Jones Shows. Beaty's show seated 2,500 people under a massive big top and featured chimpanzees Minnie and Mickey, two Bengal tigers riding on an elephant, aerial acts, and three clowns. Each show closed with Clyde himself in a battling cage act with 30 big cats.

CLYDE BEATY WAS ONE OF THE MOST FAMOUS ANIMAL TAMERS OF ALL TIME. FOR YEARS, EACH OF HIS SHOWS ENDED WITH HIM "BATTLING" AS MANY AS 30 BIG CATS.

Another well-known animal trainer who spent even more time in the midway shows was Terrell Jacobs. He'd left his home in Peru, Indiana when he was only 13 and joined the Hagenbeck-Wallace Circus. He worked the fighting lion act with the Sells-Floto Circus as an apprentice. From 1929 to 1939, Jacobs was the featured wild animal presenter for four large tent circuses, including Ringling Brothers, Barnum & Bailey. He played the San Francisco World's Fair with his animal acts and then worked independently with several other circuses.

In 1942, Patty Conklin called on him to furnish a large circus in Canada. Conklin had won a coveted contract in 1937 and was building a huge midway operation when World War II broke out, which canceled the upcoming shows. Conklin then put together a cause called the "Fair for Britain" and secured a location where Jacobs performed.

At the same time – and through 1952 – Jacobs played the annual spring circus at the Chicago Stadium. After that, he performed with

STARTING IN 1929, TERRELL JACOBS WORKED AS A LION TAMER FOR SEVERAL MAJOR CIRCUSES.

the James E. Strates Shows, and, according to *Billboard*, his show was sending locals away happy; eight out of every ten people coming through the gate were hitting the midway and attending the circus. The show boasted three working dens of lions and tigers, bears, llamas, and Baby Jean, a two-year-old elephant. She was presented in one of the rings while Jacobs worked his cage act, which featured Sheba the Lion. Trapeze and clown acts rounded out the 35-minute show, for which patrons paid a quarter for admission and an extra 20 cents if they wanted to sit down.

In 1955, Jacobs toured with Jimmy Sullivan's Finest Shows and spent the next season with the Kelly-Miller Circus. Terrell Jacobs worked one last tour in 1957 with Paul A. Miller's combined carnival and circus. He passed away later that same year.

THE WANING DAYS OF THE ANIMAL SHOWS came when some showmen decided to try offering a free circus surrounded by midway rides and joints.

One of the earliest to try this was Jay Gould. At the start of the Depression, he bought a merry-go-round and put together a combination circus and carnival. In 1938, he started taking the show on the road, doing one-night-stand engagements, such as the Jay Gould Revue and Circus. But business crashed by 1943 and closed – for a few months. A friend convinced him to try it again, and it worked this time. He operated successfully with few changes until the 1960s.

There's no question that Gould was slick. At first, he operated the show by making sure that the towns where he played guaranteed the cost of the circus part of things. He carried 1,000 chairs but soon found that many seated people couldn't see what was happening. He quickly reduced the number of chairs to only a few hundred and started renting them out for 25-cent each. If you wanted to stand, though, the show was free.

In the 1950s, Gould bought newer rides and added concessions to his operation. He started playing regular fairs, and while his show looked like a carnival, the big draw was still the free circus shows offered at 2:00 and 8:00 P.M. each day.

Paul A. Miller's Free Circus and Carnival started in 1957 and was another circus-carnival combination that offered eight major rides, eight kiddie rides, two shows, a fun house, a glass house, and 30 concessions – which makes me hungry just thinking about it. Miller booked circus acts to work on a semi-trailer stage with a ring and an animal arena on the ground in front of it.

Another profitable operation was Siebrand Brothers Carnival and Circus, which started as a "gilly carnival" in Arizona in 1916. These were shows that played in the small towns the big shows couldn't be bothered with, and they

43 | THE DEVIL'S CARNIVAL

traveled by train using baggage cars to transport their entire operation. In 1932, they switched to trucks and then, a few years later, added the circus to draw more people. It lasted until 1951.

In the 1950s, the breakup of several large truck circuses resulted in big menageries hooking up with carnivals. In 1952, Frank Bergen hired what remained of the Cole Brothers Circus – now called the Barnes Brothers Circus – for a summer tour with Bergen's World of Mirth Shows.

The biggest draw? Elephants. Even after years of rides, games, and other attractions, the circus animals still packed them in.

In 1953, Tony Diano and Ben Davenport's Diano Brothers Circus broke up mid-season, and the next year, Frank Bergen hired Diano's large menagerie – 10 elephants, a giraffe, a zebra, a rhinoceros, a hippopotamus, chimps, monkeys, and several kinds of big cats. The animal shows continued to tour with the World of Mirth Circus for the next several seasons.

Finally, in 1956, Arnold Maley and Floyd King put out two units of their King Brothers Circus on the road – but business was so bad that they abandoned equipment and animals within weeks. They were soon closed.

A couple of months later, E.J. Brady, one of the show's screwed-over investors, managed to sell some of the remaining animals to the James E. Strates Shows. Strates spent $17,00 for three elephants – Mona, Alice, and Marge – Friendly George the Hippo, a polar bear, a leopard, two lions, and a black bear.

The carnival was in Shelby, North Carolina, when the animals arrived, and Strates put them under a tent that used to house his Dancing Waters show. The elephants finished the season, moving from place to place by truck, but the next year, he purchased a railroad car for them.

The elephants were such a draw that he bought three more in February 1958 from the Pollock Brothers Circus. The animal show was a regular back-end attraction until 1969, but even after the other animals retired, the elephants were kept around for publicity. To keep them watered, fed, and cared for, a 10-cent midway grind show called "Tarzan's Elephants" featured them for several more seasons until they were eventually sold.

Because, as we all know, everybody loves the elephants.

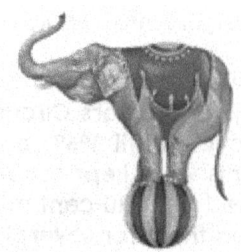

2. RUNNING AWAY TO JOIN THE CIRCUS

IN THE EARLY DAYS, THE CIRCUS WAS A WORLD separate from ordinary life. The two or three hours that audiences spent on circus grounds or under the canvas of the big top were meant to be unlike ordinary life, a time of wonder and a chance to see the impossible made real.

To actually "run away with the circus" meant leaving an ordinary life behind forever. Your past ceased to exist, and your future was wherever the wheels of the wagons or the trains would take you.

But in the very early days, many parts of what would become the essential parts of the circus were just getting started.

THE FIRST PROCESSION THAT CAN BE RIGHTLY CALLED a "circus parade" took place on May 1, 1837, when Purdy, Welch, Macomber & Company sent a group of musicians on horseback along the streets of Albany, New York, playing wind instruments. Two drummers mounted on elephants followed behind them.

This was the start of something that lasted for over a century, a form of advertising that slowly became more elaborate and attention-getting as time passed.

Horns soon gave way to bandwagons, where the emphasis was on brass instruments – lots of them. But soon, technology even changed that. In 1855 came the invention of the steam calliope, an arrangement of keyboards and whistles powered by a boiler.

A STEAM CALLIOPE USED BY THE HAGENBECK-WALLACE CIRCUS. THE CALLIOPE WOULD BECOME ESSENTIAL TO CIRCUS PARADES – A PART OF THE SHOW THAT WAS NOT TO BE MISSED.

When the pressure mounted to 120 pounds – and a key was pressed – steam was released through a valve, and a copper or brass whistle let out a screech that could be heard from a quarter mile away. Circus promoters were quick to see the value of the contraption, and it started to be used as early as 1857 to promote the Nixon & Kemp Circus, as well as others.

Thanks to their weight and how difficult they could be to use – some calliopes had 25 keys, and others had 67 – their use was limited regarding parades, but it still became an integral part of the circus experience.

The inventor, Joshua C. Stoddard, had intended it to replace church bells, but soon one had been installed on just about every paddlewheel steamboat of the day, and a stroll around a circus grounds that didn't have one playing in the background was a considered a big disappointment.

The calliope is still around today. You hear its music in popular songs and recordings playing during amusement park carousel rides. And if you have ever visited a circus – of pretty much any size – then you've heard a calliope, whether you knew it or not.

ANOTHER PART OF CIRCUS HISTORY launched in the mid-nineteenth century can be credited to a showman named Dan Rice. Born as David McLaren in New York City in 1823, he began his career in vaudeville shows as a song and danceman and a strongman billed

DAN RICE

as "The Young Hercules." In 1844, he started appearing with the Bowery Circus in Galena, Illinois, as a horseback comedian who mixed wisecracks and songs into his routine and gained a large following.

His most popular routine was as a "drunk" who wanders into the circus ring, insisting he can ride as well as anyone and demanding the chance to prove it. The performance is immortalized in a passage in Mark Twain's *Huckleberry Finn*, where Huck provides an account of the action.

When members of the circus troupe demand the "drunk" be kicked out so the show can continue, the ringmaster intervenes and suggests the troublemaker be given a chance to back up his boasting. The crowd quiets, and the drunk is helped onto a horse, which – although held steady by two circus hands – immediately starts bucking, flinging the drunk like a rag doll, but he manages to stay on.

Soon, the horse slips away from his handlers and, in Huck's words, "away he went like the very nation, round and round the ring, with that sot laying down on him and hanging to his neck, with first one leg hanging most to the ground on one side, and t'other on t'other side, and the people just crazy. It wasn't funny to me, though; I was all of a tremble to see his danger."

Before long, the drunk steadies himself and, as Huck describes, "the next minute he sprung up and dropped the bridle and stood! And the horse a-going like a house afire, too. He just stood up there, a-sailing around as easy and comfortable as if he warn't ever drunk in his life – and then he began to pull off his clothes and sling them. He shed them so thick they kind of clogged up the air, and altogether he shed seventeen suits."

Ultimately, the drunk transformed into a slim, handsome man who easily rode the horse around the ring. Then he skipped off, took a bow, and headed off to the dressing room while the crowd in the big top cheered.

That Mark Twain would take the time and trouble to describe Rice's act on the pages of what would become an American classic is proof of Rice's popularity at the time. He was making as much as $1,000 a week, which was unheard of then.

He also delighted audiences with his interactions with Lord Byron, a "learned pig" who could answer questions by grunting responses, spell out words by moving letter cards with his snout, and close the show by choosing an American flag from a dozen others and waving it about.

If you think you've never heard of Dan Rice, you'd be wrong – sort of. He's become immortalized in America's culture in an unexpected way. His favorite costume was based on the American flag. He wore a blue jacket, and his shirt and pants were striped red and white. He crowned it all off with a top hat, and with his goatee and boots, he became the unknowing model for cartoonist Thomas Nast's representation of Uncle Sam – a symbol of the United States that's still around today.

Rice's career lasted for 40 years, though he continuously bounced back and forth between success and poverty, plagued by bad business choices, poor health, a fondness for liquor, and bad luck. Later in life, he made an unsuccessful attempt to win a congressional seat in Pennsylvania and then ended his days with relatives in New Jersey. He died there, lonely and forgotten, in 1900.

DAN RICE'S FAVORITE COSTUME WAS ONE BASED ON THE AMERICAN FLAG – WHICH INFLUENCED CARTOONIST THOMAS NASH WHEN HE CREATED THE CHARACTER OF "UNCLE SAM."

IN 1859, TWO OTHER MARVELS WERE INTRODUCED to the public and became a permanent part of the circus. The most remarkable appeared on June 30 when a Frenchman who called himself Charles Blondin captured the imagination of the American public by walking a rope that stretched 1,100 feet across the chasm just downriver from Niagara Falls.

The newspapers covered this accomplishment in detail, including the *New York Daily-Tribune*, which noted, "As a mere foolhardy exploit, this feat has seldom been equaled, and as an exhibition of nerve, it stands without parallel."

The young man, whose name was Emile Gravelet, was a member of a French group of high-wire walkers who had been performing in New York since 1855, but nothing in their routines had

A STEREOSCOPE CARD OF BLONDIN'S TIGHTROPE WALK OVER NIAGARA FALLS

ever gotten the kind of attention that his tightrope walk across Niagara Falls did. The rope he walked was only three inches in diameter and was steadied by a series of lines spaced every 18 feet and anchored to spots on the opposing cliffs. His original plan was to stretch his wire across the falls, anchoring one end in the United States and the other in Canada despite the blinding spray and slippery mist there. But he was forced downstream by landowners who refused him permission because they didn't want to be "accessory to his death."

Blondin made his appearance at 4:40 P.M. before a crowd of about 4,000 who gathered on the grounds of an amusement park on the American side. He performed some introductory antics on a small rope and chatted with the crowd until about 5:15 when he stepped onto the main rope. He paused and then turned back to the crowd with a grin. "Gentlemen!" he called out in heavily accented English. "Anyone what please to cross, I carry him on my back."

When no one accepted his offer, he shrugged and started on his way, balancing on one foot at times, bouncing up and down at other times, and even lying at full length on his back.

At the midpoint -- where his weight caused the rope to sag by some 50 feet and left him an uphill climb to continue – he dropped a long cord down to the tour steamer *Maid of the Mist*, which had traveled out to a spot on the river 50 feet below his position. The ship's captain tied a bottle of wine to the cord, and Blondin hauled it up, drank the wine, tossed the bottle in the river, bowed to the crowds, and continued toward the thousands awaiting his arrival on the Canadian side.

It took him 18 minutes to traverse the falls.

After a short rest, Blondin returned to the American side, where he was greeted with cheers and the clang of a brass band. He was acclaimed as the "king of the rope" and was memorialized by a reporter for the *Tribune* when he wrote, "Thus was accomplished one of the most daring – and useless – feats that even this fast age has ever witnessed."

Blondin repeated the crossing numerous times that summer and in the following years, adding somersaults, chair balancing, and other things to his routine. He astonished luminaries like William Dean Howells – novelist and literary critic – and Edward, Prince of Wales. Howells found the whole thing so nerve-wracking that it thought the tightrope should be prohibited by law. The future king of England reportedly whispered, "Thank God it is all over," when Blondin returned to safety.

JEAN FRANCOIS GRAVELET, WHO USED THE NAME "CHARLES BLONDIN" WHEN HE PERFORMED HIS AMAZING TIGHTROPE STUNTS.

He continued to perform dazzling feats until 1896 -- less than a year before he died in London at age 74 – long after he had made tightrope walking something that occurred at every show for American circus troupes.

The second phenomenon added to the circus repertoire in 1859 came along in November when another young Frenchman, Jules Leotard, debuted an act that one reporter described as "reckless breakneck flights from trapeze to trapeze like some tropical bird swooping from branch to branch."

In the old Spanish circus, an act called "casting" existed where two acrobats hung by their legs from stationary bars and tossed a smaller acrobat back and forth between them. The smaller acrobat – called the "flier" – might do flips and turns while sailing through the air, but no one knows if Jules ever witnessed or even heard of this kind of performance – which, honestly, sounds pretty boring.

JULES LEOTARD, THE FRENCH ACROBAT WHO BROUGHT THE TRAPEZE TO THE AMERICAN CIRCUS.

Jules claimed that he'd originated his act one day while getting ready to swim at a gymnasium that his father owned in France. He was about to enter the pool, he said, when he noticed two sets of cords dangling above the water from ventilators in the roof. A picture formed in his mind – he could fix a wooden bar between each set of cords and swing from one, let go, and fly to grab the other. If he missed it, all that would happen was that he would fall into the water.

It wasn't long before Jules and his father had concocted a routine where his father swung one trapeze toward his son. Hules grabbed hold and flung himself through the air to catch a second trapeze, back, and so on. He often turned somersaults and twists as he did this in a way that resembled flight.

In place of the swimming pool, padded mattresses were spread across the stage beneath Jules in case he fell, but soon those were replaced by a net, even though an awkward tumble into a net could prove just as fatal as having no safety measures at all. It wasn't long before a "catcher" was added to the routine, and the "flying trapeze" act became another essential part of the circus.

The American circus had undergone tremendous changes in only a handful of decades. By this time, it included trapeze artists; highwire acts; animal menageries with lions, tigers, learned pigs, elephants, and more; big tops; three rings; clowns; parades; calliope music; new methods of travel; performance schedules; and clever marketing – cobbled together to create a form of entertainment like nothing Americans had ever seen before.

It was becoming what could truly be called – without any exaggeration from a pitchman – the greatest show on earth.

OF COURSE, THE CIRCUS WAS NOT THE ONLY THING that Americans were thinking about at this point in our history. Around the same time circuses were adopting trapeze acts and tightrope-walking, big things were happening, like the first oil well drilled in Titusville, Pennsylvania, in August 1859. Oil would eventually end steam engines and horse travel and change how circuses travel around the country.

On October 16, 1859, abolitionist John Brown took over a federal armory in Harper's Ferry, Virginia, hoping to begin a slave uprising in the region. The incident was quickly quashed by General Robert E. Lee – still in the U.S. Army at the time – and Brown was hanged, but it would foreshadow the horrific war that was coming.

That same year, we gained a state when Oregon joined the Union, but then we lost one the following year when South Carolina became the first state to secede after Abraham Lincoln was elected president.

Even though it seemed like the country was falling apart, there were moments worth celebrating, like the start of the Pony Express in April 1860, which carried mail between St. Joseph, Missouri, and Sacramento, California. Even better, it was replaced by telegraph lines the following year, which made communication from one side of the country much faster than the "orphans preferred" on fast horses.

The telegraph was not the only modern miracle introduced to Americans around this time. They were also getting used to elevators, sewing machines, ready-made clothing on store racks, pasteurized milk, antiseptics, and anesthesia that made dental work at least a little more bearable.

Advances in cameras, telephones, electricity, and a railroad that connected the entire nation would have to wait until after the Civil War, but the circus wouldn't use the railroads as a significant method of travel for more than a decade anyway. At this time, the shows traveled by road, which meant they moved very slowly and often at great risk to everyone involved.

An average-sized circus required at least a few dozen vehicles and many horses to move from town to town. There needed to be space for the performances, their baggage, trunks of costumes, ropes, poles, the massive canvas tent, and

CIRCUS WAGONS REQUIRED HORSES TO MOVE FROM TOWN TO TOWN ON ROADS THAT WERE OFTEN BARELY FIT FOR TRAVEL.

PAVED ROADS DID NOT EXIST IN THE MIDDLE TO LATE NINETEENTH CENTURY, SO CIRCUS WAGONS OFTEN FOUND THEMSELVES BURIED TO THE AXLES IN MUD. MANY SHOWS BECAME LOST, DELAYED, OR MISSED THEIR DATES ALTOGETHER AS THEY STRUGGLED TO GET FROM PLACE TO PLACE.

much more. They were assembled into a kind of wagon train that moved slowly along the unpaved roads which turned into impassable muck when rain started to fall. There were a few exceptions when it came to roads – like some improved turnpikes in Kentucky and the northeastern states and the 620-mile National Road that connected the Potomac and Ohio Rivers – but a network of well-marked and maintained highways was many years in the future.

After a performance ended in one town, the first vehicle sent out to the next was the "telegraph wagon," which carried a member of the production team and a local who was hired to guide the way and leave marks behind for the wagons carrying the equipment, animals, and performers to follow. At an intersection, the wagon might stop to remove a rail from a fence and lay it down to indicate which direction to go. If the company was traveling in an area where fences and wood were scarce, the guide might draw arrows on the road with flour – and, I suppose, hope it didn't rain or wasn't too windy.

It's not hard to imagine how many shows got lost on the way to engagements, took wrong turns, or became hopelessly turned around. Wagons would become stuck in the mud as deep as their axles, often so deep that the company's elephant was needed to pull them out because the horses had failed.

A circus that became lost would have no place to sleep, nothing to eat, no clean clothing, and had a very good chance of missing out on their earnings if the engagement was missed entirely.

The workmen – called roustabouts – who set up the show generally traveled on the equipment wagons, sleeping as best they could as the vehicles creaked and rocked along at just three or four miles an hour. Once they reached their destination, the drivers would nap in the wagon beds that had been emptied so the other men could raise the tents. The performers and circus workers weren't needed until closer to show time, so they may have gotten a later start, sleeping in a hotel or camp before heading out on the morning of the next show.

ROUSTABOUTS SETTING UP TENTS ON THE CIRCUS GROUNDS. THEY TRAVELED ON THE EQUIPMENT WAGONS AND USUALLY ARRIVED FIRST WHEREVER THE SHOW WAS PLAYING NEXT.

Depending on the distance that had to be covered – usually 15 miles with "big jumps" saved for Sunday, when shows were normally prohibited from playing – the wagons and members of the troupe gathered in a lot and prepared for the parade. When ready, the musicians, animal wagons, horses, and performers moved to the edge of town and began their spectacular procession along Main Street.

Of course, all this – the travel, the guide, the wagons, the tents, the parade – was only possible if the circus made it safely to their destination safe and sound. Bad roads weren't the only problems they faced while traveling around the country.

There were also bad men, too.

Far more often than they'd liked, circus troupes traveled roads that passed through isolated and often unsafe areas. Most of those encountered in such places were not law enforcement officers wearing badges – they were quite the opposite. Bandits, cutthroats, and thieves prowled the woods and roads in rural areas, stealing and killing. Most would assume that the size of a circus company would cause highway robbers to think twice before confronting them. However, the amount of valuable goods that could be taken from a traveling show often overpowered their hesitation.

A handful of circuses during this period traveled by riverboat, but they weren't any safer than their compatriots who journeyed by land. They ran into the river pirates that preyed on travelers, like those who hid out along the Ohio River at Cave-in-Rock, Illinois, which, at

WHILE MOST THE CIRCUS AND CARNIVAL GROUNDS IN RURAL AMERICA WERE PEACEFUL PLACES, THINGS COULD SOMETIMES GET OUT OF HAND, ESPECIALLY WHEN THE RUBES WERE CONVINCED THEY WERE BEING CHEATED.

one time, offered a tavern, a floating brothel, and a "circus company" about which no details remain.

For the most part, though, most rural Americans were peaceful, law-abiding, and more interested in the conditions of their own lives than in causing trouble for the only kind of entertainment that visited their small towns. Even so, once the circus arrived and the show was set up, the glittering lights and colorful music of the grounds served as a beacon for young men looking for excitement. They could often be "overzealous" when expressing their admiration for female performers and, at other times, moved to test their mettle against the circus strongman, the skilled horsemen, and even the occasional wrestling bear.

When a fight broke out, the cry of "Hey, Rube!" signaled workmen and roustabouts to grab a club or some other weapon and come running. If it turned into a brawl, local papers often carried a story detailing the incident, which in circus language was a "clem." A veteran circus promoter, P.A. Older, recalled, "In those days, it was worth a man's life to run a show. We used to have fights with rubes two or three times a week. All they used to think of was to clean out the circus."

That was the thing – a fight with a rube was never blamed on the rube. It was always the fault of the circus folks, the roustabouts, and the carnies. For this reason, it was very much in the interest of those with the circus to ensure a show went on without incident. If the authorities closed the show, there would be no day's receipts and no day's pay. And if that happened often enough, there was no circus at all.

This often meant that in rough towns, some local thugs could pass into the circus grounds with their friends without buying a ticket. It was better to lose a little cash on ticket sales than have to close a show.

And besides that, it was also often possible to make up for some of those losses in other ways. Games of chance set up in the vicinity of the big top might hand out kewpie dolls as prizes and also offer forms of outright gambling, so like as the circus "fixer" – the advance man – had assured the local sheriff that he would receive a cut of the proceeds in return for looking the other way. On the other hand, if the operator of the game was suspected of fleecing a local, the victim might return with a few pals seeking reimbursement, an encounter almost certain to kick off a spirited clem.

It was a rough-and-tumble world that many young men were introduced to in those days, when a lack of work, a dismal home life, or just a taste for adventure spurred them to do what legions of other boys would do in the years that followed – they ran away to join the circus.

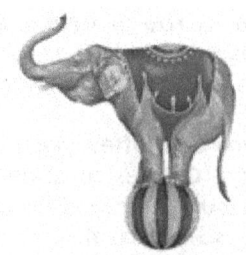

3. AMERICA'S GREATEST SHOWMAN

IRONICALLY, ONE NAME THAT IS MOST OFTEN linked to the American circus is the name of a man who didn't become involved in the circus business until it was nearly four decades old.

And he had to be lured out of retirement to do it.

However, it can be argued that the circus in America would never have captured our imaginations in the way it did if he hadn't laid the groundwork for what it eventually became.

When he finally became an official part of the circus, there was no question that the name of Phineas Taylor Barnum was already a legend in the world of American show business.

BARNUM WAS BORN IN DANBURY, CONNECTICUT, in 1810. He was the sixth of 11 children born to Philo Barnum, an unsuccessful farmer and merchant whose greatest skill seemed to be producing children. Luckily for Philo, his wife's father, Phineas Taylor, was a prosperous landowner, so his family would never starve. And while his sons spent their childhoods working on the farm, money was available for a modest and frugal lifestyle.

It would turn out that Barnum's Grandfather Phin had a larger impact on his life than he probably imagined as a boy. The elder Phineas was a free-spirited man with little interest in the latter-day Puritanism that was still very much part of life in New England in the early nineteenth century. He was a colorful storyteller and loved practical jokes, including one in which he convinced 13 friends on a weeklong fishing trip to shave only half their beards and delight in the spectacle it produced. After the laughter faded, Phin announced he would also shave his own beard but somehow lost his grip on the only razor, which fell into the water and was lost. As he had planned when their boat returned home, it was a Sunday afternoon, and all the town's barbers were closed. That meant all his friends were forced to walk down the street – and return to their wives – looking like half-bearded dimwits.

And Phin's grandson was not saved from his shenanigans. When he was a boy, Phin bestowed a parcel of land called Ivy Island on Barnum, which his grandfather assured him was one of the finest farms in the state. His father and mother often reminded Barnum of his fabulous bequest and told him they hoped he'd remember them once he reached the proper age and received his inheritance.

THERE WERE MANY INFLUENCES IN THE EARLY LIFE OF P.T. BARNUM THAT TURNED HIM INTO THE SHOWMAN THAT HE WOULD BECOME.

It wasn't until he was 12 that Barnum learned the truth. He was finally taken out to inspect Ivy Island, which was nothing more than a stretch of half-submerged, unusual swampland. Asked by his father how he liked his property, Barnum hung his head and muttered, "I'd sell it pretty cheap." Unbeknownst to him, he'd been the butt of the joke to his family for years.

It's possible that his grandfather instilled in Barnum the skill he'd perfect to bamboozle people good-naturedly. However, even if he didn't, it taught him a lesson on how easily reality could be manipulated.

Perhaps even more important to Barnum's later career would be his time as a clerk in his father's grocery store, where he learned the fine art of bargaining, trading store goods for cash and produce and items made by the customers. The customers were not above cheating the store -- perhaps by using inferior furs for hats and calling them something else -- so the store cheated them in return. They mixed sugars, teas, and liquors and gave the concoctions impressive names to convince the customers to pay too much for cheap mixtures. As

Barnum later shrugged, "Each party expected to be cheated if it was possible."

Barnum later graduated from such conniving and developed a specialty for selling lottery tickets, another form of taking his customers to the cleaners.

When he was 15, Philo died, and Barnum was so poor that he had to borrow the money for a pair of shoes to wear to his father's funeral.

Luckily, a former Danbury resident who had opened a grocery store in Brooklyn came to Barnum's rescue, hiring him as a clerk and, later, entrusting him with purchasing goods for the store. Barnum enjoyed learning the wholesale business but dreamed of working for himself.

In the summer of 1827, Barnum contracted smallpox, and after a long convalescence in Danbury, he returned to Brooklyn with enough money to start his own business. He opened a porterhouse – a tavern and steak restaurant – near the store where he'd clerked and, within months, could sell it for a nice profit. He stayed in New York for a time, working for another tavern owner, and spent much of his time attending the theater.

Early in 1828, Grandfather Phin wrote Barnum and offered him the use of a carriage house on the main street of the Danbury suburb of Bethel. He could also use the living quarters above if he wanted to establish a business there. Barnum decided to accept and returned home, converting the building into a fruit stand and confectionery. He had worked out ways to obtain a steady supply of goods from New York contacts, and for good measure, he installed a keg of ale in the corner. On his first day of business, he had drained the ale keg and took in enough money to put him on solid footing. By fall, he had added a line of lottery tickets and novelty items and began serving stewed oysters to go with the ale.

The following year, when he was 19, Barnum proposed to a tailoress named Charity Hallet. Neither of the families approved, each believing their child could do better. When Charity's mother said her daughter "was altogether too good for Taylor Barnum," Barnum heartily agreed.

Nevertheless, Charity accepted his proposal, and the two were married on

CHARITY HALLET – A PHOTO TAKEN MUCH LATER IN LIFE.

November 8, 1829. The ceremony was held in New York City and was kept a secret from Barnum's mother. After she discovered her son had gotten married, it took her a while to accept his choice, but she softened quickly and eventually loved Charity like her own daughter.

Barnum continued to operate his store in Bethel, expanding his goods to include brandy, bibles, and other books. He also dabbled in real estate and became well-known for his liberal views. He even started a liberal-leaning newspaper and opposed any ordinances designed to prevent various forms of entertainment on Sundays and laws against the sale of lottery tickets, which, of course, were a big part of his store's business.

He got into trouble with his paper several times, but when he was found to have libeled a Presbyterian church deacon -- accusing him of being guilty of "taking usury of an orphan boy" – he was thrown in jail for two months. Barnum had been outraged that the church deacon had purchased a note worth $42 for only $25 from a boy in the community.

Barnum continued to publish his newspaper from behind bars, and calling out a church official as a hypocrite made him a hero to many. When he was released, he was carried home at the head of a celebratory parade of hundreds – an occasion that gave him his first taste of celebrity.

Married and with the birth of his first child, Caroline Cordelia, in 1830, Barnum began to long for something other than a merchant's life. He wanted to conduct business faster than his mercantile would allow, buying large and selling large instead of giving out extensive credits and piling up bad debts.

When the Connecticut legislature banned the sale of lottery tickets in 1834, Barnum decided enough was enough. He sold his store, closed his newspaper, and took his young family to New York City, where he would pursue much bigger dreams – which he failed to immediately find.

He struggled, looking for work, but then, in the spring of 1835, he came into some money when some old lottery debts were paid to him, and he used the cash to open a small boardinghouse and purchase part of a nearby grocery store. It wasn't what Barnum had been chasing when he came to New York, but he had a wife and child that depended on him.

How long Barnum would have gone on renting rooms and selling groceries is impossible to guess, but everything changed for him on one hot July day when an old friend named Coley Bartram

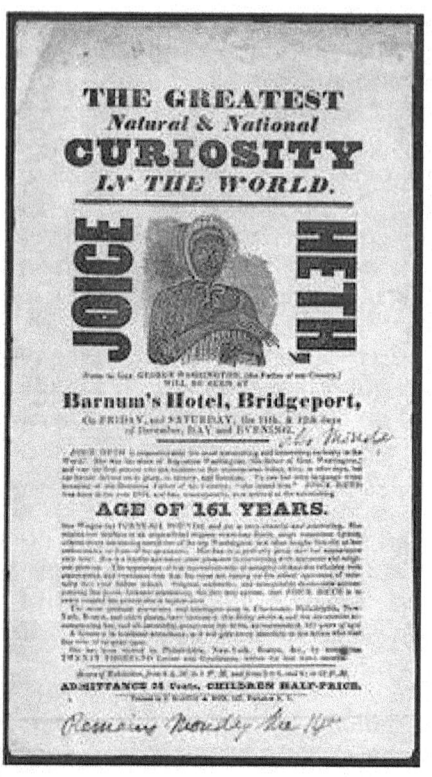

AN ADVERTISING POSTER FOR BARNUM'S FIRST PROMOTED ATTRACTION – THE 161-YEAR-OLD NURSEMAID OF GEORGE WASHINGTON.

came into his store with a proposition. He freely admitted that it was odd, but when he heard it, he thought of Barnum.

Coley explained that he owned an interest in what he described as "an extraordinary negro woman" named Joice Heth. He explained that she was 161 years old and had been George Washington's nursemaid.

Whatever Barnum was thinking about, the story was interrupted by Coley getting to the point. He said that he'd recently sold his interest in Joice to R.W. Lindsay of Kentucky, who'd brought her to Philadelphia, where he was exhibiting her as the wonder that she was. However, Coley confided in his friend that Lindsay was not much of a showman, and his heart wasn't in it. He was anxious to find a buyer for his one-woman show and return to Kentucky.

Coley then handed over a copy of a newspaper advertisement from Philadelphia that described Joice's history and listed the various "proofs" of her claims – including the original bill of sale from Augustine Washington, the former president's father, when he sold Joice Heth to his sister-in-law. According to the document, the sale was made on February 5, 1727, when Joice was described as "aged 54 years."

Barnum was already familiar with the Philadelphia exhibition -- it had been in the New York newspapers – and he was astounded by the fact that he had the chance to purchase the rights to such an amazing person. Barnum packed a bag immediately and quickly went to Philadelphia to consult with Mr. Lindsay.

At the Masonic Hall in Philadelphia, Barnum inspected Joice Heth, who he stated, "Might almost as well have been called a

THE GREATEST
Natural & National
CURIOSITY
IN THE WORLD.

thousand years old." She was blind and too feeble to do much more than wave her one good arm from the sofa where she lay, but she was quite the conversationalist, could sing several Baptist hymns, and had many detailed stories to tell of "dear little George."

Lindsay showed Barnum the fragile bill of sale, which was kept encased in glass, and by then, he'd seen enough. Lindsay demanded $3,000 for the rights to Joice Heth, but Barnum knew this was only an opening offer. He left Philadelphia with the option to purchase Joice any time over the next ten days for $1,000. He was leaving town without her because he didn't have enough money for the sale – but he soon would.

Barnum quickly sold off his interest in the grocery store and returned to Philadelphia. He arranged with Lindsay to continue the show in Philadelphia for one week and then bring what was now *his* show to New York.

P.T. Barnum had officially entered the world of show business.

He'd also technically purchased a slave. He may have reasoned that he was purchasing an "exhibit" – and Joice always maintained she was a performer and Barnum was her manager – but for all practical purposes, he had become the owner of another human being.

This is much easier for us to disparage today, looking back and applying modern standards to the early nineteenth century. By the 1830s, the abolitionist movement was gaining traction in the United States, but there was little outrage directed at Barnum or the exhibition of Joice Heth. The public's interest focused primarily on the amazing prospect of her age and her purported connection to Washington.

In New York, the exhibition offered an introduction that explained Joice's history. Then, she answered questions about her age and her relationship with Washington in a way that was, by all accounts, convincing. She paused occasionally to sing hymns, leaving audiences delighted by the experience.

After New York, the show moved on to Providence and then Boston. There, people were so intrigued by Joice that the room Barnum had rented at the city's concert hall was overrun, forcing the exhibition of Maelzel and his "automaton chess-player" out of the grand parlor. This was quite an achievement because automatons were then all the rage. They were the early version of a robot – a self-operating machine designed to carry out a series of tasks.

But Maelzel didn't mind getting bumped. He convinced Barnum that the young man would be a great showman. He could see that Barnum understood the power of the press and told him, "When your old woman dies, you come to me, and I will make your fortune. I will let you have my carousel, my automaton trumpet-player, and many curious things that will make you money."

But Barnum was already making a lot of money. The show toured almost every other city of size in Massachusetts, then Hartford, New Haven, Newark, return engagements in New York, and as far away as Albany, where Barnum spotted a juggler performing at the city museum.

He was an Italian and performed under the name Signor Antonio. His act – which included plate spinning, stilt walking, balancing the point of a knife on the end of his nose, and other feats – had never been seen anywhere else in America.

When Barnum left Albany, he took two acts with him – Joice Heth and the Italian juggler, whom he renamed a more "foreign-sounding" Signor Vivalla.

As the story continues, we must pause momentarily and wonder just how much of Joice Heth's story Barnum believed.

My guess? None of it.

In 1855, he wrote that if Joice was an imposter, who taught her all the details of the Washington family? He said he didn't know: "I taught her none of these things." A better answer probably would have been: "She was able to convince most people, so that was good enough for me."

Joice's age was finally put to rest in February 1836. She had been sent to recuperate from exhaustion at the home of Barnum's half-brother, Philo, and while she was there, she passed away. Philo had her body sent to Barnum in New York, and he made good on a promise he'd made to a friend who was a surgeon that he could perform a postmortem on Joice after she died. At the autopsy, attended by several other doctors, medical students, and newspaper editors, the surgeon made a careful examination of the arteries leading to Joice's heart. The surgeon consulted with serval colleagues who were present, and then, after the room was emptied, he delivered his opinion to Barnum – Joice Heth had been no more than 80 when she died.

Barnum later recalled that he protested to his friend that he'd hired Joice "in perfect good faith and had relied on her appearance and the documents as evidence of the truth of her story." The surgeon shrugged. He even thought Joice looked older than her years.

The revelation about Joice's real age prompted an editorial in the *New York Sun* the following day. The headline read: "Dissection of Joice Heth – Precious Humbug Exposed," but it did little harm to Barnum's reputation.

In his eyes – and in the eyes of those who had delighted in the possibility they were meeting the nursemaid of George Washington – those who had attended the performances had been offered entertainment for their money.

And if anyone felt duped and decided to complain about how gullible they had been in public, P.T. Barnum couldn't be blamed for that.

WITH JOICE HETH GONE, BARNUM TURNED TO Signor Vivalla as his star attraction. He would even go onstage sometimes as his assistant, tossing props to the juggler and offering a running commentary about the skills needed to toss around razor-sharp knives and hop around on one stilt.

At one show in Philadelphia, a local juggler named Roberts started heckling Vivalla, claiming he could put on a much better show than the Italian. Rather than have the man tossed out, Barnum devised a better idea to generate much publicity between the local man and the visiting performer. He summoned the man backstage and suggested a sort of "duel" between the two men, with a prize of $1,000 going to Roberts if he could duplicate all of Vivalla's tricks.

Roberts protested – he was a better juggler but had no idea how to walk on stilts. Barnum was concerned his plan was falling apart and suggested an alternative idea. He promised Roberts $30 if he would perform under his direction one night at the Walnut Street Theater and keep quiet about anything that happened behind the scenes.

This turned into a cooked-up rivalry between the two performers that was to be settled by a contest at the theater. Notices started appearing in newspapers about the event, promoting Roberts as an American who could beat the "foreigner" onstage. Roberts bragged that a portion would go to charity when he won the still advertised $1,000.

On the night of the battle, the theater was packed to overflowing. The contest – which was completely rigged – lasted for 40 minutes until Roberts, unable to spin two plates at once, confessed that he'd been beaten. He then was allowed to take over the stage to demonstrate the various feats he could do, which earned him deafening applause.

When even Vivalla came onstage to congratulate Roberts on his skills, the latter immediately challenged Vivalla to a rematch the following week with a $500 wager on the line, which brought cheers from the crowd.

The entire scenario, of course, had been laid out by Barnum, who had cleared $200 for the evening. This led to one contest, then another, between Vivalla and Roberts for the next month.

Eventually, though, the novelty faded. As summer 1836 approached, Barnum finally entered circus life when he signed on with a former Danbury neighbor, Aaron Turner, who ran a traveling show. In addition to bringing Signor Vivalla along with him, Barnum would serve as the show's secretary, treasurer, and ticket seller. This would earn him 20 percent of the profits. The show opened in Massachusetts – circus performances were then illegal in Connecticut – and traveled throughout the summer along the East Coast, as far south as North Carolina.

By now, Barnum felt he'd earned enough money to go off on his own. During the winter, he toured the South with a vaudeville-like show called "Barnum's Grand Scientific and Musical Theater," featuring Vivalla and an African American minstrel singer named James Sanford.

Things were going fine until they reached South Carolina, and Sanford abruptly quit the show. With half of his headliners missing, Barnum had a dilemma. He didn't want to refund a sold-out show, but where would he find a black singer and dancer just hours before the show started?

He devised a plan, but it wasn't one that would go over today. Barnum blackened his face, took the stage, and sang the songs that were advertised. To his surprise, he was applauded, and two more songs were demanded as an encore.

The good news is that Barnum never repeated his "black face" show, but he would find himself pressed into service again in the future. He also employed a magician and ventriloquist named Joe Pentland. During one performance, Pentland's small assistant, who was usually crammed into the bottom of the magician's table to help with the "disappearance" of objects by tugging them through a trapdoor in the tabletop, was nowhere to be found.

Though he could barely fit into the compartment, Barnum agreed to help. All went well for a time, with Barnum removing items and supplying balls, cups, scarves, and other things the script called for. The finale of Joe's act is for him to receive a gold watch and chain passed to him by someone in the audience. It was then Barnum's job to pull the watch down and then wind its chain around the neck of a live squirrel in a cage inside the cabinet with him. Once that was done, he was supposed to shove the squirrel with the watch around its neck back up through the trapdoor, where Joe would show it off to the crowd.

What could go wrong?

Joe called for the watch, and an audience member produced one. He placed it on the table, covered it with a vase, and then rapped on it, which was the signal for Barnum to open the trapdoor, grab the watch, and get to work. But when Barnum pulled the squirrel for its cage, it promptly sank its teeth into his thumb.

In terrible pain and unable to move in such quarters – let alone dislodge the animal from his thumb – Barnum shouted and thrashed, kicking the flimsy wood of the cabinet apart. Barnum rolled free of the splintered contraption and got the squirrel worked loose from his flesh.

As Joe Pentland gaped at him, Barnum dashed behind the stage curtain, blood dripping from his hand. Meanwhile, the squirrel vanished into the theater's rafters, the audience member's watch still hanging from its neck.

Whether the audience saw this as a disaster or merely part of the show is unknown, but Barnum later said, "If ever there was hooting and shouting in a mass of spectators, it was heard that night."

Barnum's rag-tag show continued touring the South, finally winding up in Nashville in May 1837. Exhausted, he spent the summer at home in Connecticut before loading up for another winter tour of the southern states. Things didn't go well. Eventually, he sold his horses and wagons to feed the troupe and started moving the show up and down the Mississippi by steamboat. When he finally decided he'd had enough, Barnum returned to New York City, vowing to never again work as an itinerant showman.

Back in the city, with $2,500 in his pocket, he decided to invest in some solid business enterprise. After interviewing a cast of charlatans and quacks, he settled on a German with a fledgling business that manufactured things like shoe polish, waterproof paste for leather, and mechanical greases. It took over two years for the business to fail and for his partner to flee the city after emptying the bank accounts.

Barnum, at the age of 30, had no choice but to return to the business that he knew best – show business. He struggled with only a handful of lackluster acts in a city still suffering from the effects of a recent bank panic. The only good thing about that gloomy business climate was that Barnum wasn't the only one having trouble – everyone else was, too. This meant that the value of many once notable properties in New York had been greatly diminished by the economic downturn – namely John Scudder's American Museum, a five-story building on Broadway.

Filled with an array of stuffed birds, fossils, shells, and curious minerals, the institution had steadily declined since John Scudder had died a few years before. Even though he'd invested more than $50,000 in his museum when he opened it, it was now offered for only $15,000.

But, of course, it was $15,000 more than Barnum had at that time.

However, he was determined not to let this stop him. He decided to approach the owner of the building with something he'd never tried before – honesty. He sent a letter to the owner of the building the museum was housed in – a retired merchant named Frederick Olmstead – and proposed that Olmstead purchase the museum's contents and sign them over to Barnum, who would make yearly installments until the debt was repaid. Olmstead was impressed by the young man's gumption and asked if Barnum had any references.

Barnum produced a string of people willing to attest to his character, and Olmstead was convinced to go along with the deal. He did, though, have one last request – did Barnum have a piece of real estate he might be able to offer for additional security?

Barnum did have a few properties in Danbury, but they were mortgaged to the hilt. And then he remembered that he had one fabulous piece of ground he could offer. He replied that he could offer five acres of land in Connecticut.

"What did you pay for it?" Olmstead asked him.

"It was a present from my late grandfather, Phineas Taylor," Barnum replied.

As security, he offered the merchant the desolate swampland that Phineas had given him as a long-running practical joke, and Olmstead agreed to the deal.

So, perhaps he wasn't completely honest with Olmstead, but his heart was certainly in the right place.

BARNUM'S AMERICAN MUSEUM BEGAN ON UNSURE FOOTING BUT WOULD BECOME ONE OF THE MOST POPULAR ATTRACTIONS IN NEW YORK CITY.

ON JANUARY 1, 1841, BARNUM OPENED HIS NEW American Museum. Promoting it as a place for family entertainment, enlightenment, and instructive amusement, it became an almost immediate success, with admission lines sometimes stretching around the block.

Before the museum re-opened, Barnum had moved his growing family into a ground-floor apartment attached to the building. A daughter, Helen, had been born in 1840, followed by Frances in 1842 and Pauline in 1846. This living arrangement allowed Barnum even more time to work in the museum, which he was determined to turn into the most famous place in the city.

And he did. Barnum's American Museum became known as a place that furthered the public's knowledge of art, music, and the marvels of nature, showcasing natural curiosities alongside artistic

and historic exhibits. It would remain one of the most popular attractions in the city for the next 23 years.

It would've never happened if Barnum wasn't the showman that he was. One of his first ideas was to install a series of large flags representing the nations of the world along the roofline of the building, attracting notice for blocks around. Along with the flags, he installed the first spotlight in the city, which lit up the skies every night. He also had all the building windows covered with colored paintings of the various displays inside, like polar bears, kangaroos, lions, seals, giraffes, and elephants.

By the following spring, he'd installed an outdoor garden atop the building, where guests could stroll, enjoy refreshments, and listen to always-changing brass bands. There were hot-air balloon rides from the roof by day and fireworks displays at night, and soon, there was a huge fountain that geysered from the top of the building, too.

All the excitement outside was naturally meant to lure the curious through the front doors – and to buy a ticket. The museum was promoted as having 850,000 exhibits and curiosities within the four conjoined buildings comprising the display space and the workshops where the exhibits were prepared. One department made wax figures that looked like the well-known personalities of the day. There was also a taxidermy department, an aquarium, and an elaborate set-design department that satisfied the demands of the museum's theater. There was also a host of exhibitors demonstrating various skills and crafts and new technological devices. They offered a continual run of changing exhibitions ranging from talking machines, panoramas of Niagara

Falls, Paris, and Peru, ivory carvers, glassblowers, sewing machine operators, musicians, ballerinas, Native American performers, and more.

But Barnum knew very well that educational displays would only take the museum so far. Once a visitor had looked at a stuffed bison or bear, there would be little reason to repeat the experience anytime soon. And yes, the skilled artisans and the new contraptions were interesting – and might bring people back more than once – he knew what visitors really wanted to see.

You can take the showman out of the circus, but he will always be a showman.

Barnum began importing live acts that came straight from the circuses of the day – "educated" dogs, jugglers, ventriloquists, albinos, "fat boys," giants, pantomimes, singers, dancers, and more. A visitor would rarely see the same show twice, so there was always a reason to come back another time.

Before 1841 was over, Barnum had paid off every penny of the $12,000 loan provided by Frederick Olmstead. The American Museum was the success he'd dreamed it would be; even greater fortunes were just around the corner.

And those successes would have nothing to do with educational exhibits and stuffed buffalo. His notoriety would skyrocket thanks to a dead mermaid.

ONE OF THE FIRST TRULY SPECTACULAR attractions for Barnum's Museum was a "mermaid" he purchased in 1842. Not surprisingly, it had a colorful backstory that claimed it had been purchased from a

THE FEEJEE MERMAID THAT EVENTUALLY MADE IT INTO BARNUM'S MUSEUM WAS FIRST EXHIBITED BY A SHIP'S CAPTAIN IN ENGLAND. ONCE IN NEW YORK, BARNUM TURNED IT INTO A CITYWIDE SENSATION.

Japanese fisherman by an American ship captain named Samuel Edes. He paid $6,000 for it – equal to more than $100,00 today – but didn't have the money to meet the seller's price. So, he borrowed it from the ship's expense account, which put him in hot water when the company he worked for discovered the missing cash. Rather than press charges, the ship's owners allowed him to repay the money over time, which he did by putting the mermaid on display in London.

    The mysterious mermaid received wide coverage in the press. Hundreds of people saw it in a small London pub daily – until William Clift from the Royal College of Surgeons paid his admission, examined it, and declared it a fake.

    There was no longer an audience for the mermaid in England, but the attention had worked out well for Edes. He'd paid back his "loan," earned a tidy sum, and now planned to display his oddity in America. Unfortunately, he passed away before he could put on an exhibition – and his son wanted nothing to do with it – so he sold it to Mose Kimball, a rival museum owner in Boston, who showed it to Barnum.

    Barnum was interested in displaying it, but before he did, he wanted to show it to a scientist. He consulted his resident naturalist, who proclaimed it a fake. He said it had obviously been manufactured using pieces of a fish and perhaps a small monkey. He did admit, though, that he wasn't sure how it had been done.

    "Then why do you say it's manufactured?" Barnum asked him.

    "Because I don't believe in mermaids," the naturalist replied.

Barnum scoffed. "That's no reason at all, so therefore I'll believe in the mermaid and hire it."

But Barnum still wanted a scientific stamp on his new attraction, so he looked for another scientist to examine the mermaid. He found one – and this time, the scientist proclaimed the mermaid was "absolutely real." And that was because this "scientist" was Barnum's attorney and friend, Levi Lyman, sporting a goatee and a British accent. He knew nothing, of course, about science or mermaids.

BARNUM ADVERTISED THE FEEJEE MERMAID AS A BEAUTIFUL, TOPLESS MERMAID, KNOWING THAT NO ONE WOULD PAY TO SEE THE MONSTROUS THING HE HAD ON DISPLAY.

News spread. A British naturalist had declared the "Feejee Mermaid" was genuine! Everyone wanted to see it, and crowds flooded the museum for a closer look – after coughing up their admission fee.

Barnum advertised the mermaid as a scandalously topless woman with long, flowing hair and a fishtail because he knew no one would purposely come to see the nightmare-inducing thing on display. Once they arrived and got a look at the grotesque creature, though, they were thrilled.

Barnum knew that the Feejee Mermaid was nothing more than a "humbug," but he was philosophical about it. He referred to his more questionable attractions as "skyrockets" – special features that got people in the doors. He stressed to his critics that once the public was inside, they were educated, inspired, and moved by the "moral dramas" that were produced for the stage, including "The Drunkard," "Uncle Tom's Cabin," and more.

But no matter how he portrayed himself in the press, it would always be the "humbug," the oddity, and the unusual that would excite him most.

IN NOVEMBER 1842, BARNUM WAS RETURNING FROM Albany when his trip was stalled because of a frozen river. This left him back home in Bridgeport for the night, and while there, his half-brother, Philo,

CHARLES STRATTON, THE YOUNG MAN WHO WAS SOON TO BECOME GENERAL TOM THUMB.

introduced him to a small boy named Charles Stratton – a four-year-old who was only 25 inches tall and weighed only 15 pounds.

Recognizing the shy boy as a marvel of nature, Barnum was enthralled. Charles had proportional dwarfism, or in circus parlance of the time, was a midget. He discovered that Charles had not grown at all beyond the age of seven months. Barnum later recalled, "After seeing him and talking with him, I at once determined to secure his services from his parents and to exhibit him in public."

The boy was no mere curiosity – he had extraordinary potential. In short order, he made arrangements with Charles' parents – Sherwood and Cynthia – to hire the boy for an exhibition tour of four weeks at $3 per week, plus travel, room, and board for Charles and his mother In New York.

Barnum moved Charles and Cynthia into an apartment on the fifth floor of the American Museum and set to work creating a legend.

Charles proved to be an excellent student. Barnum schooled him in grown-up manners and speech and had him practicing a series of one-line comebacks in the best vaudeville tradition. The boy was smart, funny, and, as Barnum put it, "had a love of the ludicrous." The two became friends – a friendship that would continue to grow and remain strong through their lifetimes.

Charles became known to the public as General Tom Thumb, an 11-year-old recently arriving from England. New York was fascinated with Charles, and after his first month, Barnum gave him $50 and raised his salary to $7 per week. Before the year was out, his pay had been raised to an astounding weekly salary of $25. It wasn't long before Barnum doubled that salary and started planning a European tour.

They departed in 1844 and would be out of the country for three years. When Barnum and the young general arrived in Liverpool 19 days later, Charles was smuggled off the boat and past the waiting crowds disguised as an infant in his mother's arms. Barnum had two goals for the European tour – to turn Tom Thumb into a star and to obtain an audience for the boy with Queen Victoria. He had no established contacts to assist with either of those things – he was flying by the seat of his pants – but Barnum had great faith in his showmanship skills.

He quickly secured a theater in Liverpool where Charles could appear, and during their short stint there, a London theater manager came down, was impressed, and arranged an engagement in London. The response in London was as enthusiastic as it had been in Liverpool, and offers began pouring in.

But Barnum had a better idea. He rented a furnished home in the ritzy West End and invited influential newspaper editors and members of society to visit. Word spread of Barnum's remarkable little friend, and it wasn't long before the pair received an invitation from Queen Victoria inviting them to Buckingham Palace.

BARNUM TOOK CHARLES TO EUROPE FOR THREE YEARS, TURNING HIM INTO AN INTERNATIONAL STAR AND INTRODUCING HIM TO ADORING AUDIENCES AND ROYALTY, INCLUDING QUEEN VICTORIA, WHO CONSIDERED HIM ONE OF HER FAVORITE GUESTS.

They were prepared for their visit, although little would be required of Charles except remembering to walk backward when leaving the queen's presence. It was clear to Barnum that he should not presume to go directly to the queen. Any questions she had for him would be relayed through a second party, and his responses would be made the same way.

On the night of their visit, Barnum and Charles arrived at the palace and were escorted to the Picture Gallery, where the doors were opened to reveal a group of 20 or so nobles, including Prince Albert, surrounding the queen at the far end of the room. Barnum was frozen stiff in the doorway.

THE SHOWMANSHIP OF BOTH BARNUM AND "TOM THUMB" TURNED THE TWO OF THEM INTO VERY WEALTHY MEN.

But Charles wasn't. Undaunted, he strolled into the room, made a graceful bow, and loudly announced, "Good evening, ladies and gentlemen!"

The royals burst into laughter, including the queen, who left her seat, took Charles by the hand, and led him about the gallery in conversation. Charles told her that her gallery was "first-rate," he asked where the Prince of Wales might be because he hoped to meet him. The prince was resting, he was told, but the two of them would meet very soon. Queen Victoria was utterly charmed by the boy.

After an hour of Charles singing, dancing, and doing impersonations of Napoleon and others, he and Barnum began backing out of the room – only to be interrupted by one of the queen's little dogs taking a sudden interest in him. The spectacle of Charles holding off the dog by wielding his tiny cane like a sword added the final touch to a night beyond Barnum's wildest expectations.

News of the command performance spread, and Barnum found himself having to book larger and larger halls for Tom Thumb exhibitions. Charles also visited Buckingham Palace a second time, where his wish to meet the Prince of Wales was fulfilled.

Soon, Barnum estimated that the daily gate from their shows was $500, and sometimes more. He had a small, custom-sized carriage built for Charles, pulled by four ponies, with an attendant and a driver who were children. Just rolling through the street served as a moving advertisement for future shows. But they didn't need to advertise – Tom Thumb was undoubtedly the most popular attraction in the city.

From London, they continued to every town of size in England and Scotland, with forays to Belfast and Dublin, and arrived in France, where they appeared before King Phillipe on four separate occasions. The frenzy for Tom Thumb in France was even greater than in England. Promoters were forced to try to calm advance enthusiasm for the shows so venues wouldn't be swamped.

The tour went to Belgium, where King Leopold and his family were as charmed by Charles as everyone else. With the momentum created by his fame, the pair continued to Cuba and then returned to the United States. Crowds flocked to see Charles wherever he appeared, and his popularity and celebrity were greater than any actor during his lifetime.

That was saying a lot because, in those days, stage shows were pretty much the only kind of entertainment that existed. Before Tom Thumb came along, presenting "human curiosities" was considered disreputable. It was Barnum – and General Tom Thumb – who changed all that, and soon, the popularity of American sideshows began to grow.

As the years passed, Charles' career remained strong, earning him tremendous amounts of money. When he was still a boy, his father built the family a $30,000 mansion in Bridgeport, and under Barnum's management, Charles became a wealthy man. He also inspired scores of imitators. Soon, a dozen or more other men were using military titles to promote themselves, too.

But there was only one General Tom Thumb.

Charles bought a house in the fashionable part of New York – the furniture, stairs, and doors sized for

IN 1863, CHARLES MARRIED LAVINIA WARREN, MAKING FRONT PAGES NEWS EVEN WHILE AMERICA WAS IN THE MIDDLE OF THE CIVIL WAR.

his convenience. He also owned a wardrobe of fine clothes and a yacht, and once, when Barnum got into financial trouble, Charles bailed him out.

In 1863, Charles married Lavinia Warren, another little person, and the wedding made front-page news. After the ceremony, the couple was even received at the White House by the president and first lady, Abraham and Mary Lincoln.

Barnum saw the public's excitement about the marriage and knew he could generate even more publicity if they had a baby. So, in 1865, Lavinia gave birth to a daughter – Minnie.

But the public didn't know that, in truth, Lavinia could not have children, so Barnum went to an orphanage, bought a baby, and swore the staff to secrecy. It was a publicity stunt, but the couple loved the little girl. Sadly, though, things turned tragic the following year when Minnie died.

ALTHOUGH LAVINIA WAS UNABLE TO HAVE CHILDREN, BARNUM ARRANGED FOR THE COUPLE TO "HAVE A BABY" AS PART OF A PUBLICITY STUNT.

In 1883, Charles passed away after suffering a stroke. He was only 45. More than 20,000 people attended his funeral, and Barnum -- always the showman -- commissioned a life-sized statue of Charles for his grave.

Tom Thumb changed America's entertainment history as the first human curiosity deemed socially acceptable for everyone. His life and career opened the door for many others that followed.

IN THE FOLLOWING YEARS, BARNUM returned to America and became known as one of the wealthiest men in the country. He had taken great care to build a reputation as a prominent man in New York, and his museum was as famous as it was remarkable. It was common to see his name printed and posted on broadsides and in newspapers across America. Advertisements regaled readers with the museum's wonders of the natural world, but he was just as well known for his promotion of Tom Thumb and the Feejee Mermaid.

It didn't matter to Barnum why people gave him money, he was happy to spend it.

In 1846, he chose a 17-acre site near Bridgeport and spent the next two years building "Iranistan," a Turkish-Oriental-theme palace for his family.

BARNUM'S LOST PALACE, "IRANISTAN," WHICH WOULD EVENTUALLY BURN TO THE GROUND.

In November 1848, the Barnums hosted a housewarming party for 1,000 guests at the three-story home, decorated with elaborate grillwork and dozens of minarets and towers.

It had burglar and fire alarms, heated by forced air from Barnum's gasworks, and its bathrooms were all fitted with hot and cold running water. Barnum had his own retreat – a secluded study connected to a bathing suite with a shower and multiple tubs. On the third floor was a billiards and entertainment room, linked by a spiral staircase rising inside a great central dome offering a breathtaking countryside view.

It was a "dream castle," like nothing else that existed in America at the time – so, in other words, the perfect home for P.T. Barnum.

Now almost 40, Barnum took great pride and pleasure in his new estate, but it wasn't as though he could relax and rest on his successes. There was always a drive within him to do more, and by 1849, an unlikely project had been troubling his thoughts. He had become set on bringing singing sensation Jenny Lind – known as the "Swedish Nightingale" – to America for a grand tour. She'd already captivated Europe with her otherworldly voice, but no plans had been made for American appearances.

Barnum was determined to change that, even though, at that time, he'd never even heard her sing. But that didn't matter. Jenny was the toast of England and Europe, and publicly, Barnum stated that he was endeavoring to present a higher grade of amusement than he

JENNY LIND, WHO WAS CALLED "THE SWEDISH NIGHTINGALE" WAS THE SINGING SENSATION OF THE MID-NINETEENTH CENTURY.

was generally known for. He claimed to attend the opera, lectures, and first-class concerts frequently and wanted to offer the same kind of entertainment to towns and cities across America.

But deep down, Barnum knew there were massive amounts of money to be made by bringing Jenny Lind to the United States, and he wanted to be the one to do it.

Barnum had competitors, however. He was not the only promoter who wanted to introduce her to American audiences, but he was the most clever and persistent one. After months of negotiation, the terms for the venture were reached. It was concluded that Jenny would receive $1,000 per night for her performances with all expenses paid, including those of her musical director, servants, a secretary, three musical assistants, and related transportation and board.

The contract terms were extremely beneficial to the "Swedish Nightingale." Jenny would deliver a 150-night concert tour of the United States, secured by an enormous monetary guarantee. That money would allow her to realize her dream of establishing a musical academy for girls in Sweden.

Barnum had won – he'd gotten what he wanted – but that good news was balanced by one harsh reality: the tour cost to Barnum would be $187,500, which would serve as Jenny's guarantee. A London bank would hold it until the end of the tour.

To a showman who was used to paying his expenses out of the previous night's ticket sales, it was a daunting sum – equal to $7.7 million today – but Barnum wouldn't give up. He gathered all his cash, took out a mortgage on the museum and his new home, and borrowed $20,000 from the London bankers who would serve as the trustees.

He was still short, so he went to see one of his New York bankers, who laughed him out of his office. "Mr. Barnum," he said, "it is generally believed on Wall Street that your engagement with Jenny Lind will ruin you."

Stinging, he stormed out of the office, put up a few of his properties for cash, and secured the last $5,000 he needed from an old friend.

He was celebrating his success as he returned to New York the next morning on the train. When he opened the morning paper, he discovered that his contract with the famous singer had been leaked to the press before he'd had the chance to promote it himself.

The train's conductor, an old acquaintance, noticed that Barnum was agitated and asked him what was wrong.

It was nothing, Barnum assured the conductor. It was a story about his contract with Jenny Lind, bringing her to America in August. He stared at the conductor, curious to see how excited the man would be to learn that the "Swedish Nightingale" would soon be performing for American audiences.

The conductor nodded and smiled. "Jenny Lind!" he exclaimed. "Is she a dancer?"

It was not the response that Barnum had been hoping for. He knew right then that he had a lot of work to do.

BY THE TIME JENNY'S STEAMSHIP ARRIVED IN NEW YORK on September 1, 1850, everyone knew she was coming. Barnum ensured it with ads, news stories, and accounts of her European concerts. There were said to be between 30,000 and 40,000 people waiting for her on the docks when she left the boat.

Barnum was already on it. He'd spent the previous night at a friend's home on Staten Island and had been transported to the ship before it docked. He greeted Jenny, and after exchanging pleasantries, she asked Barnum when and where he'd first heard her sing.

"I've never had the pleasure of seeing you before in my life," he replied.

Jenny was shocked. "How is it possible that you dared risk so much money on a person you've never heard sing?"

"I risked it on your reputation," Barnum smiled, "which in musical matters I would much rather trust than my own judgment."

If Jenny wondered what she'd gotten herself into, her adventure was just beginning. After guiding her past the crowds at the docks and helping her fend off the hundreds of flower bouquets that were being shoved at her, Barnum got her into his carriage and took her to the Irving House – the finest in the city at the time – where another

10,000 people were waiting for her. And they continued to wait throughout the day and into the night. At midnight, 200 New York Musical Fund Society musicians arrived to serenade her, escorted by 300 red-shirted firemen, all carrying torches that illuminated the scene.

During an auction for opening-night tickets, the winning bid was submitted by John Genin, who owned a hat shop next to Barnum's Museum. He paid $225, a sum that made him a national celebrity.

The news was also trumpeted that Barnum had torn up the contract between Jenny and himself that promised her $1,000 per show and announced he planned to split the net proceeds of each night with the singer instead. It was a gesture that allegedly prompted Jenny to vow that she would sing for Barnum anywhere "for as long as you please."

The first concert was held at Castle Garden in New York City on September 11, 1850. It quickly sold out. More than 5,000 people filled the Garden, and thousands more crowded outside, hoping to catch faint echoes of the concert.

AND THAT FIRST NIGHT WAS JUST THE BEGINNING.

Jenny sang for New York audiences five more times at the start of the tour, and each was a sold-out performance. She attracted the attention of city officials, dignitaries, and the wealthiest members of local society. Among them was newspaper publisher Horace Greeley, who'd recently fallen under the spell of another young woman who had recently arrived in the city. That young woman, Greeley believed, was as gifted as Jenny Lind, but in a much different way.

Her name was Kate Fox, and she was one of the most famous women in America in 1850. She and her sister, Margaret, had recently introduced the world to Spiritualism, a movement founded on the belief that life existed after death and that the spirit could continue to exist outside the body. Most importantly, Spiritualists maintained that these spirits could – and did – communicate with the living.

The girls quickly became celebrities after Kate and Margaret began communicating with a spirit in their parents' home in upstate New York in March 1849. There was a huge demand to see the Fox sisters talk with ghosts, and they began to be booked into theaters all over New York. The publicity around them was intense. Some newspapers hailed them as frauds and others as sensations. But people flocked to see them in massive numbers, gladly paying for the privilege. As they continued to tour, they became hugely popular, and their séances became more elaborate, with objects moving about, spirits appearing, and tables levitating.

One of their greatest supporters was Horace Greeley, who helped Kate and Margaret arrange private demonstrations for select customers like author James Fenimore Cooper and First Lady Jane Pierce, who'd lost her young son while traveling with her husband, Franklin Pierce, to Washington for his inauguration.

One of the VIP engagements that Greeley arranged for Kate was a séance with Jenny Lind while she was performing in New York. He managed this through his friendship with Barnum, who had previously met Kate and toyed with the idea of representing her and her sister. But overwhelmed with publicity for the tour with Jenny, he didn't have time. He was aware of the publicity Kate Fox could provide for Jenny. He willingly agreed to take her to a séance arranged by Kate.

KATE AND MARGARET FOX WERE NEARLY AS FAMOUS AS JENNY LIND WHEN KATE HELD A SÉANCE FOR HER, ALONG WITH NEWSPAPER PUBLISHER HORACE GREELEY AND P.T. BARNUM.

That turned out to be a little harder than he thought. Jenny, a religious woman, balked at the idea at first but then agreed to attend for the entertainment value, not planning to take it seriously. There was no question that many fashionable people had become fascinated with Spiritualism, and it had become quite the thing to attend a séance. And, like Barnum, she was aware of the publicity value.

Jenny was in a jovial mood when she took her seat at the séance table, positioned between Barnum and Greeley. As Kate contacted the spirit world, a series of rapping noises were heard in the room. Jenny suspected Greeley of tomfoolery and admonished him to keep his hands above the table where she could see them. The editor shrugged and then sat with his hands on his head while the séance continued. Kate said nothing – she just continued producing the raps.

It wasn't recorded at the time what messages Jenny received from the spirit world, but a newspaper story later stated:

It is said the sweet songstress had a very interesting interview with what she believed to be the spirits of departed friends, and when she left, she kissed little Kate, saying, "If it were possible for you to make these sounds, I know it is impossible for you to answer the questions I have asked this evening."

Jenny had been conversing in her native tongue, and she was so impressed with the startling nature of the intelligence she received that she bade Kate goodbye with eyes suffused with tears.

Jenny may have been impressed, but tears seemed unlikely. If Jenny did ask her questions in Swedish – and we don't know since everyone seems to have been using this séance for publicity – then it's interesting that she received coherent replies. There are other accounts of Kate conducting rapping dialogues in foreign languages, and delivering messages to sitters, even though she spoke only English.

Whether this happened with Jenny, however, is unknown. Whatever she was told, the séance didn't convert Jenny to Spiritualism.

However, the incident is a chance meeting between two of the most famous women in America during one brief moment in 1850.

THE TOUR WAS SOON ON ITS WAY. IT CROSSED and re-crossed the country for the next nine months, netting just under $1 million, with about $500,000 going to Barnum and $350,000 to Jenny Lind.

By May 1851, they had traveled up the Mississippi and the Ohio and returned to New York and Philadelphia, tallying more than 90 performances by the time it was over. By then, certain people close to Jenny had planted the notion that Barnum was exploiting her. She didn't need him. She could do just as well on her own.

This happened for weeks, and Barnum finally tired of the accusations. He'd made a fortune – one that he'd worked hard for – and was ready for it to end.

On the night of their 93rd performance, Jenny presented him with a note terminating their enterprise. And with that, Barnum's most ambitious undertaking so far ended.

WHILE BARNUM WAS HAPPY TO SPEND THE REST OF the summer relaxing at Iranistan, Jenny continued her performances around the

JENNY TOURED THE LARGEST HALLS IN THE COUNTRY DURING THE GRAND TOUR ARRANGED BY BARNUM. SOON AFTER THE GOT MARRIED, HOWEVER, THE TOUR CAME TO AN END AND SHE RETURNED TO SWEDEN.

United States. In 1852, while on tour in Boston, she married Otto Goldschmidt, the German pianist performing with her.

According to Barnum, he and Jenny remained friends and visited backstage at her farewell concert later that year. She told Barnum she didn't plan to sing a great deal when she returned home except for charitable purposes. Jenny never opened her school. Instead, she lived in London, had three children, and occasionally performed. In her later years, she became a professor of voice at the Royal College of Music.

Barnum, of course, wouldn't rest for long. He was soon back to work and running at full speed at the museum. New exhibits and attractions began regularly appearing, including America's first public aquarium and many other remarkable displays.

He also began adding to his repertoire of human curiosities. One of the first additions was Madame Josephine Clofulia, "the most heavily bearded woman ever presented before the public." The Lucasie family from Holland – mother, father, and daughter – were striking people with albinism.

IN 1854, BARNUM PUBLISHED THE FIRST EDITION OF HIS AUTOBIOGRAPHY. MANY UPDATED VERSIONS WOULD FOLLOW AND WOULD CONTINUE TO BE A BESTSELLER FOR DECADES TO COME. EVEN WHEN HE WAS DEALING WITH BUSINESS DOWNTURNS, HE COULD COUNT ON SALES FROM HIS BOOK.

He also organized annual beautiful baby contests, fattest baby contests, flower shows, dog shows, poultry shows, and one of the nation's first beauty pageants, which he called the "Gallery of American Beauty." For a year, he also dabbled in publishing as the editor of a pictorial weekly called the *Illustrated News*, a venture he gave up on when he discovered how much work was required to keep it going.

In 1854, Barnum crafted the first version of his memoirs – *The Life of P.T. Barnum* – which would undergo periodic revisions for the rest of his days. It was rarely out of print, sold in the museum and later at the circus, and became one of his most valuable and enduring enterprises. He was surprisingly candid in his writings, which his critics found off-putting, dismissing Barnum and his museum: "Its conceited coarseness and the disgusting way in which it glories shameless frauds upon the public have astonished us."

But others, including Mark Twain, found Barnum's honesty and wry humor irresistible. Twain admired the showman for his wit, and others did, too. They didn't see any harm in Barnum's "humbugs," believing it provided the public with the kind of distraction and entertainment missing from the drudgery of everyday life.

Many considered Barnum a con artist and grifter, but I don't agree. Barnum was a showman and entertainer, and while he often stretched the truth, colored outside the lines, and told more than a few tall tales, he was never malicious or even greedy. Barnum had a knack for making – and spending – money, and while he loved fame and fortune, none of his "humbugs" ever really hurt anyone. The only person that Barnum ever really seemed to hurt was himself.

Throughout the 1850s, Barnum became involved in several losing businesses and failed ideas. He lost $10,000 on the "Fire Annihilator," a device that purported to produce steam vapors to put out fires.

He also became involved in land speculating and developing a parcel along the Pequannock River called East Bridgeport. Trying to lure industry to the area, Barnum agreed to secure several loans -- totaling $110,000 -- for the Jerome Clock Company in return for promises from company president Chauncey Jerome that he'd relocate to East Bridgeport.

All seemed to be going well until early 1856 when Barnum received word that his credit was in question. When he investigated, he discovered that his name had been used to secure nearly half a million dollars in loans for the clock company, which had just declared bankruptcy. Chauncey Jerome had stolen the money and fled the country, leaving Barnum to take the fall.

In a matter of days, he had been completely wiped out.

Barnum lost his money and closed up his grand home, but scrambling to stay afloat, he transferred the lease for the museum to his wife and sold the museum collection to friends, who'd keep it safe. Several wealthy friends offered him interest-free loans to pay off the outstanding clock factory notes, but Barnum was adamant about wanting to manage his own recovery.

But there was one friend that Barnum didn't turn down when they wrote to him and offered help. On May 12, 1856, he received a letter from Charles Stratton – General Tom Thumb. He didn't offer money – he knew his friend wouldn't accept it – but he did offer to join Barnum on a reprise of their wildly successful European tour of a decade before.

WHEN CREDITORS AND OTHER FRIENDS ABANDONED BARNUM TO HIS DEBTS, ONLY CHARLES STEPPED IN TO SAVE HIM. KNOWING BARNUM WOULD NEVER TAKE MONEY, HE ARRANGED FOR BARNUM TO PUT TOGETHER A TOUR IN EUROPE TO HELP HIS FRIEND PAY OFF HIS BILLS.

Barnum accepted, and soon, the pair were on their way to England, Germany, and Holland. The crowds were as large as ever, and Barnum began chipping away at his debts, trying to keep a low profile in case his creditors attempted to interfere with his plans.

Eventually, Barnum returned to the United States for the wedding of his daughter, Helen, but even that happy occasion was shadowed by further tragedy. Boarded up and waiting for the sale to pay off his creditors, Iranistan caught fire on the night of December 17 after a workman left a lighted pipe inside. The home – worth $150,000 but only covered by $28,000 insurance – burned to the ground. Barnum would sell the land for $50,000, with all the proceeds going to his creditors.

In despair, Barnum returned to England in early 1858 and continued the tour with Charles in Scotland and Wales. Tom Thumb was now in his twenties but was as popular as ever. For Barnum, spending time with his old friend was the best medicine he could ask for to ease his troubles. The fact that they were making money was a happy bonus. By the time the two men returned to America, nearly all the debt in his name had been retired.

In early 1860, Barnum secured a $20,000 loan to cover the last of the money still owed on his debts, and on March 24, a few months before his 50th birthday, he signed the contract that returned the ownership of the American Museum to him.

Barnum was eager to revamp the museum and brought in several new oddities, including a display of whales and a group of Native American chiefs. In late 1960, he also arranged a six-week engagement of the famous and original "Siamese Twins," Chang and Eng Bunker.

The brothers were joined at the stomach with their livers fused in the ligament that connected them. They had emigrated from Thailand, then known as Siam. They were nearly 50 years old and show business veterans by the time they came to work with Barnum.

CHANG AND ENG BUNKER WERE THE ORIGINAL "SIAMESE TWINS." THOUGH THEY HAD TOURED ON THEIR OWN BEFORE ACCEPTING AN ENGAGEMENT AT BARNUM'S MUSEUM, HIS PROMOTION DID WONDERS FOR THEIR CAREER.

They were among the rare performers who managed themselves during their careers. They'd had a manager for their first three years of performing, but they toured on their own after finding out he was cheating them. While they were still young, their exhibitions showed off how athletic they were. Later, they learned English and told stories about their lives in a more dignified parlor setting.

The twins were remarkably distinct individuals. Eng was a quiet, deferential teetotaler, and Chang was a loud, disagreeable drunk. Their career lasted only a decade, and when they retired, they settled in North Carolina, became American citizens, bought slaves, married local sisters who also fought constantly, and fathered 21 children. Each man's wife and children lived in a separate house, and the twins alternated between them every three days.

While the engagement with Chang and Eng at the museum was a financial success, it came with conflict and stress. One night, a frightful disturbance came from the museum apartment where the two were staying. When the door was broken open, staff members were shocked to find Chang on top of Eng, choking the life out of him. While the two calmed down and the show would go on, the engagement was not extended, and the twins returned home shortly before North Carolina seceded from the Union and the Civil War began.

During the war, the pair lost most of their wealth and resumed touring for a while. Chang died in January 1874, and Eng died just a few hours later. The two men were 62.

BARNUM FARED SOMEWHAT BETTER DURING THE Civil War. He stood firmly with President Lincoln and the Union, blasting Southern sympathizers in print and staging several dramas and exhibitions at the museum supporting the Union cause.

Barnum was often criticized for his outspoken support of the Union cause, and threats were frequently made that the museum or his new home, Lindencroft, would be burned. But Barnum was willing to accept the risk, and he even accepted the draft of the new Republican party to run for the Connecticut legislature. He won the election and considered it an honor to be able to help approve the Constitutional amendment to abolish slavery. He won a second term in 1866.

He lost in his third run for the office when a Democratic landslide swept over the state, removing the governor and dooming many Republican candidates, including Barnum. He insisted he was not disappointed with the defeat, saying he would not miss "the filth and

BARNUM'S AMERICAN MUSEUM BURNED ON JULY 13, 1865, BUT WITH 25 YEARS OF HIS LIFE INVESTED IN IT AND 150 EMPLOYEES DEPENDING ON HIM, HE QUICKLY REBUILT.

scandal, the slanders and vindictiveness, the plottings and fawnings" of political life. He came away from it with a knowledge of "new phases of human nature" and said the lessons he learned about the duplicity of politics were enough to last him a lifetime.

But it wasn't just double-dealing and backstabbing that darkened Barnum's post-war days. On July 13, 1865, he was addressing the legislature about expanding the railroads when he was handed a telegram with terrible news – the American Museum had caught fire and was burning to the ground.

Barnum calmly finished his speech and then rushed to New York to find that the collection he'd put 25 years of his life and at least a half-million dollars into had been reduced to ashes. Barnum had underinsured the museum, too. He'd recover only about $40,000.

When Barnum walked dejectedly into the office of Horace Greeley, seeking advice, his friend was direct with him: "Accept this fire as a notice to quit and go fishing."

And perhaps Barnum would have accepted that advice – not really, there's no way he'd have quit – if it hadn't been for the 150 employees who depended on the museum for their livelihoods. He also correctly believed that the museum was important to New York City.

"Going fishing" was going to have to wait.

Barnum leased the former Chinese Museum buildings further uptown, and on November 13, 1865, Barnum's New American Museum was opened for business.

Among the many improvements in the new museum was the installation of a permanent animal menagerie, which he partnered with the Van Amburgh Menagerie Company. The troupe would travel during the summer and then bring the animals back to New York for display over the winter. As Barnum described, the Van Amburgh company had a menagerie "superior in extent to any other similar collection in America." It included a small African elephant and what he claimed was the only living giraffe then in the United States. There was also a collection of lions and two Bengal tigers.

Barnum also added a much larger lecture room, and as the new museum achieved even greater success than the original, he added an adjoining building to the complex. This allowed Barnum to investigate the establishment of a true national exhibition hall, which he envisioned as an American counterpart to the British Museum. He said his museum would become the "nucleus of a great free national institution."

Barnum presented his plans, which were endorsed by Horace Greeley and his *New York Tribune*, as well as a group of prominent citizens. Even President Andrew Johnson lent his approval to the project. Soon, Barnum was making the rounds in Washington, promoting the establishment of a National Museum in New York City.

However, what might have become of this grand vision will never be known. On the evening of March 2, 1868, a second fire consumed the new museum, taking with it the lives of nearly all the animals of the menagerie.

Enough was enough for Barnum, who had lost two homes and two museums to fire. He was done. There would be no more museums.

FOR A TIME, BARNUM TOOK GREELEY'S ADVICE. He didn't go fishing, but he retreated into isolation. Just two weeks after the second museum burned, his mother, Irena, died, and his wife, Charity, began suffering health issues. Her doctor suggested that living near the shore might improve her condition, so Barnum sold Lindencroft, the second of his grand homes, and moved to a temporary house he purchased on the Long Island Sound.

BARNUM'S NEW HOME, WALDEMERE, WAS BUILT IN 1868.

By the fall of 1868, he was building a new home on the water named Waldemere, or Woods-by-the-Sea. Barnum announced that it would be both a home and a giant guesthouse and if he decided to do some actual fishing, it would be the perfect spot.

But again, fishing and relaxation were not really in the 58-year-old Barnum's repertoire.

He tried traveling for the sole purpose of sightseeing, but scarcely had he gotten to Salt Lake City when he was conferring with Mormon leader Brigham Young about the possibility of exhibiting the man's dozens of wives and scores of children. Barnum suggested to Young that a traveling show might net them as much as $200,000 a year, and although Young expressed interest, nothing came of the idea.

In San Francisco, Barnum encountered a little person "more diminutive than General Tom Thumb when I first found him." Soon, "Admiral Dot" was out on a tour managed by Barnum. His old friend, Charles, undertook a new world tour, which Barnum had also arranged.

Admiral Dot's real name was Leonard Kahn, and he'd been born in 1859 – or maybe 1863, no one knows for sure – to Garbriel and Caroline Kahn. His mother gave birth to 10 children, although only three survived – all of them little people.

BARNUM'S NEXT DISCOVERY WAS "ADMIRAL DOT," WHOSE REAL NAME WAS LEONARD KAHN.

Leonard's two brothers later performed as Major Atom and General Pin. I haven't been able to verify this, but accounts say that Caroline was declared insane and jailed after she tried to drown Leonard's youngest brother when he was two years old.

After Barnum discovered Leonard, he dressed him in a complete admiral's uniform and invited the editors of all the San Francisco newspapers to meet him at the Cosmopolitan Hotel. The following news accounts created a huge demand to see the boy, and Leonard exhibited for three sold-out weeks before Barnum took him east.

He remained under Barnum's management until 1877. At that time, he joined the American Lilliputian Company. In the 1890s, he toured with a circus owned by Adam Forepaugh.

Leonard married Lottie Smartwood, also a little person, in 1892, and they had two children together, Hazel and Gabriel. Leonard died during the 1918 Spanish Flu pandemic. He was 59 years old.

BARNUM' WAS INSPIRED IN 1869 BY THE DISCOVERY of the so-called "Cardiff Giant" on a farm near Syracuse, New York. In reality, the 10-foot-long object was nothing more than a statue carved in the likeness of a man. It had been created in the pose of a man who may have died in pain and began to be exhibited as a giant "petrified man" from some previous age.

Barnum loved it. He offered to buy the object and, when turned down, had his own copy made and placed it on display in an acquaintance's museum in New York, calling his statue the "real" giant and the one displayed in Syracuse a "fake."

BARNUM WAS SO INSPIRED BY A HOAX DUBBED THE "CARDIFF GIANT" THAT HE CREATED A HOAX OF HIS OWN.

When he found out about Barnum's stunt, David Hannum, the leader of the group displaying the original Cardiff giant, made a remark that has since become legendary: "There's a sucker born every minute."

But Hannum didn't come up with the phrase. It was first uttered by Mike McDonald, a gambler and confidence man from Chicago, but somehow, the quote has been attributed to P.T. Barnum himself. He never said it, but many maintain that he could have – or even should have.

Instead, Barnum was busy revising his autobiography and toying with other schemes, like fencing off a section of the East River so he could exhibit a squad of sea lions that he dreamed of capturing off the coast of San Francisco.

He didn't do that or anything else. Barnum had lost all patience with "fishing," so it was no surprise in the fall of 1870 when W.C. Coup called with a business proposition that Barnum was in the mood to listen.

It wouldn't be long before Barnum's life would change forever. Coup and his partner, Dan Castello, were about to give him the chance to collaborate on a venture that promised to revitalize Barnum's passion for museums and menageries. It would use his love for the American Museum to foster the creation of what would become known as "The Greatest Show on Earth."

W.C. COUP, THE CIRCUS OWNER WHO CHANGED BARNUM'S LIFE AND HISTORY FOREVER.

W.C. Coup was no stranger to the circus. He had been knocking around the sawdust-strewn tents since 1853 when he was only 16. He started running sideshows for a couple of so-called "mud shows," small outfits that traveled the unpaved roads of western America. By 1869, he had worked his way up to a management position with the Yankee Robinson Wagon Circus. However, his wife finally convinced him to give up the show business life for a more reasonable existence, breeding livestock on a Wisconsin farm.

Coup gave that his best shot, but his farm was near Delavan, in southern Wisconsin, where several shows kept their winter quarters. When one of his old friends, a seasoned performer named Dan Castello, arrived in Delavan after touring the West Coast with a show of his own, the two hatched plans to charter a steamboat, load Dan's troupe on board, call themselves Dan Castello's Great Circus & Egyptian Caravan and start playing in the lumber camps that were located on the shores of nearby Lake Michigan. They did well enough, and by the time winter stopped their travels, they had convinced themselves they were simply one bold move away from fame and fortune in the circus.

Coup began working on their plan. Many years before, he had worked one season as a roustabout for a show in which P.T. Barnum was interested. He'd seen the draw of Barnum's name firsthand and was sure it would be the key ingredient to the plan he was concocting with Castello. He worked up the courage to approach Barnum with his idea. If Barnum was willing to combine his name, financial backing, and genius for picking talent, they could create the greatest traveling show ever known with their expertise in managing circuses.

Luckily for Coup and Castello, they came to Barnum when he was bored and desperate for something to do. But the great showman initially said he had no interest in the scheme, but the two men persisted, even scaling down their plan and asking for only the use of his name. Then, Barnum changed his mind and offered to invest $100,000 in their show, but still hesitated to get fully involved – but not for long.

The story goes that Coup visited Barnum one day in his office, played a game of checkers, and discussed possibilities for the show. While chatting, one of Barnum's assistants came by to drop off some papers. When the assistant overheard them talking, he joked to his boss, "I thought you were a man of leisure."

Barnum laughed and jumped up from his chair, knocking the checkers and board onto the floor. "I thought so, too!" he said.

Coup looked up and told him, "Then it's time to decide this thing. You've got $100,000 in it. If you want to get out, it's all right."

"I'm in it!" Barnum stated. "The checkers can lay where they are."

Barnum would end up with only a few small additions to the partnership, including having his son-in-law Samuel Hurd retained as the company treasurer. For only a modest three percent of the receipts, Barnum would back the show and allow the use of his name. He'd also add certain key attractions to the troupe, including the tiny Admiral Dot, his copy of the Cardiff Giant, and several other curiosities. In addition, he'd advise Coup and Castello on preparing advertising materials, playbills, and the like.

With things moving full speed ahead, the pair began assembling ten carloads of animals, circus performers, and all the paraphernalia they needed to be shipped to New York.

On April 10, 1871, P.T. Barnum's Great Traveling Museum, Menagerie, Caravan, and Hippodrome opened under three acres of canvas tents in a field in Brooklyn. Over 10,000 people attended that opening show, and thousands were turned away. The show then went on the road, traveling from Maine to Kansas, and returned to New York City in November, where it played at the 10,000-seat Empire Rink through the holidays, closing only so the performers and crew could prepare for the upcoming season.

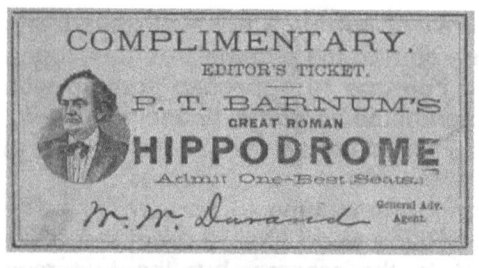

BARNUM WAS BACK ON THE ROAD AGAIN, BUT FOR THE FIRST TIME, HE WAS WITH A CIRCUS. THE BIGGEST DRAW WAS BARNUM'S NAME BUT HE BROUGHT MUCH MORE THAN THAT TO THE SHOW, AS DID COUP AND CASTELLO'S KNOWLEDGE OF BUSINESS.

Barnum brought a lot to the show besides his name. He offered two giraffes for the menagerie, although one died during the voyage across the Atlantic. He also sent representatives to Alaska to bring back sea lions and seals and discovered an Italian goat named Alexis who could ride on the back of a horse and jump through hoops and over rails without falling. The topper, though, was – regrettably – "four wild Fiji cannibals, ransomed at great cost from the hands of a royal enemy, into whose hands they had fallen, and by whom they were about to be killed and perhaps eaten."

It was definitely a different time in history.

The animals and curiosities that Barnum provided to the show were invaluable to the show itself. However, Coup and Castello's knowledge about how to tour and manage a traveling circus was equally important. Coup later said, "Mr. Barnum was absolutely ignorant about the technical details of the show, but in its place, he possessed an amount of commercial daring and business sagacity that aptly atoned for his other shortcomings."

Coup was a master at advance publicity, often hanging posters as far away as 50 miles from the towns where they'd play. It was said that Coup "hung as much paper" in a week as most shows did in a year. He has also been credited with using a train to move the circus, a plan that Barnum initially resisted. However, once he was convinced of how useful that kind of transportation could be, he was enthusiastic about it, stating that it was clear their growing show would never be efficiently transported by wagons again.

THE CIRCUS MOVED AROUND THE COUNTRY BY RAIL AND WAS A TRAVELING MIX OF BARNUM'S MUSEUM, AN ANIMAL MENAGERIE, SIDESHOW, AND CIRCUS.

Once the Barnum Show began traveling by rail, it required at least 60 to 70 freight cars, six passenger cars, and three engines. They often traveled 100 miles in a single night to hit good-sized towns every day, arriving in time to give three exhibitions and the usual street parade at 8:00 A.M. The speed of the train allowed the show to bypass smaller venues in favor of larger cities where the receipts doubled or even tripled what they could make in small towns.

When the show opened at one of its stops, it was presented in three separate tents – one for the animal menagerie, a second for the museum, and a third for the performance arena, which could seat between 5,000 and 7,500 guests. The museum was a traveling version of Barnum's former New York enterprise, containing a mix of educational exhibits, oddities, and a few outright humbugs, like the Cardiff Giant.

As we'll explore throughout this book, many see the exhibition of those with physical abnormalities as offensive today, but you must consider such exhibits from a historical perspective. During the nineteenth and early twentieth centuries – what became the heyday of the sideshows, the performers considered themselves special, even superior to those who came to gawk at them. They were referred to as "freaks," which was supposed to be an insult, but they didn't see it that way.

Most of these performers chose to put themselves on display because it was good business. A person with three legs, or pop eyes, or an unusually hairy face couldn't exactly find work behind the counter at the local drug store in those days. So, the smart, enterprising people made a very good living for themselves in the only way they could – usually making a lot more money than the fellow behind the drugstore counter.

Barnum may have been part of some things that are difficult for us to justify these days – like his ownership of Joice Heth – but, on the other hand, he helped many performers get their start in the circus business as human attractions and, in many cases, they became some of his closest friends.

In any case, in addition to human oddities, various mechanical marvels were also on display, like an automaton trumpeter, a flock of mechanized singing birds, and seven lifelike bell ringers. There was also a monkey that played the violin, a rabbit that played the tambourine, and a performance of the Last Supper, where the biblical figures ate, drank, and conversed with each other. And if the last seems less than exciting, imagine sold-out audiences flocking to see the "Pageant of the Masters" every summer, coming to see famous works of art brought to life.

The museum also boasted Egyptian mummies, various wax figures that sometimes drooped in the hot canvas tents, exotic stuffed animals, the massive teeth and jawbone of a whale, an array of Oriental weaponry, and the cross-section of a California redwood tree, hollowed out so that 20 people could stand inside and have their photographs taken.

The menagerie included camels, lions, zebras, two elephants, kangaroos, a rhino, a leopard, monkeys, and almost anything imaginable, filling about 30 cages with wildlife. The sea lions eventually made it from Alaska, although they turned out to be a great regret since they required at least 300 pounds of fish each day to keep them fed.

In addition, 60 arena performers and 75 other people were involved in the show's production. This cost them about $2,500 daily, around $64,000 today. This was an outlay that astounded other circus men, who considered the Barnum undertaking to be "madness."

But Barnum, Coup, and Castello had the last laugh. By the end of the first season's tour, they had profited over $500,000. Apparently, it wasn't madness after all.

AFTER THE 1872 SEASON, BARNUM SHIFTED GEARS AND devised a winter plan. The money was just too good. He purchased a building on Fourteenth Street in Manhattan, where he planned to offer an off-season version of the traveling show. Tragically, he'd only been open for a month before another fire occurred. This one burned the building, killed most of the animals, and destroyed the elaborate wardrobes of the performers.

But, not surprisingly, Barnum sent out an immediate call for replacements to the menagerie, and the show was back on the road for the summer of 1873 – which brought about one of the greatest innovations in circus history.

By now, the tent being used by the show had grown into an elongated oval shape that seated as many as 13,000 people. The problem was that audience members sitting on the ends often left their seats and rushed ringside to get a better view of what was happening there. Barnum and Castello devised a solution – they would mount simultaneous performances in adjoining rings.

The human performers didn't always love this since it meant the audience's attention would be divided, but for audience members, it seemed to be an added feature, offering them twice the show for the same ticket price.

In April 1874, Barnum returned to New York to oversee the opening of the new Great Roman Hippodrome, a replacement for the venue that had been most recently destroyed by fire. It was built at the site where Madison Square Garden would someday stand. The hippodrome seated 10,000 people, and the arena floor was large enough to hold what Barnum knew would be a jaw-dropping closing act – a real-life Roman chariot race.

That summer, the 64-year-old Barnum joined Coup to take the show back on the road. Barnum was feeling especially energetic because he was getting remarried in the fall. Charity had never recovered from her health problems and had died in late 1873. Barnum had spent weeks grieving her death, staying with the family of his long-time friend, John Fish. His bride-to-be was John's daughter, 24-year-old Nancy Fish. In September, they were married in a small, uncharacteristically quiet ceremony.

It turned out there was a good reason for the wedding to be so low-key. Documents found long after Barnum's death revealed that he and

BARNUM'S SECOND – MUCH YOUNGER – WIFE, NANCY FISH

WHEN COUP AND CASTELLO SOLD THEIR SHARES OF THE CIRCUS TO BARNUM, HE FOUND NEW INVESTORS AND CONTINUED ON, BIGGER AND BETTER.

(BELOW) BARNUM'S COLLECTION OF "LIVING CURIOSITIES"

Nancy had actually been married in a Valentine's Day ceremony earlier in 1874, less than three months after Charity's death. The defense for Barnum in this matter is that Charity had been an invalid and recluse for several years before she died, often having "prayed for death to come as an angel of mercy to take her home."

The elaborate hippodrome show was back on the road in 1875, along with a second show that more closely resembled a standard circus, featuring lions, clowns, acrobats, and dramatic spectacles like Native American horse riders charging after stampeding buffalo.

By this time, it had all become too much for Coup and Castello, the two men who had lured Barnum back into show business. They sold their interests to Barnum and went back to managing profitable exhibitions of their own.

After this turn of events, Barnum sold off the permanent location in New York and put his energies into the traveling show, which continued through the decade. The 1876 edition of the show was conceived as offering a "Fourth of July celebration every day," closing with the singing of "America," with the audience joining in on the chorus. The nighttime programs ended with fireworks.

Barnum had taken on several new partners, all of whom were experienced circus men – Samuel Hurd, John J. Nathans, Lewis B. June, and George F. Bailey, the nephew of the original exhibitor of the circus elephant, Hachaliah Bailey.

Doing little more than lending his name and offering direction, Barnum raked in 50 percent of the show's profits, usually making as much as nearly $87,000 yearly, more than $18 million in today's dollars. He also profited handsomely from sales of his autobiography, which sold for $1.50 per copy. It had grown to 900 gilt-edged pages, bound in muslin, that included one free ticket to the show.

It might seem as though Barnum was walking away with a larger share of profits than he deserved, but the reason for the show's success was undoubtedly advertising and publicity. In that, Barnum had no equal. He was a pioneer of the use of color lithographs, creating posters 10 feet tall and 50 feet long, and one of his most imaginative creations was a traveling display that consisted of a 64-foot-long railroad car with his portrait and dramatic representations of the show's animals and performers on both sides.

The coach served as a rolling headquarters for the circus's advertising and public relations corps. It often arrived in larger venues days ahead of the show, both as a colorful ad for the coming exhibition and a practical operations base for the publicity crew. The show spent about $100,000 on advertising each year, about one-third of the budget.

By now, Barnum's name had become legend. During a meeting with former U.S. president and Civil War general Ulysses S. Grant, Barnum told him, "General, since your journey around the world, you are the best-known man on the globe."

But Grant disagreed. "No, sir, your name is familiar to multitudes who have never heard of me. Wherever I went, among the distant nations, the fact that I was an American led to constant inquiries whether I knew Barnum."

And Grant was right. Barnum was in such great demand that his deal with his latest partners required him to appear with the show at least a dozen times each season. If he didn't, questions would follow, and it was said that more than one young visitor to the circus was heard to ask their parents, "Where's the cage that Barnum is in?"

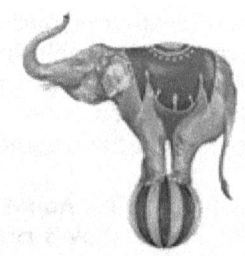

4. THE NAME THAT CAME AFTER "BARNUM"

BY 1880, BARNUM HAD COME TO BELIEVE THERE WASN'T A single traveling circus in the world that could compare to what he called the "Greatest Show on Earth."

Other show managers boasted of owning equally impressive shows, but Barnum dismissed all but a few. His closest competitor was the Great London Circus, a grand undertaking that was piloted by a man named James A. Bailey. But if Barnum was impressed with either of them, he was hesitant to say so.

But then came the "Baby Elephant."

On March 10, 1880, news broke of a baby elephant called Little Columbia, born in Philadelphia with Bailey's circus. The birth was so effectively advertised that the public became wild with excitement, and Barnum was irked by what seemed to be an insurmountable advantage Bailey and his partners had gained. Barnum stewed for two months before sending a fateful telegram offering to

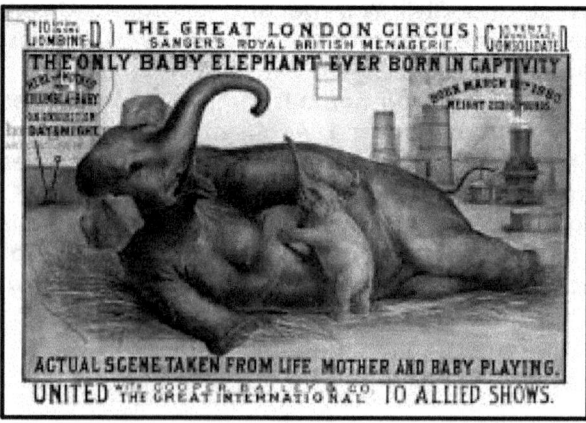

purchase Little Columbia – a telegram that Bailey turned into a marketing gold mine.

Now realizing that Bailey was a force to be reckoned with, Barnum went to work. By October, it was reported that James Bailey had bought out the interest of his partners in the Great London Circus, and soon after that, word spread that Barnum had dissolved his partnerships.

That was followed by even more startling news – James Bailey's show would be combined with those of P.T. Barnum with a series of massive consolidation shows to be given in New York in the spring. After that, one of the shows would play across America while the other toured Europe. At the end of five years, they would swap and continue to tour as the new Barnum and Bailey Circus.

The new management team would be Barnum, Bailey, and James L. Hutchinson, Bailey's former concession manager, who would serve as chief financial officer for the new combined show. Barnum would again be 50 percent owner, with Bailey and Hutchinson splitting the other half. Barnum estimated that the show's daily expenses would run at least $4,500, a figure that seemed comical to competing showmen. They said no show could hope to make any money with those costs.

But they underestimated the new partnership. Not only could they make money, but they would – by the truckload.

JAMES A. BAILEY, THE MAN WHO HAD BEEN BARNUM'S GREATEST COMPETITOR BECAME HIS ALLY AND THE BRAINS BEHIND "THE GREATEST SHOW ON EARTH."

ASK ANYONE WITH A LOVE OF CIRCUSES TO NAME THE MOST famous shows in American history, and they'll reply with "Ringling" and "Barnum and Bailey." But ironically – or maybe not, this is the circus, after all – at least one of those names was a total invention.

"James Bailey" was born James A. McGinnis on July 4, 1847, when his future partner, P.T. Barnum, was making a name for himself as a museum owner and presenter of oddities. Barnum's life and career have become the stuff of legend, but far less is known about Bailey.

He was the youngest of four brothers, orphaned before James was 10 years old. Though his father left a considerable estate of $20,000, James was sent to live in the country with his oldest sister, Catherine, and her family. Instead of being treated as a welcome addition to the family, the boy was made to work in the fields and treated like a servant. He later said that he was whipped for the slightest provocation and worked so hard that he was often late for school, which led to further beatings from his teacher.

He endured the abuse until one day in 1859 when he ran away at the age of 12. He left with only the clothing on his back and a penknife in his pocket. He managed to get himself hired on a farm, working for just $3 a month, plus room and board. His job was to follow along after the farmer with a scythe and bind the wheat into sheaves. It was brutally hard work for a young boy, but he stayed with it until the end of the harvest.

After that, he drifted to Pontiac, Michigan, where he found work as a bellhop in a small hotel, a position that required him to help in the stable, where he took a particular liking to horses.

It would be the arrival of a circus in town, though, that would change his life. The advance agent for Robinson and Lake's circus, Fred H. Bailey, arrived in town in a big red wagon and caused much excitement. Along with other local boys, James helped to post flyers around town in exchange for a ticket to the show. While hanging around the show, James met one of the owners, Bill Lake, who took a liking to him. After convincing the showman he was an orphan, James literally ran off with the circus when it left town.

He became the apprentice of the advance man Fred Bailey and Bailey his wife essentially adopted the boy. Their relationship was so close that James eventually adopted their surname. During the summers, James traveled with the show; during the winter, he found odd jobs, usually working in some kind of show business.

During the winter of 1862, Bill Lake secured a job for him as a delivery driver in Zanesville, Ohio, but young Bailey soon got tired of driving a wagon up and down the town's streets. He made his way to Nashville and got a job as an usher, but his experience and industriousness led to him being promoted to advertiser and ticket taker.

One night, a man named Green, who worked as a provisioner for the Union Army, offered Bailey a tip if he could find him a seat. He found the man a seat but refused the tip, which impressed Green so much that he hired Bailey on the spot as his clerk, which, given the hard times, was a windfall for the young man. He spent the rest of the war working for the military.

While Bailey was working as a clerk, the circus business struggled along, playing only in the North, thanks to the war. This was something that Robinson and Lake learned quickly when it began its 1861 performances in Lexington, Kentucky. Soon after putting up the tent and raising an American flag on the center pole, a group of citizens advised them to lower the colors and quickly move the show to the north side of the Ohio River. Even after the war ended, northern circuses didn't do well in the South for several years.

BY 1866 – ABOUT THE TIME P.T. BARNUM WAS PLANNING to leave the world of show business behind forever – the circus started to regain its footing in post-war America. James Bailey, now 18, was happy to quit his job as a clerk. He was soon back to work as an assistant agent for Bill Lake and advertising poster for Lake's Hippo-Olympiad show for $50 a month. Bailey proved to be a skilled assistant and was promoted to general circus agent within two years, making

$200 a month – a long way from the $3.50 he'd been making with his first job of gathering wheat into sheaves.

In 1869, when Lake's show was playing in Granby, Missouri, Lake was overseeing the circus entrance as a post-show concert was getting ready to start. A local troublemaker named Killian barged through the gate without a ticket for the second show. Killian remarked that he'd paid Lake enough money for an evening's entertainment, and if he wanted to listen to music, too, he'd damn sure do what he wanted. Lake informed Killian that he'd need to leave. He could either walk out or, Lake said and then nodded toward two burly roustabouts that stood nearby, he could be carried out.

Killian sneered and spat some tobacco juice at Lake's feet. Then he turned and left, escorted by the roustabouts. Lake thought no more about it, walked back to the gate, and started chatting with some friends.

He didn't know that Killian suddenly stopped walking, pulled a pistol from his coat, whirled around, and fired a shot over the shoulder of one of the startled roustabouts. The bullet struck Lake in the heart, and he collapsed, dead before he crumpled to the ground. Killian escaped and wouldn't be apprehended for days.

Lake's widow, Agnes, gathered the troupe together and vowed to continue. She asked those who wanted to leave to give her two weeks' notice on the spot. When no one spoke up, she broke down in tearful gratitude, and the show went on.

In the aftermath of the tragedy – and his longtime mentor gone – Bailey eventually decided to go out on his own. He scraped together his savings and purchased a 50-percent interest in a "concert privilege" with the Hemmings, Cooper, and Whitby circus. This "privilege" gave Bailey the right to the kind of "after shows" that Lake had added to his show's repertoire and allowed him to keep half the profits for himself. Such shows usually consisted of music and vaudeville acts that included dancers, comedians, singers, and, sometimes, various human "freaks."

Not much is known about Bailey's time as a concert promoter, but the tour that next season turned out to be eventful, especially after one of the troupe's partners, Harry Whitby, was shot to death taking tickets, just like Bill Lake had been the year before. Despite the tragedy, the show continued in 1872, with Bailey now working as an agent for $100 weekly, the most money paid to any general agent in circus history.

Bailey's later success in the circus business was undoubtedly because of his early experiences as a general agent or advance man.

Bailey paid his dues by posting bills and papering towns with advertisements in the days before the show's arrival. Another part of his duties involved planning the best travel routes from town to town, willing over local town officials and police officers, securing permits, leasing venues, arranging for the delivery of supplies and food for humans and animals alike, and managing all the other details needed for a smooth performance. Not to mention, most engagements started and ended in fewer than 24 hours, only to take place again the following day, six and sometimes seven times a week.

In 1873, Bailey parlayed the profits he'd made as an agent, bought out Hemmings, and became the new co-owner of the Cooper and Bailey Circus and Sanger's Royal British Menagerie. The show traveled successfully by wagon for the next three years, although that method of transportation was finally reaching its end.

By 1876, Bailey decided they also needed to transition to rail and embarked on a tour from St. Louis to San Francisco. With receipts in San Francisco topping as much as $6,000 per show, Bailey convinced his partner Cooper to undertake an even more unlikely trip.

He suggested they take the show to Australia.

After Cooper realized he wasn't joking and was assured they could make money offering something that no one in Australia had ever seen, he reluctantly agreed to his partner's seemingly ridiculous plan.

But Bailey never saw it as ridiculous. He chartered a steamship for $17,000 that would transport the company, including six elephants, a giraffe, a hippopotamus, and a rhinoceros, to Australia and New Zealand for an added series of performances.

Though business boomed in Australia, Bailey encountered problems that no one in the circus business had faced before. The ship was battered by storms.

One night, the sea crashed over the ship's bow with such force that several animal cages lashed to the deck broke free of their ropes. As Bailey, the sailors, and the circus men struggled on the storm-lashed decks, the bear cage came loose, knocked into the lions' cage, and both went overboard with the animals inside. Moments later, the rhinoceros crashed out of its enclosure, hit the ship's rail, and flew into the sea. In all, nearly half the animals were lost, and, in the aftermath, the giraffe was found dead from a broken neck.

No replacement giraffes could be found in Australia, which led to a bizarre workaround. When the ship docked in Sydney, the dead giraffe was stuffed, and a mechanical device was placed into its chest cavity. It was placed in a dimly lit cage, where its neck and head bobbed gently until a live replacement could be shipped in. None of the customers ever realized the difference.

Bailey eventually replaced all the animals, but his troubles were far from over. As the show steamed toward South America, another massive storm hit, and a wave struck the lead elephant with such force that it killed it. The company's new rhino broke free from its chains and charged another elephant, creating chaos among all the animals. But Bailey strode calmly onto the scene and directed his men to get ropes and chains around the rhino and drag it away from the elephant. Once it was subdued, the menagerie quieted down.

Bailey was only 31 when he undertook this massive endeavor. He was a small, lean man, weighing only about 130 pounds, but he never hesitated to step into the fray, leading even the most unruly and boisterous roustabouts to respect him. He was never "James," "Jim," or even "Boss," he was always "Mr. Bailey."

He was never, ever known as "McGinniss." That was a name that Bailey had come to despise. Bailey had broken away from his older sister's family and had no interest in ever contacting them again. Today, it seems impossible that a young boy could simply walk away from one life and walk into another, but – as much as some of us would have liked to -- the mid-nineteenth century was a very different time.

To "run away with the circus" back then meant to leave ordinary life behind forever. The circus stood intentionally apart from regular life. The hours an audience spent on circus grounds were meant to be an antidote to everyday life, a small window of wonder and an opportunity to see the impossible made real.

It's valid to say that when Jimmy McGinniss fled from his abusive home, he ceased to exist and was literally replaced by James Bailey. Some would find this transformation impossible or inauthentic, but the circus world was not based on the conventional.

WHEN JAMES MCGINNIS RAN AWAY FROM HIS SISTER'S ABUSIVE HOME TO JOIN THE CIRCUS, HE RE-INVENTED HIMSELF AND CREATED A LIFE THAT WAS BIGGER AND MORE SPECTACULAR THAN HE EVER COULD HAVE DREAMED AS A BOY.

To Bailey – and everyone else who did exactly what he did during the glory days of the American circus – it wasn't a transformation; it was literally a brand-new life.

BAILEY'S MONUMENTAL TOUR ON THE OTHER SIDE OF THE world was so successful that he extended it by two years, traveling from Australia and New Zealand to South America, around Cape Horn, and finally returning to New York City on December 10, 1878. He had traveled more than 76,000 miles. Despite the company's harrowing experiences with storms, the journey gave the show a notoriety and respect it had never enjoyed.

Soon after his return, Bailey got the news that a well-respected show – the Great London Circus – had fallen on hard times during a tour of the South and was stranded because of money owed to a printing company. Bailey saw this as another opportunity. Though his world tour nearly broke him financially and his return to the United States had left him almost $12,000 in debt, he was able to convince the printer who held the lien on the Great London show to take a gamble on Bailey's abilities. The printer sold Bailey the show for $25,000 and took a promissory note for the entire amount.

The 1879-1880 season of the show certainly didn't give the appearance that Bailey's finances were shaky. It was, according to all reports, "a worthy competitor of any of the shows of the period." One of the innovations he introduced that year was a steam-powered generator that illuminated a series of carbon-arc lamps to illuminate the inside of the tents. It was the first commercial use of this kind of lighting, and carbon-arc lamps would be used for sporting events and other outdoor activities well into the twentieth century.

By the end of the season, Bailey's success had turned him into one of the major players in the industry, and rival promoters understood that going up against a Cooper and Bailey show would be difficult. Bailey had not only developed a reputation as a boss who managed every aspect of the operation, keeping a close eye on the profit and loss ledger, but was also known to be ruthless. Once in South America, when the show was overextended, and there was only enough cash to get the animals back to New York, he left his performers stranded unless they paid their own fares home.

Part of Bailey's approach to business and toward the people who worked for him came from his upbringing. He was a "self-made man," there's no question about that. Like Andrew Carnegie, Thomas Edison, John D. Rockefeller, and others during the Gilded Age, he had risen above his early circumstances and turned hard work into a fortune. He felt that if he could succeed, then anyone could do it. There was no need for coddling or even pity. His tendency to obsess over even the smallest detail of the business suggests that no amount of success would ever have been enough to guard against the possibility of failure.

And then there was his coolness and reserve toward others, even those he considered friends. He'd grown up with almost no affection ever shown toward him. His parents died, and his sister and her family became monsters. When Fred Bailey and his wife took him in, he was so overwhelmed that he took their last name as his own. But even then, James didn't accept the home they likely offered. He continued to make his own way. He never learned how to give or accept affection from others.

But if Bailey had been the kind of man to discuss his feelings, he still likely would have brushed off the business fears that often plagued him. He'd already survived the Panic of 1873, the first "great depression" to strike the United States – when unemployment soared to 14 percent – so perhaps his grim stoicism served him well.

In March 1880, Bailey announced that the company's huge Indian elephant, Babe, had given birth to the first calf ever born in captivity in America. He dubbed the baby "Little Columbia," and news of the arrival spread far and wide.

The announcement gained the public's attention and promoters throughout the circus business, who knew that the baby elephant would translate directly into ticket sales.

One of the impresarios struck by Bailey's promotion was, of course, P.T. Barnum, who had been lured back into show business just four years before. He telegraphed Bailey, offering to purchase Little Columbia for the astronomical sum of $100,000 -- $20 million in today's dollars.

The telegram was a godsend for Bailey – not because he wanted

to sell the elephant, but because he knew he could use it to promote his new attraction. He dashed off a reply to Barnum that read simply, "Will not sell at any price!". Then he started distributing flyers and handbills in every city on the upcoming Cooper and Bailey tour that featured a facsimile of Barnum's telegram and the message, "Come see what Barnum would pay a king's ransom for!"

For Barnum, who never underestimated an opponent, this was a moment of great realization. Any annoyance he might have had about being bested by Bailey was replaced with a different emotion. He wrote, "I had at last met showmen worthy of my steel! Pleased to find comparatively young men with a business talent and energy approximating my own, I met them in friendly council, and we decided to join our two shows in one mammoth combination."

Barnum made the merger sound much simpler than it was, but by August 1880, a contract had been signed and an association began that changed the circus world and entertainment in America forever.

The new show was first called P.T. Barnum's and Great London Combined, but that didn't matter. What mattered was that Barnum and Bailey had now become a team.

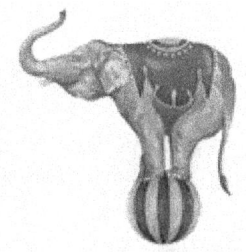

5. THE "GREATEST SHOW" BEGINS

AFTER THE MERGER OF THE TWO CIRCUSES, PLANS WERE MADE for the Great London Circus to travel to England in the spring under Barnum's supervision – but the trip had to be canceled.

In November, Barnum became sick from an intestinal blockage. Unable to eat and in terrible pain, his weight fell from 215 to 144 pounds in just one month, and for a time, doctors feared the worst. Finally, he began to improve, and doctors sent him to Florida to recuperate.

Meanwhile, planning for what was to come for the new show fell to Bailey, who announced that the two shows would be folded into one, with a grand tour of the United States to launch in 1881. Bailey announced to the press that three shows would be performed daily at each stop, catering to families and school groups with the earlier shows. He claimed that the menagerie accompanying the circus was larger than any other in the world, with the possible exceptions of the zoological gardens in London and Paris.

The entire production, he explained, would be bathed in electric light, inside and out, and much of what Bailey found to be unneeded dead weight – wax figures, stuffed animals, panoramas, and claptrap from Barnum's museums – would be removed. Perhaps most important was his announcement that, to display the biggest and best parts of both shows, the new production would be performed in three rings for the first time ever.

THE BARNUM AND BAILEY CIRCUS, THANKS TO ITS MASSIVE SIZE, HAD NO CHOICE BUT TO TRAVEL BY TRAIN. TICKET BUYERS WHO FOLLOWED THE TRAIN TO THE TOWNS WHERE THE CIRCUS PLAYED OFTEN DOUBLED THE POPULATION OF SOME COMMUNITIES.

Bailey said that the 1881 show would be remembered "in the amusement records of America as the greatest artistic success of the times."

Just in time for the opening of the late March show, Barnum returned from his convalescence in Florida to plan a torchlight parade through the streets of Manhattan. To properly promote the new undertaking, Barnum and Bailey sent invitations to the top 100 newspaper editors in the country, inviting them to the first performance, and paid for their travel to New York. It was a costly piece of advertising that was returned to them in publicity many times over.

The show traveled by train, of course, and Barnum began booking excursion trains to bring guests from miles around the various stops, often swelling the crowds to several times the population of a given town. Usually, schools and businesses closed on what was often called "Barnum Day," realizing that if they didn't, they'd see a much larger number of absentees than usual.

Beyond the sheer size and scope of the combined shows brought to the concept of the circus, Barnum and Bailey themselves brought a degree of respectability to it. Barnum, a teetotaler who often emphasized the idea of "moral character" in the dramatic performances he'd arranged, had always been a favorite of religious groups. And though Bailey, not a drinker himself, would have scoffed at the idea of presenting himself as a moral example, he was a scrupulously honest businessman. He was disgusted by the various side businesses other circus managers practiced, like allowing robbers and pickpockets to work the shows for a fee or letting gamblers set up games of chance on the grounds for a cut of their take.

Another practice that Bailey found unacceptable was the advance sale privilege, where agents bought as many tickets as they liked before a show arrived in town with the idea of selling them for as much over the face value of the ticket as they could. They got to keep whatever they conned from the customer over the ticket price.

It was also standard practice for most circuses back then to extend "privileges" to outside entities that wanted to sell food, candy, drinks, or programs – for a price. It was estimated that these outside sales might clear as much as $25,000 each season at no cost to the show. In addition, the right price paid to a local police chief would allow the circus to do all kinds of underhanded shenanigans, from games of chance to hoochie-kootchie shows and more.

But not on Bailey's watch. He never paid bribes to get police officers to look the other way and insisted that all the privileges be under the show's umbrella. Salaried employees conducted every single business transaction related to the show. Nothing was rented or sold.

The 1881 show featured such attractions as Chang Yu Sing, the seven-foot-six-inch giant – who often appeared with Tom Thumb at his side – Zazel, the Human Cannonball, who was fired out of a spring-loaded cannon to grab a trapeze bar 60 feet away, and Salamander the Fire Horse, who galloped around the ring leaping through burning hoops, traveled more than 12,00 miles during its season. It played a final date in Arkansas in November and then returned to Bridgeport for the winter.

CHANG YU SING, THE CHINESE GIANT, WAS ONE OF THE STARS OF THE BARNUM AND BAILEY SIDESHOW. HE OFTEN APPEARED WITH TOM THUMB AT HIS SIDE.

Its great success would have set the show up for a resounding follow-up season in 1882, but Barnum had to top himself by purchasing Jumbo from the London Zoo. Jumbo became a beloved figure across

JO-JO THE DOG-FACED BOY, WHOSE REAL NAME WAS FEDOR YETISHEV, WAS ADDED TO THE SHOW BY BARNUM. FEDOR PRETENDED TO BE A SAVAGE, BUT WAS ACTUALLY BRILLIANT AND SPOKE SEVERAL LANGUAGES.

America, and his death in 1885 would have ruined lesser shows, but Barnum and Bailey continued to dominate the business.

Over the next several seasons, Barnum continued to add to the repertoire of acts for the show, including human oddities like Jo-Jo the Dog-Faced Boy, who was a 16-year-old from Russia named Fedor Yetishev, whose face was covered with a thick growth of yellow hair. He was born in Russia in 1868, and his father recognized a business opportunity when he saw it.

He took his son on tour throughout Europe, but when he was old enough to tour alone, he joined Barnum in America. Barnum created a backstory that claimed Jo-Jo had been living in a cave and was captured by a hunter. The boy was a savage and couldn't be civilized, so Barnum rescued him and took him to the circus. He claimed that when Jo-Jo was upset, he would bark and growl.

Fedor played along, although he was actually brilliant, widely read, and spoke three languages. He toured the country and made a fortune but died in Greece from pneumonia in 1904.

There were also the remarkable Portuguese child cyclists, the Elliots, who ranged from six to 16 years of age. Their performances brought Barnum up before the courts on charges that he was endangering the health and safety of children. However, they were dismissed when the judges watched the Elliots in action. The well-publicized legal proceedings provided the show with a fortune in free publicity.

The show traveled with a scaled-down version of Barnum's museum, a sideshow, and two menagerie tents through which audiences passed on their way to the main tent. They were seated there around a huge oval that surrounded the three-ring extravaganza. Separating the rings from the stands was the wide hippodrome track that was used for the opening parade, equestrian performances, and races of all kinds – chariots, clowns riding ostriches,

THE CIRCUS OFFERED A "GRAND ETHNOLOGICAL CONGRESS OF NATIONS," WHICH OFFERED A COLLECTION OF THE WORLD'S "STRANGE AND SAVAGE TRIBES." NO ONE REALIZED HOW WILDLY RACIST THIS WAS AT THE TIME.

giraffes, elephants, pairs of ladies drawn from the audience, and so on.

Barnum had also secured a fabled "white" elephant from Burma – although it was mostly gray with some pale and pink splotches – and in 1884, conceived of an exhibition that can only be described as "cringe-worthy" today.

He called it the "Grand Ethnological Congress of Nations," which consisted of a parade of representatives from the "uncivilized nations," including Zulus, Nubians, Hindus, Polynesians, Filipinos, Australian Aboriginals, and Native Americans. It seems like a terrible idea today, but the spectacle was of genuine interest to the American public of the time. It was so well-received that it earned respectable reviews in the era newspapers as a "commendable display of humanity's diversity" and would be repeated in 1893 and 1904 during the World's Fairs held in Chicago and St. Louis.

It was, as I have said already, a much different time.

BARNUM AND BAILEY, DESPITE THEIR SUCCESS, PROVED TO BE an unusual pair. Back in 1880, when they negotiated their terms for a partnership, Bailey had bluntly told Barnum that he didn't care about his name – he only wanted his capital. He said, "My name as a circus man stands above yours, but I need more money, and you've got it. That's the only reason I'm entering this partnership."

It was a startling thing to say to someone like Barnum, but he was right. Bailey was strictly a circus man who knew the ins and outs of the business. Barnum was a world-renowned celebrity, but it had been many years since he'd been in the trenches, arranging routes and work schedules, writing ad copy, and directing workers at all levels. Bailey, however, was a detail-obsessed workaholic who personally called workers to get them out of bed on Saturdays and checked and re-checked every part of the operations. He typically worked 12 hours daily in his office, went home, thought about the circus, and then dreamed about it after falling asleep. Working for Bailey meant knowing how to follow orders. Some liked to say that if he directed you to hang a poster upside-down, just do it and don't argue about it. Even Barnum never referred to his partner by any other name than "Mr. Bailey."

But such intensity doesn't come without cost, especially when entering the partnership with Barnum meant doubling the size of the operation and figuring out how to add Barnum's thousands of ideas for a bigger and better show into the mix. By the end of the 1884 season, Bailey, who was still three years short of his fortieth birthday, was exhausted and near emotional and mental collapse.

The problem, Barnum wrote in a letter to Bailey's wife, Ruth, was "too much thinking." Barnum was 75, twice his partner's age, and though he had at times worked himself to the point of exhaustion, he'd found the only guaranteed cure was "brain rest and not thinking." Bailey shouldn't even be thinking about the show during the 1885 season, Barnum reassured Ruth, "It is all moving like good machinery."

Keep in mind that the 1885 season was the one where Barnum killed off Jumbo, the show's biggest attraction at the time. "Moving like good machinery" without Bailey, it was not.

During the two years that Bailey was on leave, Barnum turned to long-time circus man W.W. Cole and Bailey's old partner, James Cooper, to undertake the daily management of the show. As the operation limped along with him, Barnum finally realized how great of a manager Bailey had been. In October 1887, the pair agreed that Bailey should return to a newly reorganized operation that would tour in 1888 for the first time as the Barnum and Bailey Greatest Show on Earth.

It didn't get off to a great start.

On November 20, a fire broke out at the show's winter quarters in Bridgeport. The only four-legged survivors were a single lion and most, but not all, of the elephants. Alice, Jumbo's purported widow, died in the flames, as did the sort of "white" elephant Barnum had acquired. Another elephant, Gracie, escaped the fire by swimming out into the frigid waters of Long Island Sound, but she later died of exposure while being towed back to shore.

The surviving lion, Nimrod, was nowhere to be found after the blaze was extinguished, and it was first assumed that he'd died. He was later found in a nearby barn, though, by the farmer's wife, who went to milk the cows at first light and saw a shadowy shape gnawing on the lifeless forms of a cow and her calf. Assuming it was a large dog, she began beating the lion with a broom. When the unfazed big cat lifted his head from his meal, the poor woman realized what she'd been whacking with her broom and fled the barn, shrieking in terror.

THE WINTER QUARTERS FOR THE BARNUM AND BAILEY CIRCUS IN BRIDGEPORT.

A week later, Barnum found Bailey in his office, sorting through a stack of letters and telegrams, making notes as he did so. When Barnum asked what he was up to, Bailey coolly replied, "I'm ordering a menagerie."

"All in one day?" Barnum asked.

"Certainly," Bailey replied. "In six hours, we'll own a finer menagerie than the one we lost."

Barnum was undoubtedly impressed – it was something that he would have done himself. And soon, the Greatest Show on Earth was on the road in 1888, never missing a single performance.

AFTER THE CLOSE OF THE 1889 SEASON, BARNUM, NOW age 79, took the Greatest Show on Earth back to England for a 100-day engagement. He approached this series of shows with some trepidation, wondering about his popularity after nabbing Jumbo from the London Zoo, but his fears proved unfounded.

Audiences that packed the 12,000-seat Olympia Auditorium were thrilled with each performance – and with seeing Barnum. Each show ended with the great showman riding in a carriage around the hippodrome track, waving to the crowd. When he doffed his hat before exiting the tent, the spectators let out a deafening cheer.

When the London engagements ended, Barnum returned home to Bridgeport where, while remaining active with the business, he spent his time quietly. He suffered a stroke in November 1890 but continued to receive reports about the coming season in his bed. Barnum had been slowed down, but nothing seemed to stop him.

Until finally, death dead. Legend has it that his last words were a request to know what the receipts had been that day for the show at Madison Square Garden.

P.T. Barnum – America's undisputed "Greatest Showman," died on April 7, 1891.

Barnum's passing pushed James Bailey to the forefront of the business. Barnum had been the face of the circus – getting all the attention – but Bailey was the "man behind the curtain," the one who truly ensured everything was perfect. Barnum might have been the nation's greatest showman, but Bailey was the creator of the modern circus. And now he was at the head of the largest "Big Seven" circuses in America, all of which traveled by rail.

P.T. BARNUM – AMERICA'S "GREATEST SHOWMAN" – DIED ON APRIL 7, 1891, BRINGING AN END TO ONE ERA OF THE COUNTRY.

The Greatest Show on Earth traveled with 65 cars in 1891, followed by Adam Forepaugh's show, which traveled in 52. The Sells Brothers had 42 cars, John Robinson used 35, and William Main used 27; the two smallest competing companies – the Great Wallace and Ringling Brothers – each used only 20.

But if the position of the Ringling Brothers at the bottom of the list brought Bailey any satisfaction, it wouldn't last long. Within a few years, Bailey discovered that all the things he'd worried about during his years in the circus business couldn't match the worries caused by that struggling group of brothers.

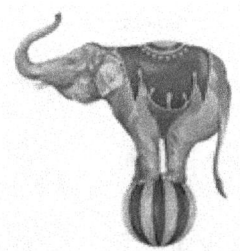

6. THE BROTHERS FROM BARABOO

YEARS LATER, JOHN RINGLING WOULD TRACE HIS FASCINATION with the circus to the summer of 1869 when he was four years old, and his four older brothers – Albert, August, Otto, and Alfred – took him along to see the arrival of a circus steamboat in McGregor, Iowa, which was then a booming town along the Mississippi River.

By then, P.T. Barnum was almost 60, still without any substantial connection to the circus, and James Bailey was 22, an assistant on a traveling show with a boss who was about to be shot by an angry customer. But this wouldn't make the much younger Ringling's passion for show business any less important in circus history.

The Ringling brothers had arrived at the dock that morning before dawn, waiting for the lights of the circus boat to appear around the river bend and for the sounds of the steam-driven calliope to ring out across the mist-shrouded water. A few moments later, Dan Rice's Brilliant Combination of Arenic Attractions arrived in McGregor.

The boys watched as the boat docked, and what passed for a circus parade in those days began with the tent wagons being dragged off and hitched to six-horse teams, followed by the exotic red and gold wagons, the colorfully dressed performers, and the white-faced clowns. The menagerie followed them – bears, camels, equestrian horses, and the elephant.

For the rest of their lives, the Ringling boys would insist that the elephant was the biggest creature they'd ever seen. And as they walked home that morning, there was only one topic of conversation between them: one day, they would have a circus of their own.

THE SEVEN RINGLING BROTHERS – AND ONE SISTER – WITH THEIR PARENTS, AUGUST AND MARIE. FIVE OF THE BROTHERS WENT INTO THE CIRCUS BUSINESS – AL, OTTO, ALF, CHARLES, AND JOHN

But starting a circus seemed like little more than a dream in those days. Though the boys' father, August, was a skilled harness maker and carriage trimmer who had immigrated from Germany in 1848, his skills at running a business fell far short of his skills with leather.

August first settled in Milwaukee, where in 1852, he met Marie Juliar, who had come to America with her parents from France seven years earlier. They married later that same year and moved to Chicago, where August began working at his trade and their first son, Albert, was born. They moved back to Milwaukee two years later, and a second son, August Jr., was born. In 1855, the family relocated to Baraboo, Wisconsin, where Otto was born, and August opened his own business. Over the following year, he expanded his business from the "One Horse Harness Shop" to the "Double Horse Harness Shop."

But his prosperity didn't last long. By 1858, he had gone out of business, and the Ringlings moved to McGregor, where Alfred, Charles, John, Henry, and the only sister, Ida, were born.

Although August had secured a comfortable frame house in the river town, there were many mouths to feed, and his harness business continued to struggle. This is why owning a circus seemed like such a distant dream to the boys – they needed to think of a practical way to help the family make more money.

But no one ever accused the Ringling brothers of being practical – or boring.

Most of the boys began plotting to make their dream of a circus into a reality. Only August Jr., who was 16, and Henry, who was much too young at two, didn't join in. The others constructed a "mammoth arena" in the family's yard made from canvas scraps, castoff carpet, and old blankets and presented their first show, charging a penny for admission.

In 1870, the population of McGregor was just over 2,000 people, and for their series of performances, the Ringlings managed to profit $8.37. This means that the boys not only attracted many of their neighbors and friends to the shows, but they also managed to bring in a fairly large percentage of the town's population. Unsurprisingly, they were encouraged enough by their success to put most of the money back into their fledgling business and purchase a huge sheet of muslin to make a serviceable tent.

Planning and practice for the 1871 season greatly distracted the brothers over the harsh winter. When the day of their first performance arrived in the spring, locals were treated to the first circus parade in Ringling history – an entourage led by Albert driving a wagon pulled by a pony that was decked out in the finest leather harness their father could offer. Albert played the bugle from his seat while his brothers followed behind, playing washboards, snares, and other instruments, all wearing plumes that matched the one that bobbed atop the wagon pony's head.

The band was followed by Otto leading the family's goat, Billy Rainbow, whom he'd spent most of the winter teaching a series of tricks.

All this was enough to entice a sizable crowd to follow them to a vacant lot where the new muslin tent was draped from a fresh-cut pine pole, topped by an American flag and strings of pennants the boys had cut from felt. A sign by the entrance announced the opening of the "Ring-Ling Circus" and stated that admission had risen to a nickel.

More than 100 people handed over nickels to Otto, who was ticket-taker that day, and filed inside to gather around the sawdust-strewn center ring, where nine-year-old Alfred was riding a pony and was billed as "The King of the Sandwich Islands." He was wearing an old Union officer's uniform, had a scrap of quilt for a cape, and had a crown cut from cardboard on his head. He led the "spec" – short for *spectacular* in circus lingo – which was the grand entrance of the performers.

The other brothers followed behind him, wearing dyed and beribboned long underwear in place of tights. John, age six, was painted with a clown face and led the family goat, bringing up the rear.

There was a smattering of applause as Alfred dismounted and bowed to the audience. Although John Ringling would forever swear that what happened next was not his intention, it would prove that he had always possessed an uncanny skill for knowing what made good entertainment.

As Alfred made his glorious bow to the crowd, John's grip on Billy Rainbow's rope loosened, and the goat charged with perfect aim. The goat's head met with Alfred's behind, and the King of the Sandwich Islands was sent sprawling into the sawdust.

Acts they had actually rehearsed followed – including a more or less successful plate-juggling routine, bareback pony riding, tumbling, trapeze work, John hamming it up as a singing clown, and more – but nothing would top the sight of Alfred taking flight after being butted by the goat and the hysterical laughter from the audience.

The boys never forgot it, and this production – as unintentionally funny as it might've been – marked the beginning of a life of showmanship for the Ringlings, who would always date their seasons from that day in McGregor, Iowa.

WHILE HIS SONS WERE ENJOYING LOCAL SUCCESS IN the circus business, August Ringling was still struggling with his own. In the fall of 1872, he took what promised to be a secure job at a carriage factory across the Mississippi River in Prairie du Chien, Wisconsin. He had barely started when the factory burned to the ground, and the economic downturn that followed ensured it would never be rebuilt.

Nevertheless, August and Marie welcomed an eighth child, Ida, to the family in early 1874 and were soon moving again, this time back to Baraboo. By then, Albert had left home to try his luck as a performer and show manager, and Otto and Gus had both worked as harness makers. Alfred and Charles were helping in their father's shop, and John, then 12, started pursuing his own ideas.

One day, his father came home from work to find that John wasn't there. There was still no sign of him the next morning either. There was no note, and no information left behind, but these were days long before the absence of a child – even one as young as 12 – raised suspicions of foul play. August put out the word to the authorities, but he felt he knew what had happened to John.

And he was right. Soon, there was word from Milwaukee. John had started a business, working out of an abandoned warehouse, where he had assembled packing crates into chairs, a table, a bed, and a workbench. He had started making what he was marketing around town as Ringling Cleanser, an abrasive powder to which he'd added a little bluing to clean pots and pans. He was doing well with it, so he wasn't happy when his parents came to collect him and take him back to Baraboo.

WHEN JOHN WAS 12, HE LEFT HOME FOR THE FIRST TIME AND WENT TO MILWAUKEE, WHERE HE STARTED HIS OWN BUSINESS. OVER THE NEXT FEW DAYS, HE RAN AWAY AT LEAST THREE TIMES, EVENTUALLY JOINING THE CIRCUS.

Over the next few years, John ran away from home at least three more times, the last when he followed a small traveling show that had played in town. He convinced the manager that he was 16 and was hired as a roustabout and ticket taker. He was supposed to get $3 a week but was seldom paid and never in full. Finally, one night, when the show was going on, John counted what was left in the money box, decided it was the amount that was owed to him, and left while the audience was still applauding the performers inside. He took off for St. Paul, but his father tracked him down again, and he found himself back in Baraboo.

There's no way to know where John might have gone next if his oldest brother, Albert, hadn't returned in 1882. After three years of traveling and managing other people's shows, he was intent on starting one of his own. He was back in Baraboo to try and convince his brothers to rekindle their dreams of circus life. What he planned eventually ended up on their handbills as "THE RINGLING BROTHERS CLASSIC AND COMIC CONCERT CO." a "refined and high-class entertainment" that included "New Faces, New Songs, Wonderful Dancers, and Noted Comedians," and offered "Two Hours of Solid Fun."

Albert also noted that it was the show's "fourth season," which he arrived at by counting the five-cent show ten years earlier. It was only a small exaggeration when he added his own three years in show business.

Alfred and Charles, both sick of harness making, immediately joined up with Albert, and as for John, there was nothing anyone could do to keep him out of it. Soon, the brothers were hard at work preparing and rehearsing for a tour, buying costumes, arranging dates, and printing posters, handbills, and signs.

By late 1882, the Ringing Brothers were finally ready to take the entertainment world by storm.

But it didn't quite work out that way.

The first "professional" show for the Ringling Brothers took place on November 27, 1882, in Mazomanie, Wisconsin, a little less than 30 miles from Baraboo – but just far enough away to discourage their friends from coming over and heckling them. But the first show was a disaster, from start to finish. Charles later admitted, "We were a confused and demoralized lot when we left the stage."

The good news is that there might have been only 59 people in attendance that night, and at least none walked out. After counting the house, they found they'd taken in $13.00 in admissions. This was balanced against the $19.90 in travel expenses, $2.00 to helpers, and $6.00 for the rental of the hall – putting them $12.90 in the hole. It wasn't an opening that would inspire a performer to keep trying, but they did it anyway.

The next night, they appeared in Spring Valley and, this time, made more than $60 with the locals applauding the singing, dancing, and juggling. Plus, they howled with laughter at every stale joke the Ringlings presented.

Over the next few months, the brothers traipsed through the wintry landscape of the Upper Midwest, often bogged down by snowstorms, sometimes having to duck out of hotels in the middle of the night without paying the bill, occasionally breaking just a little above even, and closing the season in May, when more polished shows were starting their summer tours.

This grim experience did nothing to dampen the Ringlings' enthusiasm, though. By the fall of 1883, they were on the road again, adding a married couple with circus experience to the troupe and bringing a portable organ. They'd renamed themselves the Ringling Brothers Grand Carnival of Fun.

The company struggled along through another frigid winter, and then brother Al – who had taken a lucrative position with another show for the fall – caught up with them in Lincoln, Nebraska, in January 1884. He brought his new wife, Louise, who would later become a skilled snake charmer and bareback rider. Al also brought along a veteran circus man named Yankee Robinson, who, though he'd fallen on hard times, had taken a liking to Al and was willing to join up with the Ringling Brothers in hopes of better times to come.

AL RINGLING AND HIS WIFE, LOU, WHO PERFORMED WITH THE CIRCUS AS A SNAKE CHARMER AND BAREBACK RIDER.

The result of the new additions meant a complete reorganization of the company into something vaguely resembling an actual circus. The name was changed again to Yankee Robinson's Great Show and Ringling Brothers Carnival of Comedy.

On May 19, they gave their first performance under a newly acquired big top in Baraboo, where Robinson doffed his top hat and assured the audience that despite his 40 years in the circus business, he'd finally found the troupe with which he'd stay until he died. "For I can tell you," he stated with quiet assurance," the Ringling Brothers are the future showmen of America. They are the coming men!"

There were 600 bleacher seats beneath the canvas of the tent. Robinson immediately began to make money with his share of one-third of the receipts – and he earned it when a section of seats collapsed. He was instantly on the scene, helping folks, dusting them off, cracking jokes, and ensuring tempers were cooled.

What those who attended that day saw for their 25-cent admission was not exactly the stuff of a Barnum and Bailey show or really anything that predicted the Ringlings would be the "future showmen of America." There were 21 people in the company, including

THE RINGLING BROTHERS FIRST BEGAN PUTTING ON THEIR SHOW UNDER A NEW BIG TOP IN MAY 1884.

VETERAN CIRCUS MAN YANKEE ROBINSON HELPED THE RINGLINGS GET THEIR START AND PROCLAIMED THEM, "THE FUTURE SHOWMEN OF AMERICA."

the teamsters and roustabouts, and not a single animal in the ring. The show itself consisted of some juggling and balancing acts, tumbling and acrobatics, and a contortionist, all interspersed by comic skits. John appeared as the show's only clown. Through it all, Robinson reminded the audience about the after-show concert and pestered them not to miss the sideshow, which featured an "educated pig."

Robinson's claim that the Ringlings were up-and-coming showmen one day proved true – and so did his assurances that he'd found the troupe he'd work with until he died. Not only did that come true, but it did so much sooner than he expected. In August, while on a side trip to see his son performing in a nearby show, Robinson passed away in his sleep while riding on the train.

But he'd left an impression behind on the show where he'd briefly appeared. Bettered by their time with Robinson, the Ringlings played on until early May 1885. After two weeks of rest in Baraboo, they were on the road again, having added to their educated pig – er, I mean their "trained animal exposition" – was a scrawny, forlorn-looking hyena that was billed as the "Mammoth, Marauding, Man-Eating Monstrosity, Striata Giganteum."

I hope they kept the animal behind a curtain until admissions had been paid.

By May 1886, the Ringlings had a new, larger, big top, and the company needed 15 wagons to transport the show. And, of course, they renamed it again – the Ringling Brothers Great Double Shows and Congress of Wild and Trained Animals. They now needed 18 wagons for hauling around the tent, a ticket and bandwagon, and a menagerie that had grown to include a bear, several monkeys, and an eagle. There was also a trained animal act that consisted of a donkey named January and a Shetland pony named Minnie.

WITHIN TWO YEARS, THE RINGLING BROTHERS SHOW NEEDED 18 WAGONS TO TRANSPORT THEIR CIRCUS FROM TOWN TO TOWN. THEY CERTAINLY WEREN'T THE BIGGEST IN THE BUSINESS YET, BUT THEY WERE GROWING.

Their company battled a rival company for the first time when it arrived in Vinton, Iowa, that summer. When they rolled into town, they discovered that the Reiner Brothers Great European Railroad Show had steamed into town and planned to play opposite the Ringlings. The more polished railroad show expected to trounce them, and they spent a lot of time laughing at the Ringlings and belittling their show – only to lose the contest against their rival. Otto gleefully wrote, "Today, we have fought and won a bloody battle. Now they will be as anxious to avoid us as we are to avoid them."

Bolstered by their successes, the show doubled in size for the 1887 season. They renamed themselves again, this time as the Ringling Brothers United Monster Shows, Great Double Circus, Royal European Menagerie, Museum, Caravan, and Congress of Animals.

I would not want to try to fit that onto a banner.

The mouthful of a name boasted more performers, more stunts, and a menagerie that included an elk, two lions, a kangaroo, a deer, four Shetland ponies, and the veteran bear, hyena, and monkeys. They also bought a camel while on the road, but it didn't live out the tour.

That season, the brothers incorporated their youngest brother, Henry, into the business. The 17-year-old became their advance man, mapping out the routes and setting up parades in the towns they visited. They outfitted him with new clothes and a stylish carriage, hoping it would assure town officials that he was the representative of some up-and-coming circus men.

On his first day, Henry set off in his carriage for Pardeeville, Wisconsin – and kept right on going. He spent the next six weeks on a wild bender that he capped off by selling the fine carriage, the horses, and his new clothes. Twelve years went by before Henry could get a handle on his drinking problem and fully become part of the Ringling partnership, although he never loved the business the way his brothers did.

In 1888, the Ringling Circus finally began to reach new heights. They purchased a big top worthy of its name, and among the things exhibited beneath it were Babylon and Fannie, a pair of elephants purchased from a bankrupt circus. They also added a pair of camels, a zebra, and an emu and raised the admission price to the standard of the times, which was 50 cents for all the major shows. With this, even if for no other reason, the Ringlings finally entered the big time.

That summer was one of the rainiest in years, and depressing receipts led to the Ringlings – down to their last $100 – writing home to the Bank of Baraboo to plead for a $1,000 loan. They got the money,

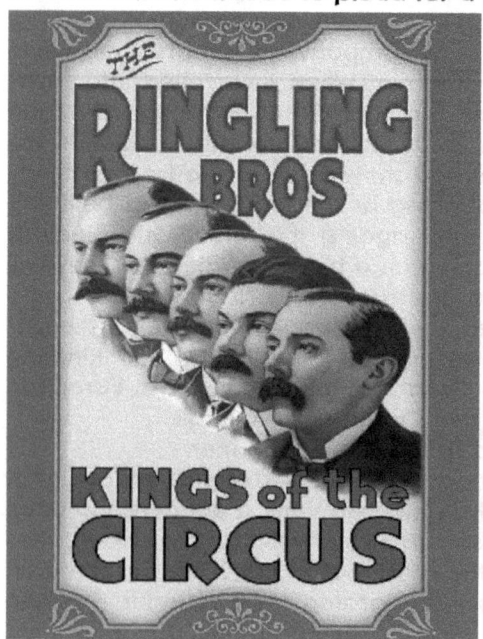

but things became even more bleak on June 23, when their circus strongman, Monsieur Dialo, a.k.a. James Richardson, got into a scuffle between two locals in Webster City, Iowa.

Thomas Baskett, a notoriously hot-headed bartender, tossed a man named Roll Brewer out of his establishment but decided that wasn't enough. He followed Brewer to the circus grounds and proceeded to beat the man mercilessly in full view of alarmed customers. When Brewer's daughter got into the fracas, trying to help her father, Baskett knocked her down with a punch and then kicked her several times. When he saw the young woman being beaten, Dialo stepped into the fray. But Baskett wasn't frightened by the burly strongman – he pulled a pistol from his waistband and shot Dialo in the stomach. It took Dialo 24 hours to die. Baskett, on the other hand, received a 15-year prison sentence for the assault.

Fortunately, the weather dried up in the following weeks, and the brothers made $3,000 during the first week of July alone. They quickly repaid the loan to the bank, hoping that what was left over would allow them to keep "feeding the elephants," as one wrote in a note to their banker.

It turned out to be enough to feed the elephants and more. They enjoyed a season that made up for the spring and took them into the 1889 season, during which they added a "Roman Hippodrome" to the show. That year was also important for adding the last Ringling brother to the company. Until then, Gus had been working as a harness maker with his father, but his brothers finally convinced him that his future was with the circus and appointed him their operations manager.

The only down note that season was the death of another longtime performer with the show – the long-suffering hyena finally met his end.

In 1890, the Ringlings took the show on the road for the first time by rail, with John in charge of the difficult task of piecing together the routes they'd need with various railroad companies and lines over which they'd need to travel. The Ringlings' 18 cars left Baraboo in early May with 54 performers, three elephants, four lions, three camels, and an assortment of other animals, which was quite a step up from the mud show they'd been just six years earlier. Even so, it was still a one-ring operation and very small compared to Barnum and Bailey or most other railroad shows.

IN 1890, THE BROTHERS BEGAN MOVING THE SHOW MY RAIL WITH JOHN IN CHARGE OF NAVIGATING THE TOUR ROUTE FOR THE SEASON.

John worked hard to navigate the show along the intricate network of American rails, trying to hit every smaller venue of any value while trying to avoid playing against the bigger shows. Proof of his abilities came when they tallied up the receipts at the end of the season and found they'd made more than enough money to expand again in 1891 as the Ringling Brothers World's Greatest Railroad Show, Real Roman Hippodrome, 3 Ring Circus, and Elevated Stages, Millionaire Menagerie, Museum and Aquarium and Spectacular Tournament Production of Caesar's Entry into Rome.

Good grief.

It was a mouthful, but the name didn't yet match its size. It was only traveling by 22 cars, much less than most circuses at the time. When the 1892 season began, the Ringling Brothers might have been the smallest of the so-called "Big Seven" – and of little concern to James Bailey – but the odds they had overcome at this point were staggering.

And soon, they would be a force that even Bailey would have to reckon with.

CIRCUS OWNER AND JAMES BAILEY COMPETITOR, ADAM FOREPAUGH.

JAMES BAILEY, MEANWHILE, WITH BARNUM GONE, WAS cementing a place for himself at the top of the circus world by acquiring the holdings of his second-most successful competitor, Adam Forepaugh, whose ads boasted that he "owned, controlled, and exhibited more wild animals and individually possessed more show property than any other person in the world."

Forepaugh, a former meat and horse dealer from Philadelphia, had always been a little rough around the edges – for instance, when Barnum bought his white elephant from Ceylon, Forepaugh simply whitewashed one of his own and called Barnum's a fake – but he'd done well for himself. He was said to be worth $5 million when he died in 1890.

Bailey purchased the Forepaugh show and kept it traveling through 1894 with his brother-in-law Joseph McCaddon in charge, but it never fared as well as it did when Forepaugh was at the helm. When Bailey finally shut it down, he transferred most of the equipment to Buffalo Bill Cody's Wild West Show, where he'd purchased an interest.

For the Ringlings, who continued to stick with the plan of avoiding conflict with Bailey and the other big shows whenever possible, their main competition was the Sells Brothers, the largest operation still standing after the Bailey-Forepaugh merger.

Like the Ringlings, Lew Sells favored the smaller towns of the Midwest and Great Plains, which often led to the two shows playing at the same venue on very close dates. The Ringlings might roll into a town to play a date ahead of Sells, only to find that their competitor's advance men had already come through, papering the town with the posters and advertisements.

WHY WASTE YOUR MONEY ON A BUNCH OF FAKES WHEN SELLS BROTHERS CIRCUS GIVES YOU TWICE AS MUCH FOR THE SAME PRICE?

That was the kind of headline that usually appeared on their ads, with additional wording like "The Ringlings are cheap crooks who try to inflate their pitiful third-rate show by extravagant FALSE claims,

as shown below." The "below" would include columns of commentary filled with wild claims and outright lies, suggesting that the Ringlings' menagerie was nothing more than two sick lions, three small elephants, and a few other miserable creatures "which would not bring $500 in the auction block, where they soon will be."

But no matter what kind of dirty tricks and harsh words were exchanged between circus men, they felt a greater kinship with each

BUFFALO BILL CODY – FAMOUS FOR HIS WILD WEST SHOW – BICKERED WITH JOHN RINGLING PUBLICLY, BUT IN PRIVATE THEY GOT ALONG WELL. THIS WAS COMMON AMONG SHOWMEN, WHO KNEW THE FEW PEOPLE THEY COULD TRUST WELL WERE OTHER SHOWMEN.

other than they did with outsiders. At one point, when the Ringlings found themselves booked in the same town with Buffalo Bill's Wild West Show, a message arrived in Baraboo from Bill himself that read: "Tell John Ringling he'd better stay out of my way, or he'll bitterly regret it."

John responded with a message of his own: "Give Colonel Cody my compliments and tell him I'm not very worried. In fact, the next time I see him, I'm going to throw him down and scalp him."

When the two finally ran into each other in a saloon in Philadelphia during another moment of dueling engagements, the only argument was over who would pay for the drinks.

But that doesn't mean that the competition between Sells and the Ringlings didn't escalate during the 1894 season, with Sells going to great lengths in Texas, Iowa, and Minnesota, where he cut the admissions for his shows in half. The Ringlings were forced to match his price, even though it meant both shows would be operating at a loss. In the South, though, both shows kept the price at 50 cents, and the Ringlings returned from the season's tour with a sizable profit.

They used their available cash to expand the show to 44 rail cars, a step that put them on par with Sells, and they made plans to open their season with a splash, playing an indoor coliseum in Chicago.

It was a momentous move for the brothers, who had been putting on a backyard show with their family goat not that many years before. They rented out Tattersall's, a barn-like structure used for horse and cattle auctions, cleaned it up and gave it a makeover. They replaced the bleachers with folding seats, hung all kinds of flags and bunting from the rafters, placed banks of potted plants and flowers, and replaced the antiquated lighting system with electric lights.

Three days before the show opened, a torchlight parade was held along the streets of Chicago with a 55-piece band, several hundred performers, the menagerie caged in horse-drawn wagons, cavorting clowns, and, of course, the necessary herd of elephants. The following show included equestrians, aerial performers, animal acts, a four-horse chariot race, and a living statue display that might have been racy if they hadn't been billed as representations of classical sculpture. Regardless, it was more nudity than most were used to seeing on display in Chicago. The showstopper was a daredevil named Speedy, who dove 80 feet from a perch in the building's rafters into a small tank of water only three and a half feet deep.

The show played to standing-room-only crowds and moved from Chicago to St. Louis, often following immediately behind Barnum and Bailey and Buffalo Bill's Wild West Show but doing equally well. By the end of the 1895 season, Ringling Brothers had transformed from a second-rate show to one on equal footing with the Sells Brothers and Barnum and Bailey.

James Bailey was feeling the heat of their meteoric rise. The success of the Ringlings led him to purchase a half interest in the Sells Brothers show. In 1896, he booked that show -- along with Buffalo Bill's – up against the Ringling show in every city possible, leading to scores of negative ad campaigns, often violent skirmishes over billboard space, and constant public relations battles.

The contest became so exhausting that both sides pulled back for 1897, agreeing there was plenty of room in the country for more than one top-notch circus. Only once that season did the Ringlings and Barnum and Bailey clash directly; that was when they were booked in Minneapolis simultaneously. By the time the Ringling advance team arrived in the city, there was no billboard or

AS COMPETITION BETWEEN THE LARGEST CIRCUSES IN THE COUNTRY HEATED UP, JAMES BAILEY MADE THJE SURPRISING DECISION TO TAKE THE GREATEST SHOW TO EUROPE FOR THE 1898 SEASON.

wall space available, leaving them with no choice but to rely on banners, small boards, and newspaper ads. Still, they drew the kind of crowds they'd hoped for, turning people away at every performance.

What Bailey did next is still a mystery. For the 1898 season, he announced he would take the Greatest Show on Earth back to Europe and leave the Forepaugh-Sells Brothers Circus and the Buffalo Bill Show to play in the United States. Some believe that Bailey was worn down by his battle with the Ringlings, while others say he simply recognized there was great money to be made by taking the show back across the Atlantic.

Bailey did have spectacular success in Europe, where he remained for the next five years. However, while he was there, the Ringlings continued to steadily grow, solidifying their spot as the premier circus operation in America.

WHILE BAILEY WAS IN EUROPE, THE RINGLINGS WERE hard at work coming up with new elements for their show. One of the additions for the new season – always effective for parades and big top processions – was a 30-piece brass band in red and gold uniforms mounted on white horses. Other additions were the so-called Bell Wagon, a 12-bell structure mounted on a wagon drawn by eight horses, and the English Derby Day Pageant, a procession of notable kinds of horse-drawn carriages, all of them filled with models dressed in the latest elegant fashions.

By 1901, the embellished Ringling show was making a circuit of the nation, traveling from Boston to San Diego, from New York to Omaha. At every stop, crowds turned out to see every part of their arrival – unloading the equipment train at dawn, hauling the poles, seats, and canvas to the grounds, and the faultless erecting of the 15,000-seat arena in just a few hours. After that, it was the arrival of the performers, the curiosities, and the animals as they paraded down Main Street towards the big top, a mind-boggling spectacle for children and adults alike.

To all but the most jaded circus men, mounting such spectacle and pageantry was just as wondrous as it was to the small-town and city folks who came out to see it. They believed the circus contributed something special to American life, introducing a bit of magnificence and beauty into people's lives – especially in the small towns – that they'd only read about but never seen.

While he was in Europe, Bailey relied on the other shows to maintain his spot at the table in the States, but without his presence, the Forepaugh-Sells Brothers and Buffalo Bill shows were little more than placeholders. When Bailey finally returned home in November 1902, he understood the need to make a grand re-entrance. With that in mind, he expanded his show to the point that moving from place to place strained even his masterful management skills.

He now needed 90 cars to transport the expanded Barnum and Bailey show, which required seven tents – the big top, menagerie, baggage stock stable, sideshow, ring stock stable, dining tent, and dressing room tent.

Bailey paid added attention to the street parade, designing the largest ornate circus wagon ever built as a centerpiece. The Hemispheres Band Wagon, which had elaborate carvings depicting various acts and animals, was 27 feet long, eight and a half feet wide, and 13 feet high – even larger than a modern Greyhound bus. The wagon was pulled by a team of 40 matched bay horses.

In addition, Bailey had hired two performers who would become legends in the circus world. While in Europe, he had been stunned by the talents of a lovely equestrian named Ella Bradna, who was recognized as the finest rider in the world at the time. Bailey persuaded her to join his show, and she brought her husband, Fred Bradna, a former German cavalry officer. The engaging and

THE HEMISPHERES BAND WAGON BECAME THE CENTERPIECE OF THE BARNUM AND BAILEY CIRCUS STREET PARADE. IT WAS LARGER THAN A GREYHOUND BUS AND WAS PULLED BY 40 MATCHED BAY HORSES.

clever man would eventually become the show's equestrian manager and, ultimately, the longtime ringmaster of the Greatest Show on Earth, earning the title of its "Field Marshall."

During his five years in Europe, Bailey – still obsessively managing every detail of his operation – impressed transportation officials with his efficiency in moving the troupe by rail. He had specially constructed 67 rail cars, and while the track gauge was the same as in the United States, tunnels and bridges were often narrower and had lower clearance heights. To avoid issues, Bailey always sent a scout train ahead on the planned route, pulling a boxcar, a flat car, and a sleeper. If the train arrived with all its cars unscathed, the remaining 66 cars followed the next day.

Such ingenuity was not lost on European military commanders, and it's said that Kaiser Wilhelm himself, astonished that an entertainer would be able to outmaneuver his artillery experts, interviewed Bailey about his methods.

Back home in 1903, though, Bailey's highly praised approach began to falter. His new circus, designed to be bigger and better than the Ringlings', was unavoidably much heavier. The bulk of the company could be carried by rail from town to town, but to get to the circus grounds and back still required a lot of old-fashioned horses. Trucks and tractors hadn't been invented yet. Thanks to a labor shortage caused by a wave of American prosperity, Bailey often had trouble breaking down the massive show and moving it to the next town in time for the parade and the afternoon and evening show.

Soon, word spread that a customer couldn't always count on his afternoon show ticket to be honored. The much lighter and faster Ringling show began to use this to their advantage, often getting into a venue before Bailey and stealing the business. Even the Ringlings would privately admit that Bailey had a more elaborate show. However, over their five years as the uncontested kings of the American circus world, they had learned to present themselves as the best in the business.

After the 1903 season, Bailey, still battling his intermittent nervous fatigue at age 57, approached the Ringlings with an offer of peace. Bailey offered them a half interest in the Forepaugh-Sells show and proposed that the three companies work out a schedule with no conflicts for the 1904 season. The Ringlings accepted, and the Forepaugh-Sells show toured for the next three seasons under the direction of Henry Ringling.

Meanwhile, Bailey's attempts to regain his competitive edge led him to make a big change in operations. After another obstacle-filled season in 1904, he decided to end the circus parade for the Greatest Show. Second thoughts about this kept him waffling for months, but early in the 1905 season, he finally followed through, shutting down the street processions and putting all his parade equipment in storage. He'd found that European audiences often just watched the parade and skipped the show, so he similarly justified his actions to the American public. However, again, the Ringlings one-upped by continuing that part of the pre-show.

IN 1906, HIS HEALTH ALREADY SHAKY, BAILEY RETURNED TO MADISON SQUARE GARDEN FOR A SHOW TO KICK OFF THE NEW SEASON AND MAY HAVE BEEN EXPOSED TO CONTAMINATED SOIL THAT WAS BROUGHT INTO THE BUILDING. HE CAME DOWN WITH AN INFECTION, WHICH KILLED HIM A SHORT TIME LATER.

Despite growing business pressures and his shaky health, Bailey kept working. Early in 1906, he was back at Madison Square Garden, engaged in rehearsals for the show that would kick off the new season. For many years after, it was widely accepted that what happened to Bailey next was the result of those rehearsals.

A large amount of topsoil was carried into the arena to prepare for the show, and all of it was possibly contaminated. Doctors who were called in to attend to a suddenly stricken Bailey found that he was suffering from erysipelas, a streptococcal infection, and they theorized he had contracted the illness after being bitten by a mosquito that had come from the muck now spread about on the venue's floor.

The disease is easily cured by antibiotics today, but they didn't exist in 1906, and Bailey, tired and weakened by stress, was confined to his home in Mount Vernon, New York, where he died five days later.

I wish I could end the story there, but to be complete, I can't. It would later turn out that Bailey hadn't been bitten by a diseased-carrying mosquito. In truth, Bailey had a nervous habit of using his fingers to yank out the hairs that protruded from his nose, often causing sores in his nasal passages that became painfully infected.

This time, the infection spread from Bailey's nose to both sides of his head, even down his right arm to his elbow. The infection turned out to be fatal.

It's a bizarre footnote to Bailey's death, but really, should his death have been anything other than one that was odd and unusual by the standards of the ordinary world? Within the circus, the unlikely and the outrageous seemed perfectly sane.

WITH THE DEATH OF JAMES BAILEY CAME THE END TO the fierce competition that had swirled to control the American circus.

After his demise, the Greatest Show struggled to operate without its leader. Bailey's brother-in-law, Joseph McCaddon, approached the Ringlings with proposals to combine the Greatest Show on Earth, the Forepaugh-Sells circus, and Buffalo Bill's Wild West Show with the Ringling operations. The brothers did agree to purchase the Forepaugh-Sells show, but McCaddon's proposal for a full-fledged merger stalled, likely over the terms of future involvement that McCaddon wanted for himself.

In 1907, a financial panic occurred, and the stock in The Greatest Show, suffering from Bailey's absence, fell to just 85 cents per share, a price at which John Ringling began to snap it up.

Soon after, John approached Bailey's widow, Ruth, and began negotiations to purchase all the operations. When he finally had his price, he went to his brothers to argue for their approval of the deal. Otto – perhaps second to John when it came to influencing their brothers – was all for it, and the others quickly agreed. On October 22, 1907, the Ringlings bought the Barnum and Bailey Greatest Show on Earth for $410,000. The two shows continued to operate and travel as separate entities for a time; however, by the end of the 1908 season, their combined profits more than repaid the Ringlings for the purchase.

The combined circus was still a little while in the future, but history had already been made with the formation of the greatest show that the world would ever know – the Ringling Brothers and Barnum and Bailey Circus was a name that everyone would soon know.

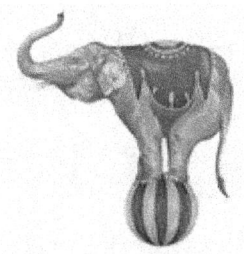

7. THE GREAT CIRCUS TRAIN WRECK OF 1918

BY THE 1870S, CIRCUS COMPANIES HAD BEEN USING THE nation's railroads for years. These were, of course, the larger shows that could afford this type of transportation – and were willing to deal with the hassle.

By then, more than 42,000 miles of railway were in operation around the country – more than double the miles of the previous decade – but many of those lines were isolated, and many others required changing cars because of the different widths between the rails on some tracks. Until 1869, the use of railroads for the industry was spotty until Dan Castello – aware of the push to link the coasts by rail – organized a transcontinental tour for his circus, traveling only by rail.

Castello's troupe left Frederick, Maryland, that spring and traveled as far west as Leavenworth, Kansas, before turning south for the winter and playing in New Orleans and other cities until the weather improved. On May 10, when the "Golden Spike" was driven in Promontory, Utah – linking east and west -- Castello's show was already in Omaha. Soon after, the show used the new railroad to take the circus for the first time to enthusiastic audiences in far-flung venues like Cheyenne, Denver, Salt Lake City, and San Francisco.

That tour was the incentive for all serious circus men to start considering the use of the railroads, and as time went on, more and more of the shows began using the rails to travel from town to town.

BY THE EARLY 1900S, EVERY CIRCUS OF ANY SIZE WAS USING THE RAILROADS TO MOVE THEIR SHOWS AROUND THE COUNTRY.

By 1919, when the Ringling Brothers and the Greatest Show finally combined into a single entity, they needed an entire train to transport the tents, rigging, performers, animals, and roustabouts, making it the largest traveling show of the day.

It continued its great success through the first few decades of the twentieth century. Even the Great Depression didn't keep customers from attending. The circus could always be counted on to take people away from their troubles for a while.

After the United States entered World War II, the attraction of the circus stayed strong for just the same reason that it survived the Depression – people needed an escape.

And wartime or not, officials knew this. Despite the travel restrictions created by the war, President Franklin D. Roosevelt made a special declaration to allow the circus to continue to use the rail system across the country.

But it was years before that – just one year before the two shows combined – that the greatest circus train disaster in American history occurred and left a record of haunting stories behind.

BEN W. WALLACE BECAME INVOLVED IN THE CIRCUS BUSINESS in the early 1880s. He'd grown up in Peru, Indiana, served in the Union Army during the Civil War, and returned home to begin a horse trading business that would become one of the largest in the state.

In 1882, Wallace, who had been interested in circuses for several years, attended a sale of equipment from the W.C. Coup show. The show had passed through Peru by rail on its way to Detroit but became stranded by unpaid bills and went bankrupt. Wallace returned from the sale with six railroad cars filled with tents, poles, costumes, and every other kind of circus equipment needed to start a new show – which he was on the verge of doing.

At another defunct circus sale in Texas, he purchased several rail cars filled with horses, then bought other animals in Chicago, and in December 1882, contracted with a local company to construct several ornate wagons.

Throughout 1883, Wallace continued gathering the pieces of his circus, hiring the best performers he could find. Finally, in the spring of 1884, he presented his first show in Peru, and then – with very little experience but a lot of enthusiasm – Wallace took his new show on the road.

BEN WALLACE STUMBLED INTO THE CIRCUS BUSINESS AFTER ATTENDING A SALE FOR A BANKRUPT SHOW AND BUYING SIX RAILROAD CARS OF EQUIPMENT ON A WHIM.

Traveling as a wagon show, Wallace and Company's Great World Menagerie spent most of its successful first season in southern Indiana, Ohio, West Virginia, and Kentucky. After another money-making season in 1885, Wallace decided it was time to expand the show and its tour route across the country. He also decided to change the name. In 1886, the Great Wallace Show took to the rails in 15 cars and traveled by train for the first time. Within a few years, the expansion paid off, and the show grew to the point that it needed 40 rail cars to handle the canvas, menagerie, performers, sideshow, and crew.

But rail travel was not without incident in those days. In July 1892, the Great Wallace Show experienced its first railroad accident. In the crash, 26 of the show's highly-trained trained horses – worth at least $5,000 – were killed. Wallace spent a lot of money and time to replace them.

A little more than a decade later, near Durand, Michigan, fate caught up with the show again. On August 7, 1903, the train arrived at the local rail yard in two separate train sections. The first section, traveling a few minutes ahead of the second, had safely arrived in Durand, but the second train failed to slow down as it approached and entered the yard. It slammed into the rear of the first train, killing 26 men, including the trainmaster and an unknown number of railroad employees. The engineer of the second train later claimed that his air

brakes failed, even though subsequent tests revealed they were in perfect working order.

At the time, this was the worst railroad wreck in circus history – but a decade and a half later, it would move to second place.

The Great Wallace Show continued its string of successes, though, and in 1907, Ben Wallace managed to purchase the highly-praised animal show of famed circus man Carl Hagenbeck for $45,000. He immediately changed the name to the Hagenbeck-Wallace Circus and began advertising it as the "world's highest-class circus." It may not have achieved quite that distinction, but it was likely close, ranking not far behind the Barnum and Bailey and Ringling Brothers' shows. By that time, the size of the enlarged circus required that it travel in two separate train sections, each numbering at least 28 cars.

Although Carl Hagenbeck wasn't happy with his name being used to promote Wallace's show – he even filed a lawsuit against him that failed in 1908 – Wallace used it to great success, even when faced with a near disaster in March 1913.

A massive spring storm system devastated the Ohio River Valley, bringing tornadoes and several inches of warm rain that fell on ground that was still frozen and snow-covered in some areas. The rain and melting snow caused the lakes, rivers, and creeks to swell and overflow their banks. They flowed into the Wabash and Miami Rivers, already above flood stage. Several thousand people died in Dayton, Ohio, and hundreds were reported dead in the circus' hometown of Peru, Indiana.

Luckily, those reports turned out to be incorrect – at least as far as the deaths in Peru went – but the flood was both deadly and costly, nonetheless. Wallace and his family didn't live on the grounds of the circus' winter quarters – he had a large home in town – but the animals were there, and so were many of the workers, 75 of whom were trapped on the property by the floodwaters.

The Wallace family home didn't come through the flood unscathed either. The water kept rising until it was knee-deep around the house, and the Wallaces sought shelter on the upper floors until the murky water began to recede.

Several days passed before anyone could see the overall damage caused by the flood. On March 29, it was announced that the Wabash River at Peru had dropped nine feet and residents were free to leave their homes and survey what had happened to their town. A death list was sent to the newspapers with 28 names on it. Homes, businesses, and factories had been wrecked by the flood, and the Hagenbeck-Wallace Circus itself sustained more than $150,000 in damages. That number included the loss of eight elephants, which had been found lying next to the Chesapeake and Ohio Railroad station, which was more than two miles downstream from the winter quarters.

Over the next few days, the newspapers reported on the cleanup efforts in the wake of the flood. It took weeks, but eventually, things started to return to normal, including with Ben Wallace's circus. After repairing damaged wagons and equipment and finding animals to replace the ones that had drowned, Hagenbeck-Wallace still managed to start its 1913 season on time.

However, the cost of reviving the circus was too much for Wallace, and in June 1913, he sold the show to Ed Ballard of French, Lick, Indiana, and his many partners. Ballard was the face of the new show, but Jerry Mugivan and Bert Bowers helped to finance the purchase. In addition, it was rumored that investors behind the scenes were Crawford Fairbanks, a well-known brewer in Terre Haute, and

Thomas Taggart, the operator of the famous mineral spa in French Lick. Taggart was wealthy and had a lot of political power, too. He had even managed to wrangle the U.S. vice presidency for Thomas Marshall in 1912. Together, these men formed the American Circus Corporation and soon began buying up other small and failing circuses to go along with Hagenbeck-Wallace.

ALTHOUGH A MILLIONAIRE BY THE TIME HE TURNED 30 AND WITH A LARGE INTEREST IN HEALTH RESORTS AND SPAS, ED BALLARD TOOK THE OPERATION OF THE HAGENBECK-WALLACE CIRCUS VERY SERIOUSLY.

To most of the men, the circus was just a business, but to Ed Ballard, owning the show became a matter of pride. Ballard was the third son of James "Big Jim" Ballard, a father from a family known for determination and hard work but not for education or wealth. It was likely Ed's mother, Mary Elizabeth Ballard, who had the most influence on the direction her third son would take. She was perhaps the most industrious member of her family and shared her work ethic with her children by example. A strict woman with strong religious beliefs, she took in laundry from all the hotels in the area. This allowed Ed's first job as a pinsetter in the bowling alley at one of the nicest local hotels.

Mary refused to allow alcohol or playing cards in her house, so the next turn of events in Ballard's life came out of nowhere. Near the end of 1893, when Ed was 19 and working as a rural mail carrier, he quit his job and became a bartender in a saloon in Paoli, Indiana. He also started running a small-stakes poker game in one of the back rooms.

After building a small nest egg, he realized he could make even more money in a larger town and soon relocated to West Baden, Indiana, where he managed the gambling operations at the Dead Rat Saloon. By the end of 1894, he owned the place.

His continued success gained the attention of the owner of the West Baden Springs Hotel, the palatial health resort and spa where Ed had once worked setting pins in the bowling alley. He was now offered the hotel's highly profitable casino manager position, and Ballard took it.

Within a decade, he was a young millionaire with interests in casinos at the hot springs in West Baden and French Lick in Indiana, Mackinac Island in Michigan, Miami Beach in Florida, and Saratoga, New York. He also owned his own hotel across the street from the West Baden Springs Resort and several dozen farm properties in southwestern Indiana. He was married in 1913 and built a large brick mansion on the avenue that separated West Baden from French Lick.

Despite his other properties, Ballard took ownership of Hagenbeck-Wallace seriously and had close ties to the show, especially since it started in Indiana with Ben Wallace.

Over the next five years, the American Circus Corporation became a massive concern, competing against the "Big Seven" with its plethora of smaller shows. But this was not a group of experienced showmen who had spent their lives in show business. They were businessmen, worried more about the bottom line than bringing magic to small-town crowds. They were only interested in making money. To protect the company as they transported performers, equipment, and animals around the country, they created a corporation that would shield them from personal liability in case anything went wrong.

And in 1918, something went very wrong.

That season, the manager of the Hagenbeck-Wallace Circus was Charles A. Gollmar. His brother, Fred, was his advance man. They had been in the business for many years, the last two survivors of four brothers who had once owned their own show. Many members of their old troupe had followed them to Hagenbeck-Wallace. In years past, the Gollmars' show had played in many of the same communities on the 1918 Hagenbeck-Wallace schedule, so they weren't strangers to the route.

But this year, the circus would be returning to Hammond, Indiana, for the first time in years. The show's last visit was on July 28, 1914 – the day Austria declared war on Serbia and set the events that began the Great War into motion. This seemed like bad luck to circus folks, and Hammond was taken off the route until 1918, when the Gollmars decided to return.

But what happened to the Hagenbeck-Wallace show on the way to that town along the Illinois-Indiana state line would be considered much worse than simply bad luck.

THE 1918 SEASON FOR THE HAGENBECK-WALLACE CIRCUS was scheduled to open on April 26 in Cincinnati, Ohio, and then move northeast through Pennsylvania, New York, and into the New England states. Then, it would turn west, playing large and small towns in

upstate New York and Canada. The route then would dip down into the states again, playing northern Ohio and lower Michigan venues before stopping for performances in Michigan City and Hammond, Indiana. After the evening show in Hammond, it was set to go to Monroe and Beloit, Wisconsin, then move on to Minnesota and the Dakotas. From there, the show would backtrack through upper Minnesota and Wisconsin again and then head south into Illinois, Iowa, and southern Indiana. It would end with a grand finale engagement on the Chicago lakefront at the end of September.

All of America's circuses struggled in 1918, especially smaller shows like Hagenbeck-Wallace. They were plagued by labor shortages caused by America's entry into the Great War and the war production efforts that had sent factories into overdrive. There were also high taxes on admissions, not to mention the Spanish Influenza pandemic that began sweeping the country. The new "Daylight Savings Time" was also enacted by the government. Evening shows started later, which meant the show ended late for customers and kept many of them away. Business was down, and it was noticeable, even just a few weeks into the season.

Ed Ballard alone had invested $300,000 in the Hagenbeck-Wallace show. The circus owned 58 rail cars, and they were moved as special trains by the railroads it relied on. They had 22 tents and 1,000 employees on the payroll, which cost $7,500 per day. This didn't include expenses like feeding and transporting the roustabouts, sideshow, and all the performers, led by the famous Rosa Rosalind, who, as the star of the cast, drew a salary of $25,000 a year.

And other performers were drawing top wages, too, like Marcelline Cevene of the Cevene Sextette, a young, beautiful tightrope walker; the Cottrell-Powell English bareback riders; the famous Flying Wards of the trapeze; and the astounding Von Ritter, who stood on his head and slid down a tight wire stretched from the highest point in the big top to the ground.

In all, the Hagenbeck-Wallace Circus went on tour with 25 different acts and advertised 60 aerialists, 60 acrobats, 60 riders, 50 clowns, and "100 – count them – 100 dancing girls!" Adding to that were the show's seven elephants, lions, tigers, zebras,

THE MAIN SHOW OF THE HAGENBECK-WALLACE CIRCUS TRAVELED IN TWO TRAIN SECTIONS – ONE WITH THE ANIMALS, LIVESTOCK, EQUIPMENT, AND THE WORKERS WHO SET UP THE SHOW AND THE SECOND WITH THE PERFORMERS, STAFF, AND MANAGEMENT.

camels, a hippopotamus, hundreds of draft horses, 20 trained trick horses, and 80 horse-drawn wagons.

The show's advance men did an admirable job of papering the towns where they planned to play with posters and handbills, using 23 billposters, six lithographers, and a press agent named Floyd King. The crew could quickly cover an area of 30 miles around where the show was scheduled to play. The advance men arrived about three weeks ahead of the show, followed by a special "excursion car" that showed up around a week in advance. The press agents on board wound up the efforts and planned the "three-mile parade" that would be held when the circus arrived.

Behind the advance cars, the main show traveled in two train sections. The first section carried all the animals, livestock, essentials for the show, and workers needed to set up the camp. When the second section arrived, men and animals were put to work unloading the wagons and equipment, and soon, the task of setting up the big top was underway. When that work was completed, the animals, wagons, and performers were dressed and formed into the parade that would travel through the community and lead the crowds back to the circus grounds.

Like other shows, life with the Hagenbeck-Wallace Circus operated within a "class system." Circus administration and owners that traveled with the show lived in private cars or compartments near the middle of the train. The cars of the performers were next, with some cars having private compartments for families and regular upper and lower berths for single performers and senior staff members. This tradition automatically shifted the less skilled workers and roustabouts into the last few sleeping cars. Generally, those in the same line of work slept and ate together, operating as a small family within the larger family of the circus community.

Circuses – including this one -- traveled from one town to another every day of the week and had, years earlier, developed a fast, efficient, and profitable routine. It was so efficient that the U.S. Army studied the methods used by circuses to develop the procedures they needed to move large, mechanized forces on military campaigns – just as European armies copied the methods of James Bailey years before.

The packing, unpacking, and constant moving and handling of tents, wagons, railroad cars, canvases, seats, ropes, poles, and pulleys meant continuous wear and tear on the property on which the show depended. Sturdy and highly portable modern equipment was a basic expense for the show, and Ed Ballard decided to try to lure in wartime audiences with a new tent, seats, and a new, updated lighting system. Those items were already ordered when the show reached Michigan City, Indiana, on June 21, 1918.

THE CIRCUS USED A SMALL ARMY OF WORKMEN AND ROUSTABOUTS TO ERECT THE BIG TOP AND OTHER TENTS ON THE LOT. THEY TRAVELED BY TRAIN FROM TOWN TO TOWN, JUST LIKE THE PERFORMERS, ANIMAL TRAINERS, AND MANAGEMENT STAFF.

Ballard normally accompanied the circus and was with it when it arrived in Michigan City. However, instead of staying for the performance, he continued by train to Chicago, where he would take possession of the new big top he ordered from U.S. Tent and Awning Company. He planned to bring the tent to the show once it was settled

ON JUNE 21, THE HAGENBECK-WALLACE CIRCUS PLAYED A CHARITY SHOW AT THE INDIANA STATE PENITENTIARY IN MICHIGAN CITY. THE NEXT STOP ON THE ROUTE WAS HAMMON, WHERE THE CIRCUS HADN'T PLAYED IN FOUR YEARS BECAUSE SOME OF THE PERFORMERS BELIEVED IT WAS A "BAD LUCK TOWN."

in Hammond, the next show on the schedule. After a Saturday evening performance, the show would stay in Hammond through Sunday, June 23, and the roustabouts would unroll the new tent to be ready for use at the next stop, Monroe, Wisconsin.

The Michigan City performance was a charity show for the inmates at the Indiana State Penitentiary, held on the afternoon of June 21. There would be no evening show, so the cast and crew would have a light day and could take their time moving on to the next town. Even so, as the last acts were going through their routines that afternoon, the process of putting the show back onto the train had already begun. Once all the tents were down, rolled, and placed on wagons that carried them up the ramps to the rail cars, the job of putting the wagons, caged animals, and equipment on board began. Those tasks were finished a few hours later, and the train was ready to move again.

There was a hiss of steam, the screech of the wheels on the tracks, and the first section of the train began to move at 1:00 A.M., heading west on the old Michigan Central Railroad tracks, which were now used by the New York Central Railroad.

There were six sleeper cars, plus all the animals and their trainers that made up the first section of the train. It would first pass through Hammond and continue to the Union Stockyards on the South

Side of Chicago, where the animals could be easily fed and watered before returning to Hammond. The second train would meet the first section when it returned.

Except for the New York Central engine, its accompanying tinder car, and New York Central caboose, all the rail cars were old, wooden-framed, limited-service cars owned by the Hagenbeck-Wallace show. Government regulations stated that any train cars owned by circuses were limited to 25 miles per hour or less.

The first train passed through Hammond when the second section departed Michigan City at 2:30 A.M. on June 22. New York Central Railroad Extra 7826 was made of seven stock cars, followed by 14 flatcars carrying gilt-covered wagons and trucks painted in Hagenbeck-Wallace yellow. Next came four old sleeping cars the circus had purchased from the Pullman Car Company. At the end was a New York Central caboose occupied by a brakeman.

The dispatch board in Michigan City marked the departure time of the second train section, but no one in the yard was sure what time the train actually cleared the yard. The train still had to be assembled, and the caboose had to be attached to the rear before it could begin its journey. Once that was completed, the second train began to move and, like the first section, was restricted to speeds under 25 miles per hour.

New York Central train conductor R.W. Johnson was in charge of Extra 7826, and riding with him in the caboose was trainmaster Fred Whipple, an overseer from the railroad for both circus train sections. The third man in the caboose was rear brakeman Oscar Timm.

In the front cab of the steam engine was the locomotive engineer, a man named Gasper, fireman Clyde Phillips, and front brakeman Curtis Aust. As far as they were concerned, this was a routine trip, and each man did his usual tasks. For Aust, this meant periodically looking back at the following cars and ensuring all was well.

Things were quiet, and the train slowly began to move. Engineer Gasper held the train's speed somewhat below its allowed rate to the slight rise in elevation called East Gary Hill. Strangely, as they started up the hill, the engine headlight burned out. Gasper dropped the speed even lower than usual so that he could climb to the front of the engine and place another lantern in the lamp case – a tricky job even in the daylight.

As the train crept through the town of Gary, Curtis Aust glanced back at the rest of the train. All was well.

With Ed Ballard away from the show, command of the circus fell to general manager Charles Gollmar. He and his wife were sleeping in their stateroom in the first sleeping car. Other car sections were occupied by family acts and some of the single female performers. More single and married couples without children were in the next sleeper, while the last two cars in front of the caboose were filled with male workers and roustabouts – or would have been if the night hadn't been so warm.

Seeking a cooler place to rest than inside the stifling sleeping cars, many workers found spots to rest and get fresh air in the wagons and trucks carried on the flatcars ahead of the sleepers.

THE TOLLISON TOWER

Once the train passed through Gary, it picked up speed to about 18 miles per hour as it passed the Tollison Switching Tower. The operator on duty there recorded when Extra 7826 passed as 3:44 A.M. He immediately picked up his telephone and called the next tower operator –

three miles west – and notified him of the circus train's approach to his location, the Ivanhoe Switch.

This area of railroad tracks was complicated – both to navigate and to describe. But it's important, so bear with me.

At some point during the preceding 20 years, a small belt line railroad, the Gary and Western line, had added a third set of east-west rails that ran alongside the

A PHOTOGRAPH OF THE AREA OF TRACKS FROM THE 1960S. THERE WERE A NUMBER OF COMPLICATED CHANGES THAT TOOK PLACE IN THIS AREA – ALTHOUGH THE CAUSE OF THE CRASH WOULD BE A SIMPLE ONE.

Michigan Central tracks. The Elgin, Joliet, and Eastern Railway also had a single north-south track that crossed the Michigan Central tracks' main line and the Gary and Western lines' single track at a 90-degree angle. By 1918, the Indiana Harbor Belt Railroad had ownership of Gary and Western. It was using it as the easiest path to route trains through its facilities at Gibson Yards and to factories in Hammond on the north side of the Grand Calumet River.

The Interlocking Tower at Ivanhoe was located just west of the spot where the Elgin, Joliet, and Eastern crossed the tracks of the Michigan Central. The distance from Ivanhoe Tower to the Michigan Central depot was only five and a half miles, and the performance grounds the circus was heading toward were within walking distance of the depot.

Inside the tower were 33 manually operated switching levers controlling the track connections to the Gary and Western line and the Elgin, Joliet, and Eastern crossover. Those switches were electrically connected to automatic signaling systems that applied to the Elgin, Joliet, and Eastern, and Michigan Central right of way. The entire West Division of the New York Central, which included the Michigan Central line -- but not the Elgin, Joliet, and Eastern line – was completely equipped with modern automatic signals. They each used red, yellow, and green lights as nighttime indicators.

The average distance for a signal is one mile in each direction of the tower. Battery-powered electrical circuits were used, and these

THE MANUAL SWITCHES INSIDE OF THE TOWER, WHICH MOVED THE RAILS FROM ONE TRACK CONNECTION TO ANOTHER.

were connected so that the signal caution position was shown for each track switch unless it was overridden by the electrically controlled clear signal.

The manually thrown levers in the tower actually moved the switch rails from one track connection to another, and those rails completed the electrical circuits that controlled the signal indicators.

Got all that? I know – hang in there. It will all make sense soon.

Automatic signal 2581 served as the signal for westbound traffic approaching Ivanhoe Tower and the Elgin, Joliet, and Eastern crossing. That signal was 5,360 feet east of what was called the home signal bridge for Ivanhoe. The home signal bridge was about 950 feet east of the tower. A matching set of signals was located at the block's western end. The tower operators at Tollison and Ivanhoe were talking to each other about the proper setting of levers when the circus train traveled between Tollison Tower and the approach signal for Ivanhoe Tower.

The destination of the Hagenbeck-Wallace train was the north side of the Grand Calumet River, near some of Hammond's busiest factories. Extra 7826 had orders to take the Gary and Western branch connection and change tracks as it approached Ivanhoe Tower. To make the change, Engineer Gasper dropped his speed to about six-miles-per-hour as the train rounded a slight curve east of the switch and passed the Ivanhoe approach signal. That signal and the one close to the tower were glowing with a green light – an indicator that all was clear to transition to the Gary and Western tracks.

Then, "something a lot worse than just bad luck" changed everything.

Brakeman Timm was looking at the north side of the train cars as they moved slowly through the curve, and he spotted a problem in the middle of the train – a "hot box." This occurs within the wheel and bearing assembly and is caused by the overheating of bearings, wheels, axles, and brakes, and could be disastrous if not addressed.

This "hot box" was on a flatcar with "Hagenbeck-Wallace No. 72 painted on its side.

Timm immediately told Conductor Johnson, and both men lit fuses to signal the engine to stop. When Gasper spotted the alert and slowed down, Timm climbed off the caboose to go back eastward on the tracks and post danger warnings for any rail traffic following them.

THE TRACKS LEADING TOWARD THE SITE OF THE DEADLY ACCIDENT.

In the locomotive, Gasper applied his air brakes as the engine made the transition from the southernmost of the Michigan Central tracks through the northernmost track and onto the Gary and Western track. The train came to a stop about 70 feet east of the Elgin, Joliet, and Eastern crossing, either unaware or unconcerned that the last few cars of the train were still on the westbound Michigan Central track.

Gasper then set the independent brake for the engine and released his automatic air brakes, expecting that the crew would soon have the situation in hand, and they could continue on their way.

Of course, he had no idea that Extra 7826 would never move under its own steam again.

THE NEW YORK CENTRAL RAILROAD SYSTEM WAS ONE of the busiest in the country, even under normal conditions. But nothing was normal in June 1918. The wartime needs of a nation involved in the war made things more hectic and usual. The need to move troops from their training camps to the ports where they'd ship out to Europe was a priority for the government, and the New York Central served as a major resource for eastward movement for those destined for the battlefields of France. Once the troop-carrying rail cars were unloaded, they were returned westward to be used for the next group of soldiers ordered across the Atlantic.

Like the circus train, Extra 8485 was the leading half of a two-part train of empty troop cars. Pulled by a New York Central main-line locomotive with a standard coal and water tender, the train was

ENGINEER ALONZO SARGENT, WHO FELL ASLEEP AT THE THROTTLE OF THE EXTRA 8485 TRAIN.

pulling 21 empty Pullman sleeper cars used for moving soldiers. They were traveling back to the Chicago area from Kalamazoo, Michigan.

The conductor in charge of Extra 8485 was also named Johnson – no relation to the man on the circus train – and when it left Kalamazoo, it included engineer Alonzo Sargent, fireman Edward Burgess, a brakeman named W.R. Jackson, flagman J.E. Moyer, and three porters whose names were not recorded. Throughout the trip, only Engineer Sargent remained in the locomotive. Since the train was empty, the rest of the crew were in the caboose. Johnson, the conductor, was the only one who moved freely around the train.

Alonzo Sargent lived in Jackson, Michigan, and had left home by train at about 5:00 P.M. on June 21. He had not slept before leaving and wouldn't have much time to sleep when he reached Kalamazoo. At 8:00 P.M., he was called to take the throttle of Extra 8485. After a quick meal, he reported to the train.

Sargent's train section was dispatched out of Kalamazoo at 10:15 P.M. but didn't leave the yard until 10:55 P.M. All along the right of way from Kalamazoo to Michigan City, the train followed a slow freight train that Sargent assumed was having problems since he'd had to stop his train twice between the southwestern Michigan towns of Dowagiac and Niles to allow the freight train some extra space.

According to Conductor Johnson's watch, the train arrived in Michigan City at 2:47 A.M. on June 22. It stopped at the standpipe in the Michigan City yard, where Burgess, the fireman, left the train. Another fireman, Gustav Klauss, took his place. Ahead, in the locomotive cab, Sargent monitored water intake into the tender, preparing to push the train out of the yard.

At 2:57, Sargent got it moving again on the route to East Gary. His speed fluctuated between 25 and 30 miles per hour with the belief that he had clear track all the way. It's unclear why he believed this because the interval between his train and the circus train was only

14 minutes when he passed through the signals at Porter. This begs the question – did anyone on the troop train know that the circus train was in front of them? No one knows.

At the approach signal to East Gary, Sargent spotted a caution signal indicating a train ahead and reduced his speed. But the signal changed to all clear before his engine passed it by, so Sargent kept going but still slowed to between 10 and 15 miles per hour as he went through Gary.

When he passed the Tollison signal, Sargent picked up speed again – all the signals showed the track was clear. At the west end of the block, though, Sargent later said that he saw a caution light displayed but expected the right of way ahead to clear quickly as it did just minutes before. Once he reached the mile-long stretch between the Tollison and the Ivanhoe blocks, Sargent again picked up speed, now running at about 25 miles per hour.

He had no idea he was now just eight minutes behind the circus train.

As Sargent steamed along the line, he reached over and closed the window on his side of the locomotive. A strong wind blew off Lake Michigan, and the air had turned frigid in the cab. He didn't know it then, but this was a fatal mistake. The cold air had been what was keeping him awake.

Soon after he closed the window, Sargent dozed off.

MEANWHILE, AT THE STALLED CIRCUS TRAIN, OSCAR TIMM, the brakeman who had first spotted the hot box in the middle of the train, was walking eastward from the caboose with a brightly lit flare in one hand and a red-and-white lantern in the other.

At that point, the rear of the caboose was sitting 990 feet east of Ivanhoe Tower on the southern set of Michigan Central tracks. The switchover from the south to the north side of the tracks was 925 feet east of the tower. The wheels of the caboose had not yet reached the Gary and Western Railway switch before it stopped. The two sleeping cars in front of it were partially on the transition rails between the southern and northern Michigan Central tracks. The sleepers in front of those were sitting on the north parallel track with the Hagenbeck-Wallace flatcars. Only the locomotive, its tender, and some wooden boxcars were fully on the Gary and Western line.

Suddenly, around the far east end of the curve, Timm saw the approaching smoke plume of the troop train even before he saw the locomotive's headlight. Timm was now at least 700 feet from the rear of the circus train. He took a moment to make sure the emergency flares were burning brightly, lit another one, and started to run toward the train that he could now clearly see bearing down on them. Judging from the smoke coming from the troop train's stack, he estimated the train's speed to be at least 25 miles per hour, but there was no indication that his efforts were doing anything to get the attention of the train's engineer. He judged that he had just enough time to jump over to the fireman's side of the track to try and alert that crew member to the danger.

Timm waved the signal lights wildly, but the train didn't slow. He jumped back onto the engineer's side of the tracks, waving his arms and shouting in frustration as the steam engine roared past him. As a last desperate measure, he even threw his burning flare at the engineer's window, but it hit the glass and bounced away in a shower of sparks.

There was nothing the brakeman could do but watch in horror as the troop train steamed past.

Several of the crew members on the Hagenbeck-Wallace train saw Timm's failed actions, including Engineer Gasper, who was looking backward from his window to see the flare that Timm threw bounce off the locomotive's window. Gasper initially believed that Timm had successfully gotten the other engineer's attention and was discarding the flare -- and did nothing.

Conductor R.W. Johnson also saw Timm's futile efforts, but he could do nothing. He was carrying the gear needed to fix the hot box on the flatcar and was halfway between the caboose and the problem car when he spotted the approaching headlight on the track behind them. He dropped the tools and ran toward the troop train, also trying to signal it.

In the locomotive with Gasper and Phillips, Brakeman Aust, the train fireman, also saw Timm trying to stop the other train. When he didn't hear the engineer on the troop train blow the whistle in response to the signal, he jumped down from the cab and started running toward the rear of the train, joining Johnson and Timm as they tried to avert the coming disaster.

The trainmaster, Fred Whipple, still inside the circus train caboose, likely had the best view of Timm's failed efforts and must have been terrified to see that the oncoming train was not slowing down and was bearing down on him.

He managed to jump – or was thrown clear – of the caboose's rear platform as the steel crumpled under the tremendous weight of the steam engine and its string of rail cars, which were still moving at 25 miles per hour as they slammed into the circus train. The caboose platform, frame, wheels, and axles were instantly twisted and pushed forward into a great steel mass that was then swept into a rolling pile caught on the front of the troop train engine. The caboose and locomotive continued to drive forward, slamming into the sleeper car in front of the caboose.

The sleeper – a two- and three-tiered bunk car for unmarried men and women – was struck by the unrecognizable shape that had once been the caboose and was driven into and under it. In an instant, the locomotive destroyed everything in its path. Walls, floorboards, frame timbers, bunks, fixtures, bedding, and people were swept into that rolling mass of destruction. While some debris was thrown aside, most of the car's contents became part of the massive moving force.

After pushing its way through the rear sleeper, the engine slammed into the next car, tearing it apart and sweeping it along into the pile being pushed by the troop train. It continued to move – the sound of bent metal, broken wood, wrenching steel, and the screams of those not killed instantly nearly deafening – and ripped its way through two more sleeping cars before finally grinding to a halt.

Still in the cab of his locomotive, Engineer Gasper later claimed he felt only a "slight shock" before his air pump started working rapidly. Phillips, who was also in the cab, agreed with Gasper. He didn't realize at that moment just how bad things were.

Those in the sleeper cars struck by the troop train, though, told a much different story – well, those who survived did.

The sleeper cars were essentially torn down the middle and then splintered into pieces as the car's smashed contents were shoved forward by the weight of the roaring engine. The most fortunate were thrown clear, while others were swept along and pushed upward to the top of the debris pile.

But some others weren't so lucky. They were trapped by the broken boards, smashed furniture, and torn bedding, pulled into the iron wheels and torn apart by the sharp angles of the caboose that looked like it had been turned inside-out.

Strangely, the circus folks caught in the tragedy always claimed they didn't remember the wreck's sounds and destruction – they only recalled the terrible scenes that followed it.

It remains unknown how – or what – caused the fire to start in the wreckage that had once been the Hagenbeck-Wallace train. Or what caused the several explosions that were heard once the debris began burning. Some believe it may have been overturned oil lamps in the sleepers or possibly the locomotive firebox that started the blaze. Others have surmised it was the electric lights in one of the

sleepers, or maybe a broken piece of metal that caused an electrical short, or a loose wire that sparked and set the lamp oil ablaze. It's a mystery, but everyone agreed that once the fire started, it spread quickly and burned very hot.

Several men – like Henry Miller, a circus lighting engineer, and I.S. Steinhouser, an assistant property man – stumbled out of the wreck in their underwear and became the first rescuers of those still trapped inside. A.F. Roberts, a ticket seller who'd been in the last sleeper, said that he'd awakened under several broken timbers but was able to escape. He later said, "I saw people burned alive in one great flaming hell. God, the awfulness of it!" He did what he could to aid the injured, but so many around him were already dead.

Joe Dierckx occupied a lower bunk at the rear of the car nearest the caboose. His partner, Max Nietzborn, was asleep next to him in the bunk and was killed. Joe's brother, Arthur, was badly injured and died a short time later.

The three men performed together as the Dierckx Brothers – a strongman act with elephants walking over a bridge held up by the legs of the men as they lay on their backs – but none of them would ever perform again.

One of the youngest rescuers was Bobbie Cottrell. Bobbie was the son of Robert Cottrell and Margaret Powell, who were part of the Powell sisters act, who had been thrilling audiences with their horse-riding skills for years. Bobbie, who was 17, attended school in Valparaiso, Indiana, and joined his parents in Michigan City. He came along for the engagement in Hammond. When the troop train slammed into theirs, Bobbie had been thrown upward through the roof that had been torn away and landed outside, shaken but uninjured. He heroically rushed into the wreckage and pulled his parents from the shattered car. Aside from some cuts and bruises, they were also unharmed. However, his Aunt Louise, sleeping across the aisle, had been instantly killed. Bobbie carried her limp body from the wrecked car before the flames reached her.

Three other young men – teenagers who had run away with the circus – also rescued crew members trapped in the train's ruins. Jimmy Mulvaney and J. Turner from Ohio and James Everett from Tennessee – all cut and bruised but not seriously injured – scrambled to save as many as possible from the fire.

Henry Miller, who had managed to drag himself from the wreckage, gathered his wits and started doing what he could to help others. He recalled seeing a waving hand protruding from under a pile of broken seats and dented paint cans. The hand belonged to a wagon man known only as "Hickory," as he pulled him free, both fell backward into a small ravine. By the time Henry crawled back up to the tracks, he saw flames sweeping through the battered cars. He continued to free as many people as he could, only pausing once when he heard a woman's voice coming from the center of the fire.

"God! Oh, God! Kill me! Kill me!" she screamed.

Miller was not the only one who later recalled the woman's terrible screams. Bud Gorman, the circus horse master, heard her, too. He woke up after the crash with a dead man lying across his chest. Beneath him, he could feel jagged wooden splinters stabbing into his back. He managed to squirm free just as he saw the flames sweeping his way. Close by, he could see other survivors – men and women alike – who were pinned under the debris and desperately trying to get free. Assisted by a handful of rescuers, their efforts were failing, and the half-conscious victims, helpless under the tangled metal and wood, were screaming: "Shoot me! Kill me! Don't let me be burned alive!"

SCENES THAT APPEARED IN NEWSPAPERS IN THE WAKE OF THE ACCIDENT. HUNDREDS RUSHED TO THE SCENE, BUT THERE WAS LITTLE THEY COULD DO BUT PULL THE BODIES OF THE DEAD FROM THE WRECKAGE.

General manager Charles Gollmar and his wife occupied a stateroom in the fourth sleeper car. This sleeper had electric lights rather than the usual oil lamps. It was a newer car than the others, with more amenities, as befitted the status of a circus boss.

But those amenities did nothing to keep the car from being ripped apart by the crash. The roof had been torn off at the moment of impact, and the troop train's engine finally stopped immediately outside the Gollmar stateroom. Neither Gollmar nor his wife were seriously injured, but an unidentified body was hurled through the splintered wall into their room. Both escaped from the car and tried to do what they could to help.

Around this same time, circus clown Lon Moore saw Mary Enos, an aerial acrobat, trying to save her husband, Eugene. She had been thrown through a hole made in the side of the sleeper when the car started to buckle and break apart. She and Lon began pulling on Eugene's extended hand. He was unconscious and was being crushed under the weight of the debris piled on top of him. Somehow, though, they managed to pull Eugene from the wreckage.

Later, when Eugene was safely in the hospital, he said he owed his life to Lon and his wife.

Lon, who was 52 years old at the time of the wreck, had already survived one train crash – the Hagenbeck-Wallace accident in Durand, Michigan, in 1903.

Lon had been sleeping in another part of the same car where the Gollmar stateroom was located. His car had been badly damaged, but the state of the car behind it was much worse. Stella Coyle and her children used one of the berths in that car. Just before the crash, Stella was taking one of the children to the washroom. Her son, who everyone called Little Joe – his father was Big Joe – was asleep in the berth when he was suddenly awakened and jolted to one side. The troop train's locomotive had just crashed into the back of the train, tearing the car apart. The boy couldn't move as much as he tried – and then he heard his father's voice.

Big Joe Coyle had been thrown clear of the wreckage with only a few cuts and scrapes, and once he realized what was happening, he went looking for his family. He called out and heard his son's voice saying, "Oh, Papa, help me out of here!" Big Joe started tearing wildly at the timbers that blocked his way. The intense heat from the flames burned both his hands, but he refused to stop fighting against the wreckage. Sadly, though, his great strength wouldn't save his son.

Little Joe screamed. "Daddy! Help me, I'm burning!"

A great wave of flame swept over the debris, and several men had to pull Big Joe – dazed and badly burned – away from the destroyed sleeping car. Much later, the remains of Little Joe were found beneath the fire-blackened bodies of Stella and their other child.

Stunned minutes passed before the men in both train crews got over the initial shock of the disaster and started functioning again. Engineer Gasper grabbed a flare and ran ahead of his engine to flag down all eastbound traffic. Brakeman Aust went with him and, after stopping an eastbound freight train, returned to the train and uncoupled the connection between the sixth and seventh cars. When he did, he realized why they'd barely felt the concussion in the locomotive cab. The first circus flatcar had absorbed most of the impact and had broken in half, lifting the leading half of the broken car into the air and the back half of the car ahead of it.

While the fireman, Phillips, stayed on the engine and kept up steam pressure so that what was left of the train could be moved once the track was cleared, Conductor R.W. Johnson was running to Ivanhoe Tower to summon help. Once he had assurances that a call had been placed, he walked back to the train, only able to think about

WHEN THE ENGINE FROM THE MILITARY TRAIN SLAMMED INTO THE BACK OF THE CIRCUS TRAIN, THE WOODEN CARS SHATTERED INTO SPLINTERS.

repairing the hot box that had forced the train to stop in the first place. There's no explanation about why this task mattered to him now, but there were unconfirmed stories that he was later heard talking to himself as he worked on it. He muttered, "I'm going to get fired for this," over and over again.

The flagman, Timm, was running back to his train when the collision occurred and found the troop train's conductor, Lewis Johnson, and the fireman, Klaus, as they climbed off the train, appearing dazed and unsteady on their feet. Timm later reported that he didn't see Engineer Sargent at all, but he quickly got busy trying to rescue anyone he found trapped in the wreckage.

Johnson and Kraus also crossed to the north side of the wreckage to help in the rescue effort. There, Johnson saw Engineer Sargent and asked him what had happened. Sargent admitted that he'd fallen asleep just before the collision, then with his head shaking, he rushed into the tangle of debris to try and help.

Brakeman Jackson ensured his rear flares were still lit and then came forward to help with the rescue efforts. On the way, he came upon Klaus, still dazed and stumbling back toward the troop train. Jackson asked him how the accident had happened, and Klaus told him the engineer had been asleep.

Flagman J.E. Moyer seems to have been the most coherent crewman on the troop train at that time. After the collision, he'd relit his lanterns and had Jackson do the same while he ran backward from the rear of the train to flag down the second section of the troop train, which he knew was only minutes behind them. Once he had that train stopped, he uncoupled its engine and directed its engineer to pull back the sleeper cars of his own train so the area around the wreck could be cleared. He later recalled that when he looked back toward the disaster site, he could see the whole sky eerily illuminated by the fire.

By then, porters from both troop train sections ran forward with blankets and mattresses they'd pulled from empty berths. At the scene, they spread the bedding on the ground next to the tracks and helped the injured and dying as best they could. Three troop train porters – Frank Clemons, L. Lewis, and W. Dodson, who were generally known as the "Texas Trio" – also joined in the rescue effort, pulling the injured and dead from the wreckage. All three burned their hands severely and were later sent to the hospital for treatment.

Frank Clemons later told a newspaper reporter what he could recall: "I didn't know what to do at first. The first woman I come to kept screaming, 'Don't touch me! Don't touch me!' The first man said, 'Let me be, I'm dying!' We saw women burning alive. It was horrible – I never want to see a train wreck again."

THE SOUND OF THE COLLISION BETWEEN THE TWO TRAINS was so deafening that it shook the glass in the windowpanes of houses near the tracks, and it brought locals outside into the darkness before dawn to see what caused the noise. The crash site was so stunning that onlookers froze at the edge of the wreck. Oscar Timm later remembered the first bystanders standing and staring at the disaster as if in a daze. "They were dumbfounded," he said. "They were unable to move. I called to some to help, which seemed to jolt other people into action."

The exact time of the accident would eventually be fixed as occurring between 3:56 and 3:59 A.M on June 22, and during the 30 minutes that followed, only the crew from the trains, the surviving circus folk, and those who lived in the nearby Ivanhoe district helped with the disaster.

But help would soon arrive. Among the first responders were William Hodges, the newly elected mayor of Gary, Indiana, and the city's fire chief, Wilfred Grant. They couldn't believe what they were looking at – shattered sleeping cars, torn and bloody people under the debris, roaring flames, and the cries of helpless and desperate victims. The smell of burning flesh filled the air.

EVEN AFTER FIREFIGHTERS AND RESCUERS ARRIVED AT THE SCENE, THEY HAD DIFFICULTY GETTING WATER ONTO THE FIRE. EVENTUALLY, A TRAIN HAD TO BACK UP TWO MILES TO REACH THE ACCIDENT SITE.

The men were initially shocked into inaction but then became aware of the many injured and stunned people taking shelter in the woods and dunes alongside the tracks. There was little the two men could do but help people move away from the danger, but their presence at the scene would soon become important as more help started to arrive.

The first official rescuers were two fire companies dispatched from Hammond. They were closely followed by another contingent of firefighters from Gary. Chief Grant took charge of all three companies and began assigning tasks. Later, when the chief from Hammond arrived, the two men split the work, each fighting the fire from the opposite direction – but it wasn't working.

Without enough water to extinguish the flames consuming the rail cars, the chiefs directed their men to get anyone out of the wreckage that could be safely reached. The intense heat kept them back for the most part, though, only getting in to remove bodies after suppressing the fire's edge with fire extinguishers and axes.

Meanwhile, in the Gibson railyard, two or three miles to the west, special rescue trains and crews were being hurriedly assembled. Even so, more time passed. It wasn't until 4:45 A.M. that the first rescue train – backing up from the Gibson roundhouse two miles away – arrived, and the water in its tender was given to the firefighters on the west side of the wreck.

One of those on the rescue train was Nick Connelly, division superintendent for the Michigan Central, who helped bring order to the scene. The rescuers carried the injured and the unconscious several hundred feet to the rescue train.

After that, they carried out the bodies of the dead.

On the east side of the wreck, the second section of the troop train had also arrived and was pressed into service as a second rescue unit. Several of the badly injured passengers were loaded onto the train, and an hour later, it was ordered back to the South Broadway crossing in Gary, where medical help had been assembled.

The evacuated victims were sent to four hospitals in Gary and St. Margaret's Hospital in Hammond. Most injured circus performers and crew were taken eastward to Gary, but nearly as many uninjured survivors went to Hammond. The Michigan Central depot in Hammond became a triage point for the injured on the way to St. Margaret's, while the uninjured joined the company members who had reached the city on the first section of the circus train.

As the wounded were being taken away, circus performers and volunteers still swarmed over the wreckage, dodging flames and burrowing into small holes to aid those pinned by the debris. At the hospital, those same folks helped the injured however they could. Among them were the cowboys from the Wild West show who had come to work for Hagenbeck-Circus. They volunteered as nurses, and the hospital staff quickly found how skilled they were at handling cuts, bruises, and minor burns.

Soon after the living, dead, and broken were evacuated from the wreck, men began the process of removing the debris from the tracks. As soon as the second troop train took its load of survivors back to Gary, the westbound track was opened, and a switch engine was dispatched with all the crew and equipment needed to remove the cars that hadn't been destroyed. They were pulled to Gary and shunted onto an empty siding in the city's railyard. Except for the troop train locomotive and its tinder – jackknifed in a southwesterly direction across both the east- and westbound tracks – most of the Michigan Central tracks going west were cleared. Only some of the still burning debris of the wooden cars was left behind.

As this was being done, another crew cleared the wreck's west side. The locomotive, tender, and baggage cars at the head of the circus were soon on their way to Hammond. That left the broken flatcar and the six others between it and the smoldering circus sleepers. After the flatcar was disconnected, the last undamaged portion of the circus train was pulled away.

With the jackknifed locomotive and the smoking embers of the wooden sleeper cars all that was left on the tracks, the tender of one

EVENTUALLY, AFTER THE BODIES WERE REMOVED FROM THE CRASH, EFFORTS BEGAN TO TRY AND CLEAR THE TRACKS OF WRECKAGE AND DEBRIS.

of the trains that brought rescue crews to the scene was pulled as close to the wreckage as possible so that the firefighters could use its water. Once the flames had cooled, a crane was used to take apart the tangled steel and wood.

During this operation, rescuers kept looking through the debris for dead and injured passengers. Several more were found, and at one spot, an axle and the attached wheels of one of the demolished sleepers had settled onto the chest of a dead man. Unfortunately, the heat was so intense that slipping a chain over the axle so a hook could lift the metal away was impossible.

With more water pouring onto the scene, work progressed faster. The charred skull of a man was found beneath the front of the locomotive, and torn-away fingers lay scattered along the tracks. One of the ghastlier sites was two men who were never identified but had been caught between two of the coaches with mattresses all around them. The mattresses had caught fire, and the expressions of terror and pain were still frozen on their blackened faces.

News of the Hagenbeck-Wallace crash had spread through most of Hammond and Gary by then. Those who hadn't heard the news – but had planned to attend a circus performance – were informed as they gathered along the circus parade route.

Most younger children were kept away from the ghastly happenings at the Michigan Central depot and the tracks leading to the accident site, but others traveled to the scene.

When they started arriving, the rescue and recovery operations were still ongoing, and the new arrivals gazed with morbid curiosity at what was happening. They watched as the evacuation of the injured and dying came to an end and then stared in fascination at the survivors who remained at the scene. They gaped at the twisted steel and smoldering wood – and at the black charred remains of the dead.

A growing number of sheriff's deputies, railroad detectives, and firefighters tried in vain to keep the onlookers away from where the work was being done. However, photographs that remain show how unsuccessful their efforts were.

Officials who gathered at the site estimated that the troop train locomotive had plowed nearly 500 feet through the sleeping cars until grinding to a stop. As it drove through the caboose and the sleeping cars, the locomotive had rolled up all the broken parts of the cars into a pile that was finally shoved under the Gollmars' sleeper. Except for the few tossed clear or pulled from the rubble, those trapped in the rolling wall of wood and metal never had a chance.

By this time, local morticians had started to arrive at the scene, standing by until the wreckage had cooled enough to allow the bodies to be removed. Their wagons took them to various undertaking parlors in Gary and Hammond.

The evening newspaper initially reported eight dead at the Gary morgue and had a bulletin inserted that added another 12 to the count. In another part of the same newspaper, a story estimated that 40 were dead, another 30 were injured and expected to die, and 80 more were injured but had a good chance at survival. Already, two men and one woman had died after reaching Hammond.

More would soon join them.

LATE ON THE MORNING OF JUNE 22, A TELEPHONE CALL finally reached Ed Ballard, the owner of the Hagenbeck-Wallace Circus. His secretary, Harry Sarig, who'd arrived in Hammond on the first section of the train, tracked him down at Chicago's Congress Hotel. Ballard immediately arranged for a car to drive him to Hammond, and when he finally reached the circus show grounds, he took charge and began restoring order to his shocked circus family.

Ballard joined the gathering of circus performers, roustabouts, and staff and started verifying the presence or absence of those who worked for the show. This was particularly difficult since some of the workmen, wagon drivers, and ticket takers came and went, depending on the town, and, as he'd soon realize, the survivors didn't even know some of their names.

But for those present, Ballard checked on them and ensured they had food and anything else they needed. For those who'd lost everything, he paid for new clothes. He visited the hospitals, making sure everyone was being well cared for. Ballard also received a lot of help from the residents and merchants of Hammond, who began helping the circus folk without being asked to do it.

And they weren't the only ones. Edward P. Neuman, president of the U.S. Tent and Awning Company of Chicago, the company scheduled to deliver the new big top to Hammond that day, also came to the show's rescue. He arrived in town that day with the new tent and a full crew of men, and they went to work. With so many of the Hagenbeck-Wallace roustabouts either dead or injured, extra help was needed to get the old tent off the spool wagons and the new canvas into place. Neuman also offered great assistance with the funeral arrangements still to follow.

Another key figure in the events that followed was Charles Gollmar, the circus general manager. He had already earned the employees' gratitude by rescuing the strongbox, which had been secured in his stateroom. The wood and metal box showed signs of scorching from the fire, and while many of the valuables inside had melted from the heat, at least nothing had been stolen.

Now Gollmar had the sad duty of determining who was still alive, what condition they were in, and where they were. He moved the ticket wagon next to the cook tent and sat inside it with the circus payroll book in hand. One by one, those at the circus grounds came to see him. The boss then verified they were alive and how they felt and asked if they wanted to remain with the show.

Later that evening, Gollmar stated that 200 of the 600 Hagenbeck-Wallace employees were missing. Most of them, he thought, were roustabouts and drivers, and only a few of them were performers. His figure of 200 included both the unidentified dead and those taken to local hospitals.

At this point, no one knew who was dead and who was alive, and, in fact, no accurate count has ever been achieved of how many circus people died that morning in the crash. The Hammond Historical Society, which would carefully research the disaster, believes the most accurate death toll is 86, but no one can ever say for sure. The lists of those who worked with and traveled with the circus weren't very detailed, and, as mentioned, many workers' proper names were never recorded.

Many of those in the sleeping car used by the roustabouts were day laborers or temporary workers. Among them were drifters, men with unknown pasts who only used assumed names or nicknames to identify themselves. To make matters worse, many bodies were torn apart by the crash or burned beyond recognition in the fire that followed.

Of the 56 bodies that were buried a few days later, only 13 of their identities were known.

THE SHOW, AS THEY SAY, MUST GO ON. ON JUNE 25, THE CIRCUS PERFORMED IN BELOIT, WISCONSIN, WITH MANY OF THE WORKERS WEARING BANDAGES OR TOO SORE AND INJURED TO DO MUCH MORE THAN WATCH.

BY THE FOLLOWING DAY, WORD OF THE HAGENBECK-WALLACE disaster was spreading around the country. The Ringling Brothers and the Barnum and Bailey Circus sent telegrams offering the show whatever assistance was needed -- animals, equipment, or performers, whatever they needed to get the circus back on the road as soon as possible.

The show, after all, must go on.

They didn't perform in Hammond, although Hagenbeck-Wallace did remain in town for an extra day, hoping that many of the injured performers would have recovered enough to join them. They had been scheduled to play in Monroe, Wisconsin, next but skipped that location in favor of the extra time it gave the show to get organized.

On June 25, the show set up in Beloit, Wisconsin, with many workers wearing bandages and many others too exhausted, sore, or injured to do more than watch the tents and equipment being put into place during the setup.

The show went on that night, and according to one account: "Except for what they read in the newspapers; the public was unable to tell that the big amusement enterprise had all but been wiped out. The music, the calliope, the bright lights, the clowns, the beautiful equestrians, and the trapeze performers were all there, and the performance took place with characteristic 'snap and pep.'"

But what the crowd didn't see was the heartbreak hidden behind the bright smiles and the greasepaint. Of the 25 acts in the show, all but one of them had been affected by the wreck. The Flying Wards were not among the trapeze artists in that performance. They had been replaced by one borrowed from another circus. The Cottrell equestrians performed that night, but since one of the sisters died in the accident, she was replaced by a stranger from another show. When the band began the tune that cued the new performer to perform a solo portion of the act, Ed Cottrell left the arena and was found crying in the dressing room.

He wasn't alone. Lon Moore, one of the many clowns who brought audiences to tears with laughter, broke down in tears of pain and sadness when he returned to his dressing room that night.

Even the men regarded as heroes after the crash were shaken by what they'd seen and experienced. Blackie Logan, a wagon driver, had dug his way into the wreckage and rescued the wife of the show's trainmaster when all hope of getting her out alive had been abandoned. And then there was Bill Curtis, who'd stayed and worked with the rescuers and firefighters until the last body was recovered. Both men were back to work but felt the tragedy's effects in mind and body.

Later that evening, a reporter asked one of the Hagenbeck-Wallace trainers how many circus animals had survived the wreck. He explained that none of the animals were killed – they were all in the first section of the train. "Only people were killed," he said. "And this place ain't the same. We ain't all here. The actors can't get their minds to working straight. It's all so-so. The lady that trains that lion over there was burned to death. Her partner ain't half doing his act. He just can't."

But as Anna Donovan, one of the wardrobe mistresses, said: "And yet, we have to go on. It's business. It's our bread and butter. We have homes to maintain and families to support and bring up. We're honest, and we pay our bills. We can't stop to mourn and put on black. We have to go on, no matter how we feel inside."

WHILE THE HAGENBECK-WALLACE CIRCUS WAS PREPARING for its show in Beloit, a coroner's inquest was being held at the Lake County Superior Courthouse in Hammond, just a few blocks from St. Margaret's Hospital. The death of strongman Arthur Dierckx was cited as the reason for the inquest, but his name was just one of many that could have been used to convene the hearing.

Lake County Deputy Coroner H.C. Green was in charge of the inquest, and he summoned a long list of witnesses who would also later appear in many of the investigations and trials that followed over the next seven years.

One of the first to testify was Dr. B.W. Chidlaw, who had submitted a deposition about Arthur Dierckx's condition when he was admitted to the hospital. Two local undertakers who operated the ambulance service followed, and then men from the troop train crew, including Ed Burgess, the fireman, brakemen Jackson and Moyer, and conductor Lewis Johnson. The jury also heard testimony from the crew of the circus train, listening closely to the accounts of Oscar Timm and R.W. Johnson.

The railroad's attorneys refused to allow Engineer Alonzo Sargent or Fireman Gustave Klauss to testify. But the coroner didn't need them. He'd gathered enough information from other witnesses that a verdict was returned that cited "carelessness and negligence" by the engineer and fireman as the cause of the crash.

On the same day as the inquest, the first lawsuit was filed by a Hagenbeck-Wallace performer against the railroad. Lawyers for George Donahue, a clown confined to St. Margaret's Hospital with a broken back, filed the suit, but he didn't live long enough to benefit from the case.

Over the next few years, many more lawsuits would be filed. By 1924, when the last of the cases was finalized, a total of 125 lawsuits had been filed, and more than $1 million had been paid out.

State and federal government findings reinforced the coroner's jury verdict. The Bureau of Safety, which was part of the Interstate Commerce Commission, and the Indiana Public Service Commission launched a joint investigation into the crash. It was completed on August 8, 1918, and ruled out any problems with the automated track signals, train cars, tower operators, or the brakes on the troop train. It placed the blame for the accident squarely on Alonzo Sargent for falling asleep and on the Hagenbeck-Wallace Circus for using wooden cars for the train instead of steel ones.

When the investigation results were announced, Sargent and Fireman Krauss were arrested, charged, and locked up in the Lake County Jail. They were denied bail until their trial, which began on April 15, 1919, in the Lake County Courthouse in Crown Point, Indiana.

It was a short trial. A day of testimony from mostly the same witnesses who testified at the coroner's jury was followed by about four hours of deliberation by the jury – and ended with that jury hopelessly deadlocked. The judge declared a mistrial, but the Lake County prosecutor declined to retry the case. It was dismissed on June 9 – and the engineer who fell asleep at the switch and killed all those people walked away without any legal consequences.

But he did pay a price. His 30-plus-year career with the railroad was over. He spent the rest of his life in Jackson, Michigan, and died at the age of 75 on May 7, 1942, still wracked by guilt for causing a calamity that killed 86 men, women, and children and injured another 127 people.

Those who knew him later said that he was haunted into his grave by that morning in 1918 – and, some claimed, literally haunted by the victims. Sargent would often tell friends and relatives that he rarely slept. When he did, he would be awakened by someone standing at the foot of the mattress, shaking the bed to get his attention. The face of that person, he claimed, was black and charred, as if they had been burned by a fire.

Was this merely his guilt talking? Causing him to see things? Perhaps – but Sargent would always believe those ghosts were real.

ON JUNE 26, 1918, THE DAY AFTER THE FIRST TRAUMATIC performance by the circus survivors in Beloit, a large funeral service was held for most of the Hagenbeck-Wallace dead. It was held at Woodlawn Cemetery in Forest Park, outside Chicago, where a benevolent organization called the Showman's League of America had purchased a plot for indigent performers earlier that year. The Showman's League, now under the direction of President John B. Warren, had been founded by William "Buffalo Bill" Cody.

At the time, Warren was on his own deathbed, but despite his doctor's orders, he insisted on directing all the necessary arrangements for the circus performers killed in the accident. Ed Ballard paid the bill for the funeral.

A LARGE COMMON GRAVE WAS OPENED AT WOODLAWN CEMETERY IN FOREST PARK, ILLINOIS, WHERE THOSE KILLED DURING THE CRASH WERE LAID TO REST. OF THE 56 BURIED THAT DAY, ONLY 13 OF THEM HAD BEEN POSITIVELY IDENTIFIED.

In a large common grave – measuring 35 feet long, 24 feet wide, and five feet deep -- the caskets of the 56 performers and crew members killed in the wreck were laid to rest. Sadly, only 13 of those buried that day had been positively identified. The other 43 had been burned beyond recognition.

They became the first performers to be buried at the plot, but since then, dozens of other circus and carnival folks have been buried at Showman's Rest. Many of their identities are also unknown. Many stones in the plot marked with notations indicate that the deceased had been a clown, a wagon driver, or had the nickname "Baldy."

But despite the many rumors that have spread over the years, no animals are buried at Showman's Rest. Claims have been made that elephants were killed in the Hagenbeck-Wallace crash, but this isn't the case. The only elephants here are the stone guardians that watch over the silent graves of Showman's Rest. At the plot's entrance are five carved marble elephants with their trunks lowered in mourning. The majestic statues pay tribute to those who lost their lives in the 1918 disaster and to the legion of performers who have followed them to the grave.

And yet, strange stories about elephants – and other animals -- persisted for years.

ONE OF THE ELEPHANTS THAT WATCH OVER SHOWMAN'S REST AT WOODLAWN CEMETERY.

Rumors spread among locals that, late at night, anyone who ventured near Showman's Rest would hear ghostly animal cries – the spirits of the circus animals that died in the crash. A North Riverside police officer would discover the source of the story. He'd heard the accounts from people and wanted to experience the haunting for himself. One early morning in 1975, he went to Showman's Rest while on duty and suddenly heard lions roaring from the area around the graves.

"I wanted to run," he later reported, "until I realized the sounds were not coming from the graves, but from off in the distance, from Brookfield Zoo."

The young police officer had just solved the mystery behind one of the greatest legends of Chicago's western suburbs. Brookfield Zoo is only about a mile from Showman's Rest, and at night, when things were quiet, sounds from the zoo carried when the winds were right. It didn't take much imagination to see the elephant statues in the moonlight, hear the distinctive sounds of circus animals, and believe that animals killed in the infamous train wreck were haunting the site.

But as that trainer told a reporter right after the wreck, "Only people were killed." And some believe the spirits of those people don't rest in peace.

THE FUNERAL SERVICE AT SHOWMAN'S REST WAS officiated by Rev. Colonel F.J. Owens, chaplain of the Showmen's League, and the service drew a crowd of over 1,500 friends, relatives, and mourners, including "Big Joe" Coyle, who was burying his entire family. Thousands of floral tributes surrounded the grave, including a massive one sent by George M. Cohan, the famous stage actor and producer. The gathering pressed in close to hear the words of sympathy from the minister, and when he finished, everyone slowly drifted away.

One person who was not present that day was Ed Ballard, Hagenbeck-Wallace's owner. He was back on the road, traveling with the partially reorganized show to the next stop on the tour. The circus needed to have a successful finish for the season. But the end of the 1918 tour on Chicago's Lake Michigan shore on September 29 would mark the last time Ballard ever traveled with the Hagenbeck-Wallace Circus.

The 1918 season hadn't made much money even before the accident. Wartime restrictions and labor shortages forced them to make cuts to the size of the show. The nation's mood at war kept many people from entertainment like the circus. It had been an unusually wet summer, dampening enthusiasm and giving people another reason to stay home. All those things, plus the accident and the $300,000 that Ballard had reportedly spent paying off claims resulting from the wreck, put Hagenbeck-Wallace into bankruptcy. When it returned to its winter quarters after the Chicago show, it went into receivership.

AFTER WHAT BECAME A DISASTROUS 1918 SEASON, THE HAGENBECK-WALLACE OPERATING COMPANY FILED FOR BANKRUPTCY, ONLY TO BE RESCUED THE FOLLOWING YEAR BY ED BALLARD.

The operating company for the show was sold on December 28 for the bargain basement price of $36,000. It included the circus name, its remaining railroad cars, all the equipment, and the animals. Ed Ballard could have bid on the show and saved it but chose not to.

Only the operating company was bankrupt, however. Despite the disastrous year, Ballard and the American Circus Corporation were just fine. Ballard had other priorities and needed to pay attention to those. With a new baby at home – he and his wife's first – and aspects of his deal to purchase the West Baden Springs Hotel still being worked out, he didn't participate in the sale. However, a few months later, he and a new set of partners again purchased the Hagenbeck-Wallace Circus and three more traveling shows for the American Circus Corporation.

In 1919, the circus was back on the road, now under the management of partner Bert Bowers. He'd cut the show down to just 30 rail cars, and the season proved more profitable than he'd imagined – but it wouldn't stay that size. In 1920, the circus was on tour again, this time hitting the railways with a larger number of cars, but all of them were made from steel. The old wooden equipment had finally been phased out.

The Hagenbeck-Wallace would never be involved in another deadly railroad accident.

The 1920s have often been regarded as the "Golden Age" of the American Circus. This was certainly evident with the American Circus Corporation. The Flying Wards were back soaring through the big top. An 18-year-old named Clyde Beatty got his first job with one of the company's circuses, cleaning out animal cages. He'd go on to become a legend. A little-known clown named Emmett Kelly joined up with another show. Another young man whose father was a clown joined another circus and grew up as a star known as "Red" Skelton. In the years to come, those performers would become nationally known celebrities, but in the 1920s, they were joined by an already famous Hollywood movie star named Tom Mix, who was an instant major attraction for the company.

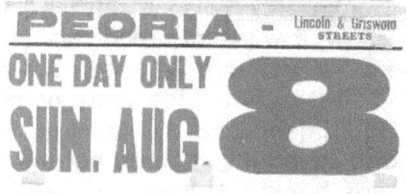

THE AMERICAN CIRCUS CORPORATION THAT WAS FORMED BY ED BALLARD AND HIS PARTNERS INTRODUCED SOME OF AMERICA'S GREATEST CIRCUS STARS, LIKE LION TAMER CLYDE BEATTY.

With five circuses going out on tour in 1928 and 1929, the American Circus Corporation was at the top of the business. Only the Ringling Brothers show could be considered true competition. But since the Ringling show only used 90 rail cars compared to the 145 cars it took to transport all of Ballard's shows, Ed felt he was really the one on top.

Then, after bringing Tom Mix on board and sneaking a contract past Ringling that put Hagenbeck-Wallace into Madison Square Garden for four weeks, Ballard received a message from Ringling. In effect, it demanded that one of them buy out the other and end the battle.

And that's what happened. Just six weeks before the Wall Street crash on October 29, 1929, the American Circus Corporation was sold to Ringling Brothers and was dissolved.

But that was not the end of the Hagenbeck-Wallace Circus – not yet. Ringling operated it as a separate show until 1936, when it was closed for good. That same year, John Ringling and Ed Ballard also died, and with them, the "Golden Age" of the American Circus died, too.

JUST SIX WEEKS BEFORE THE 1929 STOCK MARKET CRASH, ED BALLARD SOLD THE AMERICAN CIRCUS CORPORATION BUT HE WASN'T SO LUCKY WITH OTHER ASPECTS OF HIS BUSINESS. HIS WEST BADEN SPRINGS HOTEL NEVER RECOVERED FROM THE CRASH AND CLOSED IN 1932. HE LATER SOLD IT TO CATHOLIC JESUITS FOR $1.

JUST TWO YEARS LATER, ED'S LIFE WAS ENDED IN HOT SPRINGS, ARKANSAS. A MAN CALLED "SILVER BOB" HAMILTON SHOT AND KILLED HIM AT THE ARLINGTON HOTEL DURING A DISPUTE OVER A GAMBLING CLUB BOTH HAD BEEN INVOLVED IN. ED HAD SOLD THE CLUB AND HAMILTON BELIEVED HE'D BEEN OWED A PIECE OF IT. HIS MURDER MADE NATIONAL NEWS AND HUNDREDS ATTENDED HIS FUNERAL, WHICH WAS HELD IN THE ATRIUM OF HIS FORMER HOTEL IN WEST BADEN.

THE SITE OF THE HAGENBECK-WALLACE TRAIN WRECK is not easily found today. There isn't much to see at the place, and it's more than a little hard to find. The most prominent feature of the location, Ivanhoe Tower, is long gone. However, the rods that once connected the switching levers in the tower to the switching gear that moved the rails were still there when I visited the location years ago.

Also gone are the massive telephone and telegraph poles that appear in photos taken of the scene in 1918 and the houses once located nearby. Even one of the west-west tracks had been removed. The old Elgin, Joliet, and Eastern Railroad tracks are still there and still cross the former Michigan Central line at the same place they did back then, even if the railroads now have different names.

The place seems empty now, despite claims that it isn't. There is no monument, no plaque, and except for those rusted connecting rods, there is nothing left to identify it as a place where so many people died.

And yet, some claim the spirits of those killed at that lonely spot have not moved on. There are those who claim to have experienced the sounds of screams, weeping, and cries of pain in the darkness. Some say they've heard the roar of a train that never passes or have seen the headlights of the circus train locomotive moving down the tracks, disappearing at the point where a sleeping engineer allowed his steel monster to slam into the rear of the train ahead of him on that morning in 1918.

Are such stories true? Do those who died on the circus train still linger more than a century later at this stretch of tracks in northwest Indiana? Perhaps crying out for the justice the law never gave them?

I hope not.

I hope that after all this time, they have finally found some peace. To think the restless ghosts of the 86 people from the Hagenbeck-Wallace Circus who died that day were still out there roaming this desolate railroad line would be the greatest tragedy of all.

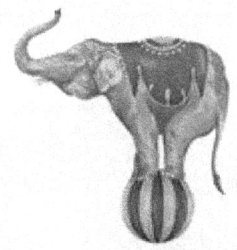

8. THE MEETING OF EMPIRES

WITH TWO MASSIVE CIRCUSES IN THE HANDS OF THE brothers from Baraboo, John Ringling began handling the routing of both shows. He had developed a near-photographic recall of the U.S. railroad system and combined that with an almost encyclopedic knowledge of economic conditions in various towns and cities.

To follow up on the success of 1908, he booked the Ringling show to open the 1909 season at Madison Square in New York, the first time the show would play in that city. At the same time, he opened the Barnum and Bailey show in Chicago. The result was underwhelming, abandoned by many in both cities who didn't get to see their favorite show. If John had felt slighted about not playing New York before that, the experiment of 1909 allowed him to get over it quickly.

Trying to prove that his decision to buy out the competition had been correct, John threw himself into overseeing both productions, leaving the details of the business management to his brothers.

One of his first decisions was to feature the equestrienne act of Ella Bradna in the Big Top's center ring, with no other acts going on to distract the audience from her performance. Wearing a low-cut sequined top, white tights, white gloves, and an ostrich fan, she was paired with Fred Derrick, who was elegantly attired in knee breeches and a tailcoat, and their act riveted guests.

Ella soared into the ring astride two white stallions, with Fred just behind her and about to jump up to stand atop her shoulders with the horses pounding around the ring beneath him. After making the leap, Fred somersaulted backward to the ground, then began a

SKILLED EQUESTRIAN ELLA BRADNA AND (BELOW) HER HUSBAND, FRED, WHO WOULD SPEND DECADES WITH THE SHOW.

series of flips and vaults on and off one of the horses. At the same time, Ella performed a veritable ballet on the other, ending with a bareback toe-dance that astonished audiences. In a finale just as exciting as fireworks closing, the two were rejoined, vaulting on and off the galloping stallions in an extended feat of athletic prowess.

While Ella was recognized as an extraordinary horsewoman, the act was designed and choreographed with a lot of help from Fred Bradna, who brought his army cavalry skills and precision to Ella's grace and elegance. By 1915, John Ringling had promoted Fred to equestrian director for the Barnum show and later for the combined shows, a position he held for over 30 years.

As many would later recall, Fred was not a big man, but he made up for what he lacked in size with his presence. He could curse in nine languages and often did so when confronting undisciplined performers. Perhaps the worst was Papa Leers, whose daughter Lucita was one of the most gifted acrobats in the Ringling show. Her act culminated with Lucita performing a full slip on a pair of Roman rings, which audiences found impressive enough. Lucita, though, then lowered the ends of a rope wound around her waist to the arena floor, where her father grabbed hold, pulled himself up, and then began his own series of acrobatics, his entire weight supported by the rope around his daughter's waist.

To Fred Bradna – and most spectators – whatever antics Papa Leers was engaged in were far less notable than the fact that a full-grown man was cavorting at the ends of a rope dangling from a young woman in a steady, full split and her legs between two dangling rings. Papa Leers, however, did everything he could to draw attention to himself, a fact that sent Fred into a hysterical rage, whispering threats of murder from beneath his top hat as Papa grinned and swung around like a chimpanzee.

Other novelties introduced by John Ringling reflected changes in the world outside the circus. Thanks to the public's fascination with the automobile, John brought two such acts to the New York opening. In one, a pair of strongmen known as the Saxons lay on their backs while property men laid out a metal bridge that used their legs as the only support stanchions. Moments later, a touring automobile with six passengers entered the big top, took a spin around the concourse, climbed the bridge, and slowly rolled over it as the Saxons held it up with their legs, supporting it all, as the *New York Times* reported, "without a quiver."

In the other auto act, the grand finale, Mademoiselle La Belle Roche drove her machine to the top of a steep incline, gunned the engine, and sped down a platform designed like a ski jump. At the bottom, the car shot off the lip of the jump, turned two back somersaults in the air, and then crashed down on its tires. The young woman behind the wheel waved brightly to the stunned crowd and sped off with resounding cheers following her out of the ring.

The New York engagement was well enough received, with the *Times* reporting the crowd left the Garden "many saying they had seen the best circus of their lives," but receipts were down, and expenses were up, an issue that followed both shows throughout the 1909 season.

Although the Ringlings were the most dominant force in the circus business, there was much competition to deal with – 30 other shows traveling that season, some with only two railroad cars compared to the 84 used by Ringling. The decline in business and an uptick in various unseemly competitive practices led the Ringlings to announce the formation of a circus owners association that would support agreements on fair trade practices. But it never got off the ground. Most prospective members were not interested in going along with the "Sunday School show" standards of the Ringlings.

John was determined that the show should have a wholesome image, especially the season he gathered 150 young dancers for a spectacle that was vaguely connected to the "splendors of the court of King Solomon." Special cars were arranged for them, and they had curfews every night. They were given daily reminders not to be seen leaving hotels in the city during the daytime because it looked crude and not to be seen with guests on the fairgrounds because it looked disreputable. Most of the dancers were happy to follow the rules to keep their jobs – but not all of them.

John's long-time valet, Taylor Gordon, remembered one girl who became unreasonable, and the boss threatened to pay off her contract and dismiss her. But she told him, "God financed me at birth – don't worry about me." She then bid him goodbye with some choice words and stomped off. Gordon remembered that the cigar in John's mouth bounced from one side of his face to the other, and his eyes were shocked like this of "a man who had been looking at the eclipse of the sun without smoked glasses."

MABLE RINGLING

Despite his insistence on proper behavior from members of the show, John didn't apply those standards to himself before or after his marriage. His wife, Mable, always had the good judgment not to question John too closely about what he might or might not have done during his many excursions around the country or across the Atlantic. She decided that if you didn't talk about it, it never happened. However, even during his bachelor days, John carefully avoided any improprieties with the women who worked for him. He confined his roaming eye to other women he might meet.

John favored the Palmer House for his lodging when the show was in Chicago and something of a contest began between him and the hotel detective there. One of the primary functions of the detective at that time was to make sure that unmarried couples were not having sex in the hotel, which was not only a criminal offense – unlawful cohabitation it was called in the books – but it also made such prominent establishments look seedy. At first, John was convinced the detective was clairvoyant because any time he managed to smuggle a woman into his room, even in the middle of the night, the door of the room flew open just as the action was getting ready to start.

In time, though, John figured it out. Once the detective was satisfied that John was in his room for the night, he would lean a matchstick against the door. If he passed by later and the matchstick had fallen, it was all the proof he needed to pound on the door and escort the offender out of the hotel. After John learned the trick, he'd wiggle his fingers beneath the bottom of the door and prop the matchstick up again.

Improprieties aside, the first decade of the new century brought many changes to Ringling's operations. Gus died in 1907 at the age of only 53, and Otto, the third oldest and the company's financial wizard, died in 1911 at just 54. Though the hard-working youngest brother, Henry, was made a full partner in Otto's place, the loss only underscored how important John's position was in the business.

In contrast to Barnum, whose measure of the quality of an act was generally limited to the amount of fanfare or business it might attract, John's time in Europe, looking for attractions, had broadened his cultural views. In 1914, he added a ballet to the show, featuring 84 ballerinas in the exhibition, when many Americans had no idea what a "ballet" might be. He was also in complete support of his brother Alf's idea to include plays in the show, including numbers such as "Joan of Arc" and "Cinderella," the latter including a cast of 1,370, along with 735 horses and – undoubtedly, the only time in the musical's history – "five herds of elephants."

It was expensive but worth it – audiences turned out in droves, and the costs were quickly earned back.

There were other parts of the show that John spent money on because he knew they were popular, but he still wasn't happy about it. At the top of that list were wild animal acts. He considered them unpredictable and dangerous. Bears,

EVEN THOUGH THEY WERE WILDLY POPULAR, JOHN RINGLING HATED BEAR ACTS, BELIEVING THE ANIMALS WERE TOO DANGEROUS.

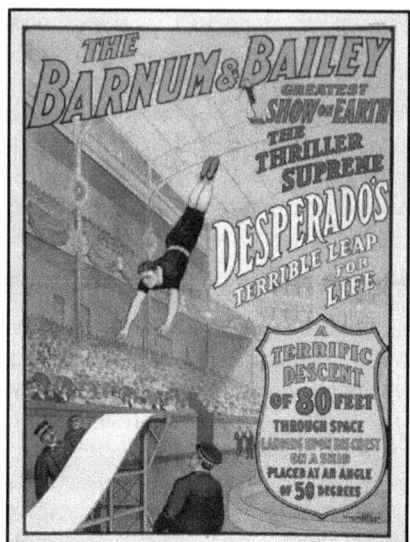

A POSTER FOR THE DEATH-DEFYING ACT OF ERNEST GADBIN, WHO USED THE STAGE NAME OF "DESPERADO"

for instance, were notoriously difficult to work with, requiring exact consistency in their routines and schedules, and were far more likely to turn on their trainers than big cats. But they had to have them – the public demanded them.

Even the act of an unhinged German acrobat named Ernest Gadbin was one he tolerated more than he felt necessary. Gadbin, who came to the show just before the United States entered World War I, used the stage name of "Desperado" and had concocted a routine in which he did a swan dive off an 80-foot platform and landed on a kind of toboggan slide that was lubricated with a cornmeal paste. He would hit the slide traveling about a mile in a minute, zoom down its length to a turned-up lip, then soar through the air to land in a waiting net. To the audience, this kind of madness was thrilling, but to John, it was only a reminder that the cornmeal paste might thicken one day and kill the German – sooner than he might expect.

As mentioned in the last chapter, this era began what's been called the "Golden Age" of the circus industry, with virtually every one of the 30 or so traveling companies offering a street parade when it arrived in town. All the big shows were going to great lengths to outdo each other in one way or another when it came to splendor, wonder, and physical feats.

The circus achieved things that put all the rest of show business to shame. It had a magic that was both universal and complex, and the first two decades of the twentieth century were a time that came before worry managed to wear that magic away. If human beings – or humans interacting with animals – learned to do something stupendous and unbelievable but real, that achievement would be presented in the flesh under the big top, where hundreds or even thousands cheered them on.

BUT, EVEN IN THOSE HALCYON DAYS, THE EVENTS OUTSIDE managed to intrude on the circus – a place that should've been immune from the worries of the outside world.

In 1916, as the nation waited for word as to whether Woodrow Wilson would run again for president, he attended a Barnum and Bailey show performance in Washington, D.C. Wilson had often expressed his dream of someday riding an elephant in the show. While John and Fred Bradna would have been happy to accommodate him, his protective detail kept it from happening. Then, on May 8, 1916, as Wilson was escorted from the performer's entrance to some reserved seats, the band struck up "Hail to the Chief." Wilson paused to raise his hat in appreciation, then spun it into the middle of the center ring. While the crowd erupted, reporters rushed to telephones to call their editors and tell them: "The President has *literally* thrown his hat into the ring!"

PRESIDENT WOODROW WILSON LITERALLY "THREW HIS HAT IN THE RING" FOR RE-ELECTION WHILE ATTENDING A CIRCUS PERFORMANCE IN WASHINGTON, D.C.

More progress slipped into the circus grounds around this time, too. The spectacle of groups of sweat-glistening roustabouts alternating blows of sledgehammers on the stakes that held the ropes of the big top would soon be replaced by a wagon-mounted pile driver device that hammered in the stakes by a four-horsepower gasoline engine. Soon, the canvas of the big top itself would be mounted on huge spools and carried about on special wagons built just for the spools, which unfurled the tents in a fraction of the time it had taken the roustabouts.

Instead of using horse teams or elephants to pull the guy lines that raised and held the huge tents, tractors were used instead. The time-consuming task of erecting the bleacher seating for thousands of spectators each time was simplified by the invention of a collapsible bleacher seat wagon. The wagon had 20- and 30-foot sections of seats that could be folded down onto their wheels and towed from one location to another, where they'd be seamlessly hooked up to other sections when they arrived.

The march of time also continued its attack on the Ringlings. On New Year's Day 1916, the oldest brother, Albert, died of a heart attack at age 64. Al's death was mourned deeply in Baraboo, for he, more than the rest of his brothers, had maintained close connections with the town he still considered home.

Then, just a little more than two years after Al's death, the youngest brother, Henry, passed away in 1918 at age 49. In 1919, middle son Alfred died, leaving Charles and John in a partnership whose holdings had grown significantly, even as those involved dwindled. When the U.S. entered the war in 1917, the Ringling Show employed about 1,000 people and traveled around the country on 92 railroad cars, with the Barnum and Bailey Show almost the same size.

NOT ONLY DID THE GREAT WAR WREAK HAVOC ON THE CIRCUS INDUSTRY AS IT LOST SO MANY WORKERS AND PERFORMERS TO THE MILITARY, BUT THE SPANISH FLU EPIDEMIC THAT FOLLOWED LED TO THE CLOSURE OF EVERY KIND OF ENTERTAINMENT VENUE IN THE COUNTRY, INCLUDING CIRCUSES.

But that soon changed. With so many workers and performers gone off to fight, the shows lacked the people to stage full programs and efficiently move around the country for the first time in their history. The canvas men were reduced from 250 to 80, while the property men dropped from 80 to 20, and most were old or unable to enlist or be drafted for physical reasons, a change from the burly personnel that had worked the fairgrounds before the war. Even the grooms who cared for the show's 535 horses were decimated as during World War I, a horse cavalry was still of vital importance to the military.

And if this wasn't enough, there was the Spanish Flu in 1918, which claimed more than 22 million lives around the world. It swept across the United States, killing tens of thousands and dragging down attendance at public venues of every kind.

After the 1918 season, the last two Ringlings made a momentous decision. Instead of returning the two big shows to their respective winter quarters – the Ringling show to Baraboo and the Barnum and

Bailey show to Bridgeport – both were sent to Connecticut, a decision that would have never gotten past Al Ringling if he'd still been alive.

But to John, the move was unavoidable. Not only would the administration and maintenance of a single operation be more practical, but Connecticut's taxes were much lower than those in Wisconsin.

Plus, the truth was that in just a few short years, the circus had lost its dominance over America's choice for popular entertainment. Moving pictures had changed from minutes-long novelties in storefront nickelodeons to full-length productions that were exhibited in actual theaters with name-brand directors like Cecil B. DeMille and D.W. Griffith producing cinematic works that were now being viewed in wonderment the way that only spectacles under a big top had been a decade earlier.

In addition, as John was aware already, getting to the theater had become much simpler. Now, even the most remote farm family could make it to the cinema in their automobile. The first Model T rolled off the assembly line in Detroit in 1908, and now, less than 20 years later, more than 15 million had been manufactured and sold. By 1929, four out of five families in America owned an automobile.

But John knew this also made it easier for families to attend the circus, too. Combining the two big shows and confining their appearances to larger population areas made sense in postwar America. There would be fewer small-town shows, but he was convinced he could build a new version of the circus that would make people come a little farther to see.

And though many in Baraboo would never get over the loss of the circus, moving the central operations to Bridgeport – close to the big population areas and transportation lines – was the best way to ensure that the circus survived in the decades to come.

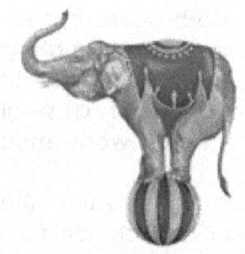

9. THE ROARING TWENTIES

THE RINGLING BROTHERS AND BARNUM & BAILEY COMBINED Shows opened for the season on March 29, 1919, with a four-week run at Madison Square Garden.

The *New York Times* called it "the biggest thing of the kind" the city had ever seen and lauded the skills of various performers, like aerialist Tiny Kline, who would remain a show business fixture long enough to perform with Tinker Bell at Disneyland in the 1960s. They also praised May Wirth, who had taken over as the show's featured equestrienne, and lovely tightrope walker Bird Millman, whose songs and graceful ballet kept the audience in rapt attention from the space above the center ring. Such diversions, along with bicycling and wire-walking bears, boxing ponies, and dogs somersaulting into a net from the aerialists' high perch, proved as popular as always.

Asked by a reporter from *American* magazine if the circus would be altered by progress, John Ringling seemed confident with his reply: "It will never be changed to any great extent, because men and women will always long to be young again."

In a way, John's claims would prove to be true. In fact, the circus would remain relatively unchanged – except for in ways that demanded it – from the golden era to the end of days. It was the world outside of the circus that changed, sometimes for the better.

There's no question that the 1920s were a boom time for the circus – as it was for pretty much everyone as the decade kicked off. As the economy boomed, people found money in their pockets that they could use to try and forget a relentless pandemic and a traumatic war that was so terrible that it was thought to be the one that would end all wars. The shows that survived the lean years at the end of the previous decade prospered, and new stars rose to capture the attention and imagination of the nation.

One of them was Mexican-born Alfredo Codona, who had joined the Barnum and Bailey show in 1911 at 18 and moved over to the Ringling Circus in 1918, where his graceful acrobatics, envied physique, and striking good looks earned him the moniker of "King of the Flying Trapeze." In 1920, he threw his first triple back-somersault, a feat referred to as the "somersault of death," which had been accomplished only a few times in circus history.

ALFREDO CODONA, "KING OF THE FLYING TRAPEZE. HE RARELY MADE MISTAKES UNDER THE BIG TOP, BUT HIS PERSONAL LIFE WAS FILLED WITH TRAGEDY.

Soon, his skill with the maneuver was effortless and one that he often repeated. He seriously miscalculated the move only once, leaving his bar at what was believed to be one-hundredth of a second too late. By the time he reached the hands of his partner and brother, Lalo, that fraction of a second had turned into a four-inch gap from where his body was and where it was supposed to be. As a result, Aldredo's head struck Lalo in the chin, knocking him unconscious. Alfredo whizzed past at 62 miles per hour, landing face down in the net with Lalo tumbling after him. Before Alfredo could scramble out of the way, Lalo's dead weight landed on the small of his back. He spent the next two weeks in the hospital while five broken bones slowly healed.

Mistakes under the big top were rare for Alfredo, but he would survive to make more than his share outside of the canvas. In 1919, a beautiful and talented aerialist and high-ring artist named Lillian Leitzel – already known as "The Queen of the Aerial Gymnasts" thanks to her legendary work in vaudeville – joined the Ringling show at the considerable salary of $250 per week. Soon, she was making twice that much, traveling in her private rail car and getting ready in her private dressing tent, which were unheard-of privileges for most performers then. As her fame grew, Lillian was pursued by men from every walk of life, including actors, senators, assorted millionaires, and titans of industry like Henry Ford, whom she kept waiting outside her tent for so long that the bouquet of roses that he'd brought for her had wilted by the time she ushered him inside.

Lillian was a diminutive four-foot-ten and wore a child's shoe size. Clad in silk tights and a sheer skirt, her long blond hair falling over a skimpy sequined top, she topped off each performance by ascending to the top of the aerialist's web, where, with no net below her, she would pass her right hand through a loop attached by a swivel to a dangling rope and begin to swing back and forth until she launched her body into a spin like that of an airplane propellor as the audience tried to call out the number of her revolutions from far below.

IN 1928, ALFREDO MARRIED "QUEEN OF THE AERIAL GYMNASTS" LILLIAN LEITZEL, WITH WHOM HE'D BEEN HAVING A TORRID AFFAIR. THE MARRIAGE QUICKLY BECAME DISASTROUS FOR ALL INVOLVED.

The technical term for this maneuver is the "full arm plange," but in simple terms, it means that each time Lillian made a revolution, her shoulder was dislocated and snapped back into place. The count of her spins by the audience often reached 100 before she stopped.

Her record was 249 – 249 shoulder dislocations and resets in a matter of minutes.

For years, she and Alfredo Codona existed within two bubbles of Ringling celebrity. However, in the end, as if it had been preordained, the King and Queen of the company's aerialists found their way to each other. In 1928, the torrid affair between two highly volatile and highly talented artists was consummated at a wedding in Chicago.

They drove away from the circus grounds with "Just Married" signs plastered across the back of the automobile. Though Lillian was in her thirties and had been twice married by that time – claiming she didn't remember the name of her first husband – she looked as radiant as a schoolgirl in a snapshot that was taken that day, while the beaming 35-year-old Alfredo looks like the excited boy next door.

But the appearance of happiness was deceiving – or at least the happy times quickly ended. The marriage was soon on the rocks. Lillian had spent two decades as the object of desire for an uncountable number of powerful and attractive men and simply couldn't turn her back on the rich and the persistent.

Alfredo, one of the most desirable celebrities of the era, came from a Latin background with little tolerance for a wayward or even flirtatious wife. Within two years, sick with jealousy, he developed a dubious plan to try and win back Lillian's attention by starting a poorly hidden affair with an Australian bareback rider named Vera Bruce, who was herself motivated by one-upping the queen of the Ringling performance world.

Things did not go well.

During the 1930 winter season, Lillian and Alfredo took on a series of European appearances – but not together.

On the night of February 12, 1931, Lillian woke from her hotel room bed after having a terrifying nightmare. It wasn't the first time she'd dreamed of falling, but this time was so real and frightening. She'd have trouble shaking off the feeling of a premonition as she rode in a cab to the Valencia Music Hall in Copenhagen, where she was scheduled to perform that night.

It was Friday the 13th.

Her performance went off without a hitch, though, and she was relieved to get through it without problems as she began the climax of the act, with her rigging man standing some 25 feet below her. As the audience's count of her speeding propellor turns neared the previously agreed-upon limit, the prop man was distracted momentarily, reaching over to guide the rope she would use to descend to the floor.

It was only a moment – but that man would relive it for the rest of his life.

WHILE ON TOUR IN 1931, LILLIAN HAD A NIGHTMARE ABOUT FALLING TO HER DEATH DURING A SHOW – A DREAM THAT CAME TRUE ON FRIDAY THE 13TH.

At that instant, the brass swivel ring, which was heated to a near-glow by the friction caused by Lillian's spinning, abruptly snapped. Lillian plunged to the arena floor 20 feet below. She landed on her shoulders and head, but to the amazement of the screaming crowd, she bounced almost instantly to her feet.

"I'm all right!" she told her rigger, planning to continue the act.

But he quickly replied, "You're not going anywhere but to the hospital." The crew promptly rushed Lillian away.

When Alfredo heard about the accident, he canceled his show at the Winter Garden in Berlin and hurried to Lillian's side, arriving the next day. But she seemed to be fine. She insisted she would soon return to work and told him he should return to Berlin and fulfill his obligations. They would speak again soon. Reluctantly, Alfredo agreed.

And then, on Sunday, February 15, Lillian suddenly lapsed into a post-concussion coma and died.

The loss destroyed Alfredo. He went into solitude for months, and when he returned, his performances had changed from graceful aerial acrobatics to dangerous stunts that defied death.

He married the Australian equestrian, Vera Bruce, but the intensity of his performances continued. Soon, he suffered a fall that permanently damaged his shoulder and grounded him for good. For a time, he and Vera toured with an equestrian show they drummed up, with him as director, but the business failed, and Alfredo found himself managing a gas station.

Not surprisingly, Vera eventually filed for divorce from a man filled with so much self-loathing that he had become intolerable. On July 30, 1937, she asked Alfredo to join her at an attorney's office to divide their property. To her shock, Alfredo quickly agreed.

When he arrived at the office, he seemed calm and prepared to

ALTHOUGH LILLIAN'S DEATH NEARLY DESTROYED ALFREDO, HE EVENTUALLY MARRIED EQUESTRIAN VERA BRUCE. THEIR MARRIAGE FAILED AND WHEN HE MET HER IN HER ATTORNEY'S OFFICE TO SIGN DIVORCE PAPERS, HE SHOT AND KILLED HER – THEN TURNED THE GUN ON HIMSELF.

face the inevitable. He asked the attorney if he might have a private word with Vera before they began, and when Vera agreed, he left the room. When the door closed behind the lawyer, Alfredo locked the door, pulled a .45-caliber pistol from his pocket, and shot Vera five times.

There was only one bullet left in the chamber – and he fired that one into his head. Alfredo died immediately, but poor Vera lingered into the next day before she succumbed to her wounds.

Ultimately, with one news story declaring that the "double tragedy" had written an epitaph to a ruined career, Alfredo Codona would be buried in an Inglewood cemetery next to the ashes of Lillian Leitzel. One word chiseled into the obelisk marks the spot: "Reunion."

John Ringling had always spoken about the circus as being something magical and pure. However, his nephew and biographer, Henry Ringling North, argued that an institution with a legacy dating back to imperial Rome would always have a dark side – an ever-present specter of death. Death was no longer inevitable in the circus, but the possibility was always there – for the high-wire walker, the acrobat performing without a net, and the animal tamer who entered a cage with no chance of fending off an animal that might decide to decapitate them with one swipe of a paw.

And there was another darkness, too, which his uncle never discussed. In the back lot of the circus, where the menagerie tents butted up against those of the roustabouts who made up the main labor force, one could say that it resembled a tented slice of hell. Most employees lacked the desire or capacity to hold down a permanent job. They were a tough and unaccountable lot, and with such a crew in tow, there were the makings of trouble every day, even though most circuses were lucky enough to have little of it.

It was also impossible for the show to leave behind the parasites that followed in its wake, like the shell-game operators, the confidence men, pickpockets, gamblers, bootleggers, and prostitutes. Every once in a while, North wrote, "We would have the engineer stop in the middle of nowhere, preferably a desert, and 'delouse' the train. We would go through it from end to end, digging the human rats out of the baggage wagons and from under cages on the flats and heaving them ungently to the ground."

The darkness would catch up to them again, eventually, but for a time, the circus could go on and at least pretend that they were bringing John Ringling's "magic and purity" to the masses.

CHARLES RINGLING

THE DEATH OF ALFRED HAD LEFT JOHN AND CHARLES AS THE last two survivors of the combined Ringling and Barnum and Bailey shows, but their relationship was not always pleasant. Charles' wife, Edith, had become irritated with John's belief that he was the most important to the show's future and his constant badgering to her husband to "keep up with him," whether in business or social affairs. If John bought anything, Charles would buy a bigger one – a yacht, a car, a house, it didn't matter.

When John took an interest in the small town of Sarasota, Florida, and started a bank there, Charles had to open a bank, too, even if there probably wasn't a need for even a single bank in town.

With John's penchant for late nights and breakfasts that might start around noon, Charles insisted that their business meetings begin promptly at 9:00 A.M. so that "things could get done." John usually only made it to the meetings by staying up all night and arriving somewhat on time.

This rivalry between brothers was most apparent in the form of the two mansions they built side by side on the bay in Sarasota – a place far away from Baraboo, Wisconsin, in an astounding number of ways.

In 1905, at the age of 39 and after a long period as a carefree bachelor, John married the lovely Almida Burton – better known as Mable – in a ceremony in Hoboken, New Jersey. By then, the show was prospering, and the brothers used the winter season to escape from cold weather and enjoy extended stays in Florida. The state had become a popular destination after railroad and hotel tycoons Henry Flagler and Henry Plant opened it up in the 1890s.

John and Mable spent a couple of winters in Tarpon Springs, a sport fishing area about 30 miles northwest of Tampa on the Gulf of Mexico but received a cool reception from the old money folks in that area. During a boating excursion arranged by fellow circus man Charles Thompson, they sailed down the coast to Sarasota, a town that Thompson highly recommended to them as a spot to spend the off-season. The people in Sarasota had no problem with "circus people."

In the fall of 1911, John bought a house from Thompson in the Shell Beach neighborhood and soon, the couple – who had never owned a house before – were calling the little town home. John soon bought up other properties in the area, and not long after that, brother Charles built his own house in Sarasota next door.

The brothers kept yachts docked at the nearby city pier, and for years up to and through the Great War, they enjoyed Sarasota as their winter getaway, although Mable increasingly started spending the rest of the year there, too. During the war, both men's boats were commissioned for use by the Navy. However, neither saw action and the Ringlings, while not excluded by what passed for "society" in the community, were largely regarded as outsiders.

Over the years, unlike most of his brothers, John had been expanding his business interests beyond just the circus. He was a part owner and board member of Madison Square Garden – along with J.P. Morgan and William Vanderbilt – and was also on the board of a prominent bank. His knowledge of the nation's rail system led to his purchase of several short-line railroads, mostly in the West, and when oil was discovered on lands next to his rights-of-ways, he began to speculate on oil leases. Eventually, John laid out plans for a community in Oklahoma oil country – called Ringling, of course – and it remains a small town on the lonesome prairie west of Ardmore.

John also owned railroads in Missouri, Ohio, Texas, and Montana, including the rather grandly named White Sulphur Springs and Yellowstone Park Railroad. The line –only 21 miles long – began in White Sulphur Springs, Montana, and ran south to connect to the Chicago, Milwaukee, St. Paul, and Pacific line, though it never went anywhere close to Yellowstone, which was more than 100 miles away. The end of the line was in the unincorporated town of Ringling, Montana. It was meant to be a jumping-off point for a resort that he planned to build in White Sulphur Springs, but an economic downturn led the development to be abandoned. Both rail lines were abandoned in the 1980s, though Ringling, Montana, lingers on as a town that never quite came into being.

While John's success as a railroad man was spotty at best, his attempt to speculate in Western land was essentially nonexistent. He did make some money in livestock trading but had little interest in it. His oil investments fared better, but one legal complication after another meant that he never saw as much of his money as he should've during his lifetime.

Sarasota, however, was another story. It became the place where his fortune grew larger than anywhere else, aside from in the circus, of course.

DOWNTOWN SARASOTA IN THE 1920S

He teamed up with a local developer named Owen Burns in the early 1920s, and John purchased the bankrupt Yacht and Automobile Club, whose holdings included a dozen or more lots in Cedar Point – now known as Golden Gate Point – near downtown and began operations to expand the footprint of what would become the John Ringling Estate. Instead of identifying him as "the noted circus man," local papers called him "the New York and Sarasota capitalist" instead. It seemed that John's days as an outsider in southwest Florida were finally over.

At this point, John was earning about $300,000 a year from the circus, another $300,000 from oil, and an equal amount from various stocks and bonds. Although this didn't put him at the same level as other tycoons of the era – Andrew Carnegie had recently died with a fortune of $450 million, and even Florida developer Henry Flagler banked around $100 million – John was more than comfortable. In fact, in 1922, he took delivery of a brand-new yacht, *Zalophus*, with six staterooms, five baths, a crew of 10, and a price tag of $200,000.

The yacht alone adds up to $3.8 million in today's money.

In 1923, both John and Charles were elected to the board of the Bank of Sarasota at a time when the so-called Florida land boom was just about to explode. There was not a lot of acreage on the mainland near Sarasota that was available for large subdivisions like those proposed for Fort Myers or for transforming the scrublands into a town that would turn into Boca Raton. But John's imagination had drifted to the islands that protected Sarasota Bay, just offshore from the town. Siesta Key, to the south, was the only one of the low-lying islands connected to the mainland by a bridge, and speculators had already bought up most of the desirable property there. But John knew that bridges were merely things that could be built and began buying up all the land he could on Bird, St. Armands, Coon, and Otter Keys, as well as several miles north on Longboat Key.

St. Armands would be the keystone to his plan, with a beautiful shopping plaza as the end point of a causeway that began on the mainland near Cedar Point and spanned the waters of the bay to connect to a string of "paradise-like, near-tropical" islands with available lots for homes. On January 1, 1925, John announced the building of the bridge to St. Armands, and on that same date, just one year and $700,000 later, he rode in the first vehicle to cross the completed span. He waved and smiled from the rear of a dark green Rolls Royce limousine.

ONE OF THE MANY TREE-LINED ROADS THAT SPRANG UP IN THE SARASOTA REGION DURING THE FLORIDA LAND BOOM OF THE 1920S.

He undoubtedly felt very confident about the future as he took that drive. In the past year, more property had changed hands in Sarasota than in any other year in its history. The town of just 5,500 people seemed on its way to great things.

An important part of John's plan remained missing, though – the construction of a new Ritz-Carlton hotel on Longboat Key, which would be adjacent to a golf course on 20 acres that John had donated. The glitzy hotel would prove that Sarasota was just as attractive to the monied set as Miami Beach and Palm Beach, already thriving on Florida's southeast coast. A permit had been issued for construction to begin on the hotel. Its cost was pegged at $3 million, with John committing $400,000 of his cash, but a subscription drive to raise the rest of the capital had stalled, enthusiasm dampened by a stock market dive in March 1926.

Determined to reenergize the prospects for his adopted city, John came up with a somewhat unusual tactic– he invited the director of the Chamber of Commerce to travel with the circus for the 1926 season. The idea was to promote Sarasota as a tourist destination and the perfect place to live in every city where the circus played. Every circus wagon was plastered with an advertisement that extolled the virtues of Sarasota, and every program included a write-up about the wonder and joy of living there.

But none of it mattered. Negative press in northern cities, spreading stories of "underwater lots" in Florida being sold multiple times in a single day until prices climbed to outrageous highs, had put a damper on land sales everywhere in the state. And then, to make matters worse, the hurricane of September 1926, which virtually flattened Coral Gables – considered the crown jewel of planned Florida cities – ended real estate speculation in the sunshine state.

Worse yet, in December, with both brothers back in Sarasota, Charles, then 62, suffered a stroke. John ran across the wide lawns that separated their homes to find his brother lying unconscious on his bed, attended by the family doctor. The room was silent except for the harsh rattle of Charle's breath.

When it stopped, the doctor rose to check his pulse, then he turned to John and shook his head.

John heaved a large breath of his own and wiped away his tears. "I'm the last one left on the lot," he said.

The Ringling Brothers – the family, not the circus – was at an end.

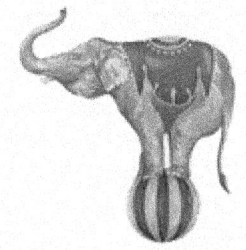

10. "THE LAST ONE LEFT ON THE LOT"

JOHN RINGLING WOULD NOT BE RUINED BY THE END OF a real estate boom. Unlike most others dealing in Florida land at the time, John's other interests – not the least of which was the circus – were too vast and too diversified for a real estate collapse to ruin him. The oil wells were still pumping, the people were still buying circus tickets, and he had partnered with legendary boxing promoter Tex Rickard to build a new version of Madison Square Garden that would seat more than 18,000 people.

Although John understood that the boom he'd envisioned for Sarasota wouldn't happen and that he needed to stop and cut his losses on the barely started Ritz-Carlton hotel project, he did not give up on the town. As 1927 approached, Ringling convinced the city to accept the gift of the $700,000 causeway he'd built to St. Armands, relieving himself of the maintenance burden. Then he called ringmaster Fred

THE RITZ-CARLTON HOTEL THAT JOHN HAD ENVISIONED FOR LONGBOAT KEY WAS NEVER COMPLETED AND WAS LATER ABANDONED. THE UNFINISHED BUILDINGS WERE FINALLY TORN DOWN IN 1964.

Bradna to Ca'd'Zan, his new Sarasota home, and unveiled his latest idea.

John was excited, and his new idea was presented in two parts. He had devised a way to reduce a significant portion of the circus overhead and deliver a tourist attraction beyond belief for his beloved adopted hometown. He told Fred that all this would be achieved by simply moving the winter headquarters of the combined shows from Bridgeport, Connecticut, to Sarasota. They'd no longer have to heat huge barns during the cold Connecticut nights, and the necessary circus staff could live far more cheaply and comfortably in Florida.

John explained that he'd found the perfect – and cheap -- location in the old Sarasota fairgrounds, which was already prepared to house more than its share of horses and domestic livestock and, with a few alterations, would also work for elephants, camels, and everything else.

But the biggest benefit in John's mind dates all the way back to the circus men of 100 years before. He knew that audiences – especially tourist audiences – would flock to the winter quarters of the Greatest Show on Earth and pay good money to see the idle circus wagons and watch the menagerie animals that were sleeping their winter away.

Fred undoubtedly agreed with the plan – Mr. Ringling was the boss – but wasn't sure where he was needed in the plan. John told him that he wanted him to know what was happening because, of course, Fred would be responsible for getting everyone and everything from one place to the other.

It was an assignment that Fred approached with little enthusiasm. After all, the Barnum and Bailey side of the company had been headquartered in Bridgeport since its earliest days and the upset over moving the Ringling headquarters from Baraboo hadn't even had time to fully die down yet. But as it turned out, no one argued against spending winters in Florida except for a guy named "Good Luck" Lombard, who ran the speakeasy that catered to the circus crowd in town. He complained nightly.

By the fall of 1927, the new Florida headquarters were finished, and a new seasonal tradition began. The season's final show took place in Tampa, just 60 miles up the road, and everyone who could find a way to get there from Sarasota found a spot under the big top that day. Both schoolchildren and workers were excused for their absences. After the show closed, huge crowds attended the celebratory arrival of the circus at its freshly landscaped, palm tree-

MOVING THE WINTER QUARTERS FOR THE CIRCUS TO SARASOTA TURNED OUT TO BE ONE OF JOHN RINGLING'S BEST IDEAS. IT NOT ONLY ALLOWED THE WORKERS AND PERFORMERS A MORE HOSPITABLE PLACE TO SPEND THE COLD WEATHER MONTHS, BUT THE QUARTERS TURNED OUT TO BE A MAJOR TOURIST ATTRACTION FOR SARASOTA AND AN OFF-SEASON MONEY MAKER FOR THE CIRCUS.

filled winter grounds, all made possible by newly minted local hero John Ringling.

In addition to the many jobs created by building the headquarters, more than 300 full-time Ringling employees came to town with their families, spending their paychecks and swelling the population with another 2,000 souls.

And John's prediction about the wave of tourists also proved true. Daily attendance at the winter quarters often topped 3,000 and averaged about 100,000 each season for the next decade. There was a little grumbling from locals about the "circus people" and the grifters and dodgers who followed them to nice weather after the season ended. However, overall, the residents slowly warmed to the idea of being the off-season home of the circus. It was clear that Sarasota would never be the next Palm Beach because of what John Ringling brought to town, but many struggling communities in Florida would have gladly traded places with them.

John had finally established himself as Sarasota's most admired citizen, but he didn't neglect the circus while he was doing so. One of his principal additions for the 1929 season was a European troupe of

PERHAPS THE GREATEST ADDITIONS TO THE CIRCUS IN 1929 WERE THE FLYING WALLENDAS, WHO BECAME AN INTEGRAL PART OF THE GREATEST SHOW ON EARTH FOR THE NEXT FIVE DECADES.

wire walkers who had become famous for creating a four-person pyramid that traveled across a high wire balanced on a bicycle. They were performing in Havana when John tracked them down and signed them after seeing their act.

Their first performance with The Greatest Show was so amazing that the audience stomped and whistled for an encore for 15 minutes after they left the ring. Fred Bradna went to look for them and found the performers sulking in their tent – in Europe, whistling, and stomping were signs that the audience was unhappy. After Fred explained everything, the troupe that became known as the Flying Wallendas happily returned to the ring and began their rise to circus legends.

Led by German-born Karl, the Wallendas went on to dazzle audiences worldwide for the next 50 years, but stardom was not achieved without problems, including a tragic accident in 1962 that killed two performers.

One of their first near misses came in 1934 when the show had been set up during bad weather on a muddy lot in Akron, Ohio. The Wallendas were on the wire, engaged in the four-person pyramid climax, rolling high above the ring with no net below them. Suddenly, a gust of wind from an approaching thunderstorm hit the big top, and the wire beneath the bicycle – fastened only to a heavy wooden slab, or "dead man" on the ground – went slack as the stakes sank into the mud.

The bicycle, with Karl riding and carrying the other three performers – including his wife, Helen -- balanced on a pole across his shoulders, pitched sideways. Karl caught the wire with one hand, then saw his wife rushing past him. He snatched her out of the air by gripping her with his legs at the last moment. Karl's brother, Herman, also managed to grab the wire as he fell, and somehow, he caught the fourth member of the troupe, Joseph Geiger, in the same way that Karl saved Helen. Herman then pulled Joseph and himself hand over hand to the platform's safety while Karl and Helen dangled from the wire until a net was hurriedly strung beneath them.

For Fred Bradna, this near tragedy was a reminder of John Ringling's constant concern for the safety of his performers. Long before, John devised a system where two telephone poles were driven deep into the ground as supports for the high-wire rig to prevent the slip that nearly killed the Wallendas.

But by 1934, though, John was no longer part of the Greatest Show on Earth – but we'll come back to that soon.

IN 1928, HOWEVER, JOHN WAS STILL TRAVELING WITH THE CIRCUS, although much of his attention was still on Sarasota, where the completion of the winter headquarters coincided with the completion of the dream house that he and Mable had started planning five years earlier.

The first house they had lived in when they moved to Sarasota in 1911, Palms Elysian, was a comfortable but rather ordinary two-story, wood-frame house with a board porch that would have looked at home on a tree-lined street in someplace like Baraboo.

That was not the kind of house John wanted in a tropical paradise like Sarasota.

By the time the 1920s had started to roar, wealthy northerners were flocking to Florida in droves and, particularly in Palm Beach, trying to outdo each other with the size, design, and lavishness of their winter homes. With support from his patron, Paris Singer, heir to the sewing machine fortune, architect Addison Mizner had become the darling of the rich on the east coast of Florida. He combined various Italian and Spanish architectural features into elaborate designs that his clients found exotic and well-suited to the Florida waterfront and climate.

The design for perhaps the most fanciful of the grand – and honestly, rather ridiculous – homes on Palm Beach Island was the 126-room Mar-a-Lago, which took three years to build. It was designed by Joseph Urban, the sometimes architect more famously known as the stage designer for the Ziegfeld Follies. He was hired by cereal fortune heiress Marjorie Post, who was looking to build "something different." Urban was happy to comply, freely borrowing from Mizner's Mediterranean concepts and adding in Moorish elements that resulted in a sprawling conglomeration of a style that doesn't have a name.

JOHN AND MABLE RINGLING'S MAGNIFICENT HOME IN SARASOTA – CA 'D ZAN, OR "HOUSE OF JOHN."

Marjorie Post – along with many other owners of questionable taste – was thrilled.

It was in this same spirit that Ringling's Sarasota home, Ca'd'Zan – or "House of John" – was built between 1924 and 1926. Its 56 rooms and 36,000 square feet were nowhere near the size of some of the monstrosities on the east side of the state, but it was just as unique and unusual as the houses built there around the same time. It is a beautiful home, and I suppose its style could best be described as "The Arabian Nights Come to Florida" or maybe "John Ringling and the Forty Thieves."

I've visited Ca'd'Zan several times, and each time is quite an experience. Entering the house is like walking onto the set of a period film. It's almost impossible to believe that this kind of opulence existed – and that people actually used to live there. Mable had adored the Tuscan villas she'd once visited and wanted something of that style in the house. The designer, Dwight James Baum, combined the elaborate detail of a Venetian palazzo for the west side, which was on the water, with a less decorative façade on the east, all surrounding a central tower that commands the approach to the home. The exterior is prominently decorated using brightly glazed terra-cotta tile, stained glass, and variegated marble.

The interior rooms are modestly sized, with most of the furniture placed by the Ringlings themselves, not by decorators. They'd acquired most of it from auctions when old estates in the Northeast were liquidated. That included the Empire-style bedroom furniture that John had purchased with the belief it belonged to Napoleon III and a barber's chair where he sat each day to be shaved. On the ceiling in the grand ballroom – the largest room in the house – were nearly two dozen canvas panels entitled *Dancers of the Nations*, painted by Willy Pogany, a book illustrator and set designed who also worked for the Ziegfeld Follies.

John had purchased and installed an intricate brass and stained-glass bar that had once stood in the Cicardi Winter Palace Restaurant in St. Louis with the idea that the house would be used for entertaining. Since Prohibition was officially in effect, he stored his wine, liquor, and other valuables in a massive vault hidden behind a false wall on the third floor. An expansive patio had been added to the western side of the house, which accommodated as many as 500 guests and offered a breathtaking view of the bay.

THE GREAT HALL INSIDE OF CA 'D ZAN, CAN SEEM OVERWHELMING TO VISITORS EVENT TODAY. IT'S HARD TO IMAGINE WHAT IT MUST HAVE BEEN LIKE IN THE 1920S.

Ca'd'Zan had cost around $1.2 million to build, with the furnishings adding another $400,000 to the tab. It's quite a number, especially for Sarasota in the 1920s, and not everyone loved the design as much as the Ringlings did. Critics considered the Florida homes of the era to be overly ornate and much too diverse to classify as anything other than something they could diplomatically call "interesting, fascinating, and awe-inspiring."

So, while not everyone agrees on the aesthetics of Ca'd'Zan, it's easier to find agreement about the other principal building on the Ringling estate. This museum housed the couple's massive art collection. In 1925, during a trip to Italy when John was buying art for

ONLY A SMALL SECTION OF THE RINGLING ART MUSEUM THAT IS ALSO LOCATED ON THE PROPERTY WHERE CA 'D ZAN STANDS TODAY. IT'S BEEN PRAISED AS ONE OF THE FINEST ART MUSEUMS IN THE COUNTRY.

the proposed Ritz-Carlton hotel, he told his advisor, Julius Bohler, that he and Mable wanted to undertake a special project that could be left to the city of Sarasota when they died – an art museum. John had never collected art before but didn't let this deter him. He had an excellent advisor in Bohler and the money to hire architects to design a building that would hold the collection that grew rapidly over the next six years.

Eventually, the U-shaped building – constructed in an Italianate style and designed a little smaller than the Ringlings had first wanted since their budget shrank before it could be completed – became home to an attached College of Art, 21 galleries, and the very large collection. In addition to the artwork on display, John included entire rooms and architectural pieces he had purchased from the Astor and Huntington Mansions in New York.

By the time the museum opened in 1930, John had collected more than 400 works, including those of Rembrandt, Franz Hals, Velazquez, El Greco, Goya, and a host of major and minor artists, as well as a collection of ancient Greek antiquities that the Metropolitan Museum had considered surplus. *Art Digest* widely praised it, and the *New York World* gushed, "John Ringling, who used to drive a circus wagon, has built one of the finest museums of art in the world."

While many of his selections were based on the artist's pedigree or Julius Bohler's advice, he often bought works simply because they appealed to him, a plan that usually worked out well. In 1929, he purchased a piece that spanned two irregularly shaped panels taken from a church in northern Italy that experts from an auction house dismissed as a worthless copy. The work was later identified as Il Guercino's *Annunciation,* and its value became unimaginable.

John paid $56 for the two panels just because he liked them.

But not all the art that John collected earned admiration. At least one of them became the source of a joke when a visitor almost as famous as the circus arrived for a visit.

Hanging in the Great Hall of Ca'd'Zan was a massive portrait that John had painted of himself. In it, he was casually posed, slightly smiling, with a hand in his pocket. It was striking and impressive, and John was very proud of it.

HUMORIST WILL ROGERS WAS JUST ONE OF THE MANY CELEBRITIES OF THE 1920S WHO SPENT TIME AT CA 'D ZAN.

Despite the preparations the Ringlings had made for their legacy in Sarasota, those things never overshadowed that Ca'd'Zan had been built for pleasure and entertaining their friends. A host of notables regularly arrived at the house for charged conversation, lavish meals, jaunts into the bay on John's yacht, and no small amount of drinking. Among the guests in those bright and shining days were the likes of Flo Ziegfeld, Tex Rickard, New York Governor Al Smith, William J. Burns of the famous Burns Detective Agency, New York Mayor Jimmy Walker, New York Giants manager John McGraw, and humorist, writer, actor, and performer, Will Rogers.

It was Will Rogers who took special note of the portrait of John Ringling hanging on the wall during a party one evening. When John asked him what he thought of it, Will replied in a way that shouldn't have been unexpected.

211 | THE DEVIL'S CARNIVAL

"Well, John," he quipped, "it's the first time I've ever seen you with your hand in your own pocket."

FOR A TIME, LIFE AT CA'D'ZAN EPITOMIZED LIFE IN AMERICA IN the Roaring Twenties, but like that dazzling decade, the party couldn't last forever.

Early in 1929, while work was still underway on the art museum, Mable, age 54, revealed that her recent spells of exhaustion and stomach difficulties were the result of the onset of Addison's disease – a failure of the adrenal glands – combined with diabetes that she had kept hidden from John for years. A recent prognosis given by her doctor was grim. And almost no sooner than she had confided in John, she found herself bedridden, and she died on June 8, 1929.

MABLE RINGLING DIED IN 1929 AFTER A LONG ILLNESS THAT SHE'D KEPT SECRET FROM JOHN. SHE FINALLY REVEALED HOW SICK SHE WAS JUST WEEKS BEFORE SHE PASSED AWAY, LEAVING HER SHOCKED AND GRIEF-STRICKEN HUSBAND BEHIND.

By all accounts, John was shocked, stunned, and grief-stricken by the speed of Mable's decline and death. John, who'd never owned a piece of black clothing in his life, was forced to borrow a pair of trousers from his butler for the funeral. He told close friends that he feared he would never be happy again and even gifted his nephew his entire wardrobe of fine suits, which were much too large for him to wear.

And a second blow came soon after Mable's passing.

Ringling was called to a meeting with the officers of the Madison Square Garden to discuss details of the circus' 1930 engagement. Whether it was his preoccupation with his wife's death or simply his indifference, John failed to appear for the meeting. When the meeting was reconvened, the directors, annoyed with John's flippant attitude about the venue, explained that the agreement making the Garden available to the circus in the following year would not include any

Friday night performances. Those would be reserved only for the presentation of highly profitable prize fights.

When John realized the directors were not only serious but absolutely unwilling to change their minds, he loudly suggested what they could do with their contract and stormed out the door. He vowed that the circus would play at the 22nd Regiment Armory, but instead of going there to see the show, he suggested the officials from Madison Square Garden – of which he was still a partial owner – go straight to hell.

Rather than take the one-way trip John suggested, the directors contacted the American Circus Corporation – as noted in an earlier chapter – and encouraged them to snap up the dates the Greatest Show had just abandoned. They were the only company that could even come close to the size and standards of the Ringling show, and soon, they were performing at the popular venue instead.

When John learned of this, and after his anger cooled, he began considering his options. For the past 50 years, either the Ringling Show, or the Barnum and Bailey Show had opened at the Garden. In fact, the Garden had been specifically built to house the circus. The very idea of another show stealing his spot was outrageous.

John calmed down, but he was still angry. He seriously considered buying the Garden outright for a moment but realized it wouldn't accomplish much since the American Circus Corporation would still have its contract. There was only one way to triumph here, so John Ringling bought the American Circus Corporation and all the shows under its umbrella.

The price was reportedly $2 million. He paid a portion in cash, and John financed the remaining $1.7 million with the Prudence Bond and Mortgage Company. Given that the American Circus Corporation was made up of five profitably operating shows with 150 rail cars, a 2,000-animal menagerie, and 4,500 employees, John believed the advice that was given to him by Wall Street analysts – even though the Ringling operations had never been offered publicly, he could simply reorganize the new company and sell its shares to the public. Given the reputation of the greatest circus man of all time, it would be a snap.

And it would have been if it wasn't 1929.

That was John Ringling's next devastating blow. How many more could he take before he was finally broken? The world was just about to find out.

The stock market, which began to become uneasy in September, crashed into oblivion on October 29 when more than 16 million shares were traded at steadily declining prices until the gains and confidence of the previous decade were destroyed. There was no hope of success for any new stock offering, and suddenly, John -- and, by extension, his personally held company – was saddled with suffocating debt at a time when even his show was having difficulty drawing crowds.

John managed to close out the dismal year of 1929 with net profits of about $1 million, but it was a drop in the bucket compared to what he now owed. By 1931, gate receipts had fallen so dramatically that the combined shows closed on September 14, the earliest date in its history.

What happened in the following months remains one of the most stunning reversals in American business history.

John had always possessed the uncanny ability to compartmentalize any setbacks or disappointments that he suffered. Even as the circus was swirling down the drain in 1931, John went to Europe to buy several paintings for the museum in Sarasota. He was determined to make sure it survived in Mable's memory, no matter what it cost him.

That same year, Alf's son, Richard, who had inherited his father's share of the company, died. He had run through an estate of $5 million, leaving his widow, Aubrey, with only one-third interest in a circus that was slowly sinking. Without batting an eye, though, John found a way to divert a little cash from the circus operations to build up a fund for Aubrey.

JOHN RINGLING'S TREACHEROUS "FRIEND," SAMUEL GUMPERTZ.

However, the true beginning of the end for John – the final blow that would break him – came in the spring of 1932 when he was diagnosed with an arterial clot in his leg. It was so serious that doctors feared it would need to be amputated. John, now 65, pulled through, but his physicians insisted that he step away from the constant stress of managing the circus and his creditors' incessant demands.

Soon after, John disappeared. He hid at the Half Moon Hotel in Coney Island, an establishment owned by an old friend and occasional fellow investor, Samuel W. Gumpertz. John was supposed to relax and take things easy. His friend assured him he would monitor things and report back when needed.

But Gumpertz turned out to be the kind of friend that makes one's enemies seem kind. An interest payment had come due on John's note with Prudence Bond – which had already been reduced to $1 million – and it had gone into default, which allowed Gumpertz and two groups of investors to purchase the note from Prudence, which was only too happy to get rid of a loan that was looking more and more as though it would never be repaid.

Gumpertz then approached Edith Ringling, the always envious wife of Charles, and Aubrey, Richard's financially struggling widow, and argued that John was sick, incapacitated, and unfit to continue running the company. If he was left to his own devices, Gumpertz assured them, he'd run what was left of the circus into the ground, and Edith and Aubrey would have nothing left.

EDITH RINGLING, CHARLES' WIDOW, WHO HAD ALWAYS BEEN RESENTFUL OF HER BROTHER-IN-LAW. GUMPERTZ FOUND IT EASY TO CONVINCE HER TO HELP HIM TAKE THE CIRCUS AWAY FROM JOHN.

And two more traitors joined his ranks.

In July 1932, Gumpertz summoned John to a meeting, which he told him was simply a planning summit about resolving the claims of the circus' creditors and getting the show back on solid ground.

But that, of course, is not what happened at the meeting.

Gumpertz now revealed to John that he and his associates, Allied Owners, had secretly purchased the note originally signed over to Ringling by Prudence Bond. Furthermore, because the note was in default, Allied was moving for the immediate settlement of that debt and planned to force the Ringling Brothers and Barnum & Baily Circus into bankruptcy.

With John seething in anger, Gumpertz played his next card – Allied would cancel the demand if certain conditions were met. The operation of the combined shows and all their holdings, he said, needed to be changed immediately from a partnership to a corporation. He added that Allied would receive 10 percent of the stock issue for its work in arranging the matter, and the remainder

AUBREY RINGLING WAS THE WIDOW OF JOHN'S NEPHEW, RICHARD, WHO DIED LEAVING HIS WIFE NOTHING BUT SHARES OF A STRUGGLING CIRCUS. HOWEVER, JOHN MANAGED TO MOVE ENOUGH MONEY AROUND TO MAKE IT SO SHE WOULDN'T BE PENNILESS. SHE RETURNED THE FAVOR BY BETRAYING HIM WITH HER VOTES.

would be divided into three equal portions – 30 percent each for Edith, Aubrey, and John.

As for the note responsible for causing the situation with the company, it would be assumed by the new corporation. However, John Ringling would be required to use all his personal assets to secure it, and those assets would be held as collateral until the debt was paid off. Gumpertz then startled his former friend with a complete list of all John's holdings – every oil well and every mile of railroad track – which he had compiled while John recovered from his illness and Edith and Aubrey plotted their betrayal.

John now found himself staring at a list of everything of value that he had acquired during a lifetime of hard work and struggle – a life that had started with him playing a co-starring role next to a goat 60 years before.

On that paper, clearly in black and white, were the details of his vast collection of art, which offered the solution to the present disaster. The sale of just a handful of them would have cleared up the whole mess, but that was unthinkable for John. He and Mable dedicated themselves to that collection and it would live on as their legacy. To hock those paintings so he could pay off the two-faced backstabber before him was a prospect he could not even consider.

Some would say that John Ringling was destroyed by stubbornness, pride, and betrayal, but I truly believe he was broken instead by his grief. It was unthinkable for him to give up the promise that he'd made to Mable, no matter how much it would cost him.

He sat at that table, silent, looking at those around him. Aubrey at least looked ashamed, but she refused to meet his eye. Edith glared at him with an expression that revealed just how she had waited to see him brought to his knees.

A different John Ringling – the *old* John Ringling – would have gotten to his feet, walked out of the meeting with a laugh, and dared Gumpertz to do his worst. A claim of default would have taken months – probably years – to work its way through the courts. By then, the nation's troubles would be over, audiences would be returning to the Greatest Show on Earth, and all the unpleasantness would be over.

But this wasn't the *old* John Ringling. He was gone. He'd been replaced by a man who was tired, alone, physically sick, and sick at heart about the magnitude of the betrayal he now faced. He'd never had a moment like this before – certainly not when his brothers were alive – and now he felt it more than ever.

He truly was the last one left in the ring.

With a sigh, John gave in to Gumpertz's demands, but with one exception. He demanded the formation of a separate entity, the Rembrandt Corporation, to which every item in his art collection was deeded. The museum and the land on which he stood had already been divested from his holdings. The remainder of his assets and stocks would become collateral for the delinquent note.

And this was how an insidious man named Samuel Gumpertz engineered the destruction of a family business and turned it into a publicly held corporation. The circus would continue for decades to come, of course, but I have always believed this was the moment when the death knell of the American circus began to chime.

For John Ringling, though, his humiliation still wasn't finished. Soon after, the first stockholder's meeting of the Ringling Brothers – Barnum & Bailey Combined Show, Inc. took place, and the first order of business on the table was moved and seconded. The resolution stipulated that John Ringling would be named president of the corporation and draw an annual salary of $5,000 per year – a number one-tenth of what he'd drawn in the past – but he would not be the general manager of operations.

That man, with complete authority over the company, would be Samuel Gumpertz.

When this was called to vote, John used his 30 percent share to vote against the motion while Edith quickly pledged her share to Gumpertz. Gumpertz naturally added his 10 percent to hers, leaving only the hapless Aubrey to vote.

This was the last position she wanted to be in. In a quiet voice, she did her best to get out of it, saying, "Now there have been enough votes cast. It's all settled, so I don't have to vote at all."

But John leaned toward her. "You will vote, Aubrey," he said to her. "I must know where you stand."

But Aubrey failed him again and turned against the man who had come to her rescue after she learned her late husband had squandered his fortune. By a margin of 70-30, John Ringling, the last brother left on the lot, was reduced to nothing more than a figurehead in the wonder he created, and the Greatest Show on Earth was transformed from a magical thing into just another business.

DESPITE THE HUMILIATING TURN OF EVENTS, JOHN DIDN'T settle into the new role intended for him. He fought against it tooth and nail, and his sheer force of will kept even those most resentful toward him from pushing back too hard. In late 1932, he was still going into the office and working on bringing the best new acts he could find into the show's roster. One of those was the Christiani family of equestrians, considered the most talented of the era.

One afternoon, while he was at his desk, a telegram arrived that John imagined had to do with his negotiations with the equestrians. He looked it over, paused, then read it again. Suddenly, John felt very dizzy. Sensing something wrong, he stood up, took a few steps toward the door, and fell to his knees. He collapsed onto the floor, the victim of a massive stroke.

Sometime later, the telegram John had been reading was found in the pocket of the suit he was wearing that day. The telegram had not come from the Christiani family or their agents but from Samuel Gumpertz. He had learned that John was negotiating with the equestrians, and he was in direct violation of his orders to stay out of circus operations. If his meddling did not stop immediately, Gumpertz warned, a stockholder's meeting would be called, and "we will turn you out."

While John did eventually recover limited use of his paralyzed right side – and his speech was restored in a few weeks – the event marked the true end of his circus career. He spent the rest of his days at Ca'd'Zan, where nephew Henry

HENRY RINGLING NORTH, WHO WENT BY THE NICKNAME OF "BUDDY," REMAINED AT HIS UNCLE'S SIDE UNTIL THE END.

Ringling North acted as his beloved uncle's "business agent, chauffeur, handyman, and sometimes cook."

Even until the end, John maintained the uncanny ability to shove all thoughts of money troubles and bad health to the back of his mind and continue to act as though he was a young man again, with money steadily rolling in. Even a heart attack that he suffered in 1934 didn't keep him down for long. Although putting enough money together for groceries wasn't always easy, John and Henry ate their meals on fine china while sipping aged wine from Venetian crystal glasses.

He loved to take long car rides in one of the elegant cars John had managed to hide from his creditors, a 1924 Rolls-Royce convertible and a Pierce-Arrow among them. They once made a 160-mile round trip to see a flowering tree that John recalled only blooming in the spring.

Another time, he was reading the morning newspaper and discovered that the Cole Brothers Circus would be appearing in the Florida Panhandle – almost 500 miles from Sarasota – and holding a parade, which had become a rarity in the circus business.

It had been 15 years since even John Ringling had seen a circus parade, so off they went. They took the open Rolls to a small Pensacola hotel with a second-story balcony overlooking Main Street, and Henry set up a comfortable chair for his uncle there. Shortly after, there came a burst of music from around the corner, followed by the appearance of the bandwagon itself, drawn by an eight-horse team, and followed by the necessary band of elephants.

The effects of the Depression were visible in the flaking paint of the wagon, and the missing spangles on the costumes, and Henry checked his uncle's face for any signs of disappointment. But he didn't need to worry. Tears were already rolling down John's cheeks.

At that moment, Henry later wrote that he realized this was not just any circus parade passing below them, but the parade of every circus John Ringling had ever known.

When the last animal, the last performer, the last wagon, and then the calliope, followed by a gaggle of children, passed by, John pushed himself out of his chair with great difficulty and reached over to grip his nephew's shoulder.

"Time to go home, Buddy," he said.

AND JOHN RINGLING DID GO HOME.

He died in New York from bronchial pneumonia on December 2, 1936, just a short time before his 71st birthday. His estate was appraised at $23.5 million, but he died with $311 in the bank.

John's initial will gave half his estate to his sister, Ida – mother of nephews Henry and John – with the other half going to the state of Florida to create an endowment for the upkeep of the Ringling Art Museum. However, most of the assets were still frozen as collateral for the note due to Allied Owners, which had been reduced to $850,000. In addition, the U.S. government filed a claim in the amount of $13.4 million for estate taxes and, since John always dismissed them as an inconvenience, unpaid income taxes. To further muddy the waters, it was discovered that just before his death, in a fit of anger over some imagined slight, he added a codicil to his will that essentially cut his sister and two nephews out of it.

The situation was made even worse by the fact that the combined shows, under the management of Samuel Gumpertz, had experienced falling profits during the lean years of the Depression, making only $60,000 a year compared to the $1 million that John had cleared in 1929. The circus business, in general, was teetering on the edge of collapse, but Gumpertz had run the combined shows into the ground – which cannot surprise anyone reading this.

JOHN RINGLING NORTH

But nephew John Ringling North refused to give up. Though his uncle's last months were marked by a steadily advancing distrust of most everyone, including his closest family, John and Henry agreed that the things John said now were not the true feelings of the man who loved them. Aging, illness, and betrayals by others had prompted John's decline, and they weren't going to allow his final days to color the feelings they had about a man they revered.

While Henry had been caring for their uncle in Florida, John North spent much of his time as a Wall Street broker struggling to keep the circus from going under. Though Ida and her sons had been cut out of the will, John had overlooked the need to rescind the position of Ida and his nephew John as executors. With the authority to liquidate and dispose of his assets, John North approached a friend at Manufacturer's Trust Company. He asked for a loan of $1 million, which he planned to use to pay off the Allied note and some other obligations. He then planned to persuade his Aunt Edith and cousin Aubrey to help him bring the circus back into a family business with himself in charge.

It worked. His aunt and cousin agreed, and the loan was obtained, the note retired, the 10 percent of stock extorted by Gumpertz was repurchased, and the circus was returned to the Ringling family. John was now president for a guaranteed five years, with Henry as his assistant and vice president. Although John North might have finally rid himself of the toxic Samuel Gumpertz and was able to beat the government down to $850,000 to settle the unpaid taxes, the new Ringling brothers soon found they faced new enemies of a different kind.

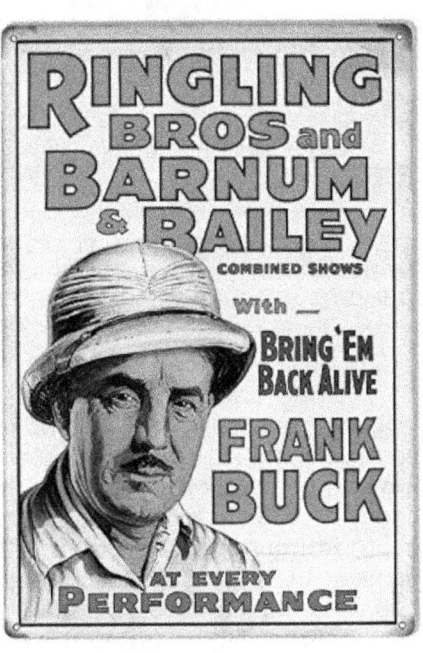

In 1938, America was still gripped by the Depression. Union organizing impeded the show for the first time when animal handlers and roustabouts went on strike during the Madison Square Garden opening. The dispute lingered into the summer, forcing John North to fold the tents for the season in June. He salvaged part of the season by sending out nonunion performers from the combined shows under the banner of the Al G. Barnes and Sells-Floto Circus, one of the holdings that his uncle had gotten when he'd bought the American Circus Corporation in 1929.

Among the star attractions at the time was Frank Buck, a long-time collector of wild animals for menageries and circuses who'd written a bestselling book in 1930 called *Bring 'Em Back Alive*. He'd also starred in several feature films about his adventures.

Although John Ringling had gotten rid of wild animal shows when he was still running the show – believing them too dangerous and unpredictable – they returned with his nephews in charge. Caged animal shows were back and included performances by Clyde Beatty, who became a legend with his "fighting act," entering a cage with as many as 40 lions and tigers, cracking a whip, and waving a chair around with a pistol strapped to his waist.

CLYDE BEATTY WAS OFTEN CRITICIZED FOR WHAT SEEMED TO BE CRUEL TRAINING METHODS WITH HIS BIG CATS, BUT BEATTY CLAIMED THE "FIGHTING" HE DID WITH THE CATS HE LOVED SO MUCH WAS JUST PART OF THE ACT. HE WAS ONLY EVER INJURED ONE TIME IN HIS CAREER, BUT DIDN'T BLAME THE LION.

Often criticized for using what appeared to be cruelty in his training methods, Beatty scoffed at the accusations. It was all for show, he explained. Any idiot who tried to control big cats that way would have to be someone interested in a quick and painful death. A whip, chair, or even a pistol would be no protection against the sudden charge of an angry big cat. The "fighting act" was just that – an "act." He liked to say he didn't teach the animals anything. You see what they can do and then develop it. He treated the animals with affection and respect, and they returned it – usually.

In 1932, as he was rehearing with his cats over the winter, a lion named Nero knocked a momentarily distracted Beatty onto the ground and bit him on the thigh. An infection developed that kept him in the hospital for weeks, but Beatty never blamed the cat. It could have easily killed him, he said. It didn't.

Traveling along as the chief animal act for John North's iteration of the combined shows – along with a fearsome and very famous gorilla named Gargantua – was the first woman to train tigers, Mabel Stark. She was billed as "The Queen of the Jungle Presenting A Notable Congress of the Earth's Most Ferocious Performing Lions and Tigers."

Mabel never used a whip or chair. Instead, she ran her animals through their routines with voice commands. The highlight of her show was a "wrestling match" between her and a Bengal tiger several times her size.

Another of the characters who became a legend for the John North show was a former cartoonist from Kansas named Emmett Kelly, whose creation of a hobo, down-on-his-luck clown struck an unforgettable chord with audiences during the Depression.

Like the bandits and bank robbers who earned folk hero status during those years, hitting back at the governments and institutions that the common folks had given them a bad deal, Americans saw Emmett's "Weary Willie" as the contrast to the happy, cavorting clowns they were used to and presentative of how so many of them were feeling on the inside. They weren't going to rob banks, but they could relate to a clown who seemed to be having a hard time.

EMMETT KELLY'S CHARACTER OF "WEARY WILLIE" MADE HIM ONE OF THE MOST FAMOUS CIRCUS CLOWNS IN HISTORY.

Emmett's style appealed to the average Joe, delighting his audiences with his low-key humor, including a routine when he patiently leaned on his shovel while his "boss" ran about trying to accomplish things. Emmett Kelly once described his character, "Weary Willie is a melancholy little hobo who always gets the short end of the stick and never has any luck, but he never loses hope, and he just keeps on trying."

In other words, he appealed to every American in the same boat during those terrible years. But his appeal wasn't limited to Americans. Once Winston Churchill came specifically to the circus to meet Kelly and laughed uproariously as he stationed himself under the hire wire acts like the Wallendas were performing and stretched a handkerchief between his hands to act as a "safety net" in case they fell.

In addition to lion tamers, animal acts, clowns, and other traditional parts of the circus, John North also sought to incorporate a bit of Broadway musical pageantry into the circus. There were showgirl dance routines and, believe it or not, even "A Ballet for the Elephant," choreographed by George Balanchine with music from

Stravinsky. Though circus purists scoffed, the poet Marianne Moore attended one of the 425 performances of this unlikely ballet and widely reported that the elephants had done their jobs. She wrote, "Their deliberate way of kneeling, on slow-sliding forelegs, like a ship's slide into the water is fine ballet."

John and Henry brought practical improvements to the circus, too. They were trying to counter the damage done to the show by the movie business and the theaters bragging about "air-conditioned comfort" since the mid-1920s. It took three flatcars to transport eight "portable" blowing units - and 50 men to maintain them - but they worked. They also introduced diesel generators, mechanized booms, mechanical stake drivers, and motorized tent rope pullers to bring the show into the modern days of the middle twentieth century.

And then came World War II.

PRESIDENT ROOSEVELT CONSIDERED THE CIRCUS TO BE AN ESSENTIAL INDUSTRY DURING WORLD WAR II SINCE IT MAINTAINED THE NATION'S MORALE. THIS ALLOWED CIRCUSES TO CONTINUE MAKING APPEARANCES AND TRAVELING BY RAIL DURING WAR TIME.

John and Henry feared the worst. They knew what the Great War had done to the circus business and feared the worst, but it never happened. President Franklin D. Roosevelt considered the circus an essential industry for maintaining the nation's morale. The gate receipts would reflect this belief. Despite everything arrayed against it - and even a tragic fire that consumed a menagerie tent and killed 65 animals in 1942 - the combined show returned a net profit of $900,000 during the season that followed the attack on Pearl Harbor.

John and Henry initially decided not to take the show on the road the next season or for the remainder of the war, citing labor shortages and safety concerns, like the difficulty of obtaining fireproof canvas since it was needed for the war effort, for instance, but Aunt Edith and Cousin Aubrey resisted. The five-year agreement that guaranteed John's place in charge of the operation had expired, and in January 1943, there was another stockholder's meeting, and John and Henry were pushed aside. Edith's son, Robert – a former opera singer with no experience – was installed as the new president of operations.

Despite this, the show did well in 1943, and 1944 began the same way. Due to the war, the show experienced regular staff shortages, which often meant problems staying on schedule and making sure equipment was properly set up and maintained. Worse yet, Robert, who had been traveling with the show and had started to acquire a decent amount of competence as operations chief, became sick and was forced to return home to Illinois. This left the operations in the hands of Jim Haley, John Ringling's former accountant – and Cousin Aubrey's new husband.

On the morning of July 6, 1944, Haley, inexperienced and somewhat clueless, accompanied the show to Hartford, Connecticut, where its 41 tents were pitched on a large lot on the edge of town.

And it was in that small city that the greatest disaster in the history of the American circus occurred.

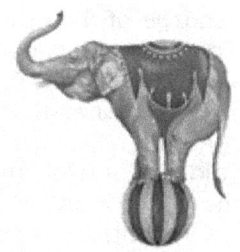

11. HELL CAME TO HARTFORD

IT WAS A PERFECT DAY.
That's how it seemed at the time. Sure, it was brutally hot, but it was July, and the sun was shining, so you expected that. Jammed side-by-side under the big top with what seemed like everyone in town, people were sweating, but they were smiling, too. The smell of animals and wood shavings was in the air, but they could also smell popcorn, hot dogs, and cotton candy.

The circus was in town – and not just any circus – it was the Greatest Show on Earth, and those who bought tickets for the matinee performance at the Barbour Street circus grounds in Hartford, Connecticut, that day were ready to be entertained.

They walked to the show, or they'd taken the bus. Those who had saved up enough ration tickets to buy gasoline had driven their cars and had parked on the lawns of residents in the neighborhood who saw the chance to make a couple of extra bucks.

They walked through the entrance as adults and children were tempted by the concessions – the hot dogs and popcorn whose aroma drifted on the breeze. There were cold drinks and ice cream cones, which melted on the hands and dripped down the arms of children.

They passed the sideshow tents, where the living skeleton, the fat lady, the jugglers, the tattooed woman, and the world's smallest people exhibited themselves for the crowds. They walked by the menagerie, where elephants, giraffes, and horses waited behind fences and where lions and tigers prowled in their cages.

THE MAIN ENTRANCE INTO THE BIG TOP ON THAT HOT AFTERNOON IN JULY 1944

White canvas walls, more than 15 feet high and attached to wagons, led the way to the main entrance of the big top, with colorful banners touting the most exotic attractions the show had to offer.

Before walking beneath the grand canvas that announced The Greatest Show on Earth, the crowds turned to the ticket wagons and handed over their money to experience the wonders inside.

And what wonders they were.

The gigantic tent slowed upward from the tops of the sidewalls to nearly 50 feet in the air. The tent had been erected over freshly mowed grass, dry from the summer heat, and over dirt that had to be watered down and covered with sawdust to keep down the dust.

MERLE EVANS' AND HIS BIG SHOW BAND, WHO MANAGED TO PROVIDE THE SOUNDTRACK FOR THAT HORRIFIC DAY.

Three rings and two stages were in place for the performers, with an oval Hippodrome track that divided the show from the seats. Until the performance began, many patrons wandered the track, gawking at the crowds, the rigging, and the nets until the ushers finally sent them to their seats.

Between the four sections of bleacher seats and the reserved seats – made up of red, wooden folding chairs – more than 7,000 people were packed into the tent for the matinee show. They were mothers, children, and grandparents – most of Hartford's able-bodied men were in the service overseas or working in one of the local war plants. There was a ripple of excitement humming through the audience. They could forget about the war for a little while.

The matinee show kicked off just a few minutes after its scheduled start time of 2:15 P.M. Merle Evans' Big Show Band at the far end of the big top, opposite the main entrance, struck up the "Star-Spangled Banner" and soon, the parade began.

Led by Ringmaster Fred Bradna, it circled the three rings, led by the steam calliope. There were performers in dazzling costumes and exotic animals like elephants, bears, horses, hippos, lions, tigers, and panthers. And, of course, there was a huge group of clowns bringing laughter to the children and adults in the audience.

It really was a perfect day – until it wasn't. No one could have predicted what would happen or that the events in Hartford would be considered the most heartbreaking in the history of the Ringling Brothers and Barnum & Bailey Circus.

Or that many of the victims who died that day would never rest in peace.

THE MATINEE SHOW WASN'T EVEN SUPPOSED TO HAPPEN.

It hadn't been on the schedule. There was supposed to have been an evening performance on July 5, but it had been canceled because the circus had arrived six hours later from Providence. So, Fred Bradna and road manager George Smith offered a special afternoon show the next day to make it up to the disappointed guests who'd planned to come the night before.

But even the matinee wasn't going according to plan. The weather forecast was calling for thunderstorms that afternoon – which was no surprise with the heat – and the two men decided they'd shorten the program a little, wait out the storm, and really razzle dazzle the crowd with the evening show.

As soon as the parade ended, prop men installed the lengths of steel runways that connected to the cages holding Alfred Court's big cat menagerie, which would soon travel from outside the tent to the center ring. Access to the track that circled the big top was limited while the runaways were in place, but there was no way to avoid it. The workers would remove the runways as soon as the act was over.

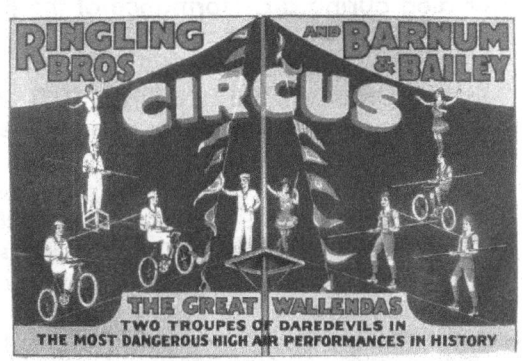

But first, high above, the famed Wallenda high-wire performers started their act two slots ahead of schedule. As usual, they performed without a net – walking on a tiny wire above 40 lions, 30 tigers, 30 leopards, and two dozen bears. That's 125 or so reasons – plus no net – not to fall.

It was during the Wallendas' performance that the fire began. Later, it was speculated that someone had dropped a cigarette into the sawdust spread on the ground, and as it smoldered, the wood shavings burned and slowly spread to the walls of the canvas tent.

And that tent was a bigger problem than anyone could have imagined.

The big top that had been raised by the roustabouts that day wasn't the new flame-resistant tent that management had recently purchased – no, that one, it turned out after the first time they used it, leaked badly. The tent used on July 6 was the old big top brought

THE BIG TOP SET UP FOR THE HARTFORD SHOW WAS NOT THE NEW FLAME-RESISTANT TENT BECAUSE, WITH RAIN IN THE FORECAST, IT WAS KNOWN TO LEAK.

back into service. This was the one that was coated with paraffin wax that had been dissolved in gasoline. It was supposed to rain that day, and everyone knew that the old tent never leaked. No one thought twice about hauling it out and using it instead of the new one.

Today, using a tent like that seems unimaginable, but at that point in its 73-year history, no patron had ever died during a performance of the Ringling Circus.

This day would change all that.

NO ONE SAW THE FIRE WHEN IT STARTED.

It's rare that anyone ever sees the start of a fire. If they did, they'd obviously put it out so that it would never be allowed to spread. Accidental fires are, by their very nature, unexpected and can't be anticipated. They start to burn and spread – just as this one did that day.

THE FAMOUS PHOTO OF EMMETT KELLY AFTER THE FIRE – "THE DAY THE CLOWN CRIED."

It started to burn unnoticed, crept to the side of the tent, and began to climb.

As the Wallendas were balancing on the wire overhead and Alfred Court's cats were being escorted back to their cages, clowns began to appear down the chute from Clown Alley.

Among them was Emmett Kelly, by now America's most famous clown. He was known for never smiling during a performance, always making everyone else laugh with his deadpan expression.

After the fire, a photographer caught a memorable shot of Kelly running toward the flames with a bucket of water and an expression of horror on his face. The image would lead to the tragedy being called "the day the clown cried."

At that moment, though, a different photographer, Dick Miller, was in the tent, snapping shots of the clowns as they tumbled into the center ring. He had just turned away when he spotted flames against the tent walls. Once he realized what he was seeing, he assumed that someone would put it out.

WHEN THE FIRE BEGAN, THE FLYING WALLENDAS WERE STILL IN THE MIDDLE OF THEIR ACT AND ALFRED COURT'S BIG CATS WERE EING RETURNED TO THEIR CAGES.

Nearby, a young girl in the bleachers felt heat behind her and turned around. She asked her mother if the tent was supposed to be on fire.

An usher in front of the bleachers saw the flames and pointed toward them – as did a man climbing back up the bleachers with a Coke he'd just bought from a vendor. He pointed with the bottle and cried out, "Fire!"

Some twisted around to see, but most of the audience kept their eyes glued on the Wallendas. They didn't want to miss even a second of their death-defying act.

But up in the air, the Wallendas spotted the flames and knew the high-wire lines were not the place to be if the tent was burning. They quickly wrapped things up and slid down the lines to the ground below.

The big top was about to plunge into chaos.

But not yet. It soon would be, many believed, under control.

The fire was still on the sidewall about six feet from the ground. It hadn't caught the roof on fire yet. There was a chance that if people got water onto it, it could be stopped there.

A trio of ushers from the north side of the big top cut behind the bleachers and grabbed the fire buckets that were underneath the seats. There were four of them, each holding four gallons of water.

The first usher hefted one and heaved the water onto the flames. It did nothing.

The fire was at eye level, about five feet high. Another usher swung his bucket, then another. The third usher threw the last one, but the fire was now out of reach. They tried to pull down the sidewall, but it was too late. The fire was eating its way toward the roof and was out of reach.

The intense heat from the flames caused the hair and clothing of the ushers to smolder. They ran outside, grabbed other water buckets, and drenched each other with them.

At this point, no one outside had any idea that a fire was burning under the big top.

AND IT'S NOT CLEAR IF ANYONE INSIDE WAS TAKING IT SERIOUSLY.

The Wallenda's escape had gotten the attention of bandleader Merle Evans, who was always alert to any deviation in the program. He looked over and spotted the flames and stopped the music with a flick of his hand. From where he stood, the fire at the other side of the tent looked small, like a "tiny ray of light across the tent."

There was a moment of stunned surprise, but most patrons barely reacted. In the bleachers, a young boy named William Epps pointed out the fire to his mother.

"Don't worry," she told him. "They'll put it out."

Surely, one of the circus crew would throw some water on it or snuff it out with an extinguisher. And yet it continued to burn.

Others thought it was part of the show, some kind of surprise. Others just failed to respond to what they were seeing, caught up in the show. They had come to see the circus, so this must be part of it. They looked and then turned back to the center ring.

Merle Evans knew the fire was not part of the performance, but he could see that the big cats were still returning to their cages. He yelled over to Fred Bradna and told him to move the cats, the tent was on fire.

Bradna saw the smoke, and while he immediately whistled to the animal trainers, he saw they were already desperately trying to hurry the rest of the big cats onto the enclosed ramp that was supposed to take them out of the tent. But time was lost when two of the leopards panicked and refused to leave. A water hose had to be turned on to prod them into the chute.

The crowds in the tent were now undecided about whether to watch the animal handlers struggle with the big cats or to watch the growing fire.

Buckets of water were still being thrown on the blaze, which had now climbed higher up the wall. Since many of the long-time crew had been drafted for the war effort, many working that day were young and inexperienced. They were running back and forth around the fire, unsure about what to do.

That may have been why there wasn't yet any panic from the audience. The fire was still small, and it was being dealt with by people who surely knew what they were doing.

They didn't.

The flames climbed higher up the side of the tent, but there was still no mass exodus toward the exits.

Merle Evans cued the band, and they struck up the disaster march – John Phillips Sousa's "Stars and Stripes Forever," a signal to circus folks that something had gone seriously wrong. The tune had been chosen because every musician knew it by heart.

Even though none of the audience members knew the song was a secret signal to the circus performers and crew, the notes of the song seemed to cause a shift among the people in the tent. The flames were now leaping toward the roof, and everyone could see them.

The crowd gasped and then let out a roar. As people in the reserved seats sprang to their feet, the chairs went over with a deafening clatter. Coke bottles rolled down the risers. Children were crying.

A group of plumed horses were waiting by the back exit, getting ready to perform, when Fred Bradna dashed out and ordered them back to the corral. The riders tugged at their reins and whirled the mounts around, but one of them, a white charger, got spooked and became tangled in the tent ropes, almost throwing the performer on his back before she got the horse under control.

In Clown Alley, Felix Adler, known as the "King of Clowns," was preparing to return to the tent. He later recalled, "We heard a roar like applause, only we knew the animal act was over and there shouldn't be applause. We knew then something was wrong. Then we smelled smoke."

Knowing the big cat act had just finished, some performers feared that a lion had gotten loose.

Emmett Kelly was in his dressing tent, enjoying a cold beer before he returned to the big top. "I heard someone say something about a fire," he said. "We were always very conscious of fire. I didn't

THE FIRE HAD ALREADY BEEN BURNING FOR SEVERAL MINUTES BEFORE ANYONE OUTSIDE THE TENT REALIZED IT WAS BURNING. ONCE FIRE AND SMOKE BEGAN TO BE SEEN COMING FROM THE TOP OF THE BIG TOP, PANIC TOOK HOLD ON THE CIRCUS GROUNDS.

see any fire, though. I thought at first it was the sideshow." He ran outside and saw smoke curling up from near the big top. He hoped it was only a straw fire but was terrified it wasn't.

Inside the big top, the animal trainers were still trying to get the big cats out of the tent. They were becoming nervous because of the cries and movements of the audience. Fred Bradna ran into the center ring, yelling for calm. Ushers did the same. "Please keep your seats?" they urged the crowd. "We know about the fire, and we'll take care of it!"

But the people in the southwest bleachers weren't interested in staying in the tent. They bolted away from the flames, running east toward the performers' entrance. Those sitting in the bottom rows had nothing in their way and an easy escape – if they moved quickly. Those who hesitated were trampled by those above them.

Many lost their balance on the narrow boards and fell. Some went through the spaces between the seats, banging their heads and getting wedged in between the seats. The next wave stomped on them as they fled.

THOSE CLOSEST TO THE EXITS FROM THE BIG TOP RUSHED TO SAFETY, WHILE HUNDREDS OF OTHERS WERE STILL TRAPPED INSIDE THE TENT WITH THE FIRE.

While most ran, others stopped, frozen, not moving, sitting or standing there entranced, as if nothing was happening.

Then, fanned by a strong wind from the storm approaching from the west, the flames began to spread with dizzying speed. Fingers of fire streaked up the canvas, climbing toward the top of the center pole. The fire fanned out across the top of the tent, and soon, as one survivor recalled, "The entire top became a mass of flames."

From outside, spectators finally saw a great burning glow beneath the tent's canvas. The material blackened and then burned, sending flames shooting into the sky. Thick clouds of black smoke poured out of the tent and now visitors on the circus grounds could hear the screams of the people inside.

The big top had turned into an inferno.

ROARING SHEETS OF FLAME, BURNING BITS OF CANVAS, and liquid paraffin rained down on the now-panicking crowd, who tumbled and fell on the bleachers or tripped over the wooden reserved seats. The luckier ones broke free or slipped through gaps in the bleachers and made it to safety. Others fought helplessly as portions of heavy canvas fell on top of them and burned them alive.

Men, women, and children were screaming, and the chairs banged and clashed as they fought past them. Over the PA system, an

PHOTOGRAPHS TAKEN FROM THE CIRCUS GROUNDS AS SMOKE ROLLED OUT OF THE BIG TOP, ACCOMPANIED BY THE SOUNDS OF THE BIG SHOW BAND AND THE SCREAMS OF THOSE TRAPPED BY THE FLAMES.

announcer asked the audience to please leave their seats in an orderly fashion. Then the power went out, cutting him off.

The track near the main door filled with people. They'd come in that way; it was the only door they knew, and they made for it, running past other, easier exits.

Above them, the top of the tent was a solid sheet of flame, making them duck, yet still they surged, many of them cut off by the animal runway still lying across the track. Before those at the front of the mass of people could turn back, they were trapped against the metal runway then crushed by the hundreds who stampeded behind them.

Near the exit, attendants cut through the ropes that held up some of the canvas barriers that had steered the audience into the tent. Once they came down, people poured through.

At the foot of the grandstands, though, things weren't that simple. The crowd piled up at the gates and pressed against the railings. Ushers shouted at them to fold down the seats, but no one could hear them. The workers tried to pull rails out of the ground, but the crowd knocked them back. Gate attendants came to their aid, holding people off as long as possible. But they were a handful of men facing thousands of panicked circusgoers.

Ushers called out, "Take it easy, take it easy, walk out quietly." Some people listened. In school, children had learned what to do in case of a wartime air raid. Adults pretended this was another drill.

As the fire ate its way across the tent, more people scrambled, bunching into a mob at the bottom of the grandstand. One mother took her young son, wrapped his arms around her neck, and told him not to let go. A man had his daughter climb onto the riser above him and climb on his back. Mothers, aunts, and grandmothers hurried the children along, strong-arming them when necessary.

In the first wave of exits from the tent, Red Cross volunteers began trying to move a group of convalescent soldiers to safety. The men had come in a large group for the circus matinee. However, many volunteers turned back to help – and so did the wounded soldiers. The men, while hampered by their injuries, couldn't be stopped from leading at least 30 children to safety, many of them burned. Once outside, the Red Cross volunteers had to restrain their patients from running back inside.

And they weren't the only heroes. An East Hartford mother lost her six-year-old, knocked out of her arms as they ran for the exit. A sailor scooped him up and carried him out. An older woman fell through some bleachers and got her foot caught so that she was hanging upside down, her face a foot from the ground. A police officer freed her and helped her outside.

As the tent burned, Merle Evans was still directing the band through "Stars and Stripes Forever," the melody now almost lost beneath the sounds of the fire. Soon, though, the music stopped, and the orchestra marched calmly out of the tent, hoping their actions would encourage the audience to do the same.

But it was much too late for that.

THOSE NOT TRAPPED BY THE BLEACHERS OF THE METAL RUNWAYS, scattered across the open arena beneath the burning tent. One West Hartford father led his two daughters out the southwest exit between the bleachers and the grandstand. Several hundred people had already fled that way, but when they were about 25 feet from safety, a man in a circus uniform held up his hands to the crowd and shouted, "You'll have to go out another entrance!"

Scraps of burning canvas were falling around them as the man in the uniform halted the crowd. The father knew that to go back into the tent meant certain death. He shoved his way to the front and told the worker, "You damn fool! We're going this way!" He pushed the man aside, but fewer than 25 people followed him. The others turned back – and what became of them is unknown.

As the fire continued to spread, the crashing of grandstand chairs drowned out the audience's shouts and cries, but the flames'

crackling muffled that sound. Groups of people were rushing forward, pressed against the railings. One woman tripped on her high heels, dropped her purse, and went down, hanging onto her son's belt. A man grabbed his daughter and wrapped her in his jacket, hoping to shield her from the heat.

They climbed over piles of seats. The chairs collapsed as people stepped on them, the wooden legs bruising and cutting shins. A foot was caught in a seat, and others tripped and fell. A few stepped on Coke bottles and twisted their ankles. And still, there were people behind them, and more behind them, all pushing and shoving toward an exit – any exit.

Many children, separated from their parents, wailed and screamed. One little boy tried to shield his fallen grandmother from the stampeding crowd, begging someone to help him get to her feet.

As the support topes burned, the tent's six huge pole began to fall, ripping apart the flaming piece of canvas as they tipped and started to topple over.

As the pieces of burning canvas fell, women, their hair and dresses on fire, shrieked and wept. Parents tossed their children into the open arms of strangers at the bottom of the bleachers, praying they'd make it to safety.

Men were flinging chairs out of the way, hurtling them back to strike others nearby. The chairs seemed light and flimsy, but they weighed eight pounds each and were built to last. One husband wielded a chair like a club, swinging it wildly to clear a path for his wife. Someone surged out of the crowd, knocked him down, and took away the chair.

Part of the crowd funneled into an aisle, pushing and shoving, but smashed against some railings and stopped. A husky sailor in a blue uniform broke through, beating his way to the front. He punched a young woman in the jaw, and she fell into some chairs. The sailor lost his footing, and then people were on top of him, heavy, pressing him down.

Someone bowled over an older man from behind, and he fell into a tangle of seats. He got up only to be knocked down again. The younger and stronger pushed past the older and weaker, knocking them back into chairs, stepping on them, and moving on.

And yet, there were still those looking out for others. A young mother hit the railing of section C with her two-year-old and could not get free. A thin man in shirtsleeves reached out and lifted both out so they could escape. He seemed calm, and his demeanor heartened her. As she ran off, he stayed there to help others.

In another section, the aisle had jammed up. A man at the bottom held everyone back until his wife could work her way down the stairs to him. He wouldn't let anyone out – he just kept calling his wife. A girl ducked under a railing and shoved him aside. Everyone started to come out.

A local man was trying to escape with a crowd pressing close behind him. He had to hold some back to let his neighbor's wife and daughter escape. When they got to him, he put out his elbows like a football blocker and cleared a path for them to the exit.

Many escaped by going over the back of the grandstand instead of trying to exit at the bottom. They jumped to the ground or climbed down the support poles that held the seats in place. Parents tried to make it a game, and some children laughed as they shimmied and slid down the poles and ropes to the ground. Adults at the bottom held the sidewall like a slide so kids could jump into it.

Some people tried to catch others who jumped. One terrified woman leaped from the top of the grandstand, and her body struck a man across the head and shoulders, almost knocking him unconscious. He later said, "If she'd have been a bigger woman, I'd have lain right there and probably have been burned to death."

A mother with five children was in section H. Three men below caught the children as they dropped. Thinking they were all safe, the mother leaped, but outside, she realized she only had four of her kids with her. She ran back into the tent and found one boy sitting on the edge of the grandstand, shaking with fright. She ordered him to jump, and he did, but there was no one to catch him, and he was badly hurt.

One woman managed to drag herself out from under the bottom of the tent, her face blackened, and her clothing charred. She stumbled to her feet and began running toward the entrance of the flaming tent before a policeman grabbed her. She thrashed in his arms, shouting, "My God! My God! My kid's in there!"

Amid this horror, Fred Bradna was still running about, pleading with people on the east side to leave through the side flaps, but they continued to jam up helplessly at the bandstand exits. Children fainted in the crush.

All the while, the fire was still burning across the top of the tent. The support poles leaned dangerously, held in place by only a few ropes and some charred strips of canvas. Once the fire breached the roof, the tent became a chimney, sucking in air through the exits and shooting it out the top. The paraffin continued to act as an accelerant, and the fresh air provided an endless supply of oxygen.

The temperatures rose inside the tent – and so did the panic.

One man in the middle of the grandstand plunged forward, knocking over chairs, women, and children without regard. When his victims fell, he stepped over them. When last seen, he was fighting and pushing to get ahead of everyone else.

A woman there with her husband and granddaughter tried to escape. Her husband lifted the girl over the railing into the arena, and she ran for the exit. The woman was making her way down when she found her path blocked by an unconscious woman. She hesitated to walk forward and step over the body, but the press of people behind her and around her kept her from bending down to offer possible aid to the fallen woman. Her indecision was painfully ended when a burning piece of canvas fell on her back, badly burning her. She had to go on, so she stepped over the woman and forced her way forward.

The rush from the tent was like a human wave being hurled along by a current. A student nurse at St. Francis Hospital and a friend were able to lift an older woman who had fallen to her knees and drag her along between them. They held her tightly until the flow carried them far enough into the open to stumble free. They left the woman in a safe place and returned inside to continue their rescue efforts.

Those who fled the grandstands continued to bunch up at the gates. At one, a chair was stuck in the opening, and the pressure from behind caused those in front to topple over it, making it so no one could get out. Even when the gates were clear, they had been purposely narrow. Trying to squeeze through, one woman was caught and crushed against a steel post, half in and half out. She stretched out a hand to a friend, and he yanked her free. The crowd immediately began to flow into the gap, tumbling onto the track.

Ushers continued to urge the audience to exit in an orderly fashion, but the crush was so tight that people were losing shoes. Some fell, and others walked on them. A woman with a child in her arms went down, and the crowd passed over her. One woman dropped her purse but knew she'd be run over if she bent down to retrieve it. A boy lost his glasses and leaned over to grab them. A man fell over him, and they both went down.

It became clear to those who weren't panicking that they had to just keep going, pushing through until they were clear of the tent. There was no stopping. Parents took advantage of anything they could to hold onto their children. When one mother's little boy got knocked down, she snatched him up by his overall straps and hauled him out like a piece of luggage. But more often, when a mother bent to rescue a child, the mass of people buried her.

The scene was beyond chaotic. Ushers, bystanders, and audience members selflessly rushed loose children to safety and returned for more. Many of those same kids were running around outside, crying, trying to find their parents. Some of them dashed straight back into the fire.

Donald Anderson, a 13-year-old boy, would receive a medal for his actions that day. When the fire broke out, he jumped from the top row of bleachers and cut a hole in the side of the tent with his pocketknife. Hundreds followed him to safety, but he was gone when the people he rescued tried to thank him. Donald had run back into the tent, cutting his way through another gap to rescue the elderly uncle who'd brought him to the circus and bringing along a four-year-old girl who'd been trampled unconscious for good measure.

THE FLAMES CLOSED IN TOWARD THE MIDDLE OF THE arena, where the steel runways for the big cats were still blocking the exits for

hundreds of people. The prop men had never had the chance to move them.

Those not smashed against the sides of the runways clambered over them, vaulting the bars and crawling on top. There were still animals inside, even as people frantically passed over the bars. One man shoved his young son on top of the cage and urged him to keep going. But the boy's foot slipped through the bars and when the boy looked down, he saw a lion directly under him, snarling, his jaw wide. The boy moved a little faster after that.

As people pounded down the grandstands, the railing at the front of one collapsed. A woman fell and dropped a child she was carrying on top of the runway. The child's arm dangled between the bars. A trainer prodded at the nearest cat, trying to distract him, to keep him moving past, but the cat turned and swiped at the child's arm, ripping off part of a sleeve with his claws. A man grabbed the screaming child and passed him to someone on the far side.

The scene in the cage where the runway began was more frightening. The fire was now directly overhead, and embers and pieces of flaming canvas were falling all around. Animal tamer May Kovar – famous daughter of two veteran big cat performers – was in the cage, driving to drive her last five panthers out of the tent. As more burning fell around her and the cats, she feared they would turn on each other – or on her – in terror.

The first four cats went peacefully, but the last panther in the cage – spooked by the fire and the flaming scraps of tent raining down – went after May. She circled it with a stick she used to gently keep the cats moving, giving it room to escape around her. When it started toward the chute, she closed in on it; this time, the panther didn't turn. She tapped it with the stick, shoved it into the runway, and shut the door behind it.

May then stepped out of the arena door and joined the trainers as they shooed the cats along the runway to the wagons. At the rear of the grandstands, where the chute entered the tent, it changed from iron bars to wooden slats—the wooden section connected with the ramp that led to individual wagons. Usually, the animals went out one by one, but not today. Two panthers who did not get along were surprised to find themselves side-by-side and began to fight. Another cat raced back in toward the cage, running under the fire and scorching its fur.

Back in the burning big top, May Kovar helped people caught at the runway, picking up children and boosting them over, but no one would remember this. The newspapers would focus solely on her heroics inside the cage, fighting her panthers while the world around her burned. A retired fire captain from New York City called her "The bravest girl I've ever seen."

But while her cats were out of the tent and safe, the runways were still there, and the crowd was larger now. Men tossed children across and then jumped over, but others struggled to get a grip on the bars, banging their knees and feet. Some slumped back, swallowed by the next wave of people as the fire drew closer.

One man caught children thrown to him and pulled the mothers over, but that kind of helpfulness was rare. Each time one young mother tried to pull herself over, people behind her, trying to climb up themselves, dragged her back. She kissed her child and told him to run, then tossed him over the top of the cage. Hands hauled her back down again. When she looked up, she saw her son had caught his foot between the bars. He dangled upside down, his hands not quite touching the ground on the other side. She started to pull herself up and over, but the boy reached between the bars and untied his shoe. It fell into the chute, and he was free.

The fire burned across the tent. The north grandstand had seated nearly 3,000 people but had emptied when the fire started. Trapped with nowhere else to go, several hundred climbed onto the seats, staying out of the flames – at first. But as the entire big top became engulfed in flames, they struggled to escape. Feet slipped between the seats, twisted so they couldn't get free. Others were stuck or jammed and couldn't move.

A teenager and her younger sister came tumbling out of the grandstand and into the massing crowd. The older girl saw men running up and down the far side of the seats, pulling people over, and she pushed her sister on top of those who had already fallen. As she lifted the girl, she looked down into the face of a young man, only slightly older than herself, unable to get up because of the layers of bodies pinning his legs. One of the men helped the younger girl across and was about to move on to someone else, but the girl held onto his hand and pulled him back toward her sister. He had to save her too, the younger girl insisted, and he did. They never knew what happened to the young man.

Black smoke filled the air as the flames burned the canvas. Pieces fell and caught in women's hair and set their light summer dresses ablaze. Paraffin continued to rain down, burning skin on contact. It sizzled as it landed on the flesh of children below, blisters dotting their arms like chicken pox.

The fire consumed the tent's roof, pole by pole, becoming hotter as it consumed wood, canvas, and rope. The heat on top of the crowd was like a broiler oven. They tried to duck away from it, but the fire found them, burning their hair, clothing, and flesh. People were literally being cooked alive.

The fire drove the crowd ahead of it toward the bandstand. People who'd believed they had time to escape now realized they'd underestimated its speed. It was moving faster, and the east end was too crowded to escape that way.

The fire was going to cut them off.

Once again, with no escape, the crowd stormed up the closest grandstand, searching for poles and ropes they could use to escape. Adults gathered at the bottom to catch the children who jumped from the back, but there weren't enough of them for everybody. One man climbed down a rope with two children on his back. People leaped for the side poles, slid down halfway, and caught their hands on the rope guide ropes. The ropes burned the flesh from their palms, and they let go from the shock and fell.

Others jumped, not bothering with poles or ropes. There were scores of bad falls, mostly among the very young and the very old. Little girls landed on their hands and broke their wrists and arms. One woman went over headfirst. An older man broke his leg and had to be helped out of the tent.

And the catchers were injured, too. They ended up with black eyes and strained backs, scratches, and bruises from being kicked.

Once they escaped from the grandstands, they still might not be safe. If there was no opening in the tent, they had to crawl beneath the canvas, but in places where the sidewall was staked tightly to the ground, there was no way to struggle under it. Boys with penknives – like the heroic Donald Anderson – saved the lives of hundreds.

Meanwhile, the tops of the bleachers were still crammed with people. Some had fallen through the boards and had gotten caught. The crowd rolled over them. Some jumped, but others refused, unsure where their children were. The surge from below pushed them over. It sent one young girl toppling. She fell 12 feet to the ground and broke her back.

Waiting for a little girl in front of her to jump, one woman saw a man shove the child off from behind. She hadn't been moving fast enough for him.

Some jumped and broke their ankles and then were unable to get up before others landed on them, knocking them unconscious or hurting them worse. People jumped over the heads of the fallen or climbed over them once they reached the ground.

One boy was knocked to the ground by a crowd stampeding over him. To escape from the feet of the mob, he crawled under the bleachers. A baby was under the boards, among the discarded programs and popcorn boxes. The boy picked it up and carried it outside. A man rushed over to him and called to a nearby barefoot woman who was crying for her baby.

Not far away, a father wandered aimlessly about the grounds, saying over and over that he thought he'd rescued his son, but when he got outside, he was holding an unknown child by the hand. Police and circus hands restrained him from running back into the flames.

Children were calling for their mothers, and mothers were calling for their children. And still, people ran out of the tent. Clowns and circus folk urged them to keep going.

"Don't look back!" one of them called.

Those coming out collided with others rushing in to find loved ones. One woman spotted a little blond girl trying to get back into the tent, crying for her grandmother. The woman held onto her.

Emmett Kelly was there, urging people to keep moving. "You can't go back in there!" he shouted.

But they could – and they did.

A man saved his children, but his wife was still inside. He left the children in the concession tent and returned to the fire. The children remained there in the shade until, minutes later, he returned with their mother.

One woman forced her way out of the tent and didn't see her niece, so she fought back through the people streaming out. She got back inside, but, unknown to her, the girl had already made it out. The woman didn't. Her body was later identified at the state armory.

A mother escaped and discovered her son and daughter were not behind her. She ran back in and burned to death with her daughter. The son escaped unharmed.

Caught in the confusion near an exit, a young man felt the grip on his cousin's hand slipping, but he had his younger brother under his other arm and couldn't let go to get a better hold of her. Bodies jostled them from all sides, and then his hand was empty. He only had his brother.

A woman with an infant in her arms had jumped from the bleachers with no one to break her fall. She tried to turn in mid-air to protect the baby and landed hard. She dragged herself under the canvas and outside, but something was wrong with her legs. She felt sharp, piercing pains with each step. Later, doctors would tell her she'd broken her pelvis, but at the time, she just had to escape from the tent.

Another mother nearby had made it out unscathed, but when she could not find her daughter, she became hysterical. "Where is my baby?" she screamed. Someone told her that her child had run back into the tent – most likely searching for her. The mother believed them and went in after the girl, disappearing into the fire and smoke.

She was never seen again.

THE WIND BLEW THE FIRE EAST, AWAY FROM THE BIG TOP, causing burning embers to fall on the women's dressing tent, which had been treated with the same paraffin mixture. An aerialist climbed a rope hand over hand, and someone passed him a bucket so he could quench the tiny fires with water.

Some of the girls had been taking bucket baths in the tent when the fire broke out. A few of them ran out into the yard stark naked. Others gathered their costumes, threw water on their trunks, and slipped under the sidewalls. A bucket brigade formed – the wardrobe mistress, two little people, and a clown – and soon, the situation was under control.

By now, people who had escaped from the big top were wandering the circus grounds, their clothing smoking. They all looked dazed and frightened. Soot was smeared on their skin. Many of them were injured and burned. In the distance, the sound of sirens rose and fell, getting closer.

But inside the big top, not much had changed – they'd just gotten worse. The fire was roaring overhead. People were screaming. Emmett Kelly held the canvas aside so folks could get out at the east end. But the fire was closer now, the heat down atop the crowd. It was making people faint. They fell, and the crowd swarmed over them. The air itself was burning people. Women ran about with their hair on fire.

Bill Curlee led his son, David, to the northeast exit. David was crying, and his father told him to stop because it wouldn't do any good. He pushed and shoved his way to an opening in the canvas and grabbed David under the arms. "Go to the car," he told the boy and tossed him outside. "I'll meet you there."

Bill started to follow but stopped. He saw another boy behind him, reached back, grabbed his wrist, and pulled. It worked. The boy was pulled free from the mob. There were more hands, more kids, and mothers holding toddlers up to him. Bill started throwing children to safety, one after another. Dozens stared as he saved countless lives, and later, they'd express their admiration for him to reporters. His story made the front page.

However, unlike Donald Anderson and May Kovar, Bill's story ended in tragedy. As he lifted a child out of the tent, his foot slipped, and he fell. The surging crowd dragged him under.

The fire was sweeping down all sides now. One woman was trying to encourage a girl to jump from the top of the grandstand, but she wouldn't, even though the fire was directly overhead. Her arms burned from trying to shield the girl, and the woman finally tossed her over and followed.

The heavy support poles overhead were now swaying, barely staying upright. The roof was fully engulfed. Several circus water trucks had made it to the big top, but they were little help. They were having trouble getting pressure.

It was too late for what little water they could offer.

Around the tent, there were many last-second rescues. A clown dragged a little boy to safety. A man picked up a girl and carried her out, the girl wildly scratching at his face. She'd been trying to find her brother.

The last ones out were burned the worst. One woman's back was red and raw from her hips to the top of her head. Another man was blackened from the waist up. An older man helped save a woman whose arms were burned to the shoulder, her skin hanging down like empty sleeves. She cried that her three children were lost.

One young woman in costume ran into the big top three times, twice coming out with children. The third time, she returned empty-handed and fell to the ground.

A man from New Britain, Connecticut, got his wife and child down the side poles and out of the tent, then went back in to save a woman and child he saw lying on the ground screaming. As he left with them, he saw at least 50 people piled up near the northeast exit.

Around the grounds, survivors wandered barefoot, their clothing in tatters, coughing up black mucus from their throats. Some fainted. There was no water to splash on their faces, so rescuers used lemonade.

Edward J. Hickey, the State Police Commissioner, and the State Fire Marshal, witnessed the last minutes of the fire on the east end of the grounds. He had been at the circus that day with his nieces and nephews.

Hickey, who would become deeply involved in not only the aftermath of the fire but the investigation that followed, later wrote: "I saw people trying to climb over the chute cages in the track on the north side, and when I left the tent, owing to the heat and fire settling, there were people piled alongside the chute cage, and these folks were flaming and burning, and shrieking and hollering. On the ground at that point, I saw a number of people who were afire and were rolling themselves on the ground. I saw from that point looking in, there were people still lying on the ground at the track at the east side whose clothing was afire, and under the stands I saw bodies on fire."

Hickey could hear the sirens of the fire trucks on their way to the circus grounds, but he knew they wouldn't be enough. He ran to look for a telephone. They were going to need more help.

INSIDE THE TENT, THE FIRE SWEPT OVER THE BANDSTAND, where Merle Evans and the other musicians tried to keep people calm as they escaped from the tent, flaming shards fell like rain. The kettle drums exploded from the heat.

Faces smudged and white uniforms scorched, the band regrouped outside and serenaded the fleeing crowd as they watched the drums and the organ burn.

By the southeast exit, a Coca-Cola stand caught on fire. The flames devoured the stacks of empty deposit bottles in yellow wooden crates. The glass melted and dripped like water.

High above, ropes dropped away, the rigging fell, and the poles slumped inward, dragging the canvas with it. The tent sagged, and then, one by one, the support poles crashed over, crushing the animal cages, the bleachers, the chairs, and the people. There was a hissing, swishing sound as the big top collapsed on itself. It fell, blanketing those still trapped in the tent under the fiery canvas coated in wax that had been applied using gasoline.

Those trapped beneath it were doomed.

Their screams were heard by those outside – men, women, and children moaning and crying for their lives. It was like howling, witnesses remembered, a terrible, eerie screeching. Several survivors said the one thing they would never forget about the circus fire as long as they lived was the sound of the animals as they burned alive in the big top's final collapse.

But there were no animals inside.

AND THEN, AS SUDDENLY AS IT HAD STARTED, IT was over. The entire big top was gone. The stands had burned, the bleachers had been reduced to ash – everything was gone. Only the dead and dying were left in the fire's wake.

The disaster was over in 15 minutes. From the moment when the first warning cries of "Fire!" were heard to the moment the big top collapsed into a smoldering ruin, just one-quarter of an hour had passed.

The survivors stared in disbelief at the ruins around them. The dead were everywhere.

Hell had come to Hartford, Connecticut, and life would never be the same.

SOON, THE SOUNDS OF WAILING SIRENS DREW CLOSER. Engine Company 7 was the first unit to arrive. As they neared the scene, they slowed. Two boys in the road pointed toward the circus, and they roared onto the grounds, headed toward the collapsed big top.

More trucks followed. Alarms had turned the big top into a five-alarm fire, and dozens of trucks raced to the grounds, arriving too late to save many lives.

All the firefighters could do was soak the blackened ruins, and even that was done with difficulty. No hydrants were on the grounds,

FROM THE FIRST CRIES OF "FIRE" TO THE TIME THE BIG TOP WAS REDUCED TO ASH, ONLY 15 MINUTES HAD PASSED, LEAVING THE DEAD AND DYING BEHIND.

so they had to run hoses extending more than 300 yards to the closest hydrants.

Ambulances lined up to take up to 682 victims to nearby hospitals. As luck would have it, the area medical centers were prepared – it was wartime, and doctors and nurses were ready to treat serious burns in case of enemy air raids.

Because most had badly burned limbs, nurses had to search for veins, especially on small children, occasionally cutting them down to get the big needles in. Nurses snipped away clothing and covered the injured with sterile sheets. The injured were given morphine, wrapped in sheets, and given plasma injections as they began long roads to recovery.

Not everyone brought in for care was burned. Some had broken ankles or wrists or bad lacerations. Others had cuts, scrapes, and bruises from being stepped on.

One 22-year-old woman had a bad combination of both – two broken ankles and burns over most of her body. She'd taken her niece to the circus as a birthday present and tried to protect her as the flames swept over them.

The hospitals quickly overflowed. Doctors were stationed at the front desks, moving the less severely to outpatient clinics, but there were still too many. The operating rooms were full, and the dying were backed up in the halls. Administrators called the Red Cross for volunteers, doctors, and nurses but were told the need would be broadcast on radio stations. It was going to take time to get help. It was a holiday week, and everyone seemed to be on vacation.

Meanwhile, hospital lobbies were mobbed by relatives of the dead and the missing, trying to find their loved ones, demanding answers, crying and wailing, standing around, and getting in the way. The

hospitals plunged into chaos. Outside, the injured and bereaved sat on the lawn. A man who drove up with his wife took one look at the jammed entrance and turned around.

As the ambulances dropped off the injured, doctors and nurses placed them on stretchers in hallways, did triage in waiting rooms, and then sent the stable patients upstairs to the wards.

The medical staff moved as fast as they could, but the hospitals were turned into war zones with all the horrors of war. A boy and his grandmother arrived at one, both burned. The boy with a possible skull fracture and his grandmother's face mostly burned away. Many of the adults were burned on the tops of their heads, thanks to the flames that had swept across the upper reaches of the big top.

One survivor later said that the South building of Hartford Hospital smelled like a roast that had been left in the oven too long.

THE DEATH TOLL FROM WHAT CAME TO BE KNOWN AS "The Great Circus Fire" changed many times in the days that followed the tragedy. The verified deaths would eventually rise to 167 --- with 67 of them being children under the age of 15. Six others were never identified and never claimed.

They'd all come to the circus that day for an afternoon of fun.

There turned out to be only one building in Hartford that was large enough for the bodies of the dead to be displayed for identification – the Connecticut State Armory. Arrangements were made for National Guard soldiers to transport the bodies there, where family members and loved ones could claim their dead.

Workers in downtown buildings would never forget the sight of the olive-drab army trucks, escorted by motorcycles when they arrived at the armory. The odor of the charred bodies was so strong that people could smell it four floors up.

A line had already formed at the front door. As the trucks passed by, turning toward a side door, relatives of the missing grimly watched them go. The trucks stopped at the west door, backed in, and their tailgates opened so soldiers and police officers could unload their terrible cargo.

Used for indoor formations, the drill floor of the armory became the temporary morgue. The room stretched over 200 feet, and the

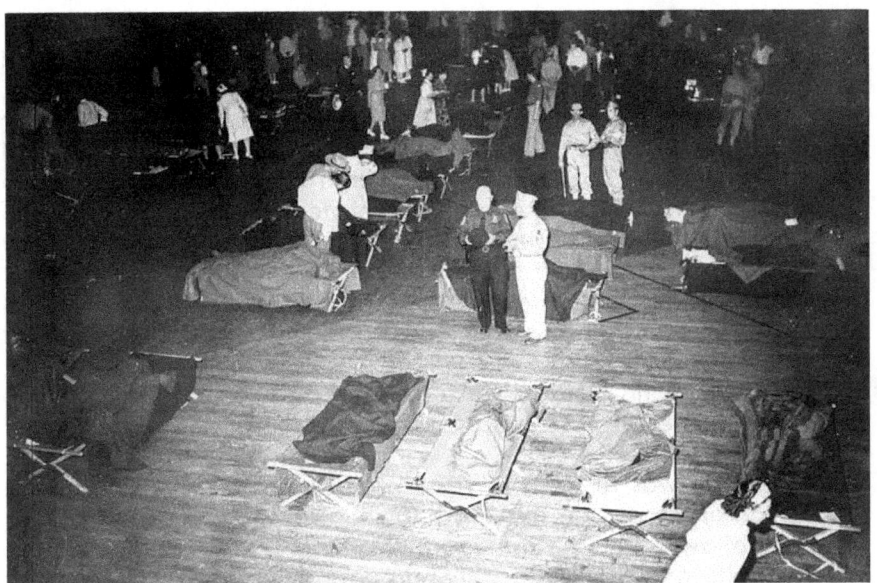

THE BODIES OF THE DEAD WERE LAID OUT FOR IDENTIFICATION AT THE CONNECTICUT STATE ARMORY.

ceiling loomed 60 feet above. A giant peaked skylight allowed sunshine into the gloomy space.

As the bodies were unloaded, State Trooper William Menser wired green tags to the wrists or ankles of the dead. The corpses were separated by sex and age, laying them out on narrow army cost. The majority were women and older girls – 75 in the northeast corner. The children were placed in three rows by the west entrance, and the ten dead men were in the middle. Many of them were faceless or missing limbs. Since the relatives would enter the room from the south, the corpses in the best shape were placed in the front rows.

The fewer the dead they saw, it was reasoned, the better.

Trooper Menser went from cot to cot with two doctors, filling in the tags with the body's probable age. He made a sheet for each victim that included height, weight, and build, noting anything that might make them recognizable to someone searching for them.

Clothing was mostly burned away in the worst cases. Occasionally, though, Menser would find a section of waistband or part of a collar but not much else.

The size of the room allowed some of the smell to dissipate, but morticians from the Newkirk and Whitney Funeral Home walked around spraying the corpses to make it easier for everyone.

After Menser completed his task, soldiers draped blankets over the dead, but in many cases, they didn't cover much. The fire had caused the muscles in the bodies to contract, pulling knees up to chests, and arms were raised as if to protect the face. Most of the badly burned were contorted and twisted, so the soldiers tented the blankets over them as best they could.

The governor was present, as were officials from the National Guard, but it was Commissioner Edward Hickey who took charge of the staff, nurses, and Red Cross volunteers. He was in his shirtsleeves, and the knees of his trousers were torn out. He'd never had a chance to change clothes after leaving the circus grounds, and he reeked of smoke or ashes.

The plan was to have relatives check in downstairs and give a description of the person they were looking for. Then, a dozen people would be allowed into the drill room at a time. There would be nurses, smelling salts, and a first aid station in case anyone was overcome. If they could not find their loved ones, they would be allowed to search again.

A check-out desk was set up by the east entrance, staffed by women at typewriters who could fill in death certificates. All bodies that were identified had to pass through that area before they were released to funeral parlors.

Then, just before the doors were opened, six priests arrived. They went from cot to cot, lifting the blankets and praying over the dead.

A soldier unlocked the gate, and the line of people outside – which stretched from the arched doorway along the walk and around the building – slowly moved into the lobby. There was little pushing, and there was almost no noise as the first group walked out onto the wood floor of the drill room and found themselves surrounded by row after row of the dead. Their footsteps echoed dully as they stepped deeper into the room. The air was still and hot.

It was an overwhelming scene for many. One young woman was positive that her mother and father were there, but after four bodies, she turned and hurried back downstairs. Others silently wept. A few cried out, and yet hardly anyone went into hysterics – possibly because the burned bodies just didn't seem human anymore. Couples searched through the rows of children. They couldn't be sure, they said, the bodies were in such bad shape.

Time passed slowly. The first identification didn't come for 35 minutes. Still, the nurses folded the blankets back, and soldiers shone their flashlights on the charred faces of the dead. And searchers reached the ends of rows and asked, "Are you sure this is all of them?"

Eventually, more names were learned, more clothing and jewelry were identified, and more tears were shed. Another truck arrived, bringing eight unidentified bodies from Municipal Hospital. The hero Bill Curlee was among them, but no one knew it yet.

Relatives and family members roamed aimlessly among the cots with handkerchiefs and scented cloths pressed to their noses. State troopers, soldiers, and nurses stayed nearby, ready to step in. The huge room was so unnaturally quiet that the occasional sob came like a shock wave, chilling the heart like an explosion.

Some identifications required only a blackened piece of jewelry, a missing tooth, or an appendectomy scar. One little girl cut her palm that morning, and her father fixed it with a Band-Aid. Her clenched fist still clutched the bandage. Otherwise, she was unrecognizable; her clothing burned away except for her black patent leather shoes.

Though no one fainted, and there was no panic, it wasn't always calm. One grief-stricken woman screamed as she identified the body of her son. She beat her forehead and wailed as a nurse took her away. Others turned and walked away swiftly, and some stood with a hand clutched over their mouth while others held their heads in despair.

One thing that struck the workers at the armory as odd was how few people were identified on that first evening. Hundreds of searchers came looking, but only two dozen or so bodies left through the checkout.

Many of the relatives were hesitant to enter the drill room, though. Their reluctance to approach the rows of cots was obvious from how slowly they walked the floor. Workers found it difficult to get some of the searchers to identify their loved ones because the bodies they were shown no longer resembled the people they knew. Some acted like they didn't understand what they were asked to do. They were not only numb but could also be combative – they'd come there hoping they *wouldn't* find the loved ones who were missing.

Others were simply in denial, unable to accept that the tragedy had actually happened – and had happened to them. One woman had gone to the circus with her 16-year-old son. The boy thought his mother was in front of him when they came out of the exit, but then he couldn't find her. Her husband visited the hospitals, then the armory.

Failing to locate her, he decided that she must have been stricken with amnesia and wandered off. She was never seen again.

The long days at the armory spawned several strange stories.

One volunteer was helping a family search for their son, and they stopped in front of a cot. The family couldn't bring themselves to pull the blanket away from the victim's face, so the volunteer did it for them. The dead boy on the cot was the volunteer's son – he'd had no idea he'd gone to the circus.

After the fire, rescuers found a woman's body that had been badly burned. Her hands were missing, her face had been scorched away, and even most of her chest was gone. But under the woman was a handbag that had been shielded from the flames. When workers opened it, they found a war rations book inside with the dead woman's name on it – or so they thought.

The woman had lived out of town in Glastonbury, so a police officer called her home, and her husband answered. The police officers gently broke the news of his wife's death.

"She's not dead," the man replied.

The police officers had seen grief and denial before, and he patiently asked the man to come to the armory and take a look at the body.

"But she's right here with me!" the husband insisted.

And she was. The husband and wife had been in the middle of the grandstand when the fire broke out. Twice, the woman had been knocked down in the crowd, but she managed to escape. Her son was safe, so she wasn't too worried that she'd lost her purse when they fled the big top.

Still, the police needed the husband to come down and officially take her name off the body. He went to the armory – with his wife – and they looked at the body that certainly wasn't hers. The next day, she was listed in the newspaper among the dead – but at least she got her purse back.

The armory spawned a few ghostly tales, too. In the years that followed the fire, it earned a reputation for its haunting. Many who spent time in or around the drill room claimed they heard voices, weeping, and crying in the echoing space. This went on for several decades, and while many dismissed the stories as nothing more than imaginations at work that turned ordinary sounds into something spectral, others weren't so sure. They believed the events of the days after the fire had left an impression behind – an indelible memory replayed repeatedly as the years passed.

However, there was also a very strange story that spread right after the fire occurred in July 1944.

A reporter who had spent most of the day in the drill room walked out onto a staircase landing to use the payphone. He had just started to dial his number when the door behind him banged open, and a man stumbled out of the drill room. His face was pale, he was breathing hard, and he half-collapsed onto the stairs.

The reporter asked him if he was all right.

"Yes, I'm all right," the man said quietly. "I found my wife and three children in there."

The man put his face in his hands and sat very still. Saddened and unsure of what to say, the reporter expressed his condolences and started to make his telephone call but stopped. It seemed heartless to be giving news to his wife while a man who lost his family in the fire was sitting just a few feet away. He placed the telephone receiver back in its cradle and turned to speak to the man again.

But the man was gone.

There was no sign of him on the stairs, and the drill room door had not been opened. The man had vanished in the moments it took for the reporter to decide against making a call and hang up the phone.

A chill went through the reporter, but he was convinced there had to be an explanation. He went to speak to the volunteers, and a check of the records revealed that no man identified a wife and three children at the armory that day.

So, who was that man? Was it some kind of sick joke?

The reporter started to walk back to the telephone on the landing when the volunteer who'd been helping him called out. She told him that she hadn't been able to find a man who'd identified his wife and three children, but she found a listing close to what he'd been looking for.

There had been a mother and her three children brought to the armory from the fire, she said, but the body of her husband had been with them. The entire family had died in the circus fire.

That was when the reporter realized who he'd seen on the staircase that day.

AMONG THE UNCLAIMED DEAD FROM THE FIRE WAS A blond-haired, blue-eyed little girl who had been trampled to death in the rush for the exits. No one recognized her or knew her name, so when she was buried, she was given a tombstone that read only "Little Miss 1565."

THE GRAVESTONE OF LITTLE MISS 1565, AN UNIDENTIFIED GIRL FROM THE FIRE AND (BELOW), ELEANOR COOK, WHO INVESTIGATOR RICK DAVEY BELIEVED WAS THE UNKNOWN GIRL.

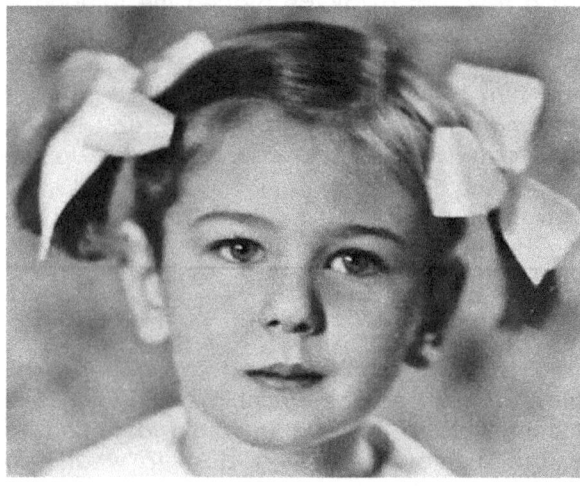

Her identity remained a mystery for decades after the fire, but in 1991, a retired Hartford fire detective named Rick Davey began his own investigation of Little Miss 1565. Her story had haunted him throughout his life, and now, with time on his hands, he decided to dig in. Through a painstaking process of interviews with survivors and by process of elimination, he concluded that the unidentified girl was Eleanor Cook – a girl who hadn't been unknown at all.

She had been eight years old in 1944 and had gone to the circus that day with her mother, Mildred, and her two brothers, Donald, 9, and Edward, 6. Edward was found dead after the fire, and Mildred, badly injured, was rushed to the hospital, where she stayed for months. Donald had somehow escaped from the fire unscathed. With Mildred incapacitated, an aunt of Eleanor, Emily Gill, was asked to view the remains of Little Miss 1565. She told officials the dead girl wasn't her niece – the hair, teeth, and clothing were all wrong. Eleanor went from being a possible fire victim to a missing person. She was never found.

Interest in Little Miss 1565 remained steady for the next half century, finally peaking when Ray Davey became obsessed with the story. He assembled all the circumstantial evidence he had that made the case for Eleanor being the unknown girl and presented it to Mildred and Donald Cook. Mildred didn't go on record, but Donald said he believed the morgue photo was his sister. State medical examiner D. H. Wayne Carver issued a revised death certificate, and Little Miss 1565 officially became Eleanor Cook.

But was she?

The information provided closure for the family, but one troubling issue remains: the dental records of Little Miss 1565 and Eleanor Cook don't match. In addition, at three feet, ten inches and weighing just 40 pounds, Little Miss 1565 was typical of a girl of six. Eleanor Cook, who was eight years old, was described as "tall for her age" and was well over four feet tall, likely weighing about 55 pounds. Physically, the two girls don't match.

And while contemporary DNA testing could likely resolve the matter, there is no one left from the family to press the issue. Although the identity of Little Miss 1565 was officially "solved" in 1991, most believe that her name remains unknown.

EVERYONE WHO WORKED FOR THE GREATEST SHOW ON EARTH escaped from the burning big top—but not because they were cowards. Emmett Kelly was only one of the clowns who led people to safety and railed performers and workers as they set up bucket lines to soak the canvas so audience members could escape.

Other crew members carried children – even adults – to safety, while others scooped up scared and crying children and stayed with them until they could be reunited with a family member or loved one.

On the night of the fire, Ringling vice president Jim Haley was arrested and charged with involuntary manslaughter. Four other circus officials joined him behind bars, as did

CIRCUS VICE PRESIDENT, JIM HALEY

Leonard Aylesworth, the man in charge of the canvas tents. He'd left Hartford after the fire and went straight to Chicago, where he met with Robert Ringling. He was arrested and charged when he returned

LEONARD AYLESWORTH, THE EQUIPMENT MAN IN CHARGE OF THE CANVAS TENTS FOR THE SHOW.

to Hartford. The courts also ordered that all circus property be impounded.

In addition to the charges, it became apparent that the legal claims against the circus would be much more than the $500,000 insurance policy it carried. Threats of litigation were already spreading, as well as fines levied against the circus for not having the right equipment to prevent fires, not having the staff to work the equipment if they had it, and even for not having "No Smoking" signs posted in the big top.

The end of the Ringling Brothers and Barnum & Bailey Circus seemed near. And if Ringling went down, it might take the entire American circus world down with it.

But this wasn't the end. It was clear to everyone that unless the circus were allowed to keep operating, none of the claims filed against them would ever be paid.

Some within the Ringling organization argued for declaring bankruptcy, but Edith and Aubrey – through Robert Ringling – forbade it. They vowed to carry on and pay every cent that was owed. The circus posted a $1 million bond and was allowed to travel to Sarasota and reorganize.

Once in their winter quarters, the circus retooled, scraping the blistered paint from the wagons, rebuilding lost props, and setting up new rigging for the wire acts. Everyone pitched in, from the bally girls to the sideshow performers, and soon it was announced that the circus would go back out on the road, but wisely not performing under a big top, even though they brought it back the next season and continued to use it for another decade. For now, though, they planned to play only in open-air arenas and ballparks. They also planned to use all-steel seats in the future, but that plan would not be realized that year. They already had a carload of flameproofing compounds heading their way.

The country's sympathies were with the victims after the fire, including the circus itself. The Ringling front office received truckloads of condolences, including one envelope from a boy in Virginia that had a quarter in it. He suggested they start a fund that was donated by all the boys and girls in America who enjoyed the circus as much as he did. Jim Haley wrote back to him, thanking him and promising they'd be back on the road again soon. He returned the boy's money, saying that he'd be the first person they called if they ran into financial trouble.

Public relations had started as an uphill battle, but now, they were winning. Haley knew that few people could hold a grudge against the circus – it was like hating ice cream, hot dogs, baseball, and apple pie.

The circus was back up and running in August, and the first show was scheduled for Akron, Ohio. They got off to a bad start, however. When the train arrived, the flats with the wagons were facing the wrong way for unloading. That section had to swing 15 miles north to another yard, uncouple the flat cars, and reattach them.

The return to performing came with its critics, notably John Ringling North, who had been sniping from the sidelines and claiming he'd told the company at the beginning of the year that shortages and war regulations made it foolish, if not dangerous, to take the show on the road. He questioned the intelligence of going out now – a position that worried Edward Rogin, the receiver in charge of collecting the money for the legal claimants. If the circus wasn't touring, it wasn't making money, and no one would get paid.

If John took control of the show again, he might let it sit until the war ended. It seemed that Edith and Aubrey would honor their debt to the survivors, but John would play hardball, and he'd already made it clear that the fire wasn't his business.

Robert Ringling accompanied the show to Akron, traveling in his private car. He oversaw the setup from the empty stands, making small talk with the performers. When everything was set, and the fireproof sideshow tent was erected, they rehearsed the entire program – twice – without costumes. The ladies wore bathing suits and shorts, and the clowns performed their antics without makeup.

In the afternoon, May Kovar ran through her routine, and during the rehearsal, a panther swiped at her and tore her baggy shorts. She tapped him with her stick and backed him onto his stand. Outside, 100 spectators pressed against the fence, hoping for a free peek.

The last rehearsal took place under the stars, and when satisfied, Robert sent the troupe to bed around midnight.

The entire circus was prepared for a grand event the following day but didn't get one. The weather for the matinee was threatening, and most didn't want to take a chance of getting wet in the open arena. On top of that, the circus grounds were seven miles from

downtown, and the only bus line that ran by the grounds was reserved for defense workers. Worse, the city was in the middle of a polio outbreak.

A crowd of only about 2,000 people showed up for the daytime show, looking even smaller than that in the wide-open area. The evening show drew about 6,500, but a rain shower ruined the opening. On Saturday, rain stopped the show twice. The show played in a steady drizzle and ended up cutting two numbers. The audience huddled under wet newspapers. In the papers the next day, Robert joked that the show would follow baseball's policy – if they hadn't completed half of the show's 22 parts before it got too wet, you got a rain check. This didn't reassure many people.

The show struggled on through the Midwest. They played 12 days at the University of Detroit stadium next. Opening night sold out, but with temperatures hovering near 100 degrees, the crowds stayed away for the remainder of time. One rainy weeknight only drew 3,500, and for one Saturday matinee, they only sold 1,500 tickets.

John Ringling North smelled blood in the water – but he'd have to wait.

The circus somehow managed to close the 1944 season with a profit and made the first payments toward what would become $4 million in claims against them for the fire. It took six years to get them all paid, but not a single person ever had to sue – all were paid without going to trial.

Late in 1944, the criminal trials of the circus officials took place. Jim Haley was convicted and received a jail sentence of a year and a day, while the others – except for David Blanchfield – received shorter terms.

Blanchfield was the only one of the defendants who had not petitioned the court to receive a suspended sentence because he was "indispensable" to the continued operations of the circus. The judge admired him for this and allowed him to go free.

Those circus officials would be the only people ever charged with a criminal offense connected to the Hartford Fire. In 1950, Robert Segee, a Native American man arrested on arson charges in Ohio, confessed to authorities that he'd set the circus fire. However, the investigation that followed failed to substantiate any of

IN 1950, ROBERT SEGEE WAS ARRESTED ON ARSON CHARGES IN OHIO AND CONFESSED TO STARTING THE HARTFORD CIRCUS FIRE, BUT HIS CONFESSION TURNED OUT TO BE FALSE. HE SPENT THE REST OF HIS LIFE IN A PSYCHIATRIC HOSPITAL.

his claims. Either way, he was in jail for other offenses, and officials ensured he stayed there. When his original prison term was up, the psychiatrist at the Ohio State Reformatory in Mansfield found Segee to be psychotic. He declared him a paranoid schizophrenic, and he was committed to the Lima State Hospital for the Criminally Insane in 1954. He never got out.

THE TRAGEDY OF THE HARTFORD CIRCUS FIRE WAS splashed across the front pages of newspapers all over the country in July 1944. It was the biggest story in the United States that wasn't about the war.

But it was more than just a newspaper story in Hartford and the surrounding area. It was a heartbreaking, earth-shattering event that somehow touched almost every family in the city in one way or another. Flags flew at half-staff for weeks, and the funeral parlors in the city were so overwhelmed that they were forced to hold services at 15-minute intervals for days.

CIRCUS DEAD AT 152; INQUIRIES PUSHED

Officials of the Big Show Face Charges of Fire Hazards—198 Remain in Hospitals

By MEYER BERGER
Special to The New York Times.

HARTFORD, July 7—Hartford and small towns fifty miles round about in this part of the Connecticut River Valley counted their dead from yesterday's circus tent fire at 152 tonight.

Most of the dead are children. Fifteen, still unidentified, were removed from the State Armory during the day. Identification experts arrived tonight to help parents claim these.

They are to be kept, meanwhile, at Hartford Municipal Hospital and other local hospitals. The unclaimed may be buried in a common grave.

Some 193 other victims of the fire, which leveled the Ringling Brothers and Barnum & Bailey circus big-top within six to ten minutes at yesterday's matinee,

The burning of the big top on the afternoon of July 6, 1944, still haunts the people of Hartford even now, all these years later. And residents weren't just haunted by bad memories and physical scars.

In the fire's immediate aftermath, stories spread like wildfire about people who'd had a near-miss that day or had been saved by some eerie happening or strange coincidence. It seemed that for every person inside the tent that day, there were five who were supposed to be there but, for some reason, didn't go. Children took the money their parents had given them to buy circus tickets for their younger siblings and spent it on ice cream, candy, or movie tickets. One woman who was going to take her grandchild but, as they waited for the bus, remembered she'd left the iron on and went home to check. Of course, they missed the bus – and their appointment with death.

One family was on the midway, heading for the big top, when the mother suddenly stopped, bent over, and collapsed on the ground. Something was wrong with her legs, and she couldn't move them. Her husband tried to help her up, but she couldn't stand – her legs just refused to work. He carried her to the car, and they rushed to see the doctor. There seemed to be no cause for the sudden paralysis, but she wouldn't regain the use of her legs for nearly a year.

A young woman from East Hartford took her three-year-old nephew to the circus that day. They stopped at the sideshow on the way to the big top, where the performers had frightened the little boy. She tried to quiet him with ice cream, but the toddler wouldn't stop crying. She finally gave up and took him home. "Saved by Sideshow Freaks," the headline about her blared the next day.

Merely coincidence? Probably, but other stories were much more unnerving.

After buying tickets for herself and her son for the matinee performance, a woman suddenly remembered a dream she'd had the night before. In it, she had seen her dead sister, dressed all in black, seated in the bleachers and watching the show. Then, her sister turned, looked at her, and shook her head from side to side, telling her not to take her seat. Frightened, the woman told her son that she'd changed her mind about the circus, and she returned to the ticket wagon and got her money back while her son protested missing the show. She was convinced the dream saved her life.

A young woman named Anna Cote also had a dream before going to the circus on July 6. She had been sleeping next to her sister Iva when Anna woke up and saw a man standing on the steps leading to her parents' room. Frightened, she scooted closer to Iva as the man stepped toward her and into the light from the window.

The man smiled and spoke. "Don't be afraid," he said, then vanished.

Anna didn't know the man, but when she described the figure to her father the next day, he knew exactly who it was. It was his father, who'd died long before his daughters were born.

IN 1946, THE BARBOUR STREET FAIRGROUND WAS TURNED INTO TEMPORARY HOUSING FOR WORLD WAR II VETERANS

Anna would think about the vision of her dead grandfather later that day when she noticed the fire that was burning under the big top. The sighting of the specter convinced her that she and her sister needed to leave as quickly as they could—which is how Anna and Iva Cote became two survivors of the Hartford Circus Fire.

Stories like these spread through the region in the wake of the fire and were joined by others – ghostly tales about those who died that day and how they'd remained behind at the site of their deaths. Screams and moans were heard sometimes, the stories claimed, as if the dead were experiencing their last moments over and over again.

But such stories were vague and usually unsubstantiated. They were the kinds of legends that have been known to haunt almost any tragic location after a disaster or terrible event occurs. Those weren't all the stories, however. There were others, and they were a little more solid than things that happen "sometimes" or were experienced by "some people." And all those stories revolved around that patch of land used as circus grounds in July 1944.

Two years after the fire, a housing project was constructed at the Barbour Street fairgrounds. It was meant to be a temporary structure that would ease the housing shortage caused by returning war veterans.

The residents of the housing project soon had strange stories to tell about their brand-new homes. They swore the place was haunted. They heard screams, they said, disembodied cries, calls for help, and women and children weeping. Some even claimed they saw apparitions of people who seemed to be smoldering or on fire.

One of the veterans who lived in the development stated that he was unlocking his door one night and saw a young boy run past his apartment. He said the boy left a trail of smoke behind him as though his clothing was on fire.

The man dropped his bag of groceries and ran after the boy, calling for him and trying to help. But when he turned a corner in the direction the boy had run, he was shocked to see no one there.

THE SCHOOL THAT NOW STANDS ON THE GROUNDS WHERE THE HARTFORD FIRE OCCURRED.

Before you think this was a guy who'd spent the afternoon in a local tavern or imagined what he'd seen because he knew about the fire that had occurred two years earlier, you should know that he had only recently moved to Hartford, knew nothing about its history, or was even aware of the fire that had occurred on the site where he now lived.

He'd been a little busy in France during July of 1944.

As planned, the temporary housing project was demolished a few years later and a school was built in its place.

You may – or may not – be surprised to hear strange happenings also began happening at the new school. Students and staff members alike now generally accept that their resident ghosts are victims of the fire who've simply never left the place where they died.

Today, a memorial to the fire victims of July 1944 stands where the Ringling Brothers big top burned to the ground. Some continue to insist that the ghosts remain, refusing to let the fire be forgotten.

They're still here, it's been said, as a reminder or a warning – a warning to all who are parents to never allow what happened to their children to happen to ours.

But, of course, those warnings come much too late. Today's children will never die inside a canvas big top at the circus. The Hartford Fire may not have brought about the death of the circus, as many feared it would, but it was certainly the beginning of the end.

12. WHAT REMAINS FROM THE ASHES

WHILE JIM HALEY WAS DOING HIS SHORT STINT IN PRISON after the fire, he found one visitor on his list that he was surprised to see – John Ringling North. At first, Jim refused to see him but then relented and the two men met in the warden's office. The two men quickly realized they had much in common and much to offer the other, regardless of their past differences. Soon, John was visiting cousin Aubrey's husband often, which is important information to know so you can understand what happened next.

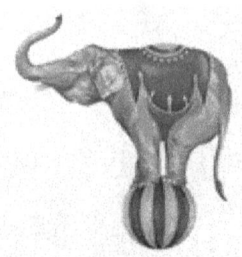

JIM HALEY WITH ONE-TIME NEMESIS, JOHN RINGLING NORTH

All the men serving time for the fire returned to work with the circus. A grand homecoming banquet greeted Jim Haley when he returned to Sarasota, but at that point, he was feeling disgruntled about the show. He'd lost weight in prison and had lost patience with his position within the company. No one had looked out for his interests, and he let Robert and Edith Ringling, as well as the circus attorneys, know how he was feeling. Among themselves, they discussed things and decided that Jim's time behind bars had affected him and that if they wanted, he'd return to being the reasonable man they knew.

He wouldn't – and they underestimated him to their regret.

In April, Jim arrived at the annual stockholder's meeting without Aubrey, who was allegedly sick. Though Edith used her shares to keep Robert as president, Jim used his wife's shares to vote for himself and John Ringling North as vice president. Victorious, Haley, and North didn't wait around to discuss the legality of the situation. They just got up and walked out of the room.

When the season opened at Madison Square Garden, both factions showed up. Edith and Robert had challenged the election in court, but the legal wheels turned very slowly, and the judge wouldn't rule for another year. Until then, they had to stand on the sidelines and watch as Jim and John ran the show for one season.

For the second year in a row, the circus skipped Connecticut. The state had passed such strict fire laws for tent shows that other circuses also stayed away. The only show that ever played in Hartford was the Shrine Circus. While reasonably well attended – and for a worthy cause – many locals stayed away, especially since the show played at the state armory building.

Before the next season was scheduled, the courts finally ruled on the case filed by Edith and Robert. It was decided that Haley had broken the law, so the presidency reverted to Robert. Two weeks later, Jim and John staged another power play and took control, with Jim Haley again as president.

Robert Ringling, never all that strong, soon suffered a stroke, and his health began to fail. Unable to continue his mother's interest, it appeared that Haley and North had finally won.

The problem was that the new president and vice president really didn't get along that well. Their partnership had served both their interests, and while it looked good on paper, it went badly in practice. They argued about basic management issues and, though technically on a lower rung of the ladder, North refused to give in to the less-experienced Haley. Plus, after being in prison, Jim trusted only himself. He was the president, and since his wife owned a larger share of the circus than North did, he was set on doing things his way.

While Jim ran the show, John worked on the other board members. He had recently won an old dereliction of duty case against Robert for $5 million and parlayed this into a compromise with his former enemy that would drop the case. By October, John had replaced Haley as president, and Robert had received the honorary

roles of vice president and chairman of the board. Jim and Aubrey, realizing they'd been beaten, sold their shares and quit the business.

John Ringling North finally owned the majority of the company again. After six long years, the circus was his again.

John was a showman in the style of his uncle or even P.T. Barnum. He was bold, abrasive, and shameless when it came to making money – and keeping it. From that point on, the relationship between Edward Rogin, the receiver in charge of paying the Hartford survivors, and John North would be difficult at best. Everyone did get paid, as we've already established, but it became much harder than needed.

Even so, a week after he took control, John announced that he intended to bring the circus back to Hartford in 1948. It made great press. Local officials welcomed the idea, saying the new fire laws were in place for just that reason.

But the citizens of Hartford weren't quite as understanding.

Despite the new laws, Ringling's innovative metal chairs, and updated safety measures, too many remembered the fire. Widows, parents, family members, and loved ones of the victims protested. They wrote letters and spoke openly. Newspaper editorials were mixed. Some agreed the time wasn't right for them to return, but the responses asked what the proper time would be.

As if to soften the opposition, the show delivered a large payment against the victim claims, and John announced that he was hoping to find a new lot in Hartford for the circus. They were ready to comply with all the new laws. Safety would be their priority.

In the end, though, the circus didn't return to Hartford. They'd tested the waters, and when a circus fan in Plainville said they had a lot they could use at any time, they accepted the offer. That summer, Ringling Brothers played Bridgeport, Waterbury, New London, and Plainville, the smallest town in which the big top had ever played. It sold out. The show returned to Plainville in 1949 for just one day, and it became a tradition. People speculated that they'd try Hartford next year, but John never said anything. He always left them guessing, all the way until the circus played in Plainville for the last time in 1956, after which traveling tent shows became a thing of the past.

Those seasons turned out to be the best post-war summers of the show. Many improvements were made, including a portable grandstand that seated 10,000 and could be erected by a few men in less than an hour.

New acts were added, too, like Unus, the "Upside-down, gravity-defying, equilibristic Wonder of the World." John North had found Unus in a Barcelona nightclub in 1946, where he'd perfected a hand-balancing routine that seemed impossible even to circus veterans. For his finale, he would show audiences nothing funny was going on by taking off his white gloves, showing them to the crowd, and then replacing them. He'd then climb onto a table next to a lamp with no shade but a large, glowing bulb. Unus would then maneuver himself into an upside-down position with only his index finger on the light – and the rest of his body pointed straight up into the air.

THE GRAVITY-DEFYING PERFORMER CALLED "UNUS" WAS ABLE TO AMAZE EVEN CIRCUS VETERANS WITH HIS SKILLS.

Having unfettered control of the family circus was the culmination of a lifelong dream for John, though he quickly began to understand that the show's golden years were in the past. As his brother, Henry, later said, "The end was written plain in our ledgers for years before it came. But we were deliberately blind."

It was just as complicated to run the circs as it had been a few decades earlier, but now it was complex in multiple ways that the Ringlings of the past had never envisioned. There were railroad operations, moving 67,000 tons of equipment and crew over 20,000 miles each year; dining operations that served about 900,000 meals each year; housing operations, which meant providing sleeping arrangements for 1,300 people in hundreds of locations over eight months; construction operations, requiring putting up and taking

down a small tented city every day; and then the entertainment business itself, which was the only one that produced an income. As costs rose over time, it became more and more difficult to end the season with a profit.

In 1929, the circus had netted $1 million from sales of $2.5 million. By 1955, sales had risen to $5 million, but the tally of costs had increased to $6 million. The circus was still paying off the Hartford victims through Edward Rogin, although he had helped them to achieve a one-off windfall. He had helped the company negotiate the dramatic rights for Cecil B. DeMille's film *The Greatest Show on Earth*, much of which was shot at the winter quarters in Sarasota. The movie grossed $20 million and won an Oscar for Best Picture.

The bad news was that while the circus was preoccupied with the movie, Gargantua, the gorilla died of pneumonia complicated by a kidney disorder and rotten wisdom teeth. Circus folks said he was a trouper to the end, holding on until the season was over.

Right after Christmas, animal trainer May Kovar was rehearsing at a wild animal farm in California. She'd left Ringling and gone out on her own, but things hadn't panned out, and she was hoping to go back to the circus with a new lion act, hoping it would solve her money troubles. Her three children were there that day, tagging along with her on what had promised to be a slow day.

IN 1955, RINGLING BROTHERS BIG CAT TRAINER MAY KOVAR WAS KILLED BY ONE OF HER LIONS – REINFORCING JOHN RINGLING'S OPINION THAT ANIMAL SHOWS WERE TOO DANGEROUS FOR THE CIRCUS.

May stepped into the cage with her stick. Outside, her grown son slid a steel door open to let in the first lion, named Sultan. It had been raining for three days, and he'd been locked up in his cage without much exercise.

And maybe that was why he rushed at May the way he did. He charged and knocked her to the ground with his paws, then closed his teeth around her throat and dragged her to the corner of the cage.

May's oldest son and her daughter ran into the cage and beat the lion with sticks but couldn't get him away from his prey. Another trainer rushed over from the elephant barn with a pitchfork and an iron pipe. He stabbed at the lion, and when it turned on him, he hit it between the eyes with the pipe. Sultan tipped back on his hind legs, stunned long enough to drag May out of the cage.

But it was too late. She was dead.

Her neck was broken, probably by the first blow.

And then, on the day after New Year's, Robert Ringling collapsed from a massive stroke and died. He was only 52. His obituary listed him as both the head of the show and an opera singer, but one line really

told the whole story: "His close associates said he never cared much for circus life."

But the show, of course, would go on.

THE NEXT SEASON KICKED OFF WITH A BANG AT MADISON Square Garden when Marilyn Monroe rode a pink elephant around the concourse for the opening spectacle. The receipts from the New York run and the movie money were enough to get them through the year.

But in 1956, even with 200 tons of "Ponderous, Performing Pachyderms" and acts like Pinito del Oro reading a newspaper while balanced on top of her head on a whizzing trapeze bar with no net below, the show was in the red by a million bucks on July 15, only halfway through the season.

"This is the end," John wrote in a telegram from Pittsburgh to his brother, Henry, on the evening of July 16, 1956.

That night, the circus gave a performance like no other in front of 10,000 adoring fans, and at 11:15 P.M., with the performers in their dressing quarters and the animals and elephants returned to their tents, the canvas big top of the Greatest Show on Earth was taken down for the final time.

JOHN NORTH RETURNED WITH THE CIRCUS TO SARASOTA, where it was sadly disbanded. For a time, he brooded and pondered a future that didn't have the circus in it, but he couldn't. He did, however, think of a letter he'd received the previous winter from a rock-n-roll promoter who correctly predicted the days of the circus as they knew it was at an end. He had some ideas that he believed could revitalize the circus business, which he wanted to discuss. John had politely brushed him off at the time but now, he was seeing things differently. He picked up the phone and made a call to Irving Feld.

Feld's background was very different from that of the Ringling family. He'd only really ever had one brush with show business back in his early years, when he and his brother had traveled the carnival circuit selling snake oil. In 1939, tired of the itinerant life, he'd borrowed $1,000 and opened a variety store in an African American neighborhood in Washington, D.C. Soon after, he was convinced to turn the place into a drugstore and lunch counter, opening the first integrated place of that kind in the city. Feld, always looking forward, thought he could make money with a record department, and soon, that part of the company turned into a chain of music stores and even his own recording label.

Before long, he was packaging tours for performers like Chubby Checker, Bill Haley & the Comets, Fats Domino, Buddy Holly, The Everly Brothers, Frankie Avalon, and others, including Paul Anka, whom he also represented as his personal manager. As he booked and routed his team of musicians, Feld picked up information that would prove to be as invaluable as John Ringling's in-depth knowledge of the American railroad system had been – an intimate knowledge of every city in the U.S. and Canada where there were large, beautiful, air-conditioned and heated indoor auditoriums where big shows could perform.

As he explained to John North, the circus could keep going, but in arenas like Madison Square Garden and the Cow Palace in San Francisco. They'd played in places like that before, but now, they confine the circus to those kinds of locations only. They'd not need to move tents or hire labor to erect them. And there'd be no more menageries, no sideshows, no cooking operations, and no hotel and travel headaches – the performers would receive travel and per diem allowances and make it to the next venue on their own. In this way, daily expenses could be cut from $25,000 to $10,000, the number of employees cut from 1,400 to 300, and the show itself would remain untouched.

In days gone by, it had been easy to find a vacant lot for a circus to set up, but those days were gone. There were more than 150 cities in the country with usable arenas, all easily accessible and plenty of parking. Every show would be indoors, which meant the circus no longer had to sit idle all winter. It could play all year round!

Feld presented John with a simple deal – Feld would book and advertise the circus and pay the venue rent. In return, the circus would pay him a fixed percentage of the gross receipts. Even though he doubted that Feld could pull off all he claimed, John saw no other reasonable option, and the deal was signed and sealed.

In 1957, the circus season began without a single railroad show in operation. The elephant corps for the Ringling Brothers and Barnum & Bailey Circus was reduced from 55 to 20 and traveled with the other train animals in baggage cars leased from the railroads. The rigging, costumes, and other necessary items were moved in trucks. Most of the personnel, including the performers, were in charge of their own travel.

In terms of the quality of the show itself, it may not have been the Greatest Show on Earth anymore, but it was at least the best circus still managing to operate. Emmett Kelly left that year to become the mascot for the Brooklyn Dodgers, but many other popular acts stayed, and new acts were recruited, like Gallan Dawn, who balanced on her head on a trapeze bar while spinning hoops on her arms and legs. There were also more clowns added, as well as a chimpanzee animal act.

Feld jockeyed at the last minute for choice arena dates, which meant the show had to crisscross the country several times as a result. Despite this, the 1957 season, which was 46 weeks long, actually made a profit, which wasn't bad since it had lost $2.5 million in the two previous years.

But the Ringling show and the circus industry, in general, had finally found itself up against a force that it couldn't beat – television. Many TV hosts, like Ed Sullivan, featured circus acts and even clowns on their shows each week for free. You could also get closer to sea creatures, lions, and tigers than at the circus by watching TV shows like *Sea Hunt*, *Flipper*, or *Disney*. So, why would audiences leave the comfort of their couches to go to the circus?

During this period, sponsored shows became popular, with charitable and civic groups like the Shriners taking over the financial responsibilities of the shows in exchange for a share of the profits. By convincing audiences they were coming out for a good cause, they often convinced them to attend shows they wouldn't have otherwise.

The 1960s were a down period for the entire industry, which did poorly financially and lost several accomplished performers to accidents.

In 1961, the Wallendas first perfected their seven-person pyramid, but the act didn't last long. On January 30, 1962, as the group carried

IN 1978, KARL WALLENDA – STILL PERFORMING IN HIS 70'S – FELL TO HIS DEATH FROM A 12-STORY TIGHTROPE IN PUERTO RICO.

out the maneuver at a Shriner's Circus in Detroit, Dieter Schepp, a nephew of Karl's who was appearing for the first time, lost his balance. The pyramid crumbled, and Karl managed to snatch his niece, Jana, by the arms, but three others fell to the concrete 40 feet below. Two died, including Dieter, and Mario Wallenda was paralyzed from the waist down.

The seven-person pyramid was never used again but Karl continued performing into his seventies. Then, on March 22, 1978, as he was walking a wire strung 12 stories above a plaza in San Juan, Puerto Rico, he lost his footing and plunged 100 feet to his death in a parking lot below.

Along with a general decline in talent, and even though the new network of arenas made things problem-free and available year-round, competition from smaller shows made it difficult for the bigger shows to plan out a long, efficient, and profitable route.

Back in 1958, Henry Ringling North retired from the circus, but John remained in charge until he realized that his uncle's oil business and property assets in Sarasota were making more money than the circus. He moved to Switzerland in 1962, and his absence saw the show steadily decline. By 1966, fewer than a dozen acts were left on the program, and the "Greatest Show on Earth" really wasn't all that great anymore.

Irving Feld, who'd grown to love the circus over the past few years, refused to let things continue to fall apart. He began

ONE OF THE GREATEST STARS OF THE RINGLING BROTHERS CIRCUS FROM THE 1970S AND 80S WAS ANIMAL TRAINER, GUNTHER GEBEL-WILLIAMS, A FLAMBOYANT PERFORMER WHO NEVER USED WHIPS OR CHAIRS, LIKE ANIMAL TAMERS OF THE PAST.

negotiating with the Ringlings to buy the circus but soon ran into a wall – John demanded $7.5 million for the operation and refused to carry a note on even a penny of it. It was a cash deal or nothing.

Feld found the necessary backing for the purchase from Judge Roy Hofheinz, builder of the Astrodome in Houston, and an elaborate ceremony was held to mark the occasion, where Feld's daughter presented him with a lion cub.

The show slowly began to regain its former status, with one of Feld's early successes being the hiring of legendary German animal trainer Gunther Gebel-Williams, whose talents with tigers, horses, and elephants, along with acrobatics led to his unquestioned status as the circus star of the era. To make the deal happen, Feld had to buy out the trainer's entire enterprise, Circus Williams, for $2 million. In return, though, Ringling audiences could thrill to see Gebel-Williams standing on one end of a teeter-totter, an elephant stomping on the other end, the performer flying through the air, turning a somersault, and landing on the back of a second elephant.

And, of course, that was just for starters. Another showstopper was a tableau he created with two horses, each with a tiger on its back, flanking an elephant with a tiger on its back, and straddled atop that tiger was the grinning Gebel-Williams. His cozy work with the big cats was much different from circus tamers of the past, like Clyde Beatty, who waved around whips and chairs and kept a pistol strapped to their hip.

Another Feld accomplishment was the creation of the Clown College in Venice, Florida, in 1968, which was conceived to provide a steady stream of performers for the circus. About 50 students were chosen from applicants each year to study costuming, makeup, and all the routines a circus clown needed to appeal to audiences. When they graduated, they received a one-year contract with Ringling. The college closed in 1997 when the demand for circus clowns finally hit an all-time low.

One of Feld's most controversial decisions was to form the show into two independent units – "Red" and "Blue." He believed that having two companies to book would make it easier for them to compete for arena dates. However, John North – ignoring that the Ringling Show and the Barnum and Bailey Show had toured separately for a decade after they merged – was outraged by the idea.

"How can there be two Greatest Shows on Earth?" he demanded from Feld. "Which one will be the greatest?"

Feld's reply would have pleased every circus man from John Ringling to James Bailey to P.T. Barnum. "Both," he said.

And Feld was right. Performers and the public alike loved both shows and Feld's marketing savvy, combined with his increased focus on concession and souvenir sales, led the show to even greater profitability, doubling the annual gross and leading to the sale of the circus to toymaker giant Mattel in 1971 for $47 million. Even though most of that was in stock, Feld had increased the worth of the circus by $40 million in just four years.

Mattel planned to use the circus to enhance its toy line, but as things developed, this proved impossible. The circus was just too complicated of an entity for them to understand. In 1982, they sold the show back to the Felds for about half what they paid for it in 1971.

In 1984, Irving Feld died from a stroke, and this left his son, Kenneth, in charge of operations. Though he was not a newcomer to the business – he'd started as a talent scout when his father bought the company in 1967 and was the creator of "Disney on Ice" – the loss of Irving Feld seemed a blow from which the circus could not recover.

Kenneth carried on, though, introducing an in-house service for making sets and costumes and even retrofitting some of the old circus train cars for use as show cars. In 1995, he directed the formation of the Center for Elephant Conservation on 200 acres of farmland in Polk City, Florida. That center, still in operation and home to about 40 elephants, was described as a gathering place for elephant behavior and conservation.

However, as well-intentioned as it might have been, the conservation center idea was not enough to save the circus elephant. In 2000, the ASPCA filed suit against Ringling Brothers for the alleged mistreatment of animals, citing undue restraint and deficiencies in health care. The suit dragged on through the courts until 2009, when it was dismissed on the grounds that the ASPCA lacked standing to bring the action. They were directed to repay Feld Entertainment $9.3 million in compensatory damages. Feld Entertainment continued its pursuit of legal fees from other organizations that had joined the suit and, in 1014, was awarded another $1.75 million from the Humane Society of the United States, the Animal Welfare Institute, the Fund for Animals, Born Free USA, and other nonprofit animal rights groups.

But this didn't stop the complaints and bad press. Other groups lined up against Ringling, protesting the use of wild and endangered species as amusement attractions. According to these activists, it didn't matter if elephants, lions, or tigers were mistreated or not. They were still suffering the rigors of circus life, which kept them confined, prevented them from socializing and moving about freely, and forced them into a life against their instincts and natures. PETA (People for the Ethical Treatment of Animals) called the circus "The Saddest Show on Earth."

No matter how well Ringling Brothers treated their elephants, there was no way to win against what was really just manufactured public outrage. In response to the growing criticism, Kenneth Feld -- along with daughters Nicole and Alana, now part of the business – announced in March 2015 that they would remove all elephants from the show. The decision was not an easy one, Kenneth said, but it was made "in the best interest of our company, our elephants, and our customers."

It turned out that wouldn't be the case.

Reaction from the animal rights groups was mostly positive, although they still complained when Kenneth announced it would take three years for them to phase out the use of the elephants. They needed time to expand the Polk City facility for the new arrivals, where costs to care for each of the animals added up to around $65,000 per year.

As it turned out, the last day for the elephants came on May 1, 2016, in Providence, Rhode Island, where six elephants danced, sat on their hind legs, and stood in line with their forelegs on one another's backs. Ringmaster Jonathan Lee Iverson thanked the elephants for more than 100 years of service to the show. "Thank you so much for so many years of joy!" he called out.

Things may have turned out well for the elephants, but they certainly did not for Ringling Brothers. The retirement of the elephants effectively ended the big business of the American circus.

The Felds had already been facing a daunting number of challenges – rising costs, the internet, railroad limitations, restrictive animal laws, a fading interest in the circus, and regulations from a

THE END CAME FOR THE RINGLING BROTHERS AND BARNUM & BAILEY CIRCUS CAME WITH THE RETIREMENT OF THE ELEPHANT HERD IN 2017.

IT'S NOT A CIRCUS WITHOUT THE ELEPHANTS.

government that no longer saw the circus as the answer to raising America's morale.

But, of course, these new challenges were just as threatening as those faced by the Ringling brothers themselves more than a century before – competition with other circuses, vaudeville, moving pictures, World War I, the Great Depression – and by their family members in the years that followed, which included union activity, World War II, suburban development, and television.

But there's one thing that I will always maintain was an advantage for the circus of the early 1900s that the modern circus of the Feld family no longer had – elephants.

It's not a circus without elephants, and no one will ever change my mind about that.

THE GREATEST SHOW ON EARTH TOOK ITS FINAL BOW ON December 21, 2017, but that was not the end of the circus itself. There are some small traditional shows still out there. They're nothing like the shows that toured the country during the heyday of the business, but at least they're still making the effort.

Most shows that call themselves a "circus" these days, though, are usually live music, dance, and acrobatics. Even the Ringling Brothers and Barnum & Bailey Circus returned in 2023 and began offering these kinds of performances, without animals, of course.

There is unlikely to ever be anything like the Greatest Show on Earth, as it was in its prime, ever again. John Ringling may have won a long, hard-fought battle to preserve the circus, but even he could not beat the passage of time. Eventually, the world would win, and the circus, as we'd once known it, was gone.

In the rise and fall of the American circus, we can see a lot of what made the circus truly an American creation. We didn't invent it. We'll credit the Romans with that or the British, who introduced horse shows. However, it was the Americans who took horses, acrobats, juggling acts, and animals and combined them with Barnum-esque elements of spectacle, oddity, and danger to make something new.

And eventually, they added elephants.

John Ringling was right when he said that the circus appealed to children as well as to the child in every person. He was also right when he claimed that the shadow of death stalked the wire walker, the high-flying acrobat, and the animal tamer. But those things combined created a sense of wonder that the ordinary limits of human capability could be transcended, even to the extent of cheating death. And then a few clowns were mixed in to remind us not to take any of it too seriously.

The glory days of the American circus are over, no matter how badly some of us don't want that to be the case. Today, a few small circuses survive, shadows of what they once were. The big shows are gone – but they're not forgotten.

They left their history, legends, and sometimes, even their ghosts behind.

PART TWO:
STEP RIGHT UP!
ALTHOUGH YOU'VE ALREADY MISSED IT!

THE AMERICAN SIDESHOW

INTRODUCTION (AGAIN)

THE BUSINESS OF EXHIBITING FREAKS AND ODDITIES in America has ridden a rollercoaster of popular interest - positive and negative - since the sideshow's modest beginnings in wagons and small tents that followed behind the early menageries and circuses. After the Civil War, the circus business grew quickly, especially after W. C. Coup figured out a way to transport the shows by railroad.

Not only did circuses expand into huge traveling enterprises, but the sideshows accompanying them began to be recognized as moneymakers who deserved their prominent spots on the show grounds. They had their own musicians and their own employees - talkers, ticket sellers, doormen, working acts, dancing girls, tent workers, concession sellers, and, of course, the performers themselves - the freaks, if you will.

The sideshow may have started with the circus, but it would eventually become synonymous with the carnival midway, a concept created by the 1893 World's Columbian Exposition in Chicago.

The first touring midway companies that emerged after the World's Fair had no rides, only shows. The shows were independently owned and operated by showmen who'd been visiting fairs on their own with various attractions for a decade or two already. Some banded together to share baggage car space - and perhaps a bottle of whiskey - on the way to the same venues. Their complaints of being treated unfairly at many fairs made a collective organization a welcome idea, so by the early 1900s, several dozen large midway

companies were traveling the country. There were also probably twice as many carnival operators playing fairs and local celebrations.

Showmen with individual attractions such as an illusion show, snake eater, or stuffed alligator could book with one midway company for a whole season. The midway owner played a pre-booked route and took care of licenses, electricity, water, and, in some cases, transportation in exchange for a percentage of the attraction's ticket sales.

Other showmen preferred to hopscotch their show ride, which meant going from one carnival company to another. A fraternity of showmen grew, and carnies, regardless of what kind of show they operated or where they went, always stuck together.

Competition was fierce, but many independent showmen continued to find value in banding together. Soon, they offered midway patrons 10 acts under a long, skinny tent for one low admission price. The 10-In-One became a carnival mainstay, just like the merry-go-round and cotton candy.

The showmen brought their skills – learned from working in vaudeville theaters, dime museums, circuses, medicine shows, and lantern slide presentations – into the new midway business. The first touring carnival companies were a melting pot of comedy acts, jugglers, acrobats, Wild West shows, glassblowers, minstrel shows, illusions, mind-reading acts, snake eaters, and hundreds of dead, stuffed pickled, embalmed, and mummified monstrosities, both human and animal. The art of the showman depended on the skill of the pitchman on the midway. Patrons rarely left a show without being talked into a special after-show or handing over some cash for a postcard, photo, or souvenir.

You never knew what you might find on the midway at the fair. Monkeys were driving little cars around a steel speedway, but those might seem tame next to jars of deformed babies or walk-through shows of embalmed gangsters and wax figures enduring the tortures of the Spanish Inquisition. Attractions were framed around any subject or curiosity the showmen believed would make money. And whether they were real or fake, they were always entertaining.

At a nickel-a-look or a dime for a laugh, how could you complain if the horse advertised with his head where his tail should be turned out to be just a horse turned backward in his stall?

Or that the "World's Smallest Woman" wasn't really that small?

Can you blame the showman if you were surprised at seeing a pickled punk in a jar after purchasing a ticket based on a banner depicting a two-headed baby on a rocking horse billed as "Real!" or "Alive, Alive, Alive!"?

But just as time doomed the circus, it would eventually come for the carnival midway, too.

Until World War I, the merry-go-round and Ferris Wheel were the main rides on the midway. After the war, new rides were designed and the business of building them boomed. New rides debuted almost every season. The baby boom of the late 1940s created a demand for kiddie rides, and every midway started featuring scaled-down versions of the main rides, including cars and boats that went around in circles and games aimed at junior patrons.

Those kids grew up wanting better, bigger, and faster rides, and eventually, high-capacity rides would dominate the carnival business—not only on the midway but also in the amusement parks.

But it was food that showed the biggest growth for the carnivals. Midways once had a grab joint or cookhouse and probably some ice cream, popcorn, hot dog, and candy apple stands. Today, food joints outnumber the games at most fairs, where you can get donuts, corn dogs, French fries, cheese on a stick, exotic meats, and every kind of fried food imaginable. Food joints changed from humble wooden stands to state-  of-the-art mobile kitchens, offering something cleaner and slicker but not quite the same as we remember.

Over the years, every aspect of the carnival business has expanded – except for the shows. Into the 1960s, patrons at fairs, both small and large, could expect to see a variety of back-end shows at every carnival.

People still flocked to see the human oddities and some of the wilder shows, but that wouldn't last forever. Just as animal rights groups ended the circus, public opinion would bring the freak shows to an end. A few held on into the 1990s – and even longer in some cases – but shows began to be packaged around illusions, freak animals, and curios in cases. By the turn of this century, the showmen who sold glances at tiny women, headless ladies, midget horses, and pickled babies in small trailers and tents had largely vanished for good.

In the final years of such shows, the pitchmen who presented the ballyhoo – the free peek at the entertainment offered inside the tent – started using the line, "See it now or miss it forever."

Truer words were never spoken.

And yet, our desire to see the "freak show" has never really gone away. We are still a country of gawkers. There's no shortage of a different kind of "freak" in our popular culture. Reality television and talk shows constantly bring the damaged lives of those looking for

their 15 minutes of fame into our living rooms daily. For all the so-called "normal" folks, the sideshow has never really gone away.

If you're like me and grew up in the fading years of the carnival sideshows, it's possible that your parents dragged you past the sideshow and its lurid banners as you were hurried on to the state fair grandstand to see the latest country singer, the demolition derby, or a tractor pull.

If that happened to you, I'm sorry. You missed out on something really great, and I hate to tell you – we're never going to get that back.

I want to think that somewhere out there, on some dusty fairground in the middle of nowhere, there are still a few midget horses, some two-headed cows, a couple of rubber aliens, a handful of deformed babies, and a girl-becoming-a-gorilla but there probably isn't.

So, think of this as your chance to see what you missed. Step right up – you may have missed it, but there are still wonders for you to behold.

13. BEFORE THE MIDWAY

JUST AS THE ROOTS OF THE AMERICAN CIRCUS CAN BE FOUND in Europe, so can the roots of the sideshow. As far back as the seventeenth century, kings and queens shared an interest with all classes of people in dwarves, giants, scaly men, and other oddities of nature. Visits to see the lions at the Tower of London in 1692 included a side trip to view a two-legged dog. The first settlers on American shores brought their fascinations with them.

England's famed St. Bartholomew Fair, which ran for more than 700 years, featured rarities like a mother and daughter with three breasts, a baby with four arms, a child with three legs and 16 toes, a pig-faced woman, a living skeleton, a lot of giants, fat men and women, and a man with one body but two heads. Such displays consistently opened the pocketbooks of the public, and at least one tradition of the midway was established by the Fair – that, dead or alive, anything with two heads was always better than one.

It was also established that the art of showing something for profit needed to start with "the story" – the tale that would entice the audience member to pay his money and enter the tent where the showman's attraction is hidden away from those who don't pay. While a street performer might offer a show and pass a hat around, the showman was careful to keep his show out of sight, where you were only allowed to see it if you paid the toll. So, the showman's spiel was the most important tool for getting the customer inside.

Making a racket with a trumpet or drum was the best way of pulling a crowd to a booth. By the 1700s, British fairs tried to license

THE "BALLY" STAGE IN FRONT OF THE ATTRACTION WAS WHERE THE TALKER TOLD HIS STORIES AND LURED THE CUSTOMERS INTO THE TENT.

showmen's use of horns and drums. The management of the 1893 Chicago World's Fair – where the word "ballyhoo" was coined – banned talkers and outside demonstrations because of the noise. Pitchmen then switched to another method – scantily-clad dancing girls giving "come in" waves in a doorway to the crowd, hoping that would fill their shows.

But mostly, it was about the talk, the patter, the spiel. In America, a portable stage set up outside an exhibit tent and in front of banners became known as the "bally stage," and door-talking became a profession. Operators were willing to pay good money to those who could tell the story and pack the spaces behind the tent flap. The authentic oddities needed little selling, but the gaffs – or hoaxes – needed a smooth man on the ballyhoo who could draw people inside using suggestive and evasive words.

In that way, the talker became one of the most important people around midway shows. Most were paid 10 percent of the door, and the good ones were never out of work.

The outside display of painted images on canvas that offered a *very* loose depiction of what was inside the tent was a necessity in the early days. Most customers then couldn't read, so letter signage was wasted on them. Pictorial banners were the midway showman's best form of advertising, and he could point to the images to reinforce his spiel.

However, American show business was slow in getting started. Those who crossed the Atlantic to the New World may have brought their interests in the odd and unusual with them, but the Puritans stalled any kind of fair where they could be seen. They'd fled England because of religious persecution, only to come to America and become persecutors themselves. It would be decades before fairs and shows became commonplace, and once they did, showmen framed their acts to appeal to women and children, keeping things tame to bring in a wider audience and not run afoul of the authorities. It would be many years before most states or communities would allow circuses and fairs to operate on Sundays.

In 1804, it seemed that pig-faced women were all the rage when it came to wholesome entertainment, but when they turned out to be bears with shaven faces, the public rebelled against such vulgar shows. They demanded moral entertainment, and even when showmen couldn't give it to them, they conned them into thinking they could. In 1860, Van Amburgh's menagerie was touring New Hampshire and Vermont, and to avoid offending the sensibilities of the area, it was dubbed "Van Amburgh's Great Moral Exhibition of Pious and Well-Disposed Animals." The show met with everyone's approval.

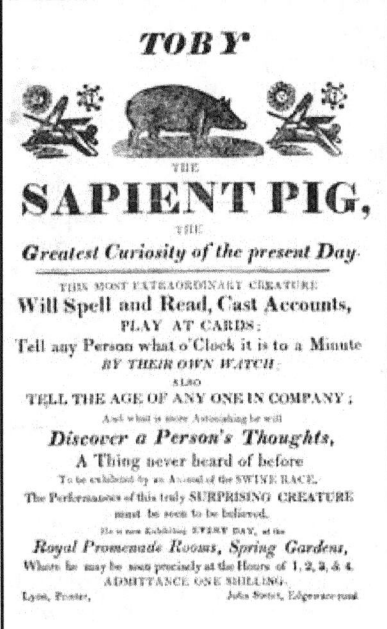

"LEARNED PIGS" WERE ALL THE RAGE IN THE EARLY TRAVELING SHOWS

Animal attractions and horse shows eventually became the circus, but elements of those shows were responsible for the kinds of attractions that would ultimately find their way to the sideshows.

The earliest was the "learned pig" exhibit. One of the routines involved a pig picking out letters laid on the ground and spelling out words, like "pork." And while pigs are smart, they're not that smart. It turns out the act was a simple one. The trainer would cue the animal by changing his breathing or making some small sound, like rubbing his fingers together.

American showman William Pinchbeck began exhibiting his "learned pig" in 1770 and developed practices that many traveling exhibitors would use. He printed handbills stating that his attraction would only be in town for a short time, so those interested should see it immediately. He developed a plan for reserved seating for those desperate for a spot when a venue had limited seating. He also emphasized that his exhibit was "Alive!" and "Real!" – terms that would eventually appear on just about every sideshow banner in the twentieth century.

Pinchbeck and other itinerant American showmen walked from town to town, which wasn't unusual then. They joined the peddlers, preachers, lawyers, and doctors who also traveled on foot. Taverns and inn owners were happy to offer a little space to the showmen, knowing that those who came to see them would buy food and drinks. That meant that by the late 1700s, puppeteers, wax figure exhibitors, along with owners of trained bears, performing dogs, and educated pigs, were showing up on tavern doorsteps and in town squares.

By the early 1800s – in larger cities at least – they were joined by the human oddities, or the "freaks." Natural curiosities like armless and legless men and women, giants, midgets, dwarves, and albino women, as well as man-made wonders like mummies and mermaids, could all be seen for a price.

As we know, P.T. Barnum dominated nineteenth-century America, cashing in on the public craze for oddities. Barnum didn't always travel either – most people came to see him at his American Museum in New York – although he was often on the road at the start of his showman career when he displayed Joice Heth, the supposedly 161-year-old nursemaid of George Washington.

For those showmen who did travel, though, steamboats and stagecoaches made life much easier, allowing them to reach more distant towns and carry a more elaborate show.

Some of the showmen traveling this way were the magic-lantern exhibitors – a kind of primitive slide show – who didn't require much gear and could make a living by performing for a few dozen people in a small space.

Another kind of show was the "Panstereorama" – miniature reproductions of towns, countries, and buildings made of paper, wood, pasteboard, and cork. While this seems like a fragile kind of thing to travel with, the exhibitors were successful. As mentioned earlier, Yankee Robinson started his career exhibiting a model known as the "Raising of Lazarus."

The "peep show" operators weren't what we'd think of today. These machines were among the most popular found on American fairgrounds of the nineteenth century. Customers peered into a lighted box and looked at pictures curated by the showmen to match the area they were traveling through. Viewers could see Presidents like Washington, Lincoln, and Grant, as well as views of the Battle of Gettysburg, the U.S. Capitol, Niagara Falls, the Hudson River, Central Park, and more. The charge for the peep shows ranged from a penny to a nickel, depending on viewing time, and showmen did terrific business, bringing in between $15 and $20 daily from fair patrons.

PEEP SHOWS OF THE NINETEENTH CENTURY ARE NOT WHAT WE THINK OF TODAY. THEY WEREN'T USUALLY RISQUE – AND INSTEAD OFFERED SCENIC AND HISTORICAL VIEWS.

An extension of the peep show was the Panorama, a much larger and more difficult exhibit to move. Touring panoramas were massive images intended to put the viewer right into the action. Many were travel scenes, like great cities or natural wonders, and others depicted historical events. Some of the most popular touring panoramas of the 1850s were The Life of Christ, Dr. Kane's Arctic Expedition, Paris, London, Pilgrim's Progress, Milton's Paradise Lost, Revolutionary War battles, and more.

This doesn't seem all that exciting until you get more details about how they worked. Amos Hubbel, who worked for P.T. Barnum, traveled in Europe with a panorama called The Burning of Moscow. It wasn't just a picture. There were animated and mechanical parts to the show, too. This panorama included moving figures of men, horses, soldiers, and ships, nearly cut from sheet brass and painted to appear lifelike.

But any moving panorama was set with a cog wheel that ran over a strip of felt, which caused the figures to move when hooked on a revolving belt that ran in front of the painted scenery. This

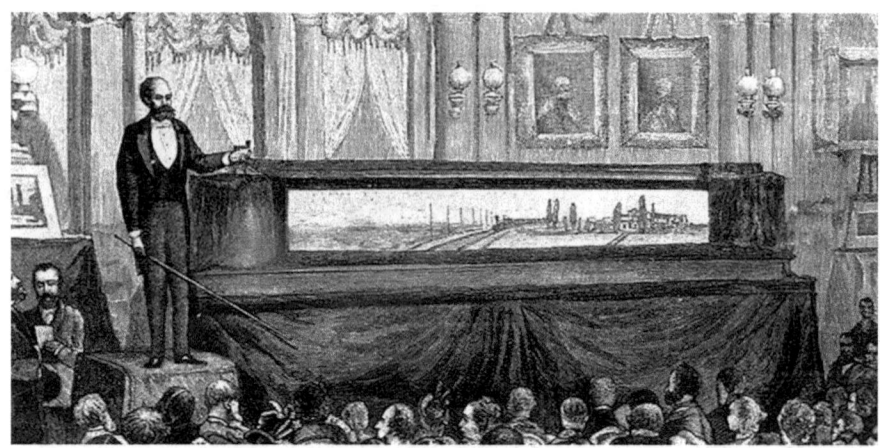

MOVING PANORAMA SHOWS COULD BE SMALLER SET-UPS LIKE THE ONE SHOWN HERE, OR COULD BE LARGE, FILLING AN ENTIRE STAGE.

allowed the showmen to display a town, city, or street scene and have a whole army marching in front of it. The movements of the soldiers, people, horses, and the guns and cannons on forts and ships were so fixed that the operators behind the scenery could puff smoke and create a booming noise with a bass drum. In the days before films and television, these kinds of shows became real crowd-pleasers.

IN THE EARLY DAYS OF AMERICAN FAIRS, IT QUICKLY became obvious to the showmen that people were happy to stare at pretty much anything – and they were glad to hand over money to do it.

They watched animal shows, magicians, ventriloquists, minstrel shows, puppet shows, "spirit manifestations," strongmen, singers, bell ringers, and just about anything else you can imagine – and many things you can't.

But there was nothing people loved to see more than human curiosities and wonders. While some performers, like Chang and Eng, the famous "Siamese Twins," were exhibited as early as 1829 when they first arrived in America, the freak show became popular just before and after the Civil War.

Pitch books – publicity booklets about curiosities on display – printed in the mid-1860s show many sideshows playing in fairs across the country. However, it was the 1880s that ushered in a new period of growth for shows. Circus and other amusement entrepreneurs had worked out the kinks of moving shows around the country by railroad by then. And fairs began boasting flying horses, striking machines, shooting galleries, weighing machines, cider presses, and fruit and popcorn stands. There were educated horses, snakes of all sizes, monkeys, birds, and tigers at even some of the smallest fairs.

Dime museums were also very popular at the time. Between 1880 and 1900, there were hundreds of such museums – at least one in every city with a population of 10,000 or more – usually located in two- or three-story buildings. Customers purchased a ticket and then started on the top floor, where the permanent collections were displayed, and then worked down to where human oddities and other performers were located. Larger museums usually had a theater where admittance to the show was free, but customers were charged a nickel if they wanted to sit down.

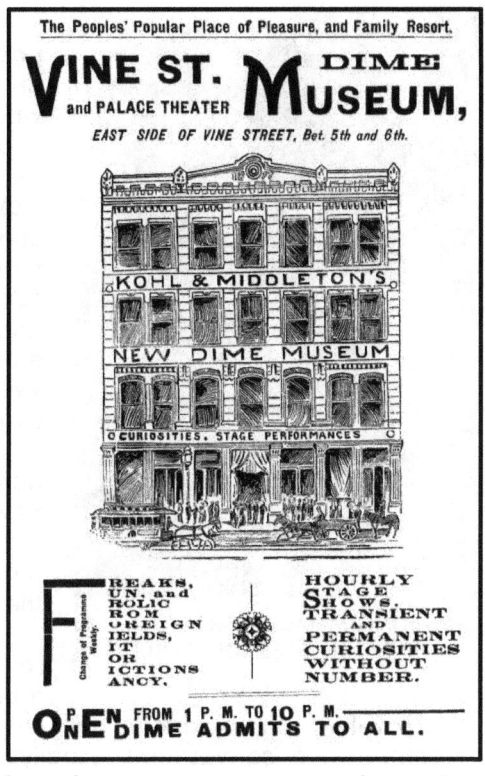

Dime museums would also book special events. In 1887, a craze developed for "Fat Lady Conventions." Managers booked in a half-dozen oversized women and featured them in various contests – like the 50-yard dash in the street outside the museum, which always drew big crowds.

The highlight of Austin and Stone's Museum in Boston in 1888 was the appearance of 12 tattooed men and women who were billed as "The Twelve Martyrs of the Needle." In 1892, Angola the Gorilla was a big draw on the museum circuit. His billing claimed he was the hero of a hard-fought battle in which he killed a bulldog in one minute 50 seconds, winning a $2,000 prize. However, what the chimpanzee – he wasn't actually a gorilla – would do with the cash is unknown. I guess it went into his owner's pocket, along with all the money the exhibit made in the museums.

TRAVELING MEDICINE SHOW WAGON OF THE NINETEENTH CENTURY

Medicine shows were also popular as touring entertainment and a great source for showmen when they wanted to recruit experienced talkers, pitchmen, and performers. Haley and Bigelow's Kickapoo Indian Medicine Show consisted of four men -- a manager who also lectured and sold snake oil, a magician, and two musicians to provide the entertainment. The show did so well that during some seasons, there were as many as 30 versions of the Kickapoo show touring across the country. Next to the newly former vaudeville theater circuits, the Kickapoo show was the biggest employer of variety acts in the 1890s.

For the last three decades or so of the nineteenth century, touring shows that were referred to as "Traveling Combinations" or "Pavilion Shows" became popular. Presented in a canvas tent, usually for a week, the shows offered performances combining a dime museum and a small circus. The tents weren't as large as those for circuses, usually only seating a few hundred. The shows often presented dramatic or comedic theatrical performances as well as sideshow acts, circus acts, illusions, and clowns. Most of their money was made selling candy, drinks, popcorn, jewelry, or through the inevitable fortune-telling concessions.

In time, most of America's touring shows would end up on the fairgrounds scattered across the nation. Others, though, remained with the traveling circuses. Most of those were independently run. They had their own tents, poles, stakes, stages, and ticket wagons.

One of the reasons that most shows ended up on fairgrounds was because the fairs themselves started advertising for support workers like banner painters, tent makers, and others, as well as for entertainment. Showmen began to use ads to look for door talkers, snare drummers, and gaff makers while also advertising their availability on the fair circuit.

Around this same time, the industry – as well as the fairgrounds – began to modernize. Wagons built-to-be show exhibits began to appear, as well as what many referred to as "uptown wagons." These wagons were often used in town to try and get the business of people who didn't come out to the fairgrounds. They would also be set up at circuses to catch the matinee and night crowds. Snakes, midgets, and animal oddities were always good attractions for the uptown wagons.

Before the 1893 World's Fair, there were maybe 50 or more independent fairground shows touring the country. They included W.D. Ament – known as "Mexican Billy – and his Wild West show; Wichita Jack's Wild West Show; C.E. Jordon who toured with his Devil Child, sea turtle, and alligator show; J.A. Jones' Museum Show; Professor E.S. O'Dell's show with a Living Vampire, mind reader, mechanical talking figure, half lady, and a midget; F.R. Blitz with his famous attraction Millie-Christine; and others.

This was around the time when showmen realized they'd reached the heights of success because show owners and fairs were directly advertised for their services and attractions in the trade papers of the day.

In the early 1900s, there were frequent ads seeking the shows of Mexican Billy, Wichita Jack, and others, but in greatest demand was Frank R. Blitz. He and his wife, Louise – who show people called Aunt Louise – were fairground show pioneers. Frank was the son of a famous musician, Signor Blitz, and had been on fairgrounds with museum-type shows since the 1870s. He and Louise knew every museum manager, sideshow exhibitor, and place in America where curiosities could be displayed for profit.

In 1878, Frank became the road manager for Millie-Christine, regarded as one of the greatest living oddities in the country. Billed as the "Famous Carolina Twins," the "Two-Headed Nightingale," and the "Double-Tongued Nightingale," Millie and Christine McCoy were African

MILLIE-CHRISTINE, THE "FAMOUS CAROLINA TWINS"

American conjoined twins born near Whiteville, North Carolina, in 1851 to enslaved parents on a plantation owned by Alexander McCoy.

The twins, who weighed 17 pounds at birth, had separate upper and lower bodies and were joined at the waist and pelvis. Although they were two separate women, they preferred to be thought of as one—or so everyone who managed them claimed.

McCoy quickly got fed up with gawkers coming to his farm and sold the girls to a man named Baxter, who wanted to exhibit them. He paid $10,000 for the twins with a note backed by a local businessman named Joseph P. Smith.

This was a time, of course, when Southern whites could legally own black people, so the girls had no choice about the direction their lives would take.

In 1853, Millie-Christine were a sensation at North Carolina's first state fair. Baxter knew he had a gold mine on his hands, and while in New Orleans, he tried to trade them for some land in Texas. Unfortunately, it turned out there was no land – Baxter had been conned. He didn't have the money to pay back Smith, and he didn't have the twins either.

Back in North Carolina, Smith paid McCoy the money owed on the debt and hired detectives to find the twins. The detective traced them to New York and found a cab driver who had driven them to the docks to catch a ship bound for Liverpool. Smith and the twins' mother sailed for England and found the girls being exhibited.

After that, Smith's wife became the twins' guardian, home-educated them, and helped Millie-Christine become skilled dancers and excellent singers. Smith died in 1860, and his son, Pearson, was given the twins in his father's will. Because of the conflict in America during the Civil War, he took the twins to Europe, and they toured the continent for years. When they returned to the United States in 1878, the girls – now on their own – hired Frank Blitz as their manager.

Over the next 27 years, he exhibited Millie-Christine as part of Blitz's Mammoth Museum, which he claimed was the largest museum tour in the country. In 1899, he booked Millie-Christine with Gaskin's Canton Carnival Co., one of the first organized carnival companies, but he preferred to book the girls independently for fairs. He felt that Millie-Christine didn't belong on the midway because there were so many fake attractions on the fairgrounds, and he feared fairgoers would assume the girls weren't authentic.

By 1909, Millie-Christine had retired from show business and bought a farm in North Carolina. They died – one day apart – in 1912.

Meanwhile, Frank stayed in the business and now sought bookings for a little person he dubbed the "Russian Prince." In the ads, the prince is shown being held in the palm of Frank's hand, with claims that the prince could generate more money in an hour than similar acts could make in a week. The Russian Prince sang, danced, built houses, bought government bonds, and entertained President Taft at the White House.

He'd also turn out to be Frank's last promotional act. Blitz died at the end of the 1910 season at the age of 57.

ONE OF THE REAL CHARACTERS OF THE FAIRGROUND CIRCUIT was W.D. Ament, who billed himself as Mexican Billy. In August 1891, he opened his 16-week fairground tour in Homer, Illinois, traveling with his massive California tent.

His Wild West show was the largest and most entertaining of its kind and was the only show selected by the Illinois State Fair out of 50 applications. The show included magicians, cowgirl singers and dancers, a tribe of Native Americans, and cowboy musical artists, with Billy himself offering sharpshooter demonstrations.

In March 1892, Mexican Billy toured west of the Mississippi for the first time, and while out in the actual "Wild West," he advertised for recruits for the show and used some genuine cowboys to break show records the following season. In 1893, he advertised himself as a "world's champion fancy rifle shot and musical artist" and promoted his wife, Princess Nanna, as a gifted mind-reader.

Billy took his show to the Midway at the Chicago World's Fair and then moved on to the California Mid-Winter Fair later that year. By 1900, he was offering Captain W.D. Ament's Vaudeville Circus, which was a combination of a circus and sideshow.

He also put the first ghost shows on the American Midway, starting in 1901. Later that same year, he also added a "Plantation" minstrel show to his tour – which, yes, is as bad as it sounds. Oddly, while the racist show was popular during that period, Billy didn't offer it for long. In 1903, he returned to offering only the ghost show – a dramatized version of a Spiritualist séance – and then, in 1909, in a complete reverse from a minstrel show, he built a theater for black audiences only in Jackson, Tennessee.

After his ghost show and carnival days, Billy ended up on the west coast. In 1922, he worked with the Foley and Burk Shows, running a large combination illusion and freak show and offering several illusions still used today, like "Sawing-A-Lady-in-Half" and "Spidora."

THE SPIDORA ILLUSION SHOW LOOKED AS SILLY IN PERSON AS IT LOOKS HERE BUT CROWDS LOVED IT ANYWAY.

Sawing a woman in half is self-explanatory, but "Spidora" was a nickname for an illusion created by a young woman's head appearing atop the body of a massive spider. "Step right up and meet Spidora, the Spider-Girl," the talker would announce to fairgoers. "Born with the head and face of a beautiful girl and the body of an ugly spider, she survives in total misery, for no man could love her."

He'd go on to explain that she lived off her earnings as a sideshow freak, eating flies and other insects – although, of course, it was just a pretty girl putting her head through an opening in black cloth, making it appear that her head was on the body of the spider. The "Spider-Girl" was proof that human beings love to be fooled - even when confronted with one of the most obvious illusions of all time.

The only thing that ever went wrong was when even some of the most gullible spectators recognized the same girl's head atop other exotic creatures, like the "Human Butterfly" or the "Snake Girl."

Billy put his show up for sale the following year, ending his long career in the carnival show world.

WHILE MEXICAN BILLY WAS ONE OF THE MOST POPULAR promoters who worked the fairgrounds circuit, J. Augustus Jones was the man who more or less wrote the book on small, two or three-car circuses. Before that, however, he started as a fairgrounds' showman. The first mention of him in the trades was in 1892 when he ran an advertisement seeking human oddities: a strong man, a fat lady, a glassblower, a woman with snakes, and curiosities of all kinds. Working out of Warren, Pennsylvania, he opened his first show in Ohio and traveled as far south that season as Virginia.

By 1894, he was running a regular show that consisted of three small animal cages, a den of snakes, and Jocko, the performing monkey. By 1895, he was promoting a "mermaid" and getting involved in the circus business.

His operation steadily grew over the next several years, and by 1910, he was running a circus that traveled on three flat cars. Within a few years, though, he was apparently in fear for his life.

Around 1915, the carnival business struggled to clean up the grift that followed their shows. Trade papers printed letters from people describing the con games they had witnessed – and there were a lot of them. After several letters appeared with complaints about his shows, Jones wrote his own letter claiming that he had no grifters on his show, and if he found out that he did – they'd be tossed off the train or thrashed to within an inch of their lives.

A short time after the letter was printed, word spread that Jones had reinforced the walls of his stateroom in the sleeping car with two inches of bullet-proof steel.

JONES WAS NOT THE ONLY CIRCUS MAN WHO GOT HIS start on the midway – many circus men decided the fairgrounds circuit was a better way to stay out of debt.

Many discovered that after going out on tour with a circus, they would have to buy things to keep up with the competition. They purchased more horses, elephants, exotic animals, and railroad cars – all to make more money. But expenses climbed with every purchase, and once what was going out began to exceed what was coming in, a showman could quickly find himself underwater. Many showmen stopped leasing out their concert, sideshow, and concession privileges and just hired managers, trying to grab a bigger cut of the money generated by these extras, but usually, that wasn't enough.

This caused many sideshow proprietors to turn to the fairground and carnival circuit. Once there, they also discovered that a one-day license for a circus to perform was more expensive than a license required for a sideshow to stay for a week.

However, there were drawbacks to this plan, as well. In the last years of the nineteenth century, one difference between circus sideshows and fairground sideshows was that few carnival shows featured authentic human oddities. In contrast, at least half the acts featured in circus sideshows were genuine. The circus showman had a limited time to fill a tent before the audience left to get their seats under the big top. Authentic freaks were a big draw, which made things easier for the talkers to turn a high percentage of people on the circus grounds into the sideshow with just one or two openings.

By contrast, the sideshow was exposed to crowds on the fairgrounds from when the fair opened until it closed, operating at a much slower pace. Fairground crowds came to be entertained, and the working and variety acts seemed to satisfy them. But as more and more shows appeared on the fairgrounds, the need for an eye-catching oddity certainly increased.

Some attractions that drew crowds in the 1890s included Congo, an armless performer, and Laloo, a young man with a second body emerging from his stomach. He became so well-known that gaff makers started creating papier-mâché licenses of him that they passed off as the real thing. Another top act was a variation of the "Tank Man" or "Man Fish," which could be any performer who could stay underwater for a long time and do unusual things in a glass tank without surfacing for air. One of the top performers in this field was Enoch, who could stay underwater for up to three and a half minutes while playing the trombone.

But soon, things would change in the carnival and sideshow world.

LITTLE EGYPT, ONE OF THE BIGGEST ATTRACTIONS ON THE MIDWAY AT THE 1893 WORLD'S FAIR IN CHICAGO.

AT THE WORLD'S FAIR IN CHICAGO IN 1893, A CONSTANT refrain from attendees was a question: "Have you seen the Midway?" People everywhere talked about going to the Fair and seeing the midway shows. The Midway was a novelty—the public had never seen so many quality attractions gathered all in one spot with the sole purpose of entertaining them. The unique ways of presenting the different shows were so intriguing to the public that even old shows seemed new. The cooch dancers, who once appeared in every sideshow and carnival girl show, were now called World's Fair Dancers. The public devoured the stories of the famous – and infamous – belly dancer Little Egypt, who had come to the fair from the exotic East, or so her publicity claimed. In truth, the scandalous dancer, Fatima Spyropoulos, was the wife of a Chicago businessman and restaurant owner.

But the crowds who came to the "Streets of Cairo" exhibit on the Midway to see her didn't know truth from fiction, and they didn't care. They just wanted to have fun and be entertained.

As the nineteenth century ended, several things fell into place that were going to usher in a new era for the carnival. The biggest obstacle to the expansion of fairground entertainment had been the lack of electricity, but that was also changing. Soon, the "electric era" revolutionized both fairgrounds and amusement parks.

Another boost to fair business was the arrival of the automobile. Families could easily drive in from surrounding towns and farms, with less time and effort than with horses and buggies. Families could return to the fair several times during the fair week. While for the showmen, it became much easier to transport animals and all the props and equipment they could possibly need.

The growth in manufacturing and commercial ventures made jobs available to those who wanted them. This meant that ordinary people had extra money for entertainment and saw it not as a waste of time but as a vital part of living a full life. By the early 1900s, employers let workers off a half day on Saturdays; some could even take small vacations.

American cities grew rapidly from 1870 to the 1920s, and local showmen stepped in to provide residents with dance halls, arcades, cinemas, amusement parks, and vaudeville theaters. People were much more accepting of the company of strangers, and by the 1890s, there were few restrictions at public events caused by gender, religion, or occupation. The only continued barrier that kept Americans from pursuing entertainment at that time was race.

Things were changing on the fairgrounds, too. Better lighting and technology led first to the first portable merry-go-rounds and then Ferris Wheels, which could be moved from place to place. However, rides and entertainment for the whole family had some segments of the public criticizing the fairground shows that had been longtime staples – the sideshows.

For instance, in 1896, a few entertainment trade papers criticized the "fakers" gathered in an open area by the horse and cattle barns in Springfield, Illinois. They were offering such shows as "A Petrified Woman, Oriental Dancing Girls, 'he, she, or it' views for scientific purposes for 10 cents extra, a lady said to have a horse's mane and a lion's claw, a Mexican wild man, a wild double-woman, and 20th Century Dancing Girls." The talkers were also openly advertising "Men Only Shows," and part of their spiel was a promise that the show was "nothing tame like ladies and children could see in downtown opera houses."

The papers took aim at the fair officials, suggesting such entertainment wouldn't do so well at the fairs if they didn't put so

much emphasis on horse racing and betting. Such things attracted a bad element – which was also drawn to shows of such scandalous nature. It suggested that the fair add dog shows, trained animals, and a more family-friendly fare instead.

That same year, the Wisconsin State Fair declared for the first time that it would have no fakers and no sideshows – "no educated pigs, no museums of anatomy, or snake ladies."

But the showmen wouldn't be off the midway for long. By the early 1900s, a fair wasn't a fair without a midway. The fairs needed to attract people and their money, which meant that midways and fairs couldn't survive without each other. That was when a love-hate relationship between carnivals and fair boards began, which continues today.

And there was nothing that attracted more people to the midway than the human oddities show did.

Customers, showmen knew, would always come to see the freaks.

14.
ALIVE!
ALIVE!
ALIVE!

DEATH AND DISEASE WERE COMMON IN AMERICA'S EARLIER days. Life was tough. Many illnesses could kill you. Medical treatment was poor. Vaccines didn't exist. People starved and froze to death. There was bad water, bad food, and bad liquor. There was rampant crime, murder, and short life spans. This was why people had so many children -- because so few of them would live to be adults. And even then, if you were lucky, you might survive for 50 years or so.

Now, imagine what life might've been like if you'd been born physically different than other people. Life just got tougher – a lot tougher.

Babies born with severe deformities were often killed at birth or left alone, without care, to die. Superstitions about such births were rampant. Many believed a deformed child was a sign from God that the parents had committed evil deeds, and the baby was their punishment. Or worse, that a deformed child was the spawn of the Devil himself.

If the child were allowed to live, they would likely be placed in an institution since it was widely believed that a deformed body also indicated a disability of the mind.

But what about those children who didn't end up locked away from society? A deformed child with parents who loved them no matter what? Or a child whose parents sold them to an entrepreneurial showman who saw their disabilities as a way to make money? Or, in the best-case scenario, the child grew up to realize that a fortune could be made by making the best of bad circumstances?

From all those circumstances, the "freak show" gained popularity in America. They were technically shows where human oddities and acts were presented for the public's awe, amazement, and entertainment for the price of admission. The performers were people with physical abnormalities that made them unusual. They were referred to as "freaks," and while that term offends people today, it was a term preferred by the performers. It had been meant as an insult but wasn't to them.

I mean, keep in mind that polite society – as well as the medical community of the day – referred to them as "monsters."

Most freak show performers *chose* to put themselves on display because it was a profitable business. For instance, if you've got three legs or an extra pair of arms growing out of your chest, you couldn't exactly work behind the counter at the local grocery store in the 1930s. So, these smart, enterprising people made a very good living for themselves in the only way they could. And they made a lot more money than the guy behind the counter at the grocery store.

As freak shows gained popularity, it created a huge demand for the unique, the bizarre, and the different – both real and fake. Now, people who had once been shunned by society could make a lucrative salary, travel, gain fame, and add quality to their lives that before joining a show seemed impossible to attain. They signed contracts, negotiated salaries, and willingly put themselves on display. In most cases, they retired financially secure with a lifetime of colorful stories to tell.

Freak shows also created a "family" of other performers for people who had spent most of their lives shunned by society. In their closed communities, they thrived, fell in love, married, and had children.

But that was most freak show performers, not all.

Others weren't so lucky. Parents or guardians sold many into the business at an age too young to understand the implications. Some were mentally challenged, and thankfully, many of them had kind managers who protected them. P.T. Barnum, for example, had a sterling reputation in the industry and treated his performers well. In other cases, though, helpless children and adults were exploited and led a miserable life. Heartless managers stole their earnings and subjected them to beatings, isolation, and poor living conditions, then dumped them in institutions after they were no longer worth exhibiting.

Freak shows themselves were usually a combination of working acts such as a sword-swallower, magician, fire-eater, and a strong man, paired with actual human oddities and with the "created freaks," such as the traditional fat lady and those with bodies covered in tattoos.

They were generally referred to as something mentioned earlier – the "Ten-In One" show. Since one sideshow could be much like the

A MIDWAY TEN-IN-ONE SHOW – THIS ONE FEATURING THE "WORLD'S SMALLEST PEOPLE" – AND ALMOST GUARANTEED TO HAVE A BLOW-OFF AT THE END

last one that hit town, the show's financial success depended on the talents of the talker, whose job was to entice the public into buying a ticket to enter the tent. Usually, the talker would be assisted by some of the performers, who appeared on the bally stage next to him to heighten interest in what was inside.

Once inside, there would be a lot of talk about the "blow-off" act, the term for a performer hyped as being so spectacular that the "marks" – the carnie term for the customers on the fairgrounds – would pay extra to see them.

After that, the Ten-In-One had a line-up that raised the stakes as the marks walked through the tent, starting with the fat lady and the strong man, then the strong man, the snake charmer, a few "gaffs" – those were the phony freaks, the genuine human oddities, and then the blow-off act, which would cost extra.

Many Ten-in-Ones also offered "cooch shows," which was a carnie slang term for "hoochie-coochie," or a performance by scantily clad dancers. More often, though, the girl shows had their own tents and tickets were sold only to adult men.

The first girl shows dated back to the mid-1800s and were known as "Posing Shows" and featured beautiful ladies posing against the painted scenery of popular historical and classical dioramas. They would often pose in silhouette behind sheer curtains in tight body stockings to give the illusion that patrons were seeing a nude woman. It was hot stuff for the time.

Later, after vaudeville shows became popular, the traveling "striptease" show was born. From the start of the twentieth century through the early 1960s, almost every traveling carnival had some kind of girl show on its midway.

A MIDWAY COOCH SHOW COULD ALWAYS BE COUNTED ON TO DRAW BIG CROWDS.

The smallest might be only one or two girls and a hand-cranked Victrola – referred to in the business as a "Single-O" – while big carnivals had elaborate revue shows that tried to outdo their competition with size and talent. In the 1930s, it wasn't unusual to have major girl shows with full orchestras, singers, and a variety of performers in colorful and sequined costumes.

But those weren't the most common shows. Most smaller carnivals with cooch shows offered things that were much racier than what you'd find on a vaudeville stage. They'd often be held in tents that were off to the side of the fairgrounds and would run what came to be known as the "Saturday Night Red Hot Ramble," where, during one late-night performance, the girls danced completely nude and, combining the act with audience participation, showed off some talents they hadn't learned in Sunday School.

The heyday of the freak show wouldn't last as long as the cooch show would, however. Until the 1940s, freak shows had been one of America's most popular forms of entertainment for nearly a century. A combination of things would bring that era to an end.

The first was the release of a film we'll discuss a little later called *Freaks*, directed by Tod Browning in 1932. The film's release– banned in many cities across the country – started a conversation about whether the freak show was still considered tasteful. Many well-meaning individuals and groups began protesting what they thought was the exploitation of the performers – even though the performers just

309 | THE DEVIL'S CARNIVAL

wanted them to mind their own business and allow them to make a living.

The next blow to the freak show was World War II. Gasoline was being rationed and this made things difficult for traveling fairground shows. After the war, inflation slowed the economy, and it became more profitable for carnivals to offer rides, games of chance, and eateries that could take up the same space as a freak show and bring in more money. Also, salaries paid to the carnies who ran the rides and games and fried the food were much lower than those paid to the stars of the sideshows.

It was television that finally finished off the freak shows. Americans now had a new form of entertainment that was beamed directly into their living room.

Freak shows could never exist today. No matter how the performers might feel, the sensitive insights and political correctness of our modern times would make it impossible for anyone to pursue being physically different as a way of making a living. Today, we see those who are disabled or different in a much different way than our ancestors did – and yet, our fascination never goes away. We may have a conflict within ourselves when we look back at yesterday's oddities with today's sensibilities, and yet we look.

So, let's not kid ourselves – we're still going to be thrilled by the sights, sounds, and history of the freak show. Enlightened and politically correct or not, we find it impossible to turn away from the lurid, shocking, and captivating glimpse into the sideshow's past.

We're the marks, folks. We've stepped right up, so toss out your nickel or your dime, grab your ticket, and let's take a trip back in time to when going to the fairgrounds to see the freak show was just a part of American life.

CONEY ISLAND FREAKS

THERE'S NO QUESTION THAT P.T. BARNUM WAS THE "FATHER" of the American freak show, but it was a man who has already appeared in these pages as a villain who made them appeal to a much wider slice of the public. His name was Samuel Gumpertz, and he was the man who brought freaks to Coney Island.

Long before Gumpertz was the foil of John Ringling, he was a boy from St. Louis who performed in Buffalo Bill's Wild West Show and managed a string of theaters in Chicago and New Orleans. He later gave Flo Ziegfeld his first job in show business, promoted strongman Eugen Sandow, and was the last manager of Harry Houdini. But in

CONEY ISLAND OPENED AS A RESORT IN 1882 BUT KICKED OFF THE ERA OF AMERICAN AMUSEMENT PARKS TWO YEARS LATER.

1904, he was hired to build and manage Dreamland, a new attraction on Coney Island, that five-mile stretch of beach where Brooklyn meets the sea.

Coney Island had opened as a resort in 1882 with only a hotel and a theater, but by 1884, it boasted the first roller coaster in the country, kicking off the era of American amusement parks.

Like other amusement parks that had opened over the last few years, Dreamland offered attractions with cultural themes. A visitor could boat through the "Canals of Venice," dine at a "Japanese Tea House," or ride a train through the "Snow-Covered Alps."

When it opened, though, its main attraction was the wildly popular miniature village called Lilliputia, sometimes nicknamed "Midget World." It was built to resemble a fifteen-century German town, except everything, including the inhabitants, was scaled down. About 300 little people were gathered from fairs, expositions, and circuses worldwide. They had their own beach, theater, and fire department, which regularly responded to false alarms to the enjoyment of the crowds. To add to the spectacle, giants were sometimes hired to stroll through town. By day, the performers entertained the paying public, but after the park closed, they lived together in a community designed just for them.

And that's when things went off the rails.

Apparently, the performers enjoyed living together a little too much. Reportedly, "lewd and immoral" behavior was widely practiced

THE DREAMLAND FREAK SHOWS AT CONEY ISLAND BECAME SOME OF THE RESORT'S MOST POPULAR ATTRACTIONS.

and then encouraged and advertised by the management to attract visitors who weren't worried about the confines of proper behavior. It was said that almost 80 percent of the babies born in the community were illegitimate.

And if you're wondering if Sam Gumpertz had anything to do with the racy advertising about Lilliputia's sexcapades, I can't say for sure. However, I do know he was once fined $100 for showing a play deemed "too suggestive even for a New York police officer."

Lilliputia didn't last long. The higher tone developers had tried to set for Dreamland had turned out to be a bust, giving Gumpertz a much freer hand to try new things and advertise the park with flyers and newspaper advertisements.

That was how he hit pay dirt by bringing a human oddities show to Coney Island.

Gumpertz personally scoured Europe, Africa, the Philippines, Asia, and Egypt for the strange and unusual. Among other things, he brought back 51 tribespeople from the Philippines and promoted them as wild and dangerous headhunters. All were friendly and had to learn to be good actors.

He exhibited people from all over the globe – in the tradition of the two recent world's fairs in Chicago and St. Louis – all to the delight of the ticket-buying public. He always managed to whisk his new arrivals through customs and past the amazed and astonished port officials whose standards had been relaxed by a few folded $10 bills.

It was said that Gumpertz was so successful with his recruitment because he genuinely liked the people he hired. He lured acts away from circuses and traveling shows, appealing to those who had grown tired of being on the road. Life was easier, and paychecks were regular. Many other performers worked for Gumpertz at Coney Island during the winter months, returning to their regular shows at the start of the new season. Many retired sideshow performers earned extra money by performing occasionally at Dreamland.

Unfortunately, Dreamland burned down on May 27, 1911 – the opening day of the season – and was never rebuilt. However, Gumpertz saw an opportunity in the park's demise. He quickly organized The Dreamland Circus Sideshow in a tent on nearby Surf Avenue, and as a newspaper of the day noted, "it opened while the park ruins are still smoking."

The freak show continued through the 1920s and kept Coney Island in business during World War I. Its success led to many rival shows appearing at Coney Island and elsewhere and created an even bigger hunger among the public for the shows that could be found every summer on fairgrounds across the country.

"CREATED FREAKS"

RUNNING AWAY TO JOIN THE TRAVELING CIRCUS OR SIDESHOW was once a life goal for some people. I think I've already confessed that it was for me, even though I was born much too late to pursue the idea realistically.

But family histories are filled with such stories. We've already seen it happen many times within these pages. For many people, taking off with a show or circus that passed through town might fill a need for adventure or offer a chance to start over. During the dark days of the Depression, running off with the circus might offer a better life than the one you left behind.

Some of those who joined up with a show became cooks, drivers, roustabouts, fed the animals, or did the laundry. Women often sold themselves to the show, became dancers in the cooch tent, or even provided sex for workers and patrons.

Others wanted to be stars but had no talents or physical abnormalities to make them memorable, so the more resourceful created physical differences that set them apart from mainstream society – they became a "created freak."

Interestingly, with most created freaks, there was an element of sex that went along with their shows. Tattooed men and women were scantily dressed to show off their body art. The more tattoos you had, the less clothing you wore. It also wasn't unheard of for some tattooed ladies performing for an all-male audience to completely disrobe after tickets were purchased and the door to the tent was closed. There's no question that the shows hinted at the nudity inside with the canvas banners outside the tent that featured the women wearing very little clothing.

A "half and half" – a person physically having male and female sexual traits – was an erotic attraction for most people of the day, especially to small-town fair attendees for whom just the idea of a woman showing a bare ankle or knee could drive them crazy. The "half and half" could be the most popular part of the sideshow, even though most of them were fakes. Even so, they could still carry a show if they could visually show off enough skin that it seemed to prove their claims.

Another wildly erotic performer was the fat lady – and she knew it. She commonly engaged audience members in good-natured flirting, guaranteeing they'd return for the next show.

Female audiences and segments of male audiences were often thrilled by the strongman, who flexed his muscles and showed off his body for the crowd's enjoyment. Many women at the time had never seen a man, except for their husband, without clothes on and now, for the price of a ticket, were able to openly stare at a half-nude man. Gay men, forced to remain in the closet back then, were just as enthralled by a mostly nude man who was displaying his body and performing acts of strength.

Prostitution on the fairgrounds was not unheard of, especially among the smaller and often seedier shows. This made extra money for the carnival and for those performers who were aging out of the show and who had hit the entertainment end of the line. Of course, staying in one place for more than a few nights could be costly and risky to the carnival if folks in town got wind of the fairground shenanigans and brought in the law, or worse, took matters into their own hands.

PART ONE:
TATTOOED PEOPLE

TATTOOS HAVE BEEN A PART OF CULTURE FOR 5,000 YEARS or more, dating back to the Polynesian, Egyptian, and Celtic people. The first American tattoo studio opened in New York in 1870, and the first electric tattooing machine arrived in 1891, cutting down the amount of pain and the time involved with getting a tattoo. By 1900, every major American city had at least one tattoo parlor, but that didn't make them mainstream.

Tattoos are widely accepted today, but during the heyday of traveling sideshows, few people had seen a tattoo, and even fewer were inked themselves. Most tattooed people in the late nineteenth and early twentieth century were sailors – or performed in the sideshow.

The first tattooed performers – or created freaks – were exhibited in America as early as the 1840s. They were paid well for their popularity, and each tattooed person tried to outdo the next. There are recorded histories of entire tattooed families performing on the sideshow circuit, little people, fat ladies, and even animals.

While male tattooed performers were popular with audiences at first, they weren't nearly as sought after as female performers. When tattooed women finally started to exhibit themselves in 1882, male performers largely disappeared.

The common term for the female performers was "tattooed ladies," and they were usually billed under their own names, even though they were often disparaged by the public – even by those who came to stare at them.

In an era when women had few lucrative employment opportunities and were often forced to marry or depend on a man for their existence, tattooed ladies and other female sideshow performers supported themselves. They made more money than most men and being financially independent meant they could choose to marry or stay single. They could also get divorced if they wanted, not worrying about the stigma that society placed on most women. With that kind of freedom – as well as by covering themselves with tattoos – the public felt compelled to look down on them, even while many women in their audiences were filled with jealousy.

AMERICA'S FIRST TATTOOED LADY

NORA HILDEBRANDT WAS BORN NORA KEATIN IN IRELAND IN 1856. Her parents emigrated to America when their daughter was only a few weeks old. They settled in the Irish slums of New York City.

Nora would go on to become America's first professionally exhibited tattooed lady. Her ink was done by her much older common-law husband, Martin Hildebrandt, who opened one of the first tattoo shops in the city. He started by tattooing Confederate and Union soldiers while he was a traveling artist during the Civil War. In New York, his customers were mostly sailors or men who'd had too much to drink. Nora's decision to embrace a career as a tattoo exhibitor can likely be attributed to the fact that she was easily influenced by Martin, who was more than 20 years older than she was – or she could have just loved tattoos and saw it as a way to earn her own money.

All of Nora's tattoos were done by hand – created before electric tattoo guns – and she first started putting them on display on March 1, 1882, at Bunnell's Dime Museum at the corner of 9th and Broadway. Borrowing from male tattoo exhibitors, she made up fanciful stories to explain her tattoos. Her stories often varied. She sometimes claimed that her father had tattooed her against her will, which was a good way to gain sympathy from a prudish Victorian public. At other times, Nora claimed that she and her father were both forcibly tattooed by savage Native Americans. In another and even more fanciful story, she claimed she had been captured by Sitting Bull, who held her family hostage. In her words, the only thing that saved them from torture and certain death was her willingness to allow her father to painfully tattoo her from head to toe while she was tied to a tree for an entire year.

And yes, people actually believed these stories – especially since Nora claimed to be able to prove it. As a result of her captivity, she now had 365 tattoos decorating her young body – one for each day she was tied to the tree.

All the stories were fictional, but they made Nora seem more like a victim than a willing participant in the tattoo process. They also added an exotic and sexual element to her performance, which made her even more popular with the naïve public. Her male customers were also very appreciative of the skimpy costumes she wore to show off her ink.

Nora exhibited at dime museums and toured primarily with the Barnum and Bailey Circus until her untimely death on April 1, 1893, from a combination of pneumonia and heart failure. She was only 37. She was buried in an unmarked grave in the Evergreens Cemetery in Brooklyn.

"LA BELLE IRENE"

IRENE WOODWARD WAS BORN IN PHILADELPHIA, PENNSYLVANIA, on August 24, 1857. Her parents, Joseph and Sarah, had six children, but only Irene and a younger brother, John, lived to adulthood.

She made her professional debut on March 21, 1882, at Bunnell's Dime Museum in New York, just three weeks after Nora Hildebrandt. She was 25 at the time but advertised as being only 19. She became extremely popular, especially after a story appeared about her in the *New York Times* calling her "the illustrated woman." She worked at other dime museums and circuses across America and then successfully toured Europe, where she was named "La Belle Irene."

At that time, she had few competitors. Nora may have been the first on the scene, but Irene was more popular in the press and with the paying public. However, both women deserve to be credited with paving the way for other tattooed ladies who followed and for

tattooed women to become some of the highest-paid performers in sideshows.

On stage, Irene's stories changed to suit her audience. Sometimes, she said that she had been saving during an Indian raid – during which her father was killed – because the tattoos her father had put on her body had frightened the savages, and they had spared the lives of Irene and her brother. Another version of her story claimed she'd spent most of her life living in a settler's wagon with her family, and her father had tattooed a spool on her arm, so he didn't lose her. Though painful, she liked the result and urged him to tattoo her more, which he did for the next six years. Her simplest story claimed that her father was a sailor and had he'd tattooed her between the ages of six and 12.

But one thing that always stayed the same in Irene's stories was that, unlike Nora Hildebrandt, Irene always proudly proclaimed that she wanted to be tattooed and had the work done willingly.

Her father hadn't done the work, however. She had been tattooed by William R. Davis and Nora's husband, Martin Hildebrandt. The facts were distorted to either sensationalize the show or to appease the morality issues that might have arisen at the time if the public thought a woman had allowed her entire body to be touched by a man other than her father or her husband.

Irene's stories also suited her needs and mixed fact with fiction, even at the end of her life. Her last interview took place on her deathbed in September 1915. She told her interviewer that she had married a printer named George Woodward when she was only 16. He introduced her to circus life and acted as her manager. They had a son, George Jr., who was born in 1878. During her two-decade career, she had played all over the country, traveling the great circus routes and touring Europe, even performing for royalty. She also claimed she'd made a fortune, but she and her husband had spent it all, and then he abandoned her, leaving her destitute. Now, she told the reporter, she was dying of stomach cancer caused by poison from the tattoo ink that had been on her body for so many years.

Irene was dying – and she had the last laugh. She passed away on October 9, 1915, in Philadelphia. She was 58. The cause of her death was a tumor in her uterus, not stomach cancer, and definitely not "tattoo ink poisoning."

While Irene claimed many inspirations for her tattoos, they were most likely her husband's idea. He probably suggested that she get tattooed for fortune, fame, and travel and to save him from a tedious life as a printer.

ANNIE HOWARD

LITTLE IS KNOWN ABOUT THE LIFE OF ANNIE HOWARD, who was regarded as one of the most beautiful women to ever exhibit in the sideshows. One thing we do know about her, though, is that she was very superstitious. Her most prominent tattoo was a good-luck horseshoe "necklace" inked around her neck.

She was born Annie Jane Morrison in Providence, Rhode Island, on January 12, 1859, and at some point, met Frank Howard Packard. Annie and Frank came from Providence, Rhode Island, and both came from a family of jewelers, so it is possible they met through relatives.

In 1876, they relocated to Chicago. It is unknown if they actually married or if their relationship was common-law. Around 1884, Frank started tattooing, and they both soon had full-body "suits" of hand-pricked tattoos. In October of that year, Frank debuted as a tattoo artist in Gregory's Dime Museum, located in Saint Louis, Missouri. That was also when he and Annie started using their stage names, Frank and Annie Howard. They traveled the Dime Circuit from 1885 to 1897 and then toured from 1897 to 1901 in Europe with the Barnum and Bailey Circus.

As with most performers of the era, they created elaborate stories to spice up the act and attract more customers. The Howards, like many others, claimed they'd been captured by savages who tattooed them against their will. Occasionally, the "savages" were Native Americans, but the Howards usually preferred stories of faraway lands and South Seas islands, even though neither of them had ever left the country. Even without the stories, Annie was offered more respect than many other tattooed ladies because she was a married woman, on display with her husband.

But Annie had first made a name for herself with a scandal. In 1882, she appeared in the newspapers after being arrested and thrown in jail. According to the reports, she was on her way to George Bunnell's Dime Museum to seek a job exhibiting her ink and was insulted on the street by a man who saw her tattoos. Annie assaulted the man, beat him badly, was arrested and charged, and then was immediately hired by Bunnell after she was released. The story immediately interested Annie, guaranteeing long lines at the ticket office.

But Annie hadn't let the truth get in the way of a good story. Annie had no tattoos on her face, neck, or hands. Wearing ordinary clothing, no one would know she was tattooed.

Her run-in with the law was nothing more than a publicity stunt, but regrettably, George Bunnell would soon make the papers himself when he was charged with "insulting" a lady on a train by "plainly exposing his person." Unlike the story about Annie, this newspaper account was unfortunately true.

Annie and Frank had one daughter, who used the stage name Ivy Howard, who traveled with them on the sideshow circuit. She started performing as a snake charmer when she was eight, but she didn't stay in the business. She later became a professional coronet player and, as far as I know, had no tattoos.

Upon returning to the United States in 1901, Frank opened a tattoo shop in Boston, Massachusetts. Annie continued to perform solo in the local Dime Museum in Boston. Their daughter worked as a clerk in a grocery store.

Annie died on January 3, 1911, and is buried in Boston. After his wife's death, Frank married Louisa Ann Morris when Frank was 57 years old, and his new wife was 37 years old.

Frank died at the age of 68 on November 18, 1925. He is buried in the family plot with Annie in North Burial Ground, located in Providence, Rhode Island. His tattoo shop was taken over in 1925 by Dad Liberty.

PRINCESS BEATRICE

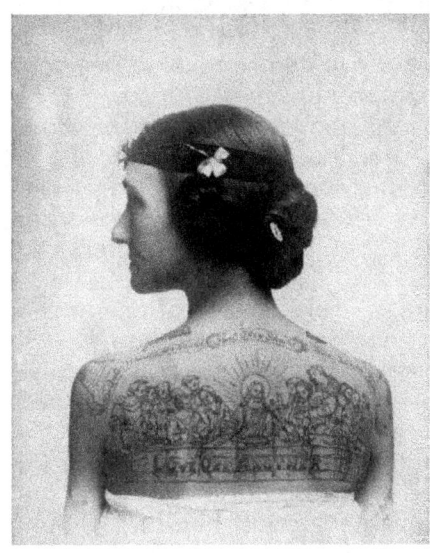

BERTHA RITCHIE WAS BORN IN NEWCASTLE, ENGLAND, IN 1878, but after her father died, her mother, Annie, moved the family to Galveston, Texas, where legends say they were quickly embraced by the elite of society in the thriving port city. There, Bertha met and married her first husband and gave birth to a son.

But her life soon took a terrible turn.

On September 8, 1900, Galveston was hit by a hurricane that remains the deadliest natural disaster in American history, killing between 6,000 and 12,000 people and devastating the area. Tragically, Bertha lost most of her family in the storm, including her mother, four sisters, and her infant son. The baby had been ripped out of her arms by the rushing water, and it was said that, in the wake of the storm, she wandered the streets of Galveston, looking into the face of each infant she saw, hoping to find her son still alive.

Bertha had been miraculously saved when a stranger dragged her out of the surging flood waters by her long hair. For the rest of her life, she was terrified of storms.

Life continued, and Bertha had another son, but her husband died soon after his birth, leaving her a widow with no money, a new baby, and no other family members to offer help or support. To make matters worse, she now was reportedly "slightly mad."

Bertha, likely more because of desperation than love, became involved with a man named John Thompson Clark, known as "J.T." He had been a friend of her late husband. They traveled together to South Africa, eventually married, and Bertha gave birth to another son, Francis, in 1906. By all accounts, the pair were happy even though J.T. was a "colorful" character with a sideshow background and very different from the kind of people Bertha had grown up around. He claimed to be the only man in the world with a tattooed scalp to go along with the tattoos that covered the rest of his body. He opened a tattoo shop in South Africa – with mostly sailors as his clients – and somehow persuaded Bertha to allow him to tattoo her. It might have been so he could use her as a source of income, displaying her for profit, or perhaps Bertha simply wanted to be covered in colorful ink like her husband was.

Among the pieces of artwork that eventually covered her body were a portrait of George Washington on her chest, *The Last Supper* on her back, and spider webs on her shoulders. She also had a memorial piece for her mother and sisters on her upper arm.

In 1914, the family fled Africa just before World War I and returned to the United States. J.T. and Bertha – now using the stage name of Princess Beatrice – exhibited together and separately with Ringling Brothers and other shows.

Bertha endured another loss in 1918 when J.T. died of pneumonia while on tour in Montreal. Bertha was a widow again, at age 40, with a 12-year-old son to support. She was lost. She had never earned her own way in life and was traumatized by the losses she had endured. She continued trying to make a living by exhibiting herself, but the paying public was more interested in the younger tattooed ladies. She was so poor that she was forced to send her son off to earn room and board working on a farm. Bertha couldn't support herself, let alone provide a stable home for a young boy.

In the early 1930s, Bertha requested a widow's military pension from J.T.'s enlistment during the Spanish-American War. She designated herself as "destitute" on the application, so it's unclear why she waited so many years to pursue it. In the end, though, she never received it. J.T. had received too many reprimands during his service to receive an honorary discharge.

Bertha died at some point in the 1950s. She had mostly been living off the charity of friends. Sadly, she has mostly been forgotten by all but the most dedicated historians of the tattooed ladies.

"LADY ARTORIA"

ANNA MAE GIBBONS WAS BORN IN 1893 IN RURAL Wisconsin, the daughter of Norwegian immigrants Frank and Mabel Burlington. In 1907, the family moved to Colville, Washington, but Frank died soon after, leaving his widow with several children to care for.

Later, during her sideshow career, Anna often told audiences the story of her childhood, claiming she ran away to join the circus at age 14, looking for adventure and travel. In truth, Anna left home at

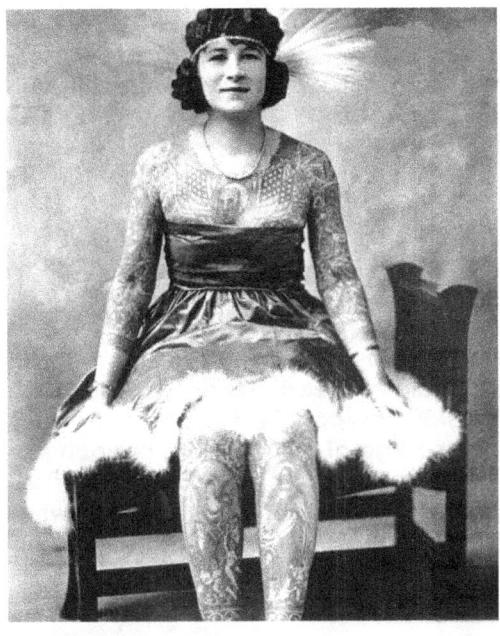

a young age, but she found odd jobs to support herself and send money home to her mother.

While working as a housekeeper in Spokane, Anna met a tattoo artist named Charles "Red" Gibbons, and they got married in 1912. Times were hard, and finding work was difficult, so the decision to ink Anna was likely financial. However, Anna always dismissed people who suggested her husband forced her to be tattooed or did it out of blind love. She always said she did it to improve her life, make money, and see the world. She never regretted her actions – always maintaining that she made much more money and had a better life than if she'd stayed home on the farm. Anna was one of the industry's highest-paid tattooed ladies, commanding a salary of between $100 and $250 a week. The job she'd had before, working as a housekeeper? It paid $5 a week.

Red created Anna's tattoos between 1920 and 1921. Believe it or not, he only tattooed as a hobby. His real job was as an oil prospector. Even so, historians state that Anna had some of the finest tattoo work on the show circuit, with Red counted as one of the best of the old-school artists.

Anna was a devout Baptist, so many of her tattoos were reproductions of religious paintings by Raphael, Michaelangelo, and Da Vinci, including *The Last Supper*, which was inked across her upper back. She also sported many patriotic designs, with colorful flags and portraits of presidents. Her artwork covered 80 percent of her body, all done by Red, who once said his wife was "crazy about the Italian masters, which likely influenced her stage name of "Lady Artoria."

Anna had a sterling reputation with every show on which she worked. She was always on time and always conducted herself in a professional manner. Once, on her way to the stage for an exhibition, she fell and broke her arm. She refused to see a doctor and have it treated until her performances were completed several hours later.

She initially retired from show business in the 1940s, but only because Red needed her. He had been robbed in 1941 and beaten so badly that he was nearly blind. A few years later, in 1946, he was badly injured in a construction accident. Anna stayed home to care for him but returned to sideshow life after Red died in 1964. She didn't return because she needed the money – Red had left her oil wells in Oklahoma – she returned because she missed the people and the carnival life.

Anna finally retired for good in the early 1980s. She moved to Tennessee to live with her only daughter, Charlene Pickle, and her family. Her show business career spanned nearly six decades, and she remains one of the most famous sideshow-tattooed ladies.

Anna died in March 1985 at the age of 91. Strangely, her obituary never mentioned her sideshow career, so it must have surprised funeral attendees to see that she was covered in colorful ink when they arrived at the open casket affair.

BETTY BROADBENT

MY FAVORITE TATTOOED LADY WAS BETTY BROADBENT, born Susan Brown in Zellwood, Florida, in 1909, although she spent her childhood living in Philadelphia.

Several stories have appeared over the years to explain why she ran off to join the sideshow when she was 17. One claims she was a member of a socially prominent Philadelphia family who tried to keep too tight of a rein on a daughter who craved adventure. Another says that she impulsively got a tattoo from an artist she encountered on the Atlantic City Boardwalk named Jack Redcloud. When she returned home, her family was so upset that she ran away after a bitter argument. We'll never know which version of the story is the truth, but basically, she fell out with her family and ran off to join the sideshow.

At a time when women – and most men, too – with tattoos were shunned by mainstream society, it's interesting to note that Betty had more than 350 tattoos all over her body. Many were portraits of famous people, including Queen Victoria, between her breasts.

Charles Wagner, a world-famous tattoo artist with a shop in the New York Bowery, did many of Betty's tattoos. He was one of the first to use an electric tattoo gun. The most heavily tattooed women of the era were usually wives of tattoo artists and were living billboards for their husbands' work. But not Betty. She just loved the process of getting tattooed and exhibiting her tattooed body. Once, she even participated in a beauty pageant alongside women without tattoos. She always believed she should have won – she didn't – but she loved the stir that her appearance caused among the audience and the press.

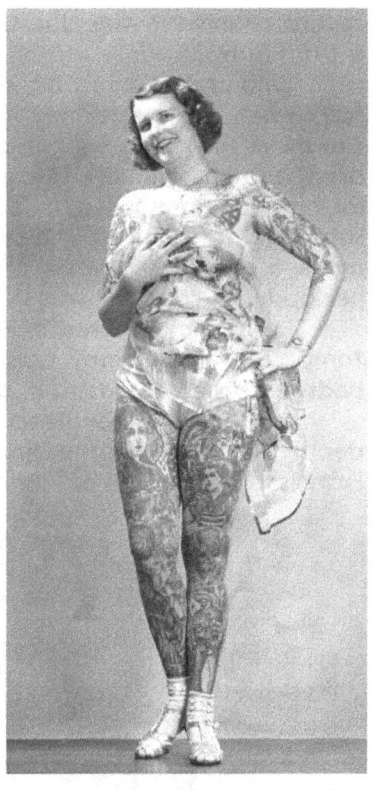

Betty joined the sideshow in 1926, and her career lasted over 40 years. She worked with every significant American circus and performed in sideshows in Australia and New Zealand. Her popularity was usually attributed to the contrast between her colorful, heavily tattooed body and her sweet face, which she kept free from ink. She earned at least $300 per week, a higher salary than any other woman of the time.

She was married three times. Her first husband, Edwin Burbank, married her when she was only 19. She married her second husband, a sideshow ventriloquist named Charles Roark, in 1940, and they toured together for many years before divorcing. She wed her third husband, Winford Brewer, in 1969 after retiring from show business.

In the early 1930s, Betty became pregnant while seeing a married sideshow rodeo cowboy named Joe Carter. It's believed the child was put up for adoption or given away to a couple she knew, but no record of this remains. Joe Carter was killed while trying to jump on a train in 1933.

One of Betty's last big shows was in 1939 at the New York World's Fair, when she performed with the John Hix "Strange As It Seems Sideshow." By then, demand for tattooed attractions had started dropping off, and the few shows still seeking tattooed ladies were looking for younger girls. So, Betty switched gears and became a successful tattoo artist. She still performed sometimes but managed to make a good living while creating the kind of art that she'd had on her body for so many years.

Betty finally retired in 1967 and settled in Riverview, Florida, near Tampa. She kept many pets and gardened as a hobby. Her flower beds were, her friends said, as magnificent as Betty was.

Betty died in her sleep in March 1983, but two years before her death, she became the first person to be inducted into the San Francisco Tattoo Hall of Fame.

"THE LAST TATTOOED LADY"

BORN LORETT LOVE IN 1915, THE WOMAN WHO GAINED fame as the last of the great tattooed ladies started in sideshows as a showgirl and a cook. She began getting ink from Gib "Tatts" Thomas, a famous Chicago artist, who did more of her extensive work for free in exchange for advertising on the trade cards she sold at her shows. He later became a traveling tattoo artist with the Ringling Brothers circus, where Lorett worked in the sideshow.

She was married to Robert Fulkerson, a U.S. Air Force captain who served during World War II and in Korea.

Lorett's career as a tattooed lady spanned a remarkable seven decades, and she was still exhibiting in 2003, four years before her death in December 2007 at the age of 92.

She and Robert are buried side-by-side at the Fairview Baptist Church Cemetery in Natchitoches Parish, Louisiana, together even at the end.

PART TWO: "IT'S NOT OVER UNTIL THE FAT LADY SINGS"

NO RESPECTABLE SHOW DURING THE HEYDAY OF THE SIDESHOWS was complete without a Fat Lady or Fat Man on the roster. Many large-sized people, tired of being stared at for free, joined the carnival and were paid well to be the source of visual amusement for the suckers who coughed up the admission price.

Many, but not all, overweight sideshow folks turned themselves into "freaks." Poor and uneducated, tired of trying to eke out a miserable living during tough times, literally ate their way into the circus. Entire oversized families joined together as a Fat attraction.

While both Fat Men and Fat Ladies were wildly popular with the public, the Fat Ladies were always more popular. Many of them added a flirtatious dialogue to their shows and dressed in risqué clothing for the times. And most were not shy about lifting their skirts to show a little more.

Since every sideshow had this kind of attraction – with wild stage names like Jolly Ollie, Baby Ruth, Dainty Dolly, Happy Val, and Tessie Ton – it's impossible to list them all. Besides that, only a few stood out as the most colorful and became major stars.

"BABY RUTH"

RUTH SMITH WAS BORN IN KEMPTON, IOWA, IN FEBRUARY 1904. She was one of the heaviest women to ever appear in the carnival and one of the most famous. True or not, most accounts record her birth weight at 16 pounds, weighed 50 pounds by the time she was one year old, and 300 pounds by age 10. By the end of her career, she reached 815 pounds, an impressive number, but she never reached her private goal of 1,000 pounds.

Of course, none of these numbers came as a surprise to her family. Ruth followed in her mother's footsteps when she joined the sideshow. Her mother had been a Fat Lady with the circus, weighing

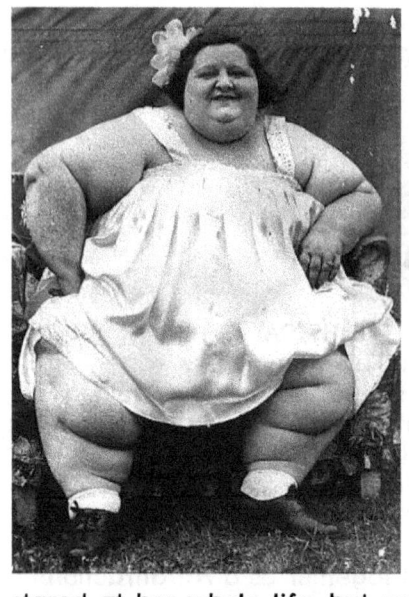

between 600 and 800 pounds and using the stage name of the "Human Blimp."

In her stage patter, Ruth always claimed that she was a light eater and that she'd inherited her size from her mother. Her father was of ordinary size, and her only sister was a fashion model. But Ruth joined the circus when she was a young girl. Her first stage name was "Ima Waddler."

If you groaned when you read that, you're not alone. Many of these bad puns were used to promote Fat Men and Fat Ladies in those days.

But Ruth enjoyed the entire experience of the sideshow from the start. She had been teased and stared at her whole life, but now she was making money just to be herself. At the height of her popularity, she made as much as $400 daily from ticket sales and sales of her photos and pitch cards.

Keep in mind that this was in the middle of the Depression.

Ruth also quickly learned how many men were attracted to large women. Reportedly, Ruth didn't mind the innuendoes and sexual advances, and her lusty exploits became well-known in the shows she worked with.

But show folks loved her for who she was. She made friends easily and was known for her generosity and for giving loans to anyone with a sob story. Ruth, though, was always paid back. No one wanted her to be upset with them.

In 1931, Ruth signed with Barnum and Bailey, and she also changed her stage name to "Baby Ruth" in honor of the popular candy bar. When she was with the circus, she met Joe Pontico, who ran the balloon concession. They were soon married and were utterly devoted to each other. Reports vary on Joe's size. Some claimed he weighed only 130 pounds, while others claimed he could have been a carnival Fat Man himself. I'd say he was probably somewhere in between if it really matters.

Later that year, Ruth contracted typhoid fever while on tour in Springfield, Missouri, and for a time, was reported to be in critical condition. Luckily, she recovered but needed to take some time off.

The newspapers ran stories about Joe taking her down to his home in Sarasota because she was down to a dainty 600 pounds. She'd lost 100 pounds during her stay in the hospital. Even so – nudge, nudge, wink, wink – they still needed to put her in the baggage car on the train to get her there.

Ruth and Joe ran an Italian restaurant in Florida during the winter season. Joe loved to cook, and Ruth loved to eat whatever he made. Her usual breakfast, she claimed, was three eggs, eight strips of bacon, four slices of toast, a glass of orange juice, and two quarts of water. Again, this was during the Depression when most people were lucky to get half that much food over a whole day.

Ruth's size was a constant problem for her in day-to-day life. She once visited her sister and fell through the floor of her house. It took a crane and a rescue crew to get her out of the hole. Her own home, a former hotel that she and Joe had purchased, had reinforced floors and sturdy, oversized furniture. She also had an enlarged shower and toilet. Like Charles "Tom Thumb" Stratton, she used the wealth she made working with the sideshows to fashion the world to fit her size.

But problems aside, Ruth was happy and comfortable with her proportions. She installed large three-way mirrors in her home and dressing room so she could see her body from every angle. She claimed to enjoy the process of gaining weight – not just eating food but also seeing the results of it appearing on her body.

One of her favorite things to say about herself was, "I once went on a starvation diet but gained nine pounds in four days and gave it up."

Ruth didn't mind how she looked, but she was bothered by how hard it became for her to move around as she got bigger. So, in April 1941, she checked into the Municipal Hospital in Tampa to have an operation to reduce her weight and improve her mobility. She was scheduled to go on tour, but her bulk made it impossible. However, the operation had to be postponed. The hospital bed collapsed under her, and a specially constructed bed had to be obtained before she could return.

Months later, in November 1941, Ruth returned to the hospital. She was taken up to her room in the freight elevator. The surgery took place the next morning, and tragically, Ruth didn't survive it. She died from complications caused by the operation on November 29. She was only 37.

Much speculation followed her death. Her doctor claimed that she failed to regain consciousness after the operation, which had removed 30 pounds of fat from her legs and stomach. The official cause of death was listed as cardiac failure, but the doctor's statement to the newspaper created doubts about its accuracy. Many believed that Ruth had choked to death coming out of the anesthesia because the medical staff was unable to turn her onto her side. Later, the doctor publicly stated that if she had not been so heavy, they could have moved her, and she might have been saved.

Today, the hospital, the doctor, and everyone in the operating room would be charged with carelessness and lack of preparation for a patient of Ruth's size. In 1941, though, everyone just shrugged and blamed everything on Ruth.

Newspapers across the country carried stories about the death of Baby Ruth, America's "Fattest Lady," and printed stories in which her weight ranged from 815 to 850 pounds.

Ruth was buried in a chromium and steel casket that cost $1,000 and needed 14 pallbearers to carry her to her grave... somewhere. The location of her burial site was never publicized and remains a mystery today.

"DOLLY DIMPLES"

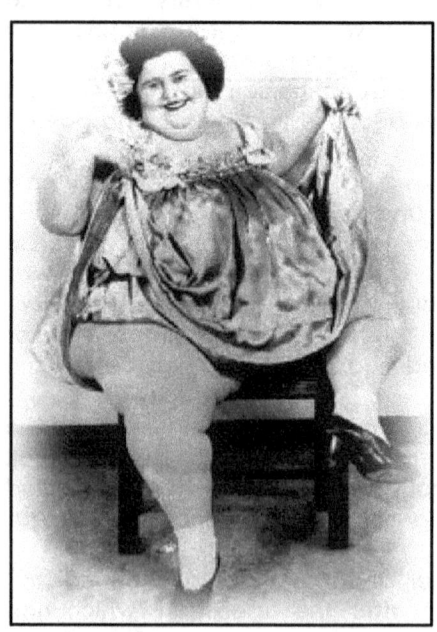

SHE ATE AT LEAST SIX TIMES A DAY, OR AT LEAST THAT'S WHAT her publicity would later say. Celesta Hermann was born in Cincinnati in 1901 with a very large appetite. Her German American parents would always say that she just loved food – and they spoiled her with it. If Celesta were teased by kids at school, her mother would bake her a special treat to make her tears go away. By age 13, she weighed 150 pounds, and by the time she dropped out of school, she was up to 295 pounds, even though she only stood four feet, eleven inches tall.

She was, as many liked to say, "as big around as she was tall."

Celesta didn't mind, but she did mind that her size kept her from finding work. No one wanted to hire someone with her girth, but many men wanted to marry her. She had many suitors, and in 1925, she chose one of them – Frank Geyer, who had never weighed more than 135 pounds during his lifetime.

Celesta later claimed she gained over 100 pounds during her first year of marriage. "I'd make a special pie or cake for Frank every day. He would eat a piece, and I would finish off the rest of it."

Legend has it that in 1927, Frank and Celesta attended a carnival, and the show's manager offered her a job on the spot. Frank supported her decision to join the show, traveled with her, acted as her agent, sold Celesta's pitch cards, and worked odd jobs for the carnival.

When she started, Celesta shared the stage with another Fat Lady, Jolly Pearl Stanley, so she adopted the name "Jolly Dolly." As her popularity grew, she gained her own spotlight and changed her stage name to "Dolly Dimples," inspired by the inch-deep dimples she had on each elbow. She kept that name for the rest of her career, which spanned two decades.

At the height of her career, Celesta weighed around 425 pounds and earned at least $300 daily. By 1950, she peaked at 555 and once said it took 12 yards of material to make her one dress.

During her heyday, she was billed as "The World's Prettiest Fat Girl" and "The World's Most Beautiful Fat Lady." Celesta's skin was always flawless, and she always maintained an hourglass figure, although, as she laughed, it was a very large hourglass.

Later, she sang and impersonated celebrities like Kate Smith – the plus-sized performer famous for her rendition of "God Bless America" – which made Celesta even more popular with the public.

There was never any suggestion from Celesta that she was "big-boned" or that her size had anything to do with heredity or gland problems. She said she just loved to eat and did so from when she got up in the morning until she went to bed at night. She claimed it took a minimum of 10,000 calories to maintain her weight – and to keep her happy. She would often amaze her audiences by eating huge amounts of food in one sitting on stage. It was the perfect plan for Dolly Dimples – the crowds paid more to see it, allowing Celesta to indulge in her love of food during the performance. She'd previously complained that she got too hungry while on stage and had trouble concentrating on her act.

Unfortunately, like many other large performers, Celesta had many health issues. She had difficulty walking because of her girth,

and her heart began to fail her. She suffered a heart attack in 1950 at age 49, and her doctors told her she had to lose weight, or she was going to die.

She was put on a baby food diet, and Celesta lost more than 400 pounds the following year. Celesta then wrote a book about her amazing weight loss called *Diet or Die: The Dolly Dimples Weight Reducing Plan*. It was published in 1968, and she spent the better part of her last years on a lecture circuit motivating others to lose weight and get healthy. She used her popularity to promote her shows, telling her audiences, "My friends told me I'd kill myself if I went on a crash diet. Well, if I do then they don't have to bring me to the cemetery on a truck. I'll fit into a hearse now."

There would be several Fat Ladies who billed themselves as "Dolly Dimples" after Cesta left the sideshow circuit, but she was by far the most famous of them. Her beloved husband, Frank, died in 1967, but Celesta traveled the world again as a widow before finally settling down to run a small art gallery in Miami for several years.

She died in February 1982 at the age of 80 – and she never gained the weight back that she'd lost.

"HAPPY JACK"

THE BEST-KNOWN FAT MAN OF THE SIDESHOW CIRCUIT ERA was undoubtedly Jack Eckert, born in Lafayette, Indiana, in 1877. He was bit by the show business bug when he was only 10 years old, eating his way to a top slot in the carnivals of the era.

Jack always claimed he would have liked a straight job, but his size stopped him from seeking ordinary employment. He was known for his outrageous costumes, often dressing as a woman or a toddler – or, on many occasions, showing up on stage in nothing but shoes.

But as wild as he could be on stage, Jack lived a pretty quiet, typical life. He was very proud of the fraternal organizations he'd joined and often hung pennants for them on stage. He billed himself as "the Largest Elk, Mosse, and Woodman of the World." Jack was married and had two children of ordinary size but was estranged from his family at the time of his death.

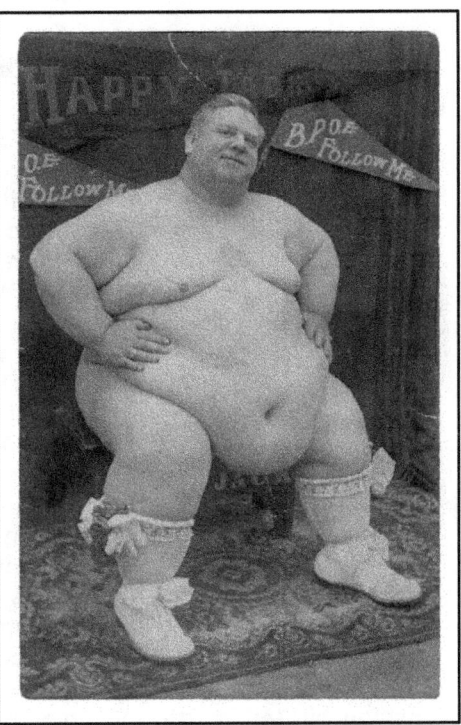

As ordinary as his daily life was, Jack was not a modest man and didn't consider himself one of those people who presented themselves as Puritan, church-going pillars of the community. Jack made a lot of extra money selling his pitch cards and noticed that his nude cards outsold his standard ones 3 to 1. He was proud of his size, and his weight fluctuated between 740 and 790 pounds. His stomach hung down to his knees, and he needed a 90-inch waist for his pants.

Unlike most of the larger folks who worked in sideshows and carnivals, Jack was healthy and somehow avoided the health and mobility issues that caused problems for others. Health issues didn't kill him – an auto accident did.

He was in Flomaton, Alabama, in February 1939 when his specially built truck collided with a freight truck. It took ten men to get him to the hospital, and he had to be placed on two beds that were strapped together. But there was nothing that could be done for him. He died from fractured ribs and internal injuries. He was 62.

His manager offered his body to Tulane University, saying that Jack had always wanted to have his body studied to explain his size, but the school turned down the offer.

Instead, his body was placed in a 500-pound cypress coffin, and Jack was buried in Mobile, Alabama. He was sent to his grave with honor from his beloved lodge brothers, the Elks, the Moose, and the Woodmen of the World.

ROBERT EARL HUGHES

ROBERT EARL HUGHES WAS BORN IN FISH HOOK, ILLINOIS – A tiny town in Pike County, north of Pittsfield – in 1926. He weighed just over 11 pounds at birth, and his parents watched in amazement as their son doubled his weight more than four times by age six. By then, he weighed 203 pounds and, at age 25, tipped the scale at 896 pounds. He was just a little over six feet tall. He'd eventually earn the title of the heaviest man in the world at 1,041 pounds.

Robert spent most of his adolescent and adult lives on the sideshow circuit. He traveled in a specially constructed trailer that accommodated his size, and stage areas and chairs had to be reinforced – or built from scratch – for his performances. He finally became so large that he could not climb the stairs to the stage and was forced to exhibit himself at ground level. He always wore the same thing – custom-made bib overalls – and they became his trademark.

Robert likely suffered from some glandular condition. It's really the only thing that would explain his extraordinary weight gain as a child. Friends and family always stated that he was a "light eater."

In 1958, Robert contracted measles while on tour in Bremen, Illinois -- in Southern Illinois, near Chester--and could not fit into an ambulance that was sent to take him to the hospital. When he finally did reach the medical center, he was too large to fit through the doors, and the beds were not strong enough to hold him. He had to be treated in his trailer, which was parked outside the hospital.

Tragically, he developed uremia and died on July 10, 1958. He was only 32. Surgeons also reported that he was suffering from a heart condition and other medical issues.

He was buried back home in Pike County at the Benville Cemetery. His custom-built coffin was the size of a piano case and had to be lowered into his grave with a crane. Friends and family wept openly. It was said during the service that Robert's heart had been as big as his body.

"THE WORLD'S LARGEST TWINS"

IF YOU WERE LIKE ME AS A KID, YOU LOVED TO THUMB through the latest *Guinness Book of World Records* when it came out each year. If you did it too, there's no way you can forget the photo of the oversized twins on a pair of mini-bikes putt-putting down the road. If you remember it, you remember Benny and Billy McCrary, history's largest set of twins.

Benny's weight was listed at 814 pounds, while Billy was a puny 784 pounds. They boasted identical 84-inch waistlines and often called themselves the McGuire Twins because they claimed announcers in other countries had difficulty pronouncing their names when they traveled the world in the 1970s as tag team wrestling partners.

The twins were born in December 1946 and grew up in Hendersonville, North Carolina. They dropped out of high school and moved to Texas, where they worked branding cattle. They were already big men. Benny once said in an interview that he and his brother had started gaining weight when they were hospitalized as young children with a severe case of German measles that damaged their pituitary glands.

By age 10, they had topped 200 pounds, and by the time they were 16, they weighed 600 pounds. They were a good-natured, fun-loving pair with many friends and a habit of teasing one another. They also considered themselves ladies' men, and most of their bickering had to do with one young woman or another.

They had an unusual career path. They performed with sideshows and carnivals and appeared in Las Vegas. They worked for Honda and did commercials and a promotional ride on their bikes from New York to Los Angeles. They also enjoyed popularity as a professional wrestling tag team and even appeared on *The Tonight Show* with Johnny Carson.

Billy died on July 14, 1979, from injuries he sustained in a motorcycle accident in Niagara Falls. He was thrown from his bike while doing one of the many stunts he and his brother had become famous for. He was 32.

Benny continued to wrestle for a while, teaming up with crowd favorites like Andre the Giant, but eventually settled back in Hendersonville, where he opened a pawn shop and worked as an auctioneer. In 1998, he and his wife moved to Walkerton, North Carolina, where he worked for a golf course. Benny died from heart failure on March 26, 2001. He was 54.

The McCrary brothers were buried together at Hendersonville's Crab Creek Baptist Cemetery. Their massive tombstone is embossed with that photo of the twins on their mini-bikes, which always made them laugh, and the words "The World's Largest Twins."

The marker is said to be the world's largest granite tombstone – 13 feet wide and weighs three tons – and is a fitting tribute to the larger-than-life twins.

PART THREE: THE "LIVING SKELETONS"

ANOTHER POPULAR "CREATED FREAK" ON THE SIDESHOW CIRCUIT was the "human" or "living skeleton." Both men and women were exhibited under this moniker, but the men far outnumbered the female performers. Displaying living skeletons next to the show's fat person was always a crowd-pleaser, especially when the publicity stunt of a phony marriage between the two was added to the mix.

Some performers suffered from medical conditions that made them thin, others suffered from diseases like scarlet fever or tuberculosis, but mostly, they starved themselves into the role.

"THE HUMAN SKELETON"

PROBABLY THE MOST FAMOUS LIVING SKELETON WAS Isaac Sprague, born in East Bridgewater, Massachusetts, in 1841. He always claimed that he was an average child until around the age of 12. He said he got a cramp one day while swimming and laid down in the shade to rest. He soon became sick, however, and he stayed ill in the weeks that followed until his weight had decreased to only 40 pounds. He claimed never to be able to gain much weight after that.

Isaac's weight loss wasn't that simple, however. He was actually afflicted by what is known as progressive muscular atrophy, a painless condition that comes on gradually and saps a person's strength. It causes severe fatigue, muscle wasting, and, in Isaac's case, severe weight loss.

When he was older, Isaac worked for his father as a cobbler apprentice and later became a grocer, but he tired easily and could not keep either job. The sideshow became an alternative for him, and in 1865, he accepted a position as a performer. It was the perfect work for him. All he had to do was sit or stand before a fascinated crowd and tell a story.

He eventually became such a popular attraction that P.T. Barnum hired Isaac to work for him. In the following publicity campaigns, he was described as five feet, five and a half inches tall and weighing only 46 pounds.

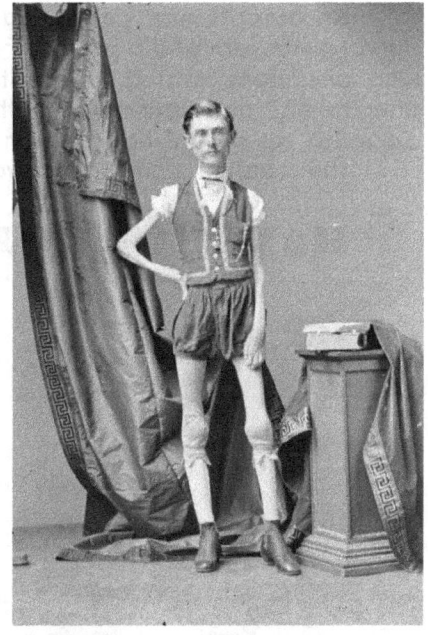

Despite his size and appearance, Isaac married a woman from Rockland, Massachusetts, and despite his lack of physical stamina, they had three sons.

Whether they were publicity stunts or not, newspaper stories later appeared that spoke of his many love interests, and he was said to have even married a few of them, including a female living skeleton and a beauty queen. No mention was ever made of a divorce from his wife.

At least one woman took the newspaper stories seriously – the beauty queen Minnie Johnson. She claimed she had married Isaac in 1883 and had lived and traveled with him during the last years of his life. When he died, she quickly filed a claim on his $10,000 estate. His first wife and his dubious second wife had to fight things out in court. The scandal created newspaper headlines like "Living Skeleton Had Skeletons in His Closet."

Isaac died in Chicago on January 4, 1887. One account said that he donated his body to Harvard Medical School, while another claimed they bought it for $1,000. Whichever it was, Isaac had already quipped to a reporter that "they can't have it until I'm done with it."

An autopsy was performed by Dr. W.E. Whitney, curator of the Harvard Museum and a professor of anatomy at the university. Several local physicians assisted him. He stated that Isaac's cause of death was pneumonia and announced the progressive muscular atrophy diagnosis. His organs had been in healthy condition.

The location where Isaac was buried remains unknown.

HANNAH AND JOHN BATTERSBY

WHETHER TRUTH OR PUBLICITY STUNT FICTION, THE MOST popular sideshow marriages were always between a Fat Lady and a living skeleton, the press never failed to write a story, and the public never got bored of reading about the unusual couple – probably because they had the "Jack Sprat" nursery rhyme and the illustration of the very thin man, and the very fat wife stuck in their heads.

Hannah Jane Perkins, 16, and John Battersby, 28, were married in February 1857 and, by all accounts, were very happy together until Hannah died in 1889. In her obituary, it was reported by her managers that she weighed 688 pounds when she'd gotten married and 800 pounds when she died. A hormonal imbalance likely caused Hannah's weight. Hannah had been a light eater unlike many sideshow Fat Ladies who ate their way into the spotlight.

Hannah had been born in Maine in 1841 and always claimed she was a normal-sized child. Nothing changed until she reached the age of 12. By the time she was in her late 20s, she was exhibiting as a Fat Lady with P.T. Barnum, and the trade cards she sold at her shows claimed she weighed 714 pounds, stood over six feet tall with broad shoulders that measured three feet wide, and had been proclaimed as the heaviest woman in the world. It was said that, at times, she couldn't fit through the doors of the places where she performed, and special accommodations had to be made for her massive bulk.

She died at age 48 in her home in Philadelphia. Her death certificate cited her cause of death as a bacterial skin infection that, most likely, was a result of a fall she'd recently taken from a stage that injured her leg.

Her husband, overcome with grief, stood guard over her body and would not allow the many reporters and curiosity-seekers who crowded the lawn in front of their home to see his wife in her oversized coffin. She was buried in the Battersby family plot at Cedar Hill Cemetery, but no stone marks her grave.

John had been born in Lancashire, England, in 1929. He claimed his weight loss began when he was a teenager, and by the time he was 23, he was exhibiting at P.T. Barnum's American Museum as a human skeleton. His trade cards listed his weight between 45 and 52 pounds, but that claim is unlikely. The truth never wrecked a good story, and entertainers were encouraged to invent any story about themselves they liked, as long as it sold tickets.

While Hannah and John were both working with Barnum, they met, fell in love, and got married. They had three children together – two daughters and a son who died in infancy.

In 1873, John sustained a spinal injury that required him to use a wheelchair for the rest of his life and to retire from the sideshow. John, Hannah and their daughter Rachael lived together in Philadelphia while John's widowed mother, his widowed sister, and his brother lived next door. Having family so close was an asset since Hannah worked and needed to travel. It was said that the couple was very close, and Hannah would often cradle John in her arms like an infant whenever he felt tired or depressed.

It was also widely reported that Hannah had once rescued John from a fire at Barnum's museum by throwing him over her shoulder and carrying him to safety. While the story is possible since the museum did burn twice, it was most likely just a story invented to increase interest in this odd but loving couple.

After Hannah's death, John moved to Almena, Kansas, to live with his daughter Rachael, who was now married. He died on February 6, 1897, just a few days short of his 68th birthday. He was buried in Fairview Cemetery in Norton County, Kansas.

In death, he is sadly far away from the woman that he loved so much.

THE FAKE AND THE NOT SO FAKE

GAFFS – THE CARNIE WORD FOR SIDESHOW FAKES – have been part of the carnival and circus from the beginning. P.T. Barnum's first attraction, Joice Heth, certainly wasn't what she was advertised to be, and when Barnum opened his American Museum, the phonier the exhibit was, the more people wanted to see it.

Two words prove that belief – Feejee Mermaid.

People wanted to see something strange and exotic, and Barnum was more than happy to show those things to the public. He never let the truth get in the way of selling a ticket, nor did any other sideshow men who followed in his wake. The performers themselves also spun tales to enhance their shows, and the details often changed to fit the tastes of different audiences.

The tradition of the sideshow was about entertainment, not truth. Almost every exhibit – no matter how real – blurred the lines of reality, and some of them stepped over the lines completely.

But as long as the audience walked away happy and felt their money had been well spent, it didn't matter if what they'd seen had been a gaff.

PART ONE:
THE BEARDED LADIES

WHEN I WAS A KID, I ALWAYS WONDERED WHERE ALL THE circus Bearded Ladies had gone. Sure, I'd seen a few women who looked like they could grow a full beard if they tried hard enough, but they were nothing like the women I'd seen in all those books about sideshow attractions. I always just assumed that maybe women had started shaving or something, so you didn't see Bearded Ladies anymore.

And then, during one of my summers with the carnival, I learned the truth --- most, although not all, sideshow Bearded Ladies weren't ladies at all. Most of them were actually effeminate men dressed in women's clothing. Thanks to the moral standards of the day, these "women" didn't have to prove they were female, and so they were allowed to continue conning the marks for as long as their careers would allow.

But not all of them were fakes. There were authentic women with beards who exhibited themselves in the sideshows, and what follows are some of the most famous of the honest-to-goodness Bearded Ladies.

ANNIE JONES

OF ALL THE AUTHENTIC BEARDED LADIES IN THE SIDESHOWS, Annie Jones was undoubtedly the most famous. She was born in Marion, Virginia, in July 1865 and suffered from a medical condition called hypertrichosis, which caused excessive hair to grow on her body.

Her parents – apparently not sure what to do with her – essentially leased her to P.T. Barnum when she was only nine months old. She began to be exhibited at his museum at age one. Her father died soon after, but her mother, Margaret, had a comfortable life since she was receiving $150 a week for Annie, a very large sum at the time.

As usual, Barnum was doing more for his performers than their own families did, providing Annie and her mother with a place to live and a tidy sum to appear with the baby on stage, where she undressed Annie and showed off her hairy arms, legs, and shoulders. By age five, Annie also had a beard and mustache and was being billed as the "Bearded Girl."

A few years later, in an incident that was most likely a publicity stunt, a New York phrenologist – a "doctor" who used the bumps on a person's head to diagnose their mental state – kidnapped Annie. Barnum and the police quickly found her being exhibited at a fair, but when the phrenologist claimed Annie as his daughter, Margaret had to sue to get the child back. Barnum, of course, paid for her attorney.

In court, the judge kept Annie secluded in a separate room, brought her in, and told her to go to her father or mother. Annie walked straight to her mother, so the judge declared the case closed, and the little girl returned home – or, well, to the apartment at Barnum's museum.

Margaret continued her role as a lousy parent in the years that followed. In census records, Annie's profession was listed as "show business," and she was living with her mother and her older spinster sister, Mary. Since neither her mother nor her sister worked, it's likely that Annie was the sole earner for the family.

But that wasn't going to last forever. When Annie was 16, she married a circus talker named Richard Elliott, but in 1895, she divorced him. In the dissolution papers, she stated that he had abandoned her – 15 years earlier. Elliott hadn't been seen since then.

Why bother to get a divorce after not seeing your husband for a decade and a half? Because Annie wanted to get married again. Her new husband was William Donovan, a wardrobe man with the Barnum show who'd been her friend for many years. Unfortunately, more heartache followed when William died a few years later.

During her time with the sideshows, Annie became the nation's top Bearded Lady and one of the chief spokespersons during what became known as the 1899 "Freak Protests."

In January, Barnum and Bailey's "Greatest Show on Earth" was a few weeks into its second winter season, and they were playing in London when the protests began. The performers in the freak show rebelled and called a meeting to protest being known as "freaks." They demanded a new name. When word of this hit the newspapers, it caused a public sensation – but all was not what it seemed.

Among the performers on the tour were Annie; Jo-Jo the Human Dog, whose face was covered with a thick growth of long silky hair; Herman the Great Expansionist, said to be able to expand his chest by more than 16 inches and break chains with its force; Charles Tripp the Armless Wonder; James Morris the Man with Elastic Skin; Hassan Ali, The Egyptian Giant; Khusania, the Hindu Dwarf; James Coffey, a Living Skeleton; and Sol Stone, known as the Lightning Calculator because of the speed with which he could solve mathematical problems.

All of them joined in the revolt. On January 6, Annie called a meeting to protest the word "freak." She outlined her objections, saying the word meant something like "fright," and if a beard made a lady frightening, then the word should also apply to a man. And no man with a beard as fine as hers, she said, would refer to himself as frightening.

The meeting approved a strong resolution, demanding that another name needed to be adopted to replace the offending word.

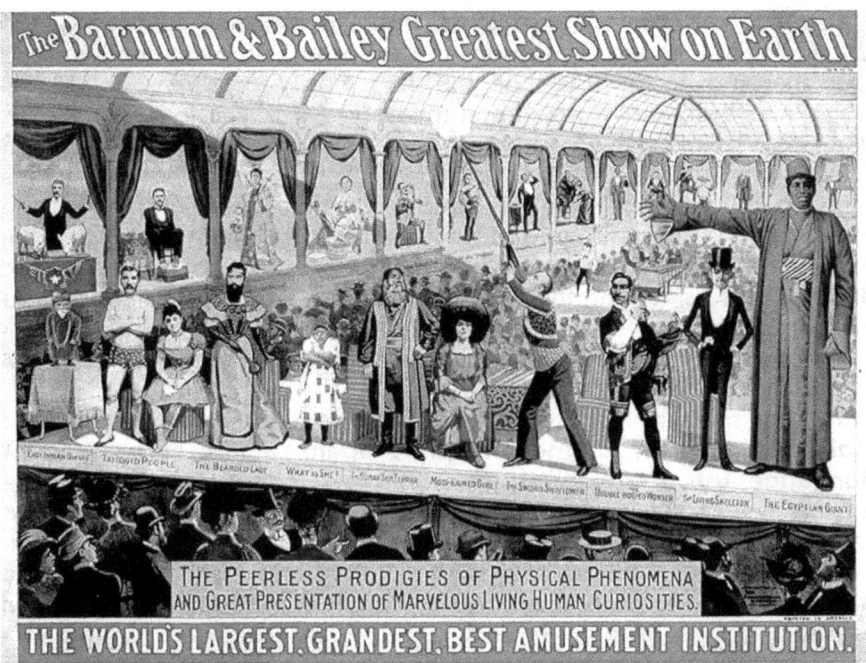

ADVERTISEMENT FOR BARNUM AND BAILEY'S "PRODIGIES" BEFORE THE ENTIRE "FREAK PROTEST" WAS EXPOSED AS A MASSIVE PUBLICITY STUNT

However, since no one could come up with an idea, the meeting was adjourned until the following day.

The news of the rebellion and suggestions that the freaks might even go on strike provoked a media frenzy across Britain. Articles were written defending and condemning the performers.

The group met again on January 15 to look over all the suggestions for a title to replace "freaks" that had come in from all over the country. The new names included Ambiguities, Anomalies, Curios, Deviations, Inexplicables, Peculiar People, Uniques, Unusuals, Vagaries, and even Whim-Wams. However, after a lengthy discussion, the possibilities were narrowed down to two – Prodigies and Human Marvels. After a vote, Prodigies came out on top.

After the vote, a delegation was dispatched to see James Bailey, who was pleased with the change. He immediately ordered all signs and publicity materials to use Prodigies instead of Freaks.

The press department, always on the lookout for a good story, immediately went into action, and news of the "Revolt of the Freaks" was published worldwide.

The Prodigies were satisfied, and life returned to normal. The show finished its winter season, toured Britain through the summer, and then moved on to Europe, the story mostly forgotten.

And that would have been the end of it if, just four years later, the circus hadn't started using the word "Freaks" again. Another protest meeting was called, this time in New York, where the circus was playing a season at Madison Square Garden. Everything about the meetings, the suggestions, and the votes was strangely similar to what had occurred in London. Many reporters were suspicious, but they put their doubts aside, and the story of a second "freaks revolt" appeared in the papers.

And then, finally, the truth came out – the whole thing had been a massive publicity stunt.

The mastermind behind it was Richard Hamilton, Barnum and Bailey's legendary, long-serving press agent. Thanks to his flair for language, use of adjectives, hyperbole, and alliteration, he was one of the best-known ad men of the era. He was said to have produced two million words of promotional copy yearly and had memorized more adjectives than any man alive. P.T. Barnum himself had once said that he owed more of his success to Hamilton than any other man on earth.

In 1899, he had been doing his job, keeping the show firmly in the headlines, and created the "freaks revolt" and got the performers to go along with the stunt. Hamilton later said it had been so successful that he was almost ashamed of himself.

The revolt had been one of Annie's last moments of glory with the sideshow. She retired soon after as a very wealthy woman. In addition to educating herself and becoming an accomplished musician, she invested her earnings wisely in real estate.

Sadly, she wouldn't have long to enjoy her fortune. She died in Brooklyn on October 22, 1902, from tuberculosis. She was buried in Evergreen Cemetery, but no tombstone marks her grave.

"MADAME DELAIT"

CLEMENTINE CLATTEAUX WAS BORN IN MARCH 1865 IN France. She had an ordinary childhood, and her beard did not begin growing until she reached puberty as a teenager. When she was 20, she married a local baker, Jacques Delait, and they opened a café and bakery in the village of Thaon-les-Vosges.

Until this time, Clementine shaved her face daily, not allowing her beard to grow. But the story went that a customer didn't believe she had a beard and wagered 500 francs that she wouldn't prove it.

But she did. And not only that, but she also allowed it to grow and become thick and luxurious. Everyone was fascinated with it, and she loved the attention it brought. She sported it around the village without embarrassment and even renamed the bakery Café de la Femme Barbee – the Café of the Bearded Woman.

In 1919, she and Jacques adopted a five-year-old girl whose parents had died during the

Spanish Influenza pandemic of the previous year. The couple had been married for 34 years but were childless.

As Clementine's fame spread, she received dozens of offers from sideshow and circus managers each week. But Jacques' health had gotten bad, and she didn't want to leave him.

After he passed away, though, Clementine traveled to England, Paris, Ireland, and eventually Coney Island for limited paid engagements. She also sold hundreds of photos of herself, typical of the day's performers.

Madame Delait – as she billed herself with the sideshows – died in 1939. Her tombstone had a simple epitaph that said it all – "Here lies Clementine Delait, the Bearded Lady."

BARONESS SIDONIA DE BARCSY

THE BARONESS SIDONIA DE BARCSY A RARE SIDESHOW performer in that she didn't have to lie to create a fantastic story for her audiences. She couldn't have made up anything that would've been stranger than the truth. In fact, her lies would have been easier to believe.

For one thing, she didn't have to make up her royal title – it was real. When she was 19, she'd married into Hungarian royal lineage when she wed Baron Antonio de Barcsy, a cavalry officer. She was

 young and beautiful, and her life became a series of privileged but routine social events.

But her life quickly changed. On February 28, 1885, the couple's first and only child – a son named Nicu – was born. He was very small, weighing less than two pounds, but he managed to flourish despite his size – and so did the soft, fuzzy beard that suddenly started to grow on Sidonia's face a few weeks after Nicu's birth. Unlike other Bearded ladies who grew dark beards and usually had excessive hair all over their bodies, Sidonia's beard was light brown, and the rest of her body remained unchanged.

When Nicu was still a baby, the family's fortunes began to change. Their money dwindled, possibly because of the social and political changes in Hungary at the time – or because Antonio was a terrible businessman and had made a series of bad investments. Whatever the reason, the family sold off most of their belongings and left Hungary in the 1890s.

Sideshows were extremely popular in Europe and America at the time. And that sparked Antoni's next business idea. He was lucky enough to have two performers living with him – a Bearded Lady and an undersized son. Antonio, a burly man his whole life, started promoting himself as a Strongman and, later, as a Fat Man. They became known as the "De Barcsy Troupe" and became successful touring Europe for more than a decade. Then, in the early 1900s, they sailed for America.

They became popular in the United States, too. How many sideshow performers in America could boast royal titles that were real? They made a handsome living, and then, in 1912, Antonio died, leaving behind his 46-year-old wife and adult son, who was still quite small.

Soon after, Sidonia met Frederick Tischu, a sideshow performer who billed himself as Charles Henry Buck, "The Long-Haired Cherokee Buck Man." He was a tall, handsome scoundrel of German heritage who didn't have a drop of Cherokee – or any other Native American – blood in his body. He was an expert at rope tricks.

To most respectable people at the time, a woman was expected to mourn her dead husband for at least two years, but the Baroness decided that she wasn't worried about scandal and quickly married the much younger Charles, who had swept her off her feet.

Sidonia and Nicu made much more money than Charles, but the "Cherokee Buck Man" had no trouble spending his new family's money. Some reporters claimed he had a drinking problem. Others stated that he was a chronic womanizer.

He was probably both because, by the winter of 1914, the family found themselves in dire straits, broke, and forced to rely on the kindness of friends and fellow performers to make it until the spring carnival season began.

When good weather arrived, the trio joined the Campbell Brothers troupe and exhibited at Coney Island. Finally, flush again, Sidonia moved to Drummond, Oklahoma, and built the town's first brick house. Cambell Brothers Circus wintered near Drummond in those days, and Sidonia always said she felt comfortable there, thanks to the kindness of the locals.

Illness eventually forced the Baroness into retirement, and money again became a problem since she was the family's biggest draw. Charles must have realized the money was running out since it was at this time that she ran off with another sideshow performer, Dolletta Boyle, "The World's Smallest Mother," one of the top earners in the business.

Sidonia never saw her younger husband again, and she died in October 1925 at the age of only 59. Many of those who knew her said that her broken heart killed her faster than her illness did. She was cremated, and her ashes were sent to New York and buried next to her first husband, Antonio.

The circus remains a large part of the heritage and history of Drummond, Oklahoma, and a huge mural there keeps the memory of the Bearded Lady of Drummond and her little son alive to this day.

PART TWO:
THE HALF AND HALFS

DURING THE HEYDAY OF THE SIDESHOW, THE HALF MAN / half woman act was one of the most popular – and probably the biggest moneymakers – on the fairground circuit, even though most of the performers were just skilled actors who put on a good show for crowds who were often embarrassed by the curiosity that brought them there. If even the seediest outfit had a good half-and-half show, that outfit would make money even if it didn't have any big draws.

A half-and-half show could – and did – carry many carnival sideshows because the public was fascinated by its entire lurid concept.

The performers were billed as "hermaphrodites," a person with both male and female organs. The word "hermaphrodite" comes from the Greek legend of Hermaphroditus, the son of Hermes and Aphrodite, who fell in love with a nymph and became both man and woman. The word was eventually replaced by the term "intersex," as ideas about sex were eclipsed by gender identity.

But there was no political correctness in advertising for the sideshows. Every possible term was used for advertising these shows – including "freaks of nature" – but they had to stop short of openly offending their audiences.

However, most sideshow half-and-halfs were nothing but fakes and grifters. Performers who truly had the external features of both sexes were rare. The vast majority were men who had purposely built up the arm, chest, and leg muscles on one side of the body while leaving the other half soft and "feminine." In this way, they could exhibit their body divided in half – the right side male and the left side female.

The shows were sexually explicit – especially for the time – but were offered in the spirit of being "scientific," which helped them to skirt the laws and the public's notions on what could and couldn't be shown on the fairgrounds.

There's no way they could get away with anything like this today.

BOBBY KORK

ONE OF THE MOST POPULAR HALF AND HALF PERFORMERS of the 1940s and 1950s was Bobby Kork, who, despite his exhibitions, dated many women and broke many hearts. He appeared naked for each show and was able to pull off the scam that he was a "hermaphrodite" for decades.

As described, Bobby built up the right side of his body, and when he performed, a realistic fake breast was glued to the left side of his chest. His genitals were then pulled back and secured with flesh-colored tape – although rumors spread that he actually achieved this with an elastic band and a cork, which inspired his "Kork" stage name.

On many occasions, Bobby had to rely on his more developed right side to fight off the more curious spectators who tried to grope him during his performances. This, of course, just added to the sensational nature of the show.

After retiring from the sideshow, Bobby became a noted photographer specializing in drag performers, and his images were eventually collected by Cornell University.

Little else is known about him – including his real name – other than he died from food poisoning. But when he died and where, or even how old he was, remains unknown.

FRANCIS-FRANCINE HODGKISS

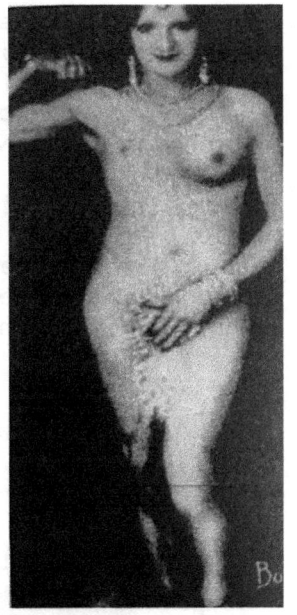

SO LITTLE IS KNOWN ABOUT FRANCIS-FRANCINE'S LIFE THAT not a single photograph of them exists, and there was little written about them in newspapers of the day.

It's believed they were a true half-and-half – a female born with both a vagina and a penis, or perhaps a very large clitoris that passed as a penis for audiences and no scrotum. They were described as having a masculine face and never developed breasts.

Sideshow history claims that Francis-Francine was placed in the sideshow by their mother after a doctor was called to examine the child after they began experiencing tremendous pain. At that point, they were discovered to be not strictly female. They were eventually studied by several doctors who were all amazed by their anatomy. Their mother quickly realized the money-making potential the child represented, and her official story was that she felt it was her duty to exhibit them in the sideshow because her child was not fake but the real thing. She added that Francis-Francine had been cruelly mocked by children and adults back home, and the carnival seemed safer for them.

In reality, the mother enjoyed the money and the lifestyle afforded to her by the sideshow circuit and didn't want to return home to her husband and her boring life.

During the Depression, Francis-Francine made over $500 a week, but the money was going to support their mother and several greedy relatives who jumped on the bandwagon. The money they had left was usually given to children's charities, or they used it to buy candy and gifts that were given to children who hung around the show.

What happened to Francis-Francine after their brief career is unknown. There's no hard information about when they were born, died, or even stopped performing. We only know they performed at a difficult time in American history and can only hope they were eventually able to get free from the clutches of their money and relatives and had a chance to enjoy a life of their own.

PART THREE: WILD MEN AND WOMEN

THE WILD MAN OR WOMAN WAS A REGULAR SIDESHOW attraction, along with other standard performers like the Fat Lady, tattooed people, sword swallowers, and hoochie-coochie girls. And why not? It was a relatively cheap act to put together, and it was easy to find someone of color to portray an exotic and dangerous inhabitant of some foreign land or to pay the part of Darwin's "missing link," especially since they faced tougher economic times than most Americans of the era did.

The "Wild Men" shows appealed to audiences because they allowed them to get close to danger without truly being at risk. They could stare at murderous "headhunters" without ever having to worry about losing their heads.

But their real appeal was a racist one. The shows addressed the pressing concerns about race that most of the predominantly white audiences of the time had about Black people, Asians, and the waves of foreigners immigrating to America. They could now stare openly at people of color presented as savages and feel justified in their belief that the white race was indeed superior.

That might not have been the intention of the owners of the sideshows, but racism was still the end result.

It is true that the choice to pose as wild men and savages was a decision made by the performers or their relatives for monetary gain, but I'm not sure that's a great defense for the wildly racist shows.

Most of the performers had little choice when it came to employment, especially those who were mentally challenged and had little control over their own destiny. Those who chose a life in the sideshow as a wild man did so because there was very little other work available for African Americans and immigrants at the time.

For many, I'm sure the money and the room and board that came from exhibiting themselves for the gawking public was preferred over other ways of making a living, but it's a shame that this kind of show had to be created to offer them a chance to work.

"THE WILD MEN OF BORNEO"

HIRAM AND BARNEY DAVIS, MENTALLY CHALLENGED BROTHERS from Connecticut, were "discovered" by Lyman Warner in 1852 when they were around 26 years old. Hiram was born in 1825, and Barney in 1927. They stood only three feet, four inches tall, and allegedly weighed only 45 pounds.

The brothers were essentially sold to Warner by their mother, Catherine Davis. By the way, she would try to regain custody of her sons several times, either because of guilt, love, or because she realized they had a very lucrative career. All her attempts failed.

By then, Warner had already started promoting them as "The Wild Men of Borneo." He claimed they were bloodthirsty wild men from the exotic land who had been captured after a fierce fight in which many sailors had been killed and maimed.

Historically, the natives of Borneo and its adjacent islands pirated European trading vessels that traveled through the region, providing the lore that the inhabitants were fierce, wild people. The sailors who returned from the region embellished the tales and helped the legend grow. Since most people of the time didn't know anything else about Borneo, it was easy to attract crowds to see the "wild men" who'd been captured there and were now on display.

There's no record of how Warner treated the brothers, but they eventually ended up in the care of P.T. Barnum, who taught them the show routines that made them a star attraction. They stayed with Barnum until Hiram died in 1905. He billed them as the twin sons of the Emperor of Borneo and the only wild men in captivity.

The two brothers possessed incredible strength. They would easily lift audience members and would wrestle any man who was brave enough – or drunk enough – to get on stage. They also performed acrobatics, danced, recited poems, and talked gibberish that spectators were assured was their native language.

In private, the brothers were quiet, soft-spoken, mild-mannered, and shy around other performers, who adored the men and always sheltered them from the crowds who tended to make them feel overwhelmed.

When Lyman Warner died, he willed the pair to his son, Hanford, who passed them on to his son, Henry, when he also died. The "Wild Men of Borneo" remained in show business for nearly 50 years and reportedly earned more than $200,000, although how much of that they were allowed to keep is unknown.

Hiram passed away in 1905 at the home of Henry Warner in Waltham, Massachusetts. He was 80 years old. Barney also died at Henry's home in 1912 at age 85.

"ZIP, THE WHAT IS IT"

WILLIAM HENRY JOHNSON – WHO'D BECOME KNOWN AS ZIP – was born in Liberty Corners, New Jersey, in 1857. His parents, William and Mahalia Johnson, were formerly enslaved people and a neighbor brought the attention of a sideshow manager to their son. While attending a traveling show passing through town, the neighbor started talking about the strange boy who lived next door. He had a cone-shaped egg head, a small face with a jutting jaw, and a long, wide nose.

Intrigued, the showman went to the Johnson house and soon had Zip in his custody. His parents had either leased him or sold him to the sideshow, depending on the story you might believe. The showman was ambitious, though, and approached none other than P.T. Barnum with his new find. And with that, Zip had a new home with the "Greatest Showman."

Barnum altered Zip's appearance by shaving his head, leaving only a small tuft of hair on top. He then fitted him with the furry monkey costume that became his trademark. He was exhibited in a cage during his early years with the show and promoted as eating only raw meat, nits, and fruit. Zip would rattle the bars of his cage and growl – all to the audience's delight.

During this time, the question "What is it?" was added to Zip's name, 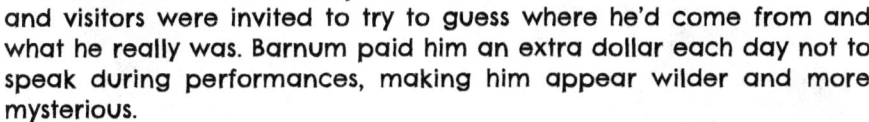 and visitors were invited to try to guess where he'd come from and what he really was. Barnum paid him an extra dollar each day not to speak during performances, making him appear wilder and more mysterious.

Zip was likely mildly developmentally challenged but still very functional and independent. His sister, Sarah, claimed in a 1926 interview that her brother would "converse like the average person and with fair reasoning power" when he came to visit her.

Zip performed for audiences for almost 70 years and thrived on the attention he received. He always carried a top pop gun with him and would jokingly threaten to shoot other performers who got too much attention. Later, he learned to play the violin, and the public never got tired of seeing him dance and play the instrument – all while sporting his comic haircut and monkey suit. He also loved a good cigar, but unless his cigars were the same brand as those smoked by circus owner John Ringling North, he'd stubbornly refuse to perform.

In his later years, Zip mostly only performed at Coney Island, and it's said that he saved the life of a small child from drowning there in 1925.

Zip died just one year later at Bellevue Hospital in New York City from chronic kidney disease. With his sister, Sarah, at his side, Zip uttered his now famous last words: "Well, we fooled them for a long time, didn't we?"

According to his tombstone, Zip was 69 when he died, but according to his death certificate, he was 83. No one knows which is correct. He was buried in New Jersey's Bound Brook Cemetery in an area set aside for the poor and for African Americans. His tombstone was simple, with no mention of his sideshow career.

His death certificate, though, was more accurate. It listed his career as a "showman."

EKO AND IKO, CANNIBALS FROM ECUADOR

ONE OF THE MOST FASCINATING – AND CONFLICTING – SIDESHOW stories is that of black albino brothers George and Willie Muse.

According to their family lore, while the parents of the two boys were working in the fields near their home in Virginia, a white man named Herman "Candy" Shelton offered George, age 8, and Willie, age 6, some candy and a ride in his truck. But he wasn't taking them for a ride – he was kidnapping them, and he later convinced them their mother was dead.

Another version of the story – which became the basis of a 1927 lawsuit – states that a sideshow promoter named Stokes kidnapped the brothers, and they were later stolen from Stokes by another crooked sideshow man, which was how "Candy" Shelton ends up in the story. The lawsuit gave birth to another version of the story that makes the boys' mother, Harriet, responsible for their sideshow career. A 1927 newspaper said she willingly signed a contract with Stokes that let him exhibit her sons on the sideshow circuit when George was 22 and Willie was 19.

The true story of what happened will never be known, but Willie Muse always claimed that "Candy" Shelton kidnapped him and his brother when they were children – and he never varied from it. If true, though, it's odd that there are no sideshow photos of the brothers that show them performing as children. Only adult photos exist, although almost all freak show kids had trade cards to sell at their shows.

Family members – who maintained the kidnapping story was the truth – claimed that Harriet never gave up hope of finding her missing sons. When the circus came to Virginia in 1927 – she lived in Roanoke then – she sought the boys out, resulting in a tearful reunion.

No matter how they ended up in the sideshow, the brothers worked for a series of shows for years but claimed they were never paid and only received room and board. Of course, this doesn't explain how they bought a house in Roanoke in 1961 after retiring from show business.

Regardless, the Muse brothers toured the world exhibiting themselves to the public. By all accounts, they enjoyed the attention and life they wanted on the road, but after they retired, they refused all interviews with reporters, preferring a quiet and private lifestyle.

George died of heart failure in 1971, but Willie outlived him. He died in 2001 at the age of 101.

THE GEEK SHOWS

STORIES OF SIDESHOW GEEKS HAVE BECOME A FASCINATING blend of fact and fiction over the years. The term "geek" was popularized by novelist William Lindsey Gresham in his 1946 book *Nightmare Alley*, which features a wild man performer cavorting in a pit of snakes and biting the heads off the creatures.

Today, we have detailed life stories for many of the sideshow performers of the past, but this has never extended to the geeks who worked the shows. Unlike the freaks, who have obvious differences or unusual talents, geeks can be easily replaced.

A typical geek show combined the snake show, and a wild man show. Snake shows had been around since the earliest days of the carnival and featured "snake charmers" or performers with an affinity – and lack of fear – when it came to snakes. But when combined with a wild man-type show, you had something very different – and much darker.

During the performance, a person on stage or in a pit would bite the head off a snake – later, carnivals used chickens – and then drink its blood. Often prolonged for maximum effect, the act of biting off the head was the climax of the performance. Audiences treated to such a scene of violence and death were mesmerized by the act. They were watching an "ordinary" person taking part in something horrific, and geek shows became a common feature of sideshows. Unlike the freaks who couldn't help their conditions, the geeks were just people doing something terrible. That caused the shows to create a very valid and real fear – that anyone, even an audience member, could become a freak.

As the wild man shows began to become tired – and recognized for their racism – many of them changed into "snake eater" or geek shows. The show consisted of a wild man sitting in a pit of snakes, one of which he eventually bites and eats. At some point, the inside showman lost control of the geek, and the creature leaped at the crowd, often scrambling out of the pit and chasing the audience out on the midway. Geek showmen called this "rousting the tip." The tent was cleared, the geek returned to the pit, and the next show began. All the commotion helped draw a crowd for the talker to direct the next bunch to the ticket box and into the tent.

Showman E.D. Conklin is considered the originator of what was first called the "Eat 'Em Alive" show. He had the first such attraction on the midway in the early 1900s. The real name of his geek, Bosco, was Will Davis, and he had worked at both the Barnum and Bailey and Ringling Brothers circuses before assuming the role of a geek.

Another famous geek was Harry Esau, who worked under the name Eau Sau and started with the Sturgis Carnival Company in 1901. He billed himself as the "original snake eater."

Carey Jones started a four-decade career as Snake-Oid in 1890 at age 11. He was still out on the road when he retired in 1934 and started running the Monster Snake Show for the Dufour and Rogers Carnival Company. When midway old-timers learned he was on the lot, they'd stop by and see him. Jones, who died in 1939, was credited with inventing the Hall of Mirrors attraction, and he opened the first movie theater in Muncie, Indiana.

THE GEEK SHOWS WERE THE BOTTOM RUNG OF SIDESHOW ATTRACTIONS, FEATURING "PERFORMERS" WHO HUDDLED IN PITS AND BIT THE HEADS OF EVERYTHING FROM CHICKENS TO LIVE SNAKES.

During the first few decades of the twentieth century, the geek show was a great moneymaker for carnivals, but as the years passed, they became one of the seedier parts of any show. Some states passed laws to ban snake eating at carnivals, but they were mostly ignored, or carnies started using chickens instead. Animal lovers attempted to discourage the killing of any animals, but that met with eye-rolling. They didn't care about the snakes any more than they cared about the geeks who performed with them.

Geeks worked under pretty terrible conditions. Their most common complaints were broken teeth and jaws or sickness from being around reptiles in such tight spaces. There was also the very real and constant danger of being bitten by a venomous snake. They weren't supposed to be venomous snakes in the pit, but mistakes happened since most geek shows went through dozens of snakes a week, and they were always buying more. In 1932, a geek who worked for the Mad Cody Fleming carnival was bitten by a rattlesnake. He was back on the job the next night, with the incident creating a lot of publicity for the show, and while he survived, many other geeks and showmen didn't.

Despite the risks, geeks earned the lowest wages on the midway since, unlike real freaks, they could be replaced at a moment's notice. There were also rumors that some geeks were not paid wages at all but instead received booze for their performances. This was allegedly said to have happened during Prohibition and after, during the Depression, when chronic drinkers were looking for free liquor. This was cheap for the show owners and allowed them to control their performers through the amount of alcohol they were promised. This provided the show with cheap, dedicated workers willing to stay no matter how horribly they were treated.

Eventually, the geek shows faded from popularity, with only a handful hanging on into the modern era. Among the showmen who stuck around was Al Renton. He grew up in St. Louis and married a woman whose parents were in vaudeville. After working at Coney Island for a time, he became a Ten-In-One operator with the Mighty Sheesley Shows for 14 years. After World War II, when his sons returned from service, he started a geek show called "Eeka," which was supposed to feature a wild woman, shown on the canvas banners outside the tent as a voluptuous woman running through a snake-filled jungle. In truth, though, Eeka was always a man wearing a wig.

Even so, Eeka became a big attraction on the carnival circuit. At one point, Al and his sons, Bobby and Chuck, each had an Eeka show on the road. When Al retired in 1954, Bobby and his wife, Betty, continued the Eeka show until 1961.

On every fairground where they played, they chose a location for the pit inside the tent and dug a deep hole. When they installed the canvas walls and floor that formed the pit, they positioned a hole in the canvas that covered it. Since the geek stayed in the pit the entire time the show was operating, he needed toilet facilities hidden out of sight of the audience, who could only see the geek through the hole.

When excitement was needed, the inside talker would bang a stick on the back of the pit and order Eeka to "get down!" They'd pretend to try and control Eeka but then scream at the audience that she was getting out of control. Then Eeka would lunge for the side of the pit and throw a piece of cut inner tube into the crowd, which sent everyone running out of the tent.

After the Rentons retired from the geek business, the only show left was the Congo, which Hezekiah Trimble ran. His show was half-magic and half-geek, telling audiences they were witnessing "voodoo, hoodoo, and conjoo." His geek did things that would probably put someone in jail today. He'd pull all the feathers off a chicken while it was still alive, stretch its neck until it broke, or simply bite its head off.

By the 1980s, though, animal rights groups began putting a damper on the traditional geek show. Hence, the operators came up with new ideas, often using seemingly drugged-out people with snakes, spiders, and more, sitting in the pit and waiting for audiences to gather. They'd clear the tent just like the geeks from a century before had done – jumping at the bars and scaring the hell out of the crowd.

And another thing stayed the same, too. It wasn't the fake snakes, the chickens, or anything else that happened in the pit that was scaring the audiences – it was still the realization of how they just might be only one lost job, one missed house payment, and one unlucky break away from becoming a sideshow geek themselves.

"WE ARE NOT AS OTHERS"
THE REAL FREAKS WITH THE AMERICAN SIDESHOWS

WHILE THE "CREATED FREAKS" WERE MONEYMAKERS ON EVERY midway across the country, the true stars of sideshows were always the real freaks, those individuals who were truly born different.

These performers did not invent themselves to make money, become famous, or travel the world. These people were born with body anomalies that separated them from society. Their life stories were beyond the imagination of those who made up colorful tales to explain why they chose to put themselves on display. Some were loved by parents who felt their child was "special." Others weren't so lucky and were shunned by their families. Some found happiness with a loving partner, while others tried in vain to find a relationship in which their physical differences would be forgotten. Some made fortunes and retired comfortably, while others lost everything to crooked managers and greedy relatives.

A few were murdered – while others committed murder.

And here are some of their stories.

PART ONE: GIANTS

WE HAVE ALWAYS BEEN FASCINATED BY GIANTS. THEY'VE appeared in both biblical stories and fairy tales as monsters to be feared, from Goliath, the offspring of angels, to Jack's nemesis at the top of that beanstalk.

But our fascination with them has always been mixed up with our fascination with those who seem to be superior to the average person. We admire – sometimes worship – the rare people who possess extraordinary physical attributes that set them apart from the rest of us mere mortals. The average person knows more about Hollywood actors and sports figures than we do about inventors, doctors, or scientists. You can't see how smart someone is at a glance, but you can certainly see what they look like.

It's a fact of human nature that we judge people at first sight. When we look at a giant of a man, we see an individual who is literally above the crowd. We immediately recognize them as someone of superior strength and ability.

The female giant – or giantess, as they were usually advertised – was not so lucky. She had already outgrown every eligible man in her town, and her life was always different from that of her male counterpart. Unlike other kinds of freaks, where the woman was more popular than the man – the Tattooed Lady, the Bearded Lady, and more – the male giant was almost more popular with the crowds.

The sideshow giant was always a moneymaking addition to any Ten-In-One show. In the controlled confines of the canvas tent, there is nothing to fear from the giant. Men and children can safely gawk at the giant for hours because he poses no personal threat. Women could stare without fear of embarrassment.

But just as it was with other freaks – the ones who might be harder to look at – the giants would have been glad to trade places with those who stared at them. Just as we can only imagine what it would be like to be so tall, they wondered what it was like not to have to duck through doorways, to be able to ride in cars, and not have to put two beds together to be able to sleep.

It's human nature to be fascinated with the sideshow giant, and it's also human nature to always want what we cannot have – even when it comes to our height.

"THE WORLD'S TALLEST MAN"

WHEN HE WAS BORN IN ALTON, ILLINOIS, IN 1918, ROBERT Pershing Wadlow weighed just over eight pounds, which was pretty average, but he wouldn't stay average for long. By the time he'd reached his first birthday, Robert weighed over 44 pounds, which was large but not alarming – not yet.

The alarm came later when he was five, weighed 105 pounds, and was five feet, four inches tall. Doctors said he was in good health, though, even if he was over six feet tall at the age of eight.

His family couldn't explain it. His parents were of normal height, and he had four younger siblings who were also of average height. But doctors were finally able to explain it when he was 12. By then, he'd become a regular visitor at Barnes Hospital in St. Louis, where his case was studied and frequent measurements were taken. Doctors believed his size was due to a deformity in his pituitary gland. There was no remedy for that in the 1920s, and it was too dangerous to attempt to operate.

When he entered school, Robert gained the attention of the entire world, although his parents vowed that he'd never work in a sideshow, believing it would keep him from living a normal life – which was really all Robert ever wanted. But performer or not, he got a lot of attention. Doctors, promoters, and fans contacted him.

Despite his size, Robert tried to be a regular kid. He lived in the small town of Alton his entire life, and folks in town, along with his family, made sure he had a sense of belonging. Robert joined the Boy Scouts when he was 13, becoming the tallest Boy Scout in history, at seven feet and four inches tall, and easily head and shoulders taller than even the tallest adult scout leader. He collected stamps, ran a soft drink stand in front of his house, and enjoyed almost anything that average boys liked.

He attended the local elementary school and graduated from Alton High School. He became a Freemason, like his dad, and enrolled at Shurtleff College in Upper Alton. In town, he was dubbed "The Gentle Giant" because of his quiet, soft-spoken manner.

Although Robert was a good student and, from all accounts, a likable and remarkably well-adjusted young man, he began to realize that his dreams of a normal career were impractical. He was, at age 18, eight feet, three and a half inches tall.

He wanted to be an attorney when he started college, but his hands were too big for even the largest pen. He couldn't sit at the desks, fit through the doorways, or use the equipment in the biology lab.

Outside of school, he couldn't sit in movie theater seats and couldn't ride in regular automobiles. When the weather was cold and sidewalks were icy, he had to walk very carefully, surrounded by his friends and holding onto their shoulders. If he fell, they would never be able to help him up, and falling from his height guaranteed broken bones.

Realizing he'd never have a regular career, he turned to the only job that was offered -- promotion and entertainment.

For years, Robert's shoes had been specially made for him by the International Shoe Company, whose popular lines included Peters and Red Goose Shoes. Now, the company agreed to not only supply Robert with his size 37 shoes -- which cost more than $150 per pair to make, which is $3,400 today -- but also to pay him to make appearances that promoted the company. He soon began traveling and appearing in the company's print and film advertising.

Robert's father, Harold, traveled with him in the family car, which had been customized to accommodate his son. He removed the front passenger seat, allowing Robert to sit in the back without being too cramped. A huge shoe of Robert's was left on display at each store he visited with a sign that promised he had tried on each and every one of them.

Obviously, Robert's height was being exploited to draw large crowds, but he refused to think of it that way. He preferred to see the exhibitions as a career in advertising instead. He was making good money, and the idea struck him that he could open a shoe store – or even a whole chain of them – that wouldn't require him to travel and put himself on display. But to do that, he needed to make a lot of money for his start-up.

The best place to do that? The circus, of course.

In 1937, Robert began making appearances for the Ringling Brothers Barnum & Bailey Circus. Robert and his family had always turned down offers to appear in sideshows, but the circus was not only giving him a lot of money but was also covering all his expenses and providing a hotel suite for Robert and his father in every city.

They also agreed to Robert's other demands – that he not be part of the circus sideshow but would appear in the center ring of the show three times each day. He would also be wearing an ordinary business suit, not the tall hats and shoes that exaggerated the heights of other circus giants.

He didn't need any of that, especially since Robert was still growing.

Robert continued to work for the circus for the next couple of years, visiting 41 of the 48 states and the District of Columbia. He and his father traveled more than 300,000 miles and visited over 800 cities. Door frames, elevators, awnings, and hanging lights were still a problem, and to ride in an automobile, he almost had to fold himself in two. Three beds turned crossways provided him with the only sleeping arrangements he could use in a hotel room.

By 1940, Robert reached his full height of eight feet, 11 and a half inches. He weighed 490 pounds, had to wear braces on his legs, and often was forced to walk with a cane.

That summer, he was making his usual personal appearances and was in Manistee, Michigan, on July 4. Robert and his father were scheduled to ride in a parade, but Harold noticed that Robert wasn't eating during lunch. Later, he complained that he didn't feel well, but with their car trapped in the parade route, it took several hours to get him to a doctor.

By then, Robert's condition had worsened. He was rushed to the hospital with a high fever. It turned out one of his leg braces had rubbed off his skin, and the wound became infected. Robert had poor sensation in his legs and didn't feel the problem caused by the brace.

His fever climbed to 106 degrees, and he spent the next few days in terrible pain from the infection. Fearing the worst, Harold called his wife, and she rushed to Michigan. As Robert's condition worsened, doctors performed emergency surgery on his foot, but by then, it was too late.

On the morning of July 15, 1940, Robert died in his sleep.

Robert's body was returned to Alton for burial, and huge crowds came to the Streeper Funeral home and lined the streets in his honor. A special casket was built for him that was 10 feet long and 32 inches wide – too wide to fit through the doors of the church.

Robert was buried with full Masonic honors in the Upper Alton Cemetery. It required 12 pallbearers and an additional eight men to manage his casket.

At Robert's request, special measures were taken to protect his remains. He'd once read about Charles Byrne, the famous Irish Giant, whose bones had been stolen after his death. Robert didn't want to take any chances, and his coffin was encased in concrete.

Since his death, Robert has become known all over the world, but in Alton, Illinois, he's a native son and local folk hero. But no matter how much he managed to achieve in his short life, he was never satisfied with what he'd done. He would've gladly traded all the money and the fame for a single day of what he really wanted – an ordinary life.

"THE TEXAS GIANT"

JACOB RHEUBEN EHRLICH WAS BORN IN DENVER IN 1906 and weighed only four pounds. For the first few years of his life, Jacob was small for his age – and then he turned seven. Within two years, he was over six feet tall, and by the time he was 13, he had grown another foot. By then, his parents, who were Jewish immigrants, had moved the family to El Paso, Texas, and locals started calling the boy "Pecos Bill," a name he stuck with for years.

Around this time, Jacob and his father traveled to Los Angeles. Over seven feet tall at the time, he attracted the attention of Jerry Ash and Zion Meyers, who ran a small motion picture studio called Century Comedies. They offered Jacob a job, and after convincing his father that this was a good opportunity, he was allowed to stay. Jacob took the screen name Jack Earle when he started working in the silent film industry.

Over the next few years, he appeared in many films -- like *Hansel and Gretel* in 1923 and *Jack and the Beanstalk* in 1924 – and attended school.

His movie career came to an end during the making of his 49th picture when he fell from a collapsed scaffolding one day on set. He woke up in the hospital with a broken nose and blurred eyesight and, within three days, was completely blind. Jack's doctor found a pituitary tumor pressing on his optic nerve, so Jack underwent radiation treatments over the next four months. His eyesight returned, and it's been speculated that the treatments may have stopped his growth at eight feet and six and a half inches.

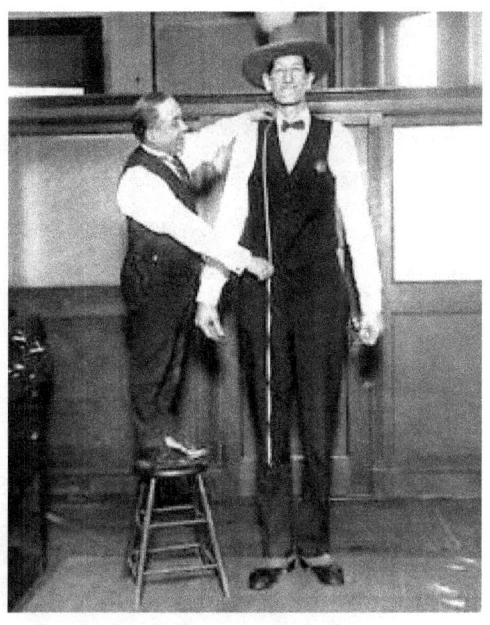

After that, Jack returned to Texas, where he graduated from the University of Texas El Paso, the tallest person ever to do so.

When the Ringling Brothers Barnum & Bailey Circus came to El Paso, one of the highlights of the sideshow was Jim Tarver, a giant being billed as "the world's tallest man." Jack's friends challenged him to go and see just how tall the giant was, and at seven feet five inches tall, Tarver was still more than a foot shorter than Jack. Circus managers hired Jack on the spot, offering him a one-year contract that turned into the next 14 years of his life.

Jack appeared in the sideshow during most of that time – but he never loved it. He soon lost count of the number of stages he stood on for hours at a time. He suffered from claustrophobia and hated people staring at him all the time. Traveling, especially by rail, was torturous to him, even though he had a special sleeper car that had a higher-than-usual roof to accommodate his height.

Despite his unhappiness, Jack was considered one of the most talented in a long line of Ringling Brothers giants. And it wasn't just his appearances on stage. He wrote poetry and John Ringling himself

arranged for him to go to art school to study sculpture after seeing his work in clay of an Australian bushman exhibited by the show. At art school, Jack became interested in painting and studied with Mexican painter Emilio Cahero.

Jack also made many close friends during his time with the sideshow, most of them among the little people in the troupe. He often appeared with "Major Mite," whose real name was Clarence Chesterfield. He was two feet, two inches tall, and Jack frequently held him in the palm of his hand to show off the massive span of his fingers.

His closest friends were the "Dancing Dolls" – Harry, Daisy, Tiny, and Grace – a famous family of little people. It became a familiar sight to see the giant walking between the tents, his big voice booming in reply to a remark from Harry or one of the others who was perched on his shoulder.

Jack and Harry had become friends during the giant's first season with the circus. Feeling uneasy about going on stage, Harry simply pointed out to him that there were more "freaks" in the audience than there were on the sideshow platform.

A friendship was born, and every winter, Jack traveled down to stay with the Dolls at their home in Sarasota, Florida.

Jack stayed with the circus until 1940. By then, he'd become disenchanted with the life of a sideshow freak. He was tired of the hours on stage, of the thoughtless youngsters who banged on his shins to prove he wasn't standing on stilts, the drunks looking for a fight, and the constant embarrassing or just plain stupid questions like, "How's the weather up there?"

After announcing his retirement, he told a reporter: "Learning to overcome the hardships of traveling – such as having to buy my socks a gross at a time and sleeping doubled up in train berths wasn't the chief difficulty. It was psychological – getting people to realize that, despite my size, I was just a normal person trying to earn a normal living in a normal manner."

After leaving the sideshow, Jack moved back to California, where a friend who worked for the Roma Wine Company persuaded him to take a three-month promotional tour with the company. Jack enjoyed the job so much that he decided to stay. He became the "world's tallest traveling salesman" and made quite an impression on customers by arriving in a customized Pontiac and leaving them with a nine-inch-long business car. He traveled the country, lecturing on the importance of the American wine industry during wartime.

Jack enjoyed his years with Roma Wine in San Francisco. The company had a special chair made for him, constructed to fit his large frame. He spent hours in it, working or painting watercolors and oils that he always gave away. At Christmas time, he put on a beard and red coat and played Santa Claus for the children of his co-workers and at orphanages and hospitals in the city.

Jack occupied a large suite at the Palace Hotel and slept in a nine-by-six-foot bed that boasted the "largest sheets in the world." Among the personal possessions he'd collected were a shotgun with a stock as large as a canoe paddle, special coat hangers that were big enough for his suit, extra-long fishing rods, and custom-made belts, shoes, and suspenders.

Part of his route included Humboldt in far Northern California, and when there, he always stayed at the Humboldt Inn, where he was a favorite guest; they'd had a special bed made for him. Jack spent about 11 months every year on the road, traveling through 46 states and crisscrossing the country three or four times a year.

And he loved it.

Just as he had done while he was with the circus sideshow, he sold thousands of his "lucky" giant's rings for 25 cents. (I've got one of them!) When he met someone who still carried one of the rings, he'd always offer to buy it back if it hadn't brought the person good luck.

Jack finally retired in 1951, settling down on a ranch in El Paso. He continued to spend his time visiting orphanages and children's hospitals, entertaining hundreds of kids with stories of the circus and magical giants.

Jack died of kidney failure on July 18, 1952. He was only 46 years old but had managed to pack several lifetimes into only four and a half decades on earth.

"THE SAINTLY GIANTESS"

ELLA KATE EWING WAS BORN IN LA GRANGE, MISSOURI, IN March 1872, the only child of Benjamin and Anna Ewing. Her father was tall, but not unusually so, at six feet and two inches in height. Ella was an average-sized baby, weighing six and a half pounds at birth. It wasn't until just before her seventh birthday that her parents began to become a little concerned. By the time she turned 10, she was not only taller than all the children in her class but taller than her teacher, her parents, and all the grown men in the Gorin, Missouri area, where the family had moved when Ella was a baby.

She was now six feet, nine inches in her stocking feet – but she wasn't done growing yet.

Ella would always maintain throughout her life that she led a lonely childhood. Her size made going to school difficult, and her father had to build a special desk for her since she couldn't fit in any of those in the classroom. Children her age were usually afraid of her, and her height made her too ungainly to take part in any of their schoolyard games. The older girls avoided her because, despite her height, she was still a little girl. She soon became the butt of jokes and pranks, which brought her to tears, causing more laughter at her expense.

Her life finally took a turn for the better when she went with her parents to the county fair. While she was in awe of the sights and sounds of the fairground, Ella found herself a large attraction. A showman approached her father with a lucrative offer to exhibit Ella, but Benjamin initially turned him down. Ella was shy, he knew and had always been hurt by her classmate's taunts and strangers' stares. But the showman didn't give up. He returned with a contract and a higher offer of $50 a week, which Benjamin couldn't pass up. Ella first appeared in the sideshow at age 17 and her mother – or sometimes both parents – traveled with her on the road.

At first, the young woman was stung by being heralded as a "freak," but she eventually learned to see her height as a gift – especially because it was making her a fortune. And that fortune grew when she signed her next contract with P.T. Barnum and became one of his main attractions in America and Europe.

Ella became popular on the circus and fair circuit, and she became known as "The Saintly Giantess" because of her quiet and dignified manner on stage. Advertisements called her "a veritable Amazon, well proportioned, beautiful, and well educated." One of the stunts used to increase ticket sales was to have Ella hold a $500 bill above her head and offer the money to anyone who, standing with their feet flat on the ground, could take the bill from her hand.

Ella always dressed elegantly on stage, which wasn't easy to do. It took 30 yards of material to make her a gown, and she wore size 24 custom-made shoes. She always wore many rings on her fingers to disguise how long they were, but even the rings had to be custom-made, or jewelers had to put pieces into the rings to make them fit.

Oddly, all of Ella's fingers were the same size, with the exception of her little finger. Another peculiarity of her size was that above the waistline, she remained almost average in size, except that her arms and hands grew in proportion to her legs, which gave her an unusual, gangly look.

Life on the road was never easy for her. Beds and train berths were too short, doorways and ceilings were too low, and dining chairs made even having dinner troublesome. Using a standard bathtub was impossible. She always said that she could seldom get comfortable on tour, even though Barnum did his best. She also preferred the country to any city in the world and missed home when she was away, even though her favorite cousin, Teent Blackwood, traveled with her after her mother's death. Anna had died in March 1900 while they were in Chicago on tour.

Ella had always dreamed of owning land and her own home, and it eventually came true. She saved enough to buy 120 acres in Gorin and had a house specially built for her. The doors of her home were 10 feet high, and the furniture was constructed to Ella's specifications. She no longer had to push two beds together to get some sleep.

She loved to horseback ride when she was home, and though she weighed over 250 pounds, her weight and size were never a problem for the large horses that she bought. She was particular about her diet. She ate no salt and little meat but loved fruit and cakes.

Ella had been raised a Baptist and remained very religious. She refused to exhibit on Sundays but rarely went to church because she always feared being there would be too much of a distraction.

She never married, but she had two important romantic relationships in her life. She vowed she'd never marry until she found a man as tall as she was – but she still came close when she met Edward Beaupre, a cowboy called "The Montana Giant," who was only a few inches shorter than Ella. After only a few months, the two became engaged, a date was set, and the preparations were made, but Ella changed her mind at the last minute. It turned out that it would have been more of a business arrangement than a real marriage – a chance for husband and wife giants to go on tour together. That wasn't how Ella envisioned a happy marriage.

The other romantic interest in her life was a giant named Louis Wilkes. Ella turned down his offer of marriage, and Louis spent several years following her around Germany and Austria while she was on tour. Louis died in 1907, reportedly obsessed with Ella until the end.

Ella herself died of pulmonary tuberculosis in January 1913. She was only 40 years old.

Ella was buried in Gorin, Missouri, and the Embalming Burial Case Company of Burlington, Iowa, put its entire work crew together and in one night, they made her massive casket. Her father feared that someone might dig up her remains, so he had it encased in concrete.

Benjamin Ewing died in Ella's specially-made home in 1933, and it burned to the ground three decades later. It had been in disrepair for years by that time, and, sadly, all efforts to find the funds to preserve it as the home of "The Saintly Giantess" had failed.

ANNA SWAN AND "THE KENTUCKY GIANT"

ANNA SWAN WAS BORN IN AUGUST 1846 AT MILL BROOK, Nova Scotia, in Canada to – once again – normal-sized parents. She had 11 siblings, all of average size, but Anna, the third child, was 18 pounds at both. By the time she was four, her parents were already putting her on display in Halifax, where she was billed as the "Infant Giantess." And the name was earned – she was four feet, six inches tall, and weighed close to 100 pounds. Anna's appearance caused quite a stir, and word spread of her size in the newspapers of the day.

When Anna started school, she usually had to sit on the floor because none of the desks for grammar school children had been built to suit her. When allowed, she sat outside and listened to the teach through the window since it was the only way she could be comfortable.

In 1863, Anna, now 17, was persuaded by P.T. Barnum to come to New York and appear at his  museum. By then, she was already over seven feet tall and weighed 350 pounds. He offered her a respectable salary of $23 a month, plus food, lodging, a personal maid, and a complete wardrobe. Anna accepted, but her parents insisted that she also have a tutor and a music coach so that she could continue her education and musical training.

Anna dreamed of becoming a schoolteacher, and I can only imagine that she would have had no trouble keeping the attention of her class.

At the American Museum, Anna was billed as "The Tallest Girl in the World" and was an immediate success. Audiences flocked to the museum's lecture hall to see the giantess, listen to her sing, speak about the history of giants, and perform scenes from various plays.

She eventually grew to a height of seven feet, eleven-and-a-half inches tall, and weighed around 415 pounds. The show advertisements at the time claimed it took "100 yards of satin, 50 yards of lace, and cost $1,000 to make each of Anna's dresses."

I think it's fair to say this was a bit of an exaggeration, especially since Barnum was paying for her wardrobe.

Barnum often paired Anna with various little people, like Commodore Nutt, who was 29 inches tall. The visual results, as you might imagine, were stunning. Eventually, Anna earned a salary of $1,000 a month, plus all the perks, and decided to give up her plans of teaching.

Anna remained at Barnum's museum for two years until the fire that destroyed the building on July 13, 1865. Anna, as well as many other performers, lived in the apartments on the top floor. If newspaper accounts are to be believed, Anna barely escaped alive and would have died if not for the heroics of museum staff members and bystanders who rescued her. Anna returned to her parents' home in Nova Scotia while Barnum rebuilt.

She returned when he opened the new museum a few months later and stayed there – along with touring – until March 3, 1868, when a second fire destroyed the museum, this time for good. He made the decision not to rebuild and take his show of oddities on the road instead.

MARTIN VAN BUREN BATES – WHO WOULD BECOME KNOWN AS "The Kentucky Giant" – was born near Whitesburg, Kentucky, to normal-sized parents. His father, John, was a wealthy farmer, and his mother, Sarah, was a beloved figure in the community. They had a large family, and all the children, aside from Martin, were average-sized. Martin was the youngest child, and sadly, his father died when he was only six.

Coincidentally, this was about the age when Martin began to grow. He would later claim that his growth occurred at such a rate that his mother was alarmed, fearing that he might also die. For the next two years, she refused to allow him to play outside or do any physical work on the farm. Once she realized he wasn't dying – he was just getting very tall – she released him from his confinement.

By age 13, Martin was over six feet tall and weighed close to 300 pounds, larger than any man in town. He attended the local school along with all his brothers. The family saw no need to educate the girls, and his mother and sisters were unable to read or write despite the wealth of the family.

When the Civil War began, Martin was at home, working on his family's farm. He and his older brother, Robert, joined Co. A, 7th Battalion of the Confederate Calvary, and fought side-by-side throughout the war. Martin eventually reached the rank of lieutenant, and Robert was promoted to captain. Later in life, though, Martin would adopt the title of captain for himself and claim the promotion was due to bravery on the battlefield.

The brothers were both captured in April 1863 in Piketon, Kentucky, by Union forces and were sent as prisoners of war to Camp Chase in Ohio. During the winter that followed, hundreds of prisoners there died during a smallpox epidemic, but the Bates brothers survived. In November 1864, Union and Confederate authorities agreed on a prisoner exchange in hopes of alleviating the suffering of sick prisoners on both sides. A total of 10,000 prisoners were exchanged, and Martin and Robert were among them – although during his colorful biographies told on stage, Martin would always insist they escaped from the camp.

Kentucky had been divided by the war. Officially, it was a neutral border state, but it leaned toward the Confederacy. There were many Union sympathizers, however, which led to local bloodshed. Rumor has it that Martin led a gang of men who hunted down and hanged eight Union supporters, forcing their wives and children to watch, in revenge for the murder of his brother, James, who was a Confederate soldier.

After the war, Martin left home. His mother had died in 1865, and he felt that he had nothing to keep him there. The South had been devastated, and he was unable to find a way to make a living. After arriving in Cincinnati, Ohio, he joined a sideshow and began touring as "The Kentucky Giant."

By now, he had reached his full height of seven feet, nine inches, and weighed close to 500 pounds. His decision to become a sideshow performer was a good one. Not only did he start earning a very good wage, but he also met the woman who became the love of his life – Anna Swan.

ANNA AND MARTIN MARRIED IN JUNE 1871. THEY MET in 1869 while on the sideshow circuit. Martin was two inches shorter than his bride, and friends good-naturedly teased him that he'd have to stand on his tiptoes to kiss her at the altar.

The wedding was a lavish affair, billed as the nuptials of "The Tallest Couple in the World." Millie-Christine McKoy, conjoined twins billed as the "The Two-Headed Nightingale," performed for the audience.

Shortly before the wedding, the engaged couple had given a command performance for Queen Victoria and the Prince of Wales – who became King Edward VII when his mother died in 1901 – while in Europe. The queen presented both Anna and Martin with giant-sized gold watches as wedding gifts. They were reportedly as large as saucers. Anna also received a six-foot gold chain for her watch, a diamond ring, and an elegant wedding dress.

Anna and Martin had two children together. Unfortunately, both were unusually large. A daughter was born in May 1872, but she died at birth. The baby was 27 inches long and weighed 18 pounds. In January 1879, Anna gave birth to a boy that was 30 inches long and weighed almost 24 pounds. He also died just 11 hours after he was born.

A WEDDING PHOTOGRAPH OF ANNA AND MARTIN IN JUNE 1871.

After the loss of their first child, Anna and Martin were deeply depressed. Anna was also exhausted, and the demanding life she spent on the road made her contemplate retirement. Martin, hoping to let Anna rest for a time, bought a 130-acre farm in Seville, Ohio, and he stocked it with the best breed of cattle.

Around this time, another source of Anna's weakness was discovered – she had tuberculosis. Luckily, there was a large inland lake near their home that was said to have a beneficial climate for sufferers of her disease.

The couple settled into a home that had been custom-built to fit them. It had 14-foot ceilings and doorways that were eight and a half feet tall and extra wide. The furniture had also been designed for them and crafted in England. All the chairs, couches, and beds were extra-large and highly reinforced. The back of the house was designed in more ordinary proportions for the comfort and convenience of friends and family who came to visit, as well as for the couple's household staff. Martin also purchased a custom-built carriage for Anna and himself, pulled by massive horses.

Those closest to the couple stated that this was the happiest time in their lives. Anna even purchased a pet monkey she named Buttons. Former sideshow friends often visited the couple and bragged about how entertaining they were. Anna was a skilled cook and made elaborate dinners for their friends.

After months of rest, Anna and Martin decided to go back out on the road. They toured with the W.W. Cole Circus for the 1878, 1879, and 1880 seasons, but the 1879 season was cut short for Anna when she learned she was pregnant again. As mentioned, this child also tragically died.

She toured one more season with her husband before ending her sideshow career for good. Anna was a highly intelligent, well-educated, and talented woman. She was a gifted singer, pianist, and actress who was known for her charm, grace, and generosity. She freely shared the money she made with family members, friends, and people in need in her community. She also achieved her original career by becoming a Sunday School teacher near the end of her life.

Anna died on August 5, 1888, at her home in Ohio. Her heart had failed due to a complication from her thyroid irregularity. She was one day away from her 42nd birthday.

Martin wired a company in Cleveland and gave them the measurements needed for Anna's casket. The funeral was delayed when the company first sent a standard-sized coffin, believing the measurements they'd first received had been a mistake. She was buried in Mound Hill Cemetery in Seville, and Martin erected a 15-foot monument on her grave.

AFTER ANNA'S DEATH, MARTIN CONTINUED TO LIVE IN THE house that he'd shared with Anna until he remarried in 1901 at the age of 63. His new bride, Lavonne Weatherby, was almost 30 years younger and the daughter of a minister.

She was five feet, two inches tall and weighed 135 pounds.

Lavonne refused to live in the oversized home where he had lived with Anna, so the couple moved into town. Friends claimed that Martin was very uncomfortable in the new cramped house and hated the place. To make matters worse, thanks to her strict upbringing, Lavonne did not approve of dancing, drinking, or social events.

Captain Bates, as people in town affectionately called him, probably should've given his second marriage a little more thought.

Martin had many friends in Seville, even though he had a reputation for being opinionated and easily irritated as he got older. He developed a habit of wearing his old Confederate uniform just to irritate people. Yet, he was generous to those in need and loaned money freely to his friends, rarely asking for repayment. He was especially fond of children and always kept candy in his pockets for them. Even at his advanced age, he hoped that he and Lavonne would have a child, but they did not.

As with most giants, Martin developed problems with his knees and legs and eventually needed a cane. After a long illness, he died in January 1919 from kidney disease. He was 82. He remembered the problems that had come up when trying to purchase Anna's casket, so he had built his own years before and kept it in a storage shed for when it was needed. It would take 12 men to lift that casket, and then the doors of the hearse had to be tied with rope because the box was too long and protruded from the back. He was buried next to Anna at Mound Hill Cemetery.

Lavonne died in 1940 and was buried elsewhere. She'd been left with most of Anna's jewelry after Martin died, but disapproving of Anna, Martin, and their sinful career in the sideshow, she'd sold it off long before she died.

PART TWO:
THE LITTLE PEOPLE

WE DON'T USE TERMS LIKE "MIDGET" AND "DWARF" these days as an identity for little people, but historically, they were commonly used in circuses and sideshows and day-to-day life. Because of how they were used in advertising, promotion, and in descriptions, they may slip into these pages in a few spots, but I'll do my best to keep it to a minimum.

In the parlance of the sideshow, a "midget" was the word used to describe a person who was proportionally sized to their small stature. The term "dwarf" indicated individuals of short stature but those with shortened legs and upper limbs. As a group, they were very popular in the circuses and carnivals, and it was rare to find a sideshow that didn't present them.

And their popularity began with the little person who started it all – Charles Stratton, the man who made a fortune as "General Tom Thumb."

"TOM THUMB"

WHILE THE STORY OF HOW CHARLES BECAME "TOM THUMB" appeared earlier in the book, I thought it was worthwhile to look a little closer at Charles' personal life, including his marriage to Lavinia Warren.

Charles was always considered P.T. Barnum's biggest star and his greatest discovery. Between the two of them, they made the exhibiting of oddities acceptable to the public, and "Tom Thumb" became a bigger attraction than most actors of the day. His appearances were widely covered in the newspapers, and he had thousands of fans in every city and, of course, in England, where he was a favorite of Queen Victoria and the royal family.

On February 10, 1863, Charles was one-half of the most important and highly publicized social event of the New York City season. It was the "Fairy Wedding" of Charles and Lavinia, which was held at Grace Church and followed by a wedding reception with over 2,000 guests – all of whom paid $75 a person to be there.

CHARLES AND LAVINIA

Lavinia's sister, Minnie, was her maid of honor, and Commodore Nutt – another little person who took a military title in the tradition of "General Thumb" – was Charles's best man. Famed Civil War photographer Matthew Brady took the wedding photographs.

Charles' new wife, Lavinia, had been born on October 31, 1842. Her parents were of average size, as were all her siblings, with the exception of a younger sister, Minnie, who was also a little person.

Lavinia had been teaching school in her hometown of Middleborough, Massachusetts when she was persuaded to join a sideshow by a distant relative, who quickly turned out to be a crook. Even so, she enjoyed the attention she received with the sideshow and boldly wrote a letter of introduction to P.T. Barnum. After meeting her, the showman quickly offered her a contract in 1862.

Lavinia was a beautiful, perfectly proportioned young woman who just happened to be 32 inches tall and weighed 29 pounds. Soon after signing with Barnum, she met Charles Stratton, and he proposed that they get married.

Their engagement and wedding were widely reported, bringing the nation some good news during the dark days of the Civil War.

They received many expensive and fabulous wedding gifts, including an elegant set of parlor furniture – scaled down to their size – in ebony and gold, a miniature silver horse and carriage crafted by Tiffany & Company, and a small billiards table with balls, cues, and a rack to match.

Thrilled with the financial success of the wedding, Barnum urged the couple to start a family to keep the interest of the paying public, but that was never going to happen. Charles cared very much for Lavinia – and those feelings were returned – but both understood the marriage was about business. The marriage was reportedly never consummated, and the pair lived as good friends only.

But in 1865, Lavinia gave birth to a baby girl. She was named after Lavinia's sister, Minnie.

Well, not exactly. Barnum, never one to let real life stand in the way of making money, went to an orphanage, bought a baby, and swore the staff to secrecy. Since the public expected the daughter of two little people to be as small as her parents, it became a problem with the orphan girl started to grow. When that happened, she was replaced with another smaller child. The replaced child was either returned to the orphanage or, more often, raised by another family in the circus. After three years, the public's interest in the child waned, and so the Minnie tragically "died." She left the public spotlight, and this callous publicity stunt came to an end.

Charles and Lavinia spent the next three years touring England and Europe and then began a three-year tour of the world, appearing 1,471 times in 587 cities. In 1881, they rejoined Barnum soon after the death of Lavinia's sister, Minnie, who died in childbirth. Barnum convinced the still-grieving couple to return for a final season of exhibitions as a way to cope with their sadness and loss.

Minnie also had a career in sideshows. She was born in 1849, and in addition to working with P.T. Barnum, she also performed on stage and was an accomplished singer. Minnie was even smaller than her sister - and arguably more beautiful - but she was shy and not as outgoing as Lavinia.

In July 1877, though, Minnie married Edmund Newell, whom she had met while touring with Barnum. Edmund was also a little person who was usually billed as "General Grant, Jr."

Sadly, Minnie died on July 23, 1878, while giving birth to a full-sized six-pound baby. She was only 29 years old and had only been married for a year.

Charles and Lavinia agreed to Barnum's plan, but while on their advertised final tour in January 1883, a fire broke out in the Milwaukee hotel where they were staying. Charles and Lavinia narrowly escaped death, as did their beloved manager, Sylvester Bleeker. Tragically, though, Bleeker's wife died trying to escape the fire, jumping to her death.

LAVINIA'S SISTER, MINNIE, WHO DIED DURING CHILDBIRTH IN 1878

Charles never recovered from the trauma of the incident. Just six months later, in July 1883, he died from a sudden stroke at the age of just 46. His wife of 25 years was on tour and away from home when he died.

After his death, Lavinia lived in retirement until she remarried Count Primo Magri, an Italian little person. They toured together in the United States and Europe until, strangely, in her later years, Lavinia grew another 11 inches, and her weight increased to 50 pounds. But her fortune had already been made, and she had no reason to return to the road.

She passed away in November 1919 at the age of 78. She was buried at Mountain Grove Cemetery in Bridgeport, not far from the final resting place of Tom Thumb.

"ADMIRAL DOT"

THE MOST FAMOUS OF THE MILITARY-TITLED PERFORMERS who followed after "General Thumb" was Leopold Kahn, who was born in San Francisco in 1858. His parent, Jewish immigrants, were average-sized, and he was their only child.

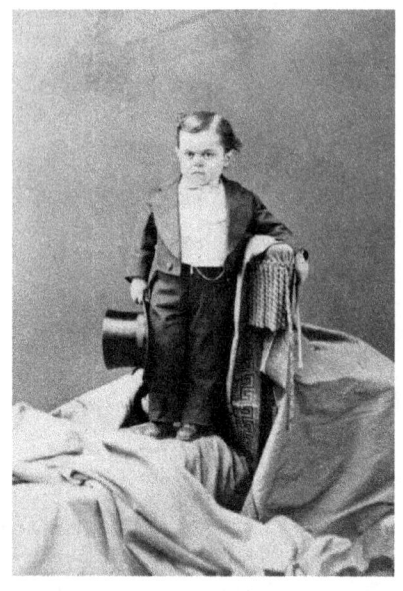

In 1870, P.T. Barnum was on a western business trip with friends when Leopold's father approached him in hopes that the showman might be interested in exhibiting his son. Barnum, after making a fortune with Tom Thumb, quickly offered the family a contract and gave Leopold the stage name of "Admiral Dot."

Promoters claimed he was only 25 inches in height, weighed 15 pounds, and was 13 years old when he began working in the sideshow. He originally appeared on stage with his mother.

Leopold grew taller as he aged, but his career still lasted for almost two decades. Part of his success was because of Barnum's ability to market him creatively by pairing him with other small performers like Major Atom.

However, the largest part of his success came from his ability to keep audiences entertained by altering his routines. When he started, he dressed in a British naval uniform and sang, danced, and played musical instruments.

After Barnum lost his museum to fire a second time, he decided to take his show on the road, and he widely advertised his latest discovery, Admiral Dot, along with Chang and Eng, the famous "Siamese Twins," Bearded Lady Annie Jones, Anna Swan, and Zip, the "What Is It?" Leopold stayed with Barnum until the late 1880s when he joined the Locke and Davis Royal Lilliputian Opera Company, which featured only little people in their productions.

It was with the opera company that he met his future wife, a little person named Lottie Smartwood. They married on August 14, 1892, at the Victoria Hall on Lexington Avenue in New York City. Lottie converted to Judaism, and the couple honeymooned on Coney Island. They toured America and Europe together but eventually grew tired of the travel and retired to White Plains, New York.

Using the fortune they'd made on the sideshow circuit, they became the proprietors of The Admiral Dot Hotel, which the locals dubbed the "Pee-Wee Hotel." It had 48 rooms and included a ballroom, banquet hall, restaurant, and bowling alley, and it did a brisk business.

But in February 1911, tragedy struck when the hotel burned down – despite the fact that the brick building with its asbestos roof was supposed to be fireproof. In addition to it being their business, the hotel was also the home of the couple and Hazel and Gabriel, their two normal-sized children. Luckily, the Kahns had deeds to many properties in the city and were financially comfortable without the income from the hotel. They moved to a beautiful home on South Broadway, where they remained until their deaths.

For Leopold, death came in 1918 during the influenza pandemic that spread across the country. In a matter of hours, he went from excellent health to being a very sick man with a fever of 105 degrees. He became delirious before he died on October 26. He was 54 years old. Sadly, his daughter, Hazel, also died from influenza a few days later.

Lottie continued to grow as an adult and eventually reached a height of a little over four feet tall. In 1943, after 25 years as a widow, she married a man named Edward Lappe, who was two feet taller than she was. Sadly, he died just two years later. Lottie died in December 1950 at the age of 81.

"THE TINIEST MOTHER IN MEDICAL HISTORY"

DOLLETTA DODD – WHOSE NAME CAME UP EARLIER IN OUR section about Bearded Ladies – was a dwarf born in October 1881 in Quincy, Illinois. She was one of 10 children born to average-sized parents, Benjamin and Anna Dodd. Her siblings were all normally sized, and while there is no record of her birth weight, she must have been a very small infant since she was given the name "Dolletta." Her family called her by her nickname, "Dolly."

While married to her first husband – also a dwarf – she gave birth to two typically sized children – a daughter, Luciea, and a son, Charles. It's impossible to know much about her marriage, but it must not have been great. By 1920, she was divorced, and she and her children were living in the home of a married sister and her husband.

Dolly was working in the sideshows at this time, where she took up with a fellow performer who was not only married but a loser and degenerate. His name was Frederick Tischu, but he went by the name Charles Harry Buck. He was a cowboy trick roper who used the name "The Long-Haired Cherokee Buck Man," even though he didn't have a drop of Native American blood in him. His wife at the time was Bearded Lady Baroness Sidonia de Barcsy, whom he treated terribly and stole most of her money when he was on his way out of town with Dolly.

It's hard to say whether Charles fell in love with Dolly or with Dolly's money. By then, he had pretty much cleaned out his wife. At the time, Sidonia was sick and wasn't able to perform as much as she had in the past. Dolly, on the other hand, was making top dollar as "The Tiniest Mother in the World." The pair had one child together, a girl they named Dotella.

I'm sure that it's hard to believe, but "The Long-Haired Cherokee Buck Man" turned out to be a menace. By 1940, Dolly was living in Missouri with her son and his wife. He managed as girl's show in the carnival, and Dolly was still performing. She referred to herself as a "widow," mostly because she didn't want to deal with her former lover, who was now "married" to Dolly's oldest daughter, Luciea, who was 17 years his junior. Charles Harry Buck and his stepdaughter had three children together.

Later in life, Charles became known as "The Old Indian Doctor" and practiced "medicine" out of a broken-down bus. He died in Port Arthur, Texas, in 1951. He and Luciea were still together.

As for Dolly, she died in Joplin, Missouri, in January 1948 at the age of 66.

LYA GRAF

BORN IN GERMANY IN 1910, LYA SCHWARTZ WAS NOT ONLY A well-known performer for several years, but she also became involved in a scandal that rocked the early 1930s before tragically going to her death a few years later.

Lya was a half-German little person who performed with Ringling Brothers and Barnum & Bailey Circus and at Coney Island. Little is known about her early life or her sideshow career before she came to America in March 1931. Two years later, she became involved in what has become the most infamous publicity stunt in the history of sideshows.

In 1933, J.P. Morgan, Jr. was the richest man in the world and was on the hot seat before the Senate Securities and Exchange Commission being grilled about his responsibility in the 1929 stock market crash that had caused bank failures, massive unemployment, and the worst depression in U.S. history. He admitted under oath that he and his partners had not paid any taxes in 1931 and 1932, at the height of the Depression, and also admitted guilt in several stock fraud schemes that had contributed to the economic crash. Morgan had quickly become a very unpopular public figure and scapegoat for the troubles that were plaguing the country.

On the morning of June 1, 1933, Morgan and his assistants sat waiting for another brutal day of questioning to begin. Lya was in town with the circus, but she had no reason to be at the U.S. Senate building. However, an enterprising circus publicity man with Ringling Brothers named Frank Braden – along with Jerry Doyle, an editor at the *Washington Times* – came up with a strange plan.

It resulted in Lya suddenly being plopped on J.P. Morgan's knee.

The press immediately reacted, taking scores of photos and rushing the weird little story to the press. Reporters claimed that Morgan first thought 23-year-old Lya was a child, and he asked her where she lived, to which she replied, "I live in a tent, sir. More simple conversation followed until a "flustered Morgan" realized that Lya was a little person.

In the photos, Lya looks amused, and Morgan looks like a kindly older man. America had been given a look behind the curtain of what they assumed was a sinister and black-hearted banker, only to discover that he was a mortal man. The photos and the story humanized the monster, and the public's hearts softened toward him. The story appeared in newspapers across the country and was repeatedly referred to for decades after the incident.

THE INFAMOUS PHOTO OF LYA AND J.P. MORGAN BEGAN AS AN EMBARASSMENT AND THEN MANAGED TO HUMANIZE THE BANKER.

Initially, Morgan was embarrassed by what happened, but his partners were thrilled. The heat from the Senate hearings had been greatly reduced, and later, Morgan began to see the humor and the benefit of the stunt.

Frank Braden loved being part of the incident but would always claim that the press got it wrong, even the part about Lya living in a tent. He claimed a reporter named Ray Tucker had made up the quote to sensationalize his story. According to Braden, Lya, advertised as the world's smallest woman, simply wanted to meet the world's richest man. He also claimed that Morgan knew exactly who she was and had agreed to the meeting in advance.

You know – in the middle of contentious Senate hearings, as anyone would do. I find Braden's protests about the publicity stunt a little hard to believe.

But the story gets much worse from here. In 1935, Lya and her family returned to Germany, only to find it was a much different place than the one they had left. Adolph Hitler was now in control of Germany, and the Nuremberg laws had deprived Jews of their German citizenship. In addition, "freaks" were among those who did not fit into Hitler's idea of a master race. Lya and her mother, who was also a little person, found themselves in immediate danger.

The family was arrested in 1937 and sent to the Auschwitz concentration camp, where they were put to death in the gas chambers, along with at least 10,000 others who had the bad luck to be born different in Nazi Germany.

PART THREE:
VERY SPECIAL PEOPLE

WHEN I WAS GROWING UP, I READ A LOT OF COMIC BOOKS. I still love them, but back then – and this would have been in the late 1970s -- I pored over every issue I picked up, reading them over and over again until the next issue in whatever series I was hooked on at the time came out. Those who have never read comics will never have the great memories the rest of us have of the advertisements that appeared between the stories back then. I still remember a lot of them – sea monkeys, x-ray specs, Charles Atlas Fitness Programs, plastic soldiers, spud guns, rubber masks, switchblade combs, hypnotic coins, itching powder, joy buzzers, and more – but most of them I didn't buy.

I was smart enough to know that most of them would be junk when they arrived, but that wasn't the only reason. When I was a kid, mail order was tough. You had to save up your allowance money and give it to your mom so that she could write a check for you to put in the mail. And if she didn't approve of what you wanted to buy, then you were on your own. You had to take a chance and send cash, hoping that you'd get whatever you ordered.

So, if you ordered something you saw in a comic book ad, you had to *really* want it. And when I saw this particular book, I knew I wanted it. It was expensive -- $6.95, plus shipping and handling – but I had to have it. The photos that were part of the ad promised that the pages of the book would be filled with even better things.

The book was called *Very Special People* by Frederick Drimmer, and it promised "The Struggles, Loves, And Triumphs of Human Oddities." It was a book about "freaks," which is what we still called human oddities then – and there was nothing else like it when it was published in 1973. There were still sideshows around in those days –

and still plenty of performers – but the book told the stories of the most famous freaks in history.

And it made a very strong impression on me – as you have likely already realized. I mean, there's a reason why this part of the book includes the stories of Robert Wadlow, Jack Earle, Tom Thumb, the Hilton Sisters, Grace McDaniels, and so many others. They served as my introduction to the freak show, thanks to *Very Special People*.

I've always wondered if my fascination with the book made me just as bad as the people who came to gawk and stare at the sideshow performers on stage.

Probably so.

But I guess I wasn't alone. Since the beginning of history, we've always belittled and looked down on the oddity. Essentially, it's because they're different, but let's be honest, we're also afraid of them and happy that whatever happened to them didn't happen to us. We avoid the oddity but then flock to see them perform. We may shudder with horror and cover our eyes with our fingers, but we always peek out between them, morbidly fascinated by someone so different than we are.

We use excuses and say we study such curiosities for scientific reasons or to try and understand them, but most of us do it for reasons that we don't really understand. It's part of our nature. As Clyde Ingalls, the longtime sideshow boss for the Ringling Brothers Circus, put it, "When I look at the freaks, it makes me content by comparison to be less than perfect."

To put it bluntly – deep down, we stare at the freaks because it makes us feel better about ourselves.

And when I say "we," I mean the "rubes" and "marks" – the people who used to pay their money to buy tickets to the show. These days, we're the people who stare at the photos of the old-time freaks because they're not around for us to gape at anymore.

To the people who worked in the carnivals and sideshows, human oddities were taken for granted. Other performers didn't stare at them, and neither did those who ran the rides, operated the grab joints, or worked the illusion shows. To them, what we consider normalcy didn't mean much. To that entire community, we were the "freaks" – they weren't.

Keep that in mind as you turn through the pages ahead. Every one of these people, no matter how strange or unusual they look to you, were also regular folks who laughed, loved, and lived a life that few of us can even imagine.

"THE OHIO BIG FOOT GIRL"

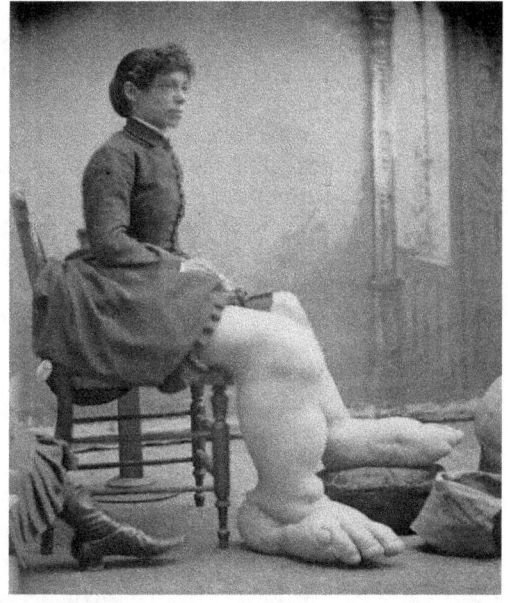

FANNY MILLS WAS BORN IN SUSSEX, ENGLAND, IN 1859, but her family immigrated to Sandusky, Ohio, when she was young. She had five siblings, but only Fanny could be deemed unusual. She suffered from what was known as Milroy's Disease, a condition that restricts the development of vessels in the legs and causes fluids to build up.

Her parents started to notice something odd about Fanny's right leg when she was a young child. The leg appeared to swell at an alarming leg, and in less than two years, the left leg did the same. Her mother told a fanciful story about how she had been marked when she was pregnant with Fanny because her husband had bullied her into caring for a horse with a swollen, infected leg.

Obviously, that was not the reason for Fanny's condition.

When Fanny became an adult, she was a petite 115-pound woman – except for her legs and feet, which were massive. While photographs of her do tend to exaggerate their condition, it was said that her left foot was 19 inches long and seven inches wide and weighed 26 pounds. Her right foot was only slightly smaller. On her trade cards – which tended not to be completely accurate – it was claimed that her big toe was 11 inches in circumference.

On another, it said that Fanny wore a size 30 shoe. Needless to say, shoes had to be specially made for her, which started stories about how it took three goat skins to make her a single pair of shoes and that she used pillowcases for stockings.

Most of her days were spent in pain. She could walk, but with great difficulty, and even using a walking stick didn't help. She spent most of her days in a chair, immobile.

As local stories about Fanny's condition spread, they got the attention of sideshow managers who were always looking for new attractions. Fanny, shy and awkward her entire life, turned down all their offers until her father died in 1885. She needed the money, and the sideshow offered her a way to pay the bills and care for her family.

Billed as "The Ohio Big Foot Girl," she was soon making the money she needed, as much as $150 per week. If Fanny wasn't so shy, though, other performers told her, she could make even more. She found it difficult to spice up her show by talking and joking with the crowds who came to see her. So, her promoters came up with their own idea. They concocted a publicity scheme that claimed her father was offering $5,000 to any man who would marry his daughter and take care of the family farm.

Of course, her father was dead, and there was no $5,000, but why let that get in the way of a clever idea?

The catchy line on the advertising poster read: "Don't let two big feet stand between you and wedlock tinged with fortune?" The stunt packed the shows, and newspapers continued the charade by claiming that Fanny was turning down every man who applied for one reason or another.

But Fanny actually did get married, even though it was kept secret for a long time so that the publicity stunt could run its course. Her husband – who did not receive a $5,000 reward – was a neighbor named William Brown, who was 20 years old than Fanny. He was the brother of a woman named Mary Brown, whom Fanny had hired to help her at home and on the road. Fanny most likely fell in love with William, the first and only man who'd even shown a romantic interest in her. How did William feel? No one knows for sure but he likely married her to get access to the substantial money she was making in the sideshow. As a bonus, she was usually out of town for six months out of the year on tour.

William had a reputation in town as a spoiled, selfish man who was too lazy to work his dairy farm hard enough to make it profitable. Why work hard when you can marry into money instead?

In August 1887, Fanny gave birth to a stillborn baby. She blamed herself for the death, believing her disease had somehow caused it, which is unlikely. Sadly, she never even had time to mourn her loss. Needing money for her family – and her shiftless husband – she went back to the sideshow within just a few weeks. She remained a performer until health issues forced her to retire in 1892.

Fanny died in 1899 because of an abnormally low level of white cells in her blood that caused her immune system to be compromised – a side effect of Milroy's Disease. She was only 39.

She was buried in Oakland Cemetery in Sandusky, but her grave is unmarked. William didn't want to go to the expense of having a tombstone made.

"THE FOUR-LEGGED GIRL FROM TEXAS"

JOSEPHINE MYRTLE CORBIN WAS BORN IN MAY 1868, and it's safe to say that her family had never seen anything quite like her before. Her parents, William and Nancy, had married three years earlier in Blount, Alabama. William had fought for the Confederacy during the Civil War, and like most southern men who returned home, he discovered there weren't many ways to make a living in the devasted South.

Again, it's safe to say that her parents were shocked when they first saw their newborn daughter, but William quickly understood that this child was going to be a money-making opportunity for his soon-to-be-growing family. They'd later have more children, none of whom were as unusual as Myrtle was. Legends claim that William first started charging neighbors and gawkers who showed up at the door, hoping to get a glimpse of his infant.

You see, Myrtle was born with an extra set of legs – and not just that. She had four legs, 16 toes – five toes on her larger outer feet and three toes on her smaller inner feet – and two vaginas. She had been born with what was called "dipygus," a rare deformity where the body is typically developed from the waist up but forks left and right below the waist. The pelvis and legs are duplicated with this condition, and, in humans, the inner two of the four duplications develop smaller than normal.

The condition was also called "monster twinned below" – a type of conjoined twin, but in Myrtle's case, she only had half of a sister to deal with.

Myrtle had two pelvises positioned side-by-side, and each of her smaller inner legs was paired with one of the outer legs. She could move the smaller legs, but they were weak and too short to be used for walking. Her larger right foot was a club foot, so this complicated her mobility even more. She could walk, but she was slow and moved with a lot of difficulty and had trouble standing for any length of time.

When she was older, Myrtle was studied by numerous doctors and experts. It was determined that both of her vaginas menstruated, which indicated that both sides of Myrtle were able to function sexually. She could become pregnant from either set of legs. During her performances, she always claimed that she gave birth from both sides, but this might have been something she said to enhance her show because she once confided to doctors that she almost always had sex on her right side. Myrtle did have eight children – although only four of them survived. Obviously, there were complications caused by her deformity.

She grew up as an attraction long before she ever set foot on a stage. When she was a teenager, she caught the eye of P.T. Barnum and began touring with his show in America and Europe. She was very popular and earned a lucrative salary, especially for a young girl. She would dress her tiny half-twin in matching socks, shoes, and bloomers, which made the twin seem more "human" to the fascinated ticket buyers. Thanks to her popularity, many fake four-legged performers started appearing on the fairground circuit, but they never appealed to audiences the way Myrtle did.

Myrtle retired from the sideshow in 1886 at the age of 18. She might have been homesick, or perhaps she'd made the money she needed to help her family.

Or maybe her father just needed to get a job.

The most likely reason for leaving the sideshow circuit, though, was that she fell in love. Within a month of her retirement, she married a 19-year-old farmer named James Bicknell.

As mentioned, Myrtle had four children who survived their births, with her last child, Lillian, being born in 1909. A few years later, Myrtle went back to the sideshow, exhibiting at Huber's Museum at Coney Island. She also signed a contract with Ringling Brothers, commanding a salary of $450 a week.

Myrtle died at her home in Cleburne, Texas, in May 1928, just a few weeks short of her 60th birthday. The cause of her death was a medical condition that affected her larger right leg. She suffered for eight months before she passed away.

Her father, William, who had lived off his daughter's money throughout her life, died in March 1923, just a few years before Myrtle passed away. His wife quickly applied for a war pension available to widows in indigent circumstances, even though it didn't seem like she should have needed it since Myrtle was still alive at the time of her father's passing. Both of her parents had been coming to Myrtle with their hands out for decades, which was likely one of the reasons she returned to the sideshow after Lillian was born.

Was Nancy just trying to get money from the government fraudulently? Or had the money well for Myrtle's parents finally run dry by then?

I'd like to think that after nearly 60 years, Myrtle had finally cut them off.

"SEALO, THE SEAL BOY"

STANISLAUS BERENT WAS BORN IN PITTSBURGH, PENNSYLVANIA, in May 1903, with a condition known as phocomelia, a very rare congenital disorder that caused the malformation of one or more limbs. In Stanley's case, his upper arms hadn't fully formed, so sections of his arms were missing, causing his hands to be attached to his trunk. Phocomelia is usually the result of environmental influences such as the drug thalidomide, but it can also be inherited. When Stanley was a boy, most people just referred to it as "seal limbs" – hence the name that he'd later perform under.

Little is known about Stanley's younger days, but the story goes that he was discovered while selling newspapers when he was about 30, and he went from there to appear on many of the major sideshows of the day. He toured the country, as well as Europe and parts of South America.

By all accounts, he was one of the most well-liked performers on the circuit. He was outgoing, always smiling and laughing, and had a great sensor of humor. His only vices, he liked to brag, were cards, cigars, and his signature drink – a "boilermaker" – which was a glass of beer and a shot of whiskey. Stanley had a stick with a hook on it that allowed him to play cards, drink, and zip and unzip his pants without help, even after consuming one too many boilermakers, which he often did.

In 1952, Stanley made his television debut on a quiz show called *True or False*, along with a panel of five other carnival performers. They challenged six young women dubbed "Radio Beauties."

Unlike the sideshow performers of the nineteenth and early twentieth centuries, there weren't many newspaper articles about Stanley. Time and public attitudes about sideshow performers had changed by the time Stanley was at the height of his popularity. The exception came in 1972 when Stanley and a little person named Norbert Terhune challenged an obscure 1921 Florida law that prohibited freak shows. The two men had been working with World Fair Freaks and Attractions, Inc. when it had been closed down by the police. Their lawsuit forced the Florida Supreme Court to strike down the las as unconstitutional and rule that "the state has no business telling persons they cannot earn an honest living. One who is disabled or in an unfortunate position because of physical handicaps or deformities, not of his own choosing, must be allowed a reasonable chance withing his capacities to earn a livelihood."

For a brief time, "Sealo" became a household name as newspapers and television stations spread the story across the nation.

Stanley retired to Gibsonton, Florida, in the mid-1970s but returned home to Pittsburgh when his health started to decline. He passed away in December 1980 and was buried in the Christ Our Redeemer Cemetery.

Unfortunately, though, even though he was one of the most beloved sideshow performers of the mid-twentieth century, there is no stone marking his grave.

"THE PENGUIN GIRL"

STANLEY BERENT WASN'T THE ONLY SIDESHOW PERFORMER of the time to become popular as a performer with "seal limbs." Ruth Davis was born around 1910 with the same congenital disorder. Her left arm and both legs were affected, plus her fingers on both hands and all her toes were fused together. Her stunted limbs, combined with her average-sized torso, gave Ruth the appearance of a penguin. She even waddled when she walked.

The stage name of "Penguin Girl" was an easy one.

Little is known about Ruth, however. We know nothing about her early life – like where or when she was born – and what happened to her after she retired from the sideshow circuit. Most of what is known appears in Ward Hall's book, *My Very Unusual Friends*, which writes that Ruth was married to Earl Davis, who was billed in sideshows as "Hoppy the Frog." They apparently made a good sideshow couple, playing in the better shows during the 1930s and 1940s. The couple then retired to California in the mid-1950s to raise Ruth's son, who'd been born without any congenital disabilities around 1944.

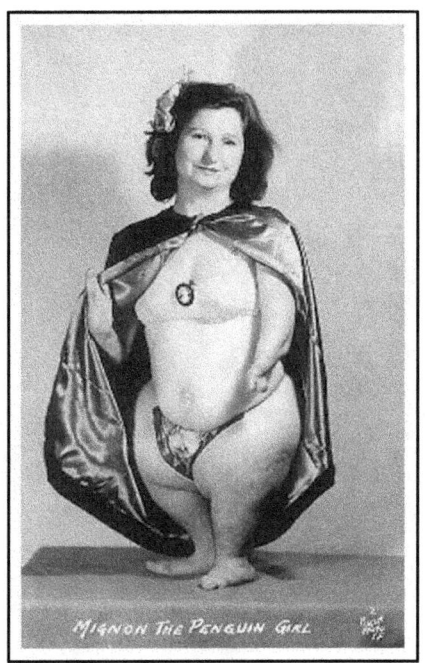

After that, Ruth just seemed to waddle off into history. Where or when she died remains a mystery.

"THE CAMEL GIRL"

BORN IN TENNESSEE IN 1873, ELLA HARPER WAS BORN WITH a condition known as genu recurvatum, which loosely translates to "backward-bending knee." This is a rare deformity in the knee joint that causes the knee to only bend backward. It's a condition that causes great pain later on in life.

No one knows for sure when Ella first started to appear in sideshows, but in 1882, she was featured as one of the stars of the W.H. Harris's Nickel Plate Circus. This is the text that appeared on Ella's trade cards four years later, in 1886:

I am called the Camel Girl because my knees turn backward. I can walk best on my hands and feet as you see me in the picture. I

have traveled considerably in the show business for the past four years and now, this is 1886 and I intend to quit the show business and go to school and fit myself for another occupation.

Nothing is known about what happened to Ella after 1886, and very few photos of her are known to exist – however, the one of her on her hands and feet that appeared on her trade cards had become one of the most famous "freak" photos in history.

Despite the fame of the photo, the young woman who appears in it is a mystery.

"THE LIVING HALF-LADY"

IN THE LATE 1800S AND EARLY 1900S, "LIVING HALF-LADIES" were big draws for sideshows and circuses. They were advertised under a variety of colorful names like Thuma, Thepia, Roila, Flora, Fauna, Zanzille, Mythia, and many others.

Unfortunately, the performers were mostly fakes. These gaffs were usually poorly constructed, put together using wood, paint, chicken wire, and fabric. They were designed to look like half of a woman, but most were so badly put together that they couldn't have fooled even a mostly blind, drunk, or stupid carnival-goer.

The performers used magic tricks to pull off the half-lady act. The most common illusions used a shelf, a table top, or a swing to carry out the trick, all using mirrors, painted screens, dark fabric, and such. These are the same kind of tricks used in more modern times to create the illusions of headless girls, "Spider women," and more.

A showman named Wesley Jakes is credited with creating the "living half lady" illusion, but he wasn't exactly celebrated for it. Are you wondering what I mean by that? Well, here's a bit of his obituary from 1900:

Wesley Jakes is dead. Many a man more widely mourned has done less for his fellow human beings. He invented the 'Cardiff Giant' and the 'living half-lady' and other harmless and interesting frauds. He was reduced to poverty, and when he died was a glass blower in a Chicago museum.

One of the most tragic "living half-lady" stories was that of Belle Carter, whose real name was Estelle Doane. She was a performer who had been performing the illusion for a few years before she checked into a hotel in Lima, Ohio, on July 30, 1890. She had traveled there to meet her lover, Max Cohen, but unknown to Belle, he had second thoughts about her and left town a few days before she arrived. He left no forwarding address. Belle received the terrible news when she reached the hotel, and that night, grieving her lost love, drank a bottle of strychnine and died.

In her trunk, they found very little but numerous photographs of her as a "living half-lady."

But let me make it clear that there were some "living half-ladies" who were the real thing. One of the most famous was Madame Gabrielle De Fuller. We don't know much about her, aside from what was on her trade cards, but we know she was born in Switzerland, exhibited at Coney Island, and traveled with the Ringling Brothers Circus.

MADAME GABRIELLE DE FULLER, AN AUTHENTIC "HALF-LADY"

She was no illusion or poorly-constructed gaff. Madame Gabrielle was quite beautiful and was only 32 inches in height. She was married at least once – although some accounts sat two or three times – and was popular in the United States between 1913 and 1926. She gained a reputation as a pianist, composer, and one of the few "living half-ladies" in the American sideshow.

THE GIBB SISTERS

Mary and Margaret Gibb "American Siamese Twins"

"THE AGONY WAS TERRIBLE."

Those were the words of Margaret Gibb, the mother of two cojoined twins, in a newspaper interview about the birth of her daughters on May 20, 1912. After the babies were born, she immediately lapsed into unconsciousness, but she survived – one of the few women in the United States at the time who did. For months after the birth, she refused to see or talk with anyone. She wanted to be alone and grieve over the fact that her children would never be "normal." But, as she'd later claim, her feeling of being cursed slowly changed into feeling she was blessed instead.

I would imagine that was around the time she realized there was money to be made from the births of her unusual daughters.

Mary and Margaret – yes, the same name as her mother – were joined at the base of the spine near the hips. The shared a common circulatory system but were unable to feel each other's pain. Early on, doctors warned that separating the twins would lead to the death or one or both of them, so he advised against it. The twins always claimed they didn't mind. "We are perfectly happy as we are," they said.

Mary and Margaret grew up in Holyoke, Massachusetts, with their mother, father, John Gibb, and their younger sister, Dorothy, who was born 10 years after the twins. At times, their father's brother lived with the family, too. They continued to live with their family throughout their entire lives, although their father died in 1947. Their mother outlived them by two years.

The twins were nervously sheltered by their parents. They never attended public school; instead, they received their education from a series of private tutors. They seldom left home and weren't allowed any childhood friends. Later in life, Mary and Margaret said they never minded being stared at, but their parents were opposed to the public gawking at their young daughters – for free, anyway.

When the girls turned 15, their parents finally decided to embrace the money-making opportunity that life had given them. In the 1920 U.S. Census, John Gibb's profession was listed as a "finisher" in a woolen mill. By the 1930 census, though, that had changed to "vaudeville manager."

The career of the Gibb Sisters began in 1927 on a Lowe's Theater stage and at Coney Island. For two years, they performed an act that consisted of dancing and playing the piano. In 1930, the family traveled to Europe and exhibited in France, Belgium, and Switzerland. The twins also debuted that year in the new "talking pictures." Then, starting in 1934, they began touring with the Ringling Brothers and Barnum & Bailey Circus and then with the Cole Brothers Circus.

Neither Mary nor Margaret ever married. In 1929, when Margaret was 17, several newspaper stories reported she had found a doctor to separate her from Mary because she'd fallen in love with a Mexico City man named Carlos Josefe and wanted to marry him. Dr. Francis P. Westin, the doctor Margaret had found to perform the operation, was hounded by reporters. However, the only thing he'd say to the press was that "the proposed operation would be very hazardous."

On March 8, she and her parents – and with Mary, of course – traveled from New York to Newark, New Jersey, and applied for a marriage license. The story died down in a few months, though, and the wedding never took place. Sadly, it looks as though the intended marriage was nothing more than a publicity stunt to generate publicity for the twins.

In 1933, they made the newspapers again when the twins registered to vote but found officials reluctant to allow it since Mary and Margaret couldn't vote without seeing the other's ballot. Or so reporters – or a publicity man from the circus – claimed. It wasn't true. They cast their votes in the next Holyoke municipal election.

Their sideshow career continued for the next seven years, and then, in 1941, they decided to retire and return home.

By then, audience tastes had changed. Vaudeville was on its way out, and movies were the biggest thing. Mary and Margaret were nice,

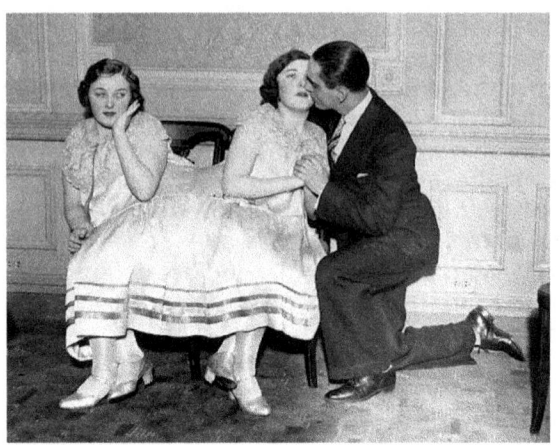

NEITHER MARY NOR MARGARET EVER MARRIED, ALTHOUGH A PUBLICITY STUNT IN 1929 MADE IT LOOK AS THOUGH THE ONLY REASON MARGARET DIDN'T MARRY A MEXICO CITY MAN WAS BECAUSE NO DOCTOR COULD BE FOUND TO SEPARATE THE SISTERS.

wholesome girls from a small town. Plus, in all honesty, they were only mildly pretty and had very little musical talent. They were no longer able to attract the size of crowds that were now heading into theaters to see the Hollywood stars with real talent.

On April 16, 1942, the twins opened the "Mary-Margaret Gift Shoppe" in Holyoke, and it remained in business for almost eight years, closing in 1949. The twins claimed they just wanted to have a quiet life now that their sideshow career was over, and so they did.

After the gift shop closed, the twins largely vanished for the next 18 years. They weren't seen around town at all, except on rare occasions when they were on their way to the Presbyterian Church. When once asked by an interested reporter how they spent their time, they responded, "When one sleeps, the other will read. When one sews, the other plays solitaire. When one plays piano, the other sings." The girls both loved movies but Mary enjoyed action movies and westerns, while Margaret preferred romantic films. "One will nap if we don't like the movie we are watching," they said but agreed they each liked to cook.

As they got older, they began to suffer from health issues – well, Mary did. In 1946, Margaret had a stone removed from her bladder, and in 1953, she had a tumor removed. While the girls did not share each other's pain, Mary had to be anesthetized during the operations along with Margaret, and both suffered some post-operation complications because they shared the came circulatory system.

Mary and Margaret died on January 8, 1967, at the Holyoke Hospital, where they had been patients for eight days, suffering from hypertension and heart disease. Margaret died first, followed by Mary a short time later. An autopsy discovered that Margaret had bladder cancer that had spread to her lungs, as well as the lungs of her sister. They were 54 years old when they died.

They were buried together, of course, but that's just as well. As Mary once told a reporter, "We never had a cross word between us."

"THE MAN WITH TWO FACES"

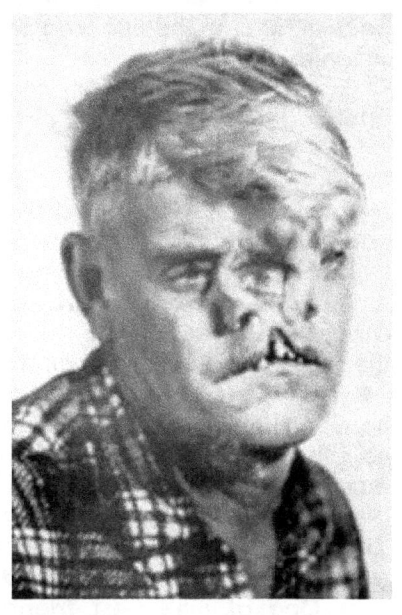

THE LIFE STORY OF BILL DURKS IS PROOF THAT "FREAK SHOWS" weren't always the horrible, shameful things that our modern definition of political correctness claims they were.

What do I mean by that? You'll see as you continue, but it's safe to say that the "freak show" literally saved Bill's life.

Bill was born in April 1913 in Jasper, Alabama. He had four siblings who were born without any physical differences, but the same couldn't be said for Bill.

He suffered from frontonasal dysplasia, a very rare birth disorder that causes severe head and facial abnormalities. Bill had widely spaced eyes, a flat, wide nose, and a vertical groove down the middle of the face. To be blunt, it looked as though he had been hit in the face with an ax. It was split in half from his eyebrows to his upper lip, with a wide gap down the middle. His eyes were spaced far apart, and he had what appeared to be two noses, one nostril on each side of his facial rift. He also had a deeply cleft lip that exposed abnormally spaced front teeth, and this made his speech so difficult to understand that most believed Bill was mentally impaired – he wasn't.

To make matters worse, he was born with a hooded-skin film over his eyes that had to be removed surgically when he was a small child. It was botched, which left him blind in one eye.

And if all this wasn't enough, Bill had the misfortune to be born into a family of poverty-stricken sharecroppers who were deeply ashamed of him. They believed he was a curse from God for their past sins. Bill never went to school. His parents worked him in the fields instead, keeping the "monster" hidden from everyone.

The isolation, the rejection and hatred from his family, his inability to speak clearly, his inability to read or write, and the likely cruelty from people in town destroyed any chance that Bill might have had to connect with other people. He was painfully shy and always kept his head bowed and wore a large-brimmed hat to try and hide his face. He once said in an interview that he never got used to the pain of seeing the shocked look on someone's face when they first saw him.

Bill's life dramatically changed, though, in the late 1950s when he attended a local carnival, and a showman spotted him in the crowd. I don't imagine it took too much convincing to get him to leave his hellish home life behind and go out on the road with the sideshow.

At first, he was billed as the "Man with Three Eyes" because Bill came up with the idea of painting a third eye in the split between his two noses. Even the eye wasn't all that believable; his unusual face thrilled and amazed the crowds who came to see him, and he became a popular attraction for the next two decades, touring with some of the biggest shows on the circuit.

Early on, a few of his managers took advantage of the fact that he was illiterate and stole from him, but Bill was fond of saying that he still made more money from those thieves than he would have made on an Alabama farm – and the work was a whole lot easier.

With the sideshow, Bill finally found acceptance and a real family. He made good money, had many friends, found fame, got to travel all over the country, and most importantly, found love.

One of Bill's best friends was Melvin Burkhart, the "Original Human Blockhead." He performed by hammering nails into his face and head. Melvin introduced Bill to Millie, the "Alligator-Skinned Woman." She was also part of the sideshow and had a rare skin condition that gave her a reptile-like appearance. She was 18 years older than Bill, but the two fell in love, got married in 1960, and remained completely devoted to each other until Millie's death in June 1968, which was brought on by a violent asthma attack.

Bill was devastated by her death but was eventually convinced to continue performing to help him cope with the loss. He stayed with the sideshow for five more years and even played a small part as a sanitarium patient in the Brian De Palma film *Sisters* in 1973.

He retired to Gibsonton, Florida, and died there in May 1975. He was 66 years old. No one knows where Bill – or his wife, Millie – was buried.

"THE MULE-FACE WOMAN"

ONE OF THE SADDEST SIDESHOW STORIES IS THAT OF GRACE McDaniels, although not because of the way she was treated as an exhibitor. In fact, those were the only happy times she knew during her life.

Hardly anything is known about the life and death of Grace McDaniel. No birth certificate, marriage certificate, or death certificates were left behind as public records. She isn't listed in any U.S. census. All that remains is what she had printed on her trade cards and the statements of those who knew and worked with her on the show circuit.

What we do know is that Grace was born in 1888 on a farm near the tiny town of Numa, Iowa. It was discovered at birth that she had a rare disorder known as Sturge-Webber syndrome, a condition that caused large, wine-colored birthmarks to appear on her head and face. The syndrome is not an inherited one, so her unsuspecting parents were likely shocked by their baby's appearance. Common side effects of the condition include seizures, weakness on one side of the body, and often serious learning disabilities.

Grace had more of the post-wine birthmarks than most others with this syndrome, but that wasn't the worst of it. She also had the misfortune also to be born with another genetic facial disorder called neurofibromatosis, which causes the growth of fibrous tumors in soft tissue and bone – tumors that get larger with age. Eventually, they would make it so that Grace had difficulty speaking and being understood. Her jaw became barely mobile, which affected how much she could eat. She lost most of her teeth over time as the jaw, and the roof of her mouth expanded.

We cannot imagine what life must've been like for Grace growing up in rural Iowa in the late 1800s. As an adult, she was shy, quiet, and extremely embarrassed and hurt by people's reaction when they saw her face.

As a result, she isolated herself, living with her aging parents until 1935, when she joined the F.W. Miller's Freak Show. Legend persists that Grace joined the show after winning an "Ugliest Woman Contest" that was held at a local fair, but this is likely just sideshow hype, especially considering Grace's introverted personality and embarrassment at being called ugly.

It's more likely that a show manager heard of Grace, met her, and convinced her to join his lineup, knowing she would be a money-maker – and that this happened well before 1935.

Since Grace gave birth to an illegitimate son while on the road with the sideshow, there's no way this happened after 1935 because she would have been 47 years old by then. Logically, she had to be much younger when she ran off to join the show. A better guess is that she joined up with the sideshow in the early 1920s because there is a record of her with the Morris & Castle Show in Aberdeen, South Dakota, in July 1926. In 1933, she exhibited with Ripley's Odditorium and was also the main attraction that year with Charlie Pyle's Chamber of Horrors at the Chicago World's Fair.

There's no question that Grace's life was better on the show circuit, but even then, it wasn't ideal. She was usually billed as the "Mule-Faced Woman," and talkers outside the tent where she exhibited spent each day proclaiming loudly to the public that she was "grotesque and ugly beyond description" to sell tickets. She never got used to that, even though she understood the reasons for the pitch. She was often brought to tears while listening to the rehearsed pre-show description of her, and friends said she usually sat with her fingers in her ears to avoid hearing the hurtful spiel.

When she performed, Grace usually took the stage with a veil over her lower face, which the talker would dramatically lift once all the paying customers were assembled in the tent. Other times, she would be seated with her back to the crowd and then turn slowly around when given her cue. There are claims that some spectators actually fainted when they saw her, but that's likely hype – much like the stories that she was "constantly courted by roguish men with nose bags of oats at the stage door."

Grace never stopped being upset by remarks about her looks, especially because – according to sideshow friends – she took great pride in her appearance. She was always clean, took great care in dressing, styled her hair, and used makeup to cover the purple birthmarks on her face. But no makeup was able to hide her disfigurement, and her efforts to make herself look better when on stage just served to give heartless spectators even more excuses to taunt her.

With everything she endured in life, it's amazing that Grace was always described as a kind, gentle, generous woman who loved needlework, cooking, and preparing large meals for her friends even though eating solid food was difficult for her to eat because of her condition.

Grace never married, but she had a son in 1930. No one knows who the father was, but rumors claimed he'd been a drunken carnival worker who took advantage of her, stole her money, got her pregnant, and then ran off. Other accounts claim he drunkenly seduced her one night to win a bet and left the show the next day because of his embarrassment after being taunted by other sideshow workers.

After her son was born, she always signed her name as "Mrs." on her trade cards, either because of the shame of having an illegitimate son or to protect her son from public criticism.

Grace's baby turned out to be a perfect son she named Elmer. His birth record doesn't exist, so his date of birth is unknown, but his mother considered him a gift from God. She adored him, letting him do anything he wanted, believing the boy could do no wrong. Not surprisingly, he grew into a selfish, spoiled young man who turned dangerously mean when he drank or was using drugs, which seemed to be most of the time.

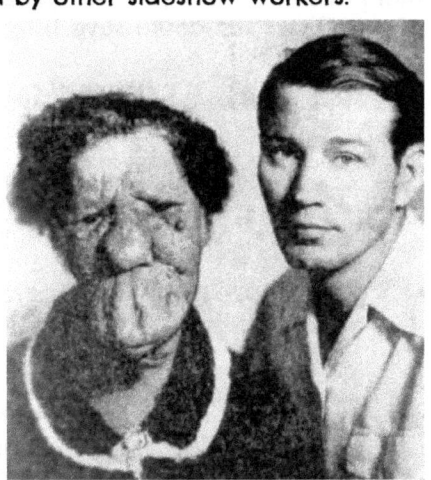

GRACE AND HER "PERFECT" SON, ELMER

There were reports of him often beating his mother, sometimes so viciously that she required medical attention. He berated her in front of others, called her vile names, stole from her, and squandered much of her earnings on gambling, alcohol, drugs, and an assortment of sleazy women and prostitutes.

Even then, Grace failed to see his failings. She began refusing to work for anyone who wouldn't also hire Elmer, insisting they were a package deal. Elmer became her manager – which just made it easier for him to steal from her – and when he stole from the shows where she performed, Grace quietly paid the money back. The show owners just learned to look the other way, knowing that if they fired Elmer, they'd lose one of their major attractions.

Grace continued to perform until late 1954. Even at the age of 64, she was still commanding $400 a week as a top attraction.

Both mother and son died in 1958, although when and where each passed away is unknown. It is believed that Grace died first, though, and Elmer died at some point later from sclerosis of the liver.

Had Grace still been alive when Elmer died, there would have undoubtedly been a lavish funeral and a large monument for the son she loved. As it is, both are likely buried somewhere in unmarked graves.

It's a sad ending to a life that was filled with so much tragedy that not even a few years of happiness with the carnival and the birth of a beloved son could save it.

"THE APE WOMAN"

MOST PEOPLE WOULD ASSUME THAT A WOMAN LIKE JULIA Pastrana never had a chance in life. Born in Sinaloa, Mexico, in 1834 to poverty-stricken parents, she was born with two severe conditions – one of which was not even recognized in her lifetime.

Doctors who examined her were baffled. One even offered the opinion that she was the product of a human mating with an orangutan. A condition that Julia actually suffered from was hypertrichosis, which left her face and body covered in thick, straight black hair. The other condition was gingival hyperplasia, which made her lips and gums thick and gave her an exaggerated, jutting jaw – hence the stage name of the "Ape Woman."

In 1854, Julia was a young woman when she was discovered by a Mexican customs administrator named Theodore Lent. He brought her to the United States and began exhibiting her around the country. They later traveled to Canada and Europe together, with Lent acting as her manager. In 1857, while in New York, they married.

Sadly, it's believed that even though Julia was in love with him, Lent simply married her so that he could legally control the impressive amount of money she was making with the sideshows. He taught her to sing and to dance to increase that revenue even more.

At some point, while they were on tour, Julia became pregnant but died in Moscow on March 26, 1860, from complications after the birth of a son who was also covered in thick black hair, just like his mother. The child died a few days later.

Not exactly a grieving husband and father, Lent had the bodies of both his wife and child mummified and enclosed in a glass case so that he could exhibit them.

He soon married a Bearded lady, gave her the stage name Zenora Pastrana, and claimed she was Julia's sister.

The bodies of Julia and her son changed ownership many times in the decades that followed. Vandals damaged the baby's remains beyond repair. However, Julia's body ended up in a storeroom at the University of Oslo in Norway for years.

On February 12, 2013, Julia's remains were finally brought back to Mexico, and after a Catholic mass, she was buried in a cemetery near the town where she was born. She was laid to rest in a white coffin covered with red roses while traditional music played.

Theodore Lent also got what he deserved. In 1884, he was committed to a mental institution and remained there until his unknown date of death. Records of his burial were lost to time.

"LIONEL, THE LION-FACED BOY"

BORN IN RUSSIA IN 1893 WITH HYERTRICHOSIS – OR WHAT SOME call "Werewolf Syndrome" – Empl Stephan Bibrowski had hair that grew all over his body, including his face. One newspaper described him as a boy who had "a soft while silky mane," which, of course, helped explain his stage name as the "Lion-Faced Boy." He was usually exhibited in full dress, preferring long-sleeved, button-up military-type costumes that emphasized his lion-like face. This also hid the fact that he also had hair that covered the rest of his body, although none of it was as long as what grew on his face.

Lionel was 10 years old when he first arrived in New York in 1903. He came to America with his 58-year-old German manager and guardian, Edouard Friederich. He had already been performing in Europe for years. His parents had literally sold him to Friederich, but by all appearances, he treated the boy like a son. Lionel had caught the eye of P.T. Barnum, who quickly contracted with Lionel's manager

to bring him to the United States and perform with the Barnum and Bailey Circus.

He became an immediate success, and newspapers raved about the crowds of people who came to see him and went away, agreeing that Lionel was "the strangest of them all."

And he was an enigma. He had the appearance of a wild and dangerous animal, yet he was gentle, well-behaved, and impeccably dressed. He spoke German, English, French, and Russian and could both read and write.

He was undoubtedly better educated than all the people who flocked to see him.

Part of every performer's act was their interaction with the audience, and Lionel didn't disappoint. He explained that his appearance had been caused by an incident that occurred five months before he was born when his mother saw his father, who was a lion tamer, eaten alive by his big cats. The sight so traumatized her that he was born covered with lion's hair. At this point in his presentation, he would show a photograph of himself at age three to show the fascinated audience that he had always been as he was that day – covered in animal hair.

When he got bored, he'd change things up. Sometimes, he claimed to be born in Poland and, at other times, in Germany. He'd also add more color to his fabricated story, especially on opening days, so that he could generate more sales and interest. Sometimes, he claimed to be able to see in the dark, like a cat, or claim he was married to a perfectly normal woman. The only thing odd about her was her abnormal love of cats.

Barnum – who could always be counted for a publicity stunt or two – once got into the act with his own story. While Lionel was in Albany, New York, in 1906, he leaked to the press that Lionel had attracted the unwanted advances of a wealthy older woman who had fallen madly in love with him, even though Lionel was only 13 at the time. She had to be dragged away from him, in tears, after his show and had been sending him letters of a scandalous nature ever since. The press and the public alike were shocked – and titillated – by the story because even then, sex and scandal sold tickets.

Lionel toured most of Europe, but he did several American tours, mostly with Barnum and Bailey, and had one longtime engagement with the Coney Island Dreamland Circus in New Jersey.

As far as is known, Lionel never married and never had children, and the date, place, and cause of his death aren't clear. However, two accounts of his passing have been told.

One states that Lionel died of a heart attack in Italy or Germany in 1932. The second claims he died in a Nazi concentration camp during World War II. In 1932, Lionel would have only been 39 years old, and while it is possible to die from a heart attack at that young age, it's unlikely.

Lionel preferred Germany to other countries, even becoming a citizen around 1930. His guardian was German, so he spent a great deal of time in the country and was comfortable with the language, customs, and geography. But Germany during Hitler's rise to power would not have been a safe place for someone like Lionel. He was of Jewish descent and a "freak," which would have doubly put his life in danger.

We'll never know about Lionel's final days, his death, or his resting place, but he'll remain one of the most curious sideshow performers in history.

THE LIFE AND WELL-DESERVED DEATH OF THE "LOBSTER BOY"

THERE'S NO QUESTION THAT IN ALMOST EVERY CASE, I FIND myself cheering on the so-called "freaks" of the sideshows, always hoping they triumph over a society that wants to keep them down.

But not when it comes to Grady Stiles, Jr.

It speaks volumes that most of his family plotted against him and paid to have him killed. Apparently, when he was sober – which wasn't often – he was a likable enough man that he could convince his first wife to marry him for a second time. Even she would realize that she should have known better because when his true colors showed again, she decided to have him murdered instead of bothering with a divorce attorney.

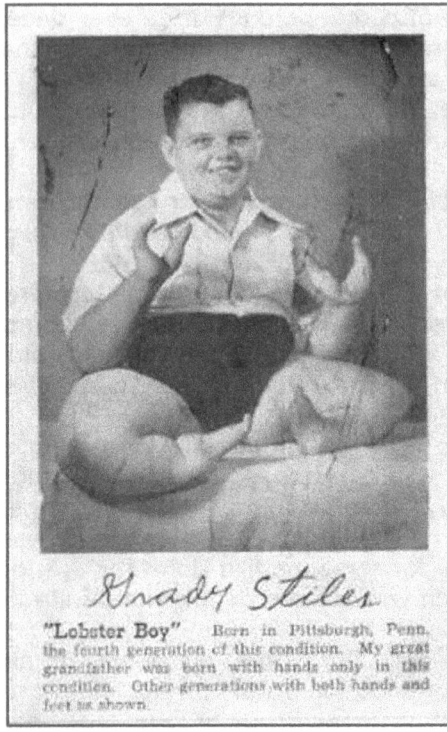

Grady Stiles

"Lobster Boy" Born in Pittsburgh, Penn. the fourth generation of this condition. My great grandfather was born with hands only in this condition. Other generations with both hands and feet as shown.

AS FAR BACK AS 1805, A PECULIAR PHYSICAL CONDITION known as ectrodactyly began afflicting the Stiles family, this rare congenital deformity made hands look like lobster claws with middle fingers that are either missing or seemingly fused to the thumb and pinky finger.

While most people would see the condition as a handicap, it became an opportunity for later members of the Stiles family. As the years passed, more and more members of the family came along with unusual hands and feet. Grady Stiles, Sr. – born in 1912 – decided to cash in on the condition and started exhibiting in the sideshows. The family became a popular carnival staple in the twentieth century until Grady's son would ruin the family name forever.

Grady, Jr. – who would become known as "Lobster Boy" – was born in Pittsburgh in July 1937. Like his father's, his hands were split down the middle and fused to form two-digit "claws." In addition, his feet were small, flipper-like appendages at the end of shortened legs. For most of his life, he used a wheelchair in public but got around in private by crawling, using his upper body to pull across the floor with impressive strength. Her performed almost all day-to-day tasks by deftly using his "claws," and as he grew up, he became alarmingly strong, which he would demonstrate during homicidal rages later in life.

Throughout his childhood, Grady and his family toured on the carnival circuit and spent the offseason in Gibsonton, Florida – a place the carnies called "Gibb Town." The family did well, making between $50,000 and $80,000 per season.

Growing up in the sideshows, it wasn't surprising that he fell in love with another carnie when he was a young man. Her name was Maria Teresa Herzog, and she had run away to join the circus as a teenager. She wasn't part of any act. Maria usually just worked in grab joints or helped wherever she was needed. She returned Grady's affections, and the two were married.

They were later divorced, and Frady married Barbara Browning, but after they split up, he convinced Maria to marry him again. Altogether, Grady had four children. Two of them – Glen and Donna – were spared the family deformity. However, his son, Grady III, and his daughter, Cathy, were born with ectrodactyly and were introduced to the family business.

As I mentioned earlier, Grady could be a monster when he drank. When he was drunk, he became abusive toward his wife and children – physically, verbally, and emotionally – and when he wasn't performing, he was always drunk. The kids were frequently seen with bruises on their bodies, black eyes, and scrapes. At one point, he allegedly used his claw-like hand to try and rip his wife's IUD out of her body during a fight. He often used those claws to choke her into unconsciousness.

And yet, the worst was yet to come. His oldest daughter, Donna, became romantically involved with a young man named Jack Layne, whom Grady didn't approve of. The pair continued to see each other despite Grady's anger over their relationship, and eventually, they became engaged to be married.

No one knows for sure what exactly happened – either Grady went to see Jack at his home or invited the young man over to his house under the guise of giving his blessing for the wedding that was happening the next day.

It was September 2, 1978, and it became the day that Grady picked up his shotgun and murdered his daughter's fiancée in cold blood.

Grady was arrested and went to trial. He freely admitted to the murder without any remorse. However, he pointed out that he couldn't possibly be sent to prison – no jail could handle his disability, and to confine him in prison would be cruel and unusual punishment. He had also, by this time, started suffering from cirrhosis of the liver from his drinking and hand emphysema from decades of cigarette smoking.

The authorities were stumped. They had no counterargument. Most prisons were ill-equipped to deal with disabilities, especially something as rare as the one that affected Grady Stiles, Jr. He was sentenced to 15 years of probation and was released to return home.

By now, "Lobster Boy" had divorced his first wife, married another woman, abused her, and continued to subject his children to his drunken rages. His second wife left him, too. And then, for reasons that no one – in the Stiles family or outside of it – has been able to understand, his first wife, Maria, agreed to marry him again in 1989.

She may have had the patience of a saint, but Maria – as well as her now-grown children – had their limits. Grady had evaded prison and now had a sense of being above the law, so his brutality toward his family became more severe.

Marie bore the brunt of his abuse until, finally, she couldn't take any more.

By the fall of 1992, the family was living in a trailer at 11117 Inglewood Street in Gibsonton, Florida. For three years, Grady had continued to brutalize his wife and his children on the rare occasions when they came around. One night, Maria sat down with her 20-year-old son from another marriage, Glenn, and told him that something needed to be done about Grady. Glenn was also a sideshow performer – "The Human Blockhead" – and his father, Henry, had been a little person. He knew someone who could help her.

A 17-year-old neighbor, Chris Wyant, agreed to kill Grady. Maria gave him $1,500, and he had a friend purchase a .32-caliber Colt automatic, which he planned to do the job with.

On the night of November 29, while Grady was watching television in his underwear and drinking his last beer, Chris entered the Stiles' trailer and shot him twice in the back of the head.

"Lobster Boy" never saw it coming.

But he should have because not a single person who was arrested for killing him denied the murder – or regretted it.

The trial became a feeding frenzy for the media with headlines like "Human Blockhead Convicted of Murder of Lobster Boy." During the proceedings, Maria spoke at length about Grady's abusive history. "My husband was going to kill my family," she told the court, "I believe that from the bottom of my heart."

Her daughter, Cathy, testified, too. In court, she testified that he father "was like Satan himself."

The jury convicted Chris Wyant of second-degree murder, and he was sentenced to 27 years in prison. The judge, sympathetic toward Maria, handed down a sentence of 12 years for her. Glenn's sentence was the harshest. He ended up with first-degree murder charges, plus conspiracy, and was sentenced to life in prison with no chance for parole for 25 years. Maria had tried to get him to take a plea bargain, but he refused.

As most of his family was being tried for his murder, Grady Stiles, Jr. was being laid to rest at the Showman Rest Cemetery in Tampa.

Or really, laid to "unrest," as it turned out.

Grady was so disliked, not just by his family but by the whole sideshow community, that the funeral home that handled the arrangements was unable to find anyone willing to be a pallbearer.

PART FOUR: TOD BROWNING'S "FREAKS"

IN 1932, WHEN THE FILM *FREAKS* WAS RELEASED IN THEATER, sideshows were still an acceptable form of entertainment in circuses, carnivals, and on the midways across America.

These were also the early days of the Hollywood silver screen. "Talking pictures" were now all the rage, and theaters had opened all over the country that were dedicated to nothing but films.

But these two forms of entertainment – freaks and movies – were never supposed to merge. Monsters and sinister figures were constantly appearing in Hollywood pictures, but those monsters weren't real. They were make-believe – something you couldn't say about the performers with disabilities who were appearing on America's sideshow stages. Hollywood shunned performers who looked like they did. They wanted beautiful people on the big screen – not human oddities.

Even today, casting directors would prefer to cast a "normal" actor in makeup and costume to play the role of someone different. The early thought seemed to be that freaks were too shocking to put into movies. Today, producers and directors aren't worried about being too shocking – they're worried about being politically correct. They try to avoid controversy, maybe not in the script, but certainly

DIRECTOR TOD BROWNING

when it comes to hiring the actors. It's better to create a freak for a role than be accused of exploiting someone with a disability.

And, of course, there's always the Hollywood conception that those who look different or have physically different bodies must be evil. There's the suggestion that an unusual face hides a dark heart and a menacing intent. Those with abnormal bodies or distorted faces inevitably become villains – or worse, the mentally impaired.

But there has been one exception to this rule in the history of Hollywood films, and it was the movie Freaks, directed by Tod Browning, the same director who'd thrilled audiences the previous year with *Dracula*.

But when it was released, this movie was no Dracula. Unlike Browning's last film, this wasn't a box office success, loved by audiences and critics alike.

Freaks was a controversial failure, and one that I believe planted the seed that would eventually bring about the end of the carnival and circus sideshows.

Today, it's a cult classic, but in 1932, censors and critics immediately forced the film to undergo extensive cuts, trimming it down from 90 to only 60 minutes. Even then, audiences hated it, and the film ended up losing a staggering $164,000, which was a tremendous amount at the time. Unfortunately, most of the material that was cut from the movie is lost today.

In many parts of the country, the film was outright banned and remained banned for years. In England, it was kept out of theaters until 1963, and it was banned in Sweden, Finland, and Ireland. In Canada, it was called "brutal and grotesque." Distributors tried changing its name, hoping to generate business, calling it *Forbidden Love, Nature's Mistakes,* and *The Monster Show.*

Before *Freaks*, Tod Browning had been heralded as an up-and-coming director, achieving success through collaborations with Lon Chaney and, of course, with *Dracula*, starring Bela Lugosi. But after

Freaks was released, he had trouble finding work, and the film is thought to be responsible for bringing his career to an early end.

And that's unfortunate because this film is really something special in a lot of different ways.

SPOILER ALERT: If you have never seen *Freaks*, then I need you to go and find a copy of it and watch it. Buy it, rent it, watch it on streaming, find a DVD or Blu-ray copy, or even an old VHS tape. I don't care – if you're reading this book, you need to see the movie.

First off, Browning used real professional sideshow performers in the film. These were people who never would have been cast in a Hollywood production under other circumstances, but in this case, the cast could basically play themselves. They were portrayed in the film in a dignified manner – especially by 1930s standards – and they were paid well for their performances.

Best of all, the storyline of the film called for the "normal" beautiful people to be the villains. The "abnormal" human oddities were the heroes, and not only that, but the villains get what's coming to them in the end.

And when the evil Cleopatra gets what she deserved, it's one of the most startling and blood-chilling images that had appeared onscreen up until that time – and it's still pretty frightening after all these years.

Do yourself a favor and seek this film out. You won't be sorry. No one has ever attempted to remake this film, and no one ever will. There would be no way to recapture the originality of it, its moral center, or the powerful visual shock of that ending.

And there would also be no way ever to assemble a cast like this one again – a unique and talented group of people like nothing that we'll ever see again.

What follows is a brief look at some of the stories of the cast of *Freaks*. Be warned as you read them – these stories don't always have happy endings.

VIOLET AND DAISY HILTON
"SAN ANTONIO'S SIAMESE TWINS"

VIOLET AND DAISY SKINNER WERE BORN IN BRIGHTON, East Essex, England, in February 1908. Their mother was an unmarried barmaid who promptly sold her two-week-old conjoined twins to Mary Hilton,

 the midwife who had delivered them. She knew what a moneymaking opportunity she had on her hands and began training them to sing and play music as soon as they were able to stand.

The girls began to be exhibited around the age of three by Mary and her husband, whom the twins were forced to call "Auntie" and "Sir." They were badly mistreated for years – beaten when they made mistakes in their shows, isolated and kept from making friends, and saw very little of the money they made, even though they were making a fortune for the Hiltons.

When they were eight, the twins came to America when the Hiltons decided to settle in San Antonio, Texas. They performed for vaudeville audiences and traveled the country, sharing billing with performers like Harry Houdini, who taught the twins self-hypnosis as a way for them to have time alone mentally. It was also Houdini who, when the girls got older, encouraged them to obtain their freedom from the Hiltons, who were still treating them poorly and stealing most of their earnings.

When they were teenagers, Daisy dyed her hair blond, then later red, to distinguish herself from Violet. Daisy also did most of the talking while Violet was quiet. As they faced front, by the way, Violet was on the left, and Daisy was on the right.

Their personalities may have been quite different, but they had a shared dislike of doctors since most of them usually wanted to study the pair to see if it was possible to separate them surgically. That was a thought, surprisingly, that terrified the sisters. They were extremely close – and not just physically – and friends were always amazed to find that they seemed to be able to communicate with one another without saying a word.

In 1931, when the girls were 23, they finally followed Houdini's advice, consulted a lawyer named Martin J. Arnold, and successfully sued for their independence. Mary Hilton had died, but she had willed the twins to her husband and her daughter, Edith as if they were property.

Of course, for most of their lives, they'd been treated that way.

Violet and Daisy were by then making $500 or more every week, making them some of the highest-paid sideshow performers in the country in the 1920s, and now they were allowed to keep it.

Violet and Daisy were joined at the hip, and when they reached adulthood, they both stood just under five feet tall and weighed around 100 pounds each. The bones of their lower spine were joined, and they shared a common blood and nervous system, which resulted in shared sexual sensations which, if the stories are to be believed, they put to good use.

The girls were beautiful, and they became notorious for their dating practices and scandalous affairs. They competed to see who could attract the most men, and rumors spread that not all the men who spent time with them were single.

Both twins were eventually married. Daisy briefly married a performer named Buddy Sawyer, but he moved out after 10 days, saying that she was a lovely girl but that "he guessed he just wasn't the kind of fella to marry a Siamese twin."

Violet was married in the Cotton Bowl in Dallas during the Texas Centennial of 1936, but this was likely a publicity stunt since the marriage was annulled a short time later.

After touring for many years, the girls struggled to make a living as they got older. They appeared in *Freaks* – a box office and critical failure – and then in 1951, they appeared in *Chained for Life*, which was loosely based on their life story. It was not exactly a smashing success. The film was poorly produced and directed, and the girls gave a performance that even the kindest critics said was awful.

Things didn't improve for them much after that. They were ill-equipped to manage their own careers and finances and were taken in several times by romantic suitors and show business crooks who bilked them out of large sums of money. Violet and Daisy made and lost several fortunes in their lifetimes and, by the mid-1950s, were living in poverty, largely forgotten by the world.

They tried several times for a comeback. They opened a snack bar in Miami, but it failed, and then they began making personal appearances at mostly small-town theaters and drive-ins that were showing double-bill screenings of *Freaks* and *Chained for Life*.

The last public appearance of the Hilton Sisters was in 1962 when they were promoting the double feature at a drive-in near Charlotte, North Carolina. Their tour manager abandoned them there, taking off with their money and leaving them stranded and broke in a little town called Monroe.

Luckily, kind people in town helped them find a place to stay and sent them to the local grocery store to look for work. The owner of the store always remembered the day they'd walked into his store looking for a job. They were wearing makeup and had bright red toenails, but their hair was dirty, and their clothing was wrinkled.

They offered him two employees for the price of one.

He got a laugh out of that one and hired them on the spot. They worked in the store for the next seven years, never talking about their show business background. Many of the store's customers never realized that the two sisters working side by side were Siamese twins until January 4, 1969, when Violet and Daisy failed to show up for work. They were found on found dead in their apartment, victims of influenza. They were 60 years old.

It was a tragic end to a not-always-happy story.

JOHNNY ECK
"THE HALF BOY"

BUT NOT ALL THE STORIES OF PERFORMERS FROM *FREAKS* were sad. John Eckhardt, Jr. was born in Baltimore in 1911, seemingly without legs and the lower part of his abdomen, but he never let that slow him down.

Johnny was a second-born fraternal twin. His brother, Robert, had no disabilities, and neither did his older sister, Carrie, who had been born 12 years earlier. Johnny had a condition called sacral agenesis, a spinal deformity. Although he didn't appear to have legs – he did. They were small, unusable ones that he kept concealed under clothing that was specially made for him.

When he was born, doctors told his parents that he wouldn't survive, but Johnny thrived and was walking on his hands by age one. Later, his mother made him special gloves that he could wear as shoes.

His parents made sure that he had a regular childhood, and his mother liked to tell everyone that her son could do anything any other child could do – and Johnny could do many things better.

He started in show business at the age of 12, working in a dime museum, and by 18, he was already a seasoned professional, billed as

"Johnny Eck, the Half-Boy." He traveled with the John M. Sheesley Circus for a few years and then moved on to bigger and bigger shows. His twin brother, Robert, eventually joined him on the road, and they performed together for most of their lives. They were famous for a magic trick they did with Johnny working as the top section of a volunteer – played by Robert – who was sawn in half. It was said that the only time the twins were separated was when Johnny was filming *Freaks* in 1932.

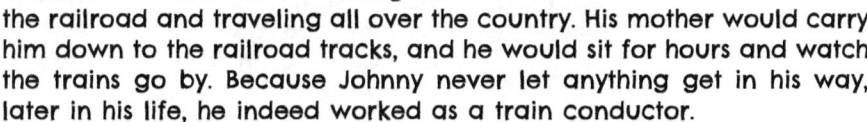

As a child, Johnny had always dreamed of somehow working for the railroad and traveling all over the country. His mother would carry him down to the railroad tracks, and he would sit for hours and watch the trains go by. Because Johnny never let anything get in his way, later in his life, he indeed worked as a train conductor.

He performed in sideshows for years, touring the country and making a very good living. Tod Browning, who directed Freaks, said that Johnny was an excellent actor and that had he not been born with a disability, he would have undoubtedly been a film star.

In the late 1930s, Johnny appeared regularly at Robert L. Ripley's Believe It Or Not! Odditoriums and in 1938, climbed the stairs to the top of the Washington Monument on his hands. Robert Ripley called Johnny "the most remarkable man alive" – and he was.

Johnny never saw himself as handicapped – only unique. He was a remarkable talent, funny, and the center of attention everywhere he went. He was an accomplished writer, artist, photographer, magician, puppeteer, expert model maker, race car driver, swimmer, and gymnast. His friends maintained that he had an unsinkable spirit that inspired everyone around him. He traveled the world, and he made a lot of money, achieving more in his lifetime than most people with legs.

But even Johnny Eck's story has a tragic final act.

His always positive outlook on life came to an end in 1987 when thieves broke into Johnny and Robert's home. Not satisfied with just robbing the two 76-year-old brothers, they beat them severely. Johnny never seemed to recover from the physical and mental trauma and spent the last few years of his life in almost total seclusion.

He died of a heart attack in January 1991, at the same hour in Baltimore, where he'd been born. He was 70 years old. His twin brother, Robert, died four years later, and they're buried side by side in Green Mount Cemetery.

THE EARLES / THE DOLLS
HARRY, GRACIE, DAISY & TINY

HARRY EARLES WAS THE SECOND OLDEST SIBLING IN THE FAMILY. He'd been born Kurt Fritz Scheider in Germany on April 3, 1902. He came to America with his sister, Freida – who took the stage name of Gracie – in 1915. They had gotten their start in show business in Germany, where they'd worked the sideshows as Hans and Gretel, the "smallest dancing couple on Earth."

In America, they also toured in a sideshow, working for their sponsor, Burt Earles, and adopted his surname to seem more Americanized. Their standard shows involved dancing, singing, and horseback riding.

Harry and Gracie had made a name for themselves as popular performers before Hilda joined the show in 1925. She took the stage name of Daisy and was often referred to as the "midget Mae West," thanks to her good looks and sultry manner. Daisy had so much fun that she soon convinced their last sister, Elly, to come to America and join the rest of her siblings. She took the stage name of Tiny.

The four managed to get a lucrative contract with the Ringling Brothers and Barnum & Bailey Circus, but they also worked in the movies, appearing in comedies with Laurel and Hardy. Around 1939, though, they left the movie business, preferring life with the circus, where they made a lot more money for less work.

It was also around this same time that Burt Earles died, and the family adopted the new surname of Doll. They claimed audiences always said they looked like "dolls," so the siblings decided the new name was a good one.

Although friendly and always spoken about in glowing terms, the Earles spent most of their time with each other. Daisy was the only sibling to get married, but she divorced her average-sized husband after less than a year. When working on the film *The Wizard of Oz*, the siblings had their own apartment. They reportedly didn't fraternize much with the rest of the Munchkin cast due to their alleged immoral behavior and questionable antics.

By 1958, the quartet had become tired of life on the road, retired, and had a custom home built for them in Sarasota, Florida. It had an added attraction that they opened to the public called "The Doll's House."

The four of them lived together for the rest of their lives. Gracie died in November 1970, followed by Daisy in March 1980, Harry in May 1985, and Tiny in September 2004, when she was 90 years old.

ANGELO ROSSITTO
"LITTLE MO"

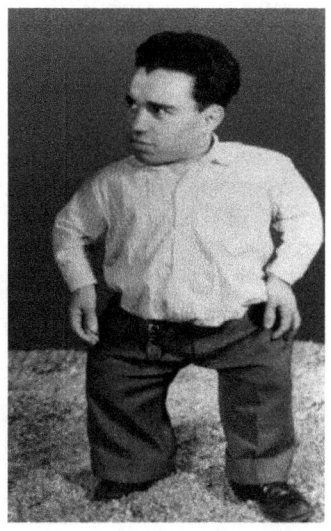

BORN ANGELO SAVATORE ROSSITTO IN OMAHA, NEBRASKA, in February 1908, he went on to Hollywood in the 1920s to become a star. Legend has it that he was selling newspapers one day on the street when he was discovered by John Barrymore, who got him his first film role.

If this story wasn't true, it should have been.

He started showing up in movies when he was still in his teens, usually appearing in highly visible supporting roles or as an unusual extra. He stood only two feet, 11 inches tall, but he became a popular and highly sought-after performer because of his appearance and his talent. His dark hair, olive skin, and dramatic facial features made him a natural for the roles he was cast in, and he had a reputation for being highly professional on the set.

Angelo's first film role was in a silent movie in 1927. However, he kept working steadily for the next 60 years, appearing in feature films – in addition to *Freaks* – like *The Baron of Arizona, Dementia, Invasion of the Saucer Men, Something Wicked This Way Comes*, and dozens of others, like *Mad Max Beyond Thunderdome*, where he played the smaller half of "Master Blaster." He also appeared in television shows like *Gunsmoke, The Man from U.N.C.L.E., Baretta, the Rockford Files, The Incredible Hulk*, and more.

He acted alongside Hollywood legends like Lon Chaney, John Barrymore, Bela Lugosi, James Arness, James Garner, and Mel Gibson. He was a stunt double for Shirley Temple until she outgrew him.

He played a wide range of characters like a gnome, a pygmy, a villain, a monster, and an alien. He appeared in comedies, dramas, science fiction flicks, mysteries, fantasy films, and horror movies. He could never be considered a household name – despite his impressive list of film and TV credits – but he was always one of those guys you'd see onscreen and think, "Hey, I know that guy."

Angelo appeared in more than 200 productions during his career, but most of them only required a few days or weeks at a time. So, Angelo had a "day job" from the 1930s through the 1960s, running a newsstand just outside one of the studio's gates. He often joked that when he was needed for a film, someone would just come to get him at the newsstand, and he'd close early for the day.

One of Angelo's final films was *Mad Max Beyond Thunderdome*, and no one knew that he was almost completely blind at the time of that performance.

He passed away just six years after that film was released, in September 1991, from complications during surgery. He was 83 years old.

FRANCES O'CONNOR
"THE ARMLESS GIRL"

FRANCES BELLE O'CONNOR WAS BORN IN SEPTEMBER 1914 in Granite City, Minnesota, and to her parents' surprise, she had no arms. But even as a small child, she never let that slow her down.

Frances compensated for her missing arms by becoming extremely adept at using her feet. She learned to sew, dress herself, feed herself, and even shoot a gun without assistance. Frances always credited her mother's love and support for her success and for making her self-reliant. She was not a person who ever felt sorry for herself, and everyone who knew her always spoke fondly of her upbeat manner and sense of humor.

Her entry into show business was with the Al G. Barnes Circus in Sheridan, Wyoming. Her mother, not surprisingly, became her manager and stayed in that role for Frances' entire career. She also toured with the Sells-Floto Circus, Ringling Brothers, and Cole Brothers Circus. She signed autographs for her fans with her feet, who always marveled at her excellent penmanship. Her small part in *Freaks* showed her eating and drinking with her feet.

Frances had many male admirers. She was a very pretty young woman with a sweet disposition, plus it didn't hurt that she was innocently able to show a lot of leg in her performances. She received a few dozen marriage proposals during her career, but she never married, instead preferring to live with the mother she adored. After she passed away, Frances retired from show business.

She died in Long Beach, California, in January 1982.

KOO KOO
"THE BIRD GIRL FROM MARS"

HER NAME OBVIOUSLY WASN'T "KOO KOO." IT WAS JUST the name that everyone seemed to know. She was born Minnie Woolsey in New Mexico in 1880 and had a small part in *Freaks*.

But that's one of the few things we know about her life.

She was afflicted by what is known as Harper's Syndrome, a form of dwarfism that's characterized by multiple anomalies such as short stature, a beak-like nose, large ears, an absence of hair and teeth, and intellectual disability. Sadly, Minnie was afflicted with all these anomalies and was almost blind, too.

421 | THE DEVIL'S CARNIVAL

Her managers took advantage of her odd appearance by dressing her in various bird costumes and directing her to strut around the stage and dance. At other shows, she just sat quietly and stared out into space through her large, oversized glasses with very thick lenses.

Reportedly, she spent at least part or most of her life in an institution. I don't think there's any doubt that she has taken advantage of and used to make money for someone – although certainly not for herself.

The date and place of her death is unknown.

ELIZABETH "BETTY" GREEN "BIRD GIRL"

THE EARLY YEARS OF BETTY'S LIFE ARE A MYSTERY. Little is known about her background or how she got started in the sideshow business. By most accounts, she was not actually a "freak" at all. However, she was just a tiny, odd-looking woman who capitalized on her unusual looks, accentuating them with facial gestures, a shaved head, and the costumes she chose to wear.

According to Freaks director Tod Browning, "Betty was a Jewish girl from Springfield, Massachusetts, who owned five apartment houses."

Truth or fiction? No one knows. There's no record of where she went after the film was completed, but it seems likely that Betty simply went home and lived the rest of her life as an ordinary person with an extraordinary appearance.

JOSEPHINE - JOSEPH

BORN IN POLAND IN 1913, JOSEPHINE-JOSEPH'S FATHER was a simple Jewish farmer who likely never expected how his child would make a name for themselves in America.

Although Josephine-Joseph claimed to be a hermaphrodite, most reports state they were a clever impersonator, a homosexual, or a transvestite. Although a handful of what were called "half and halfs" were true hermaphrodites, most were simply blow-off acts. However, the sexual lure of the possibility, plus the tantalizing look at parts of the human body usually clothed in public in that day, made the half-and-half acts very popular – so popular they could often carry an entire show.

Very little is known about Josephine-Joseph, including their true name. They always claimed in interviews that they had been raised as an average boy until the age of 12 when they started to exhibit feminine traits on the left side of the body. The story, though, was likely untrue and was repeated for audiences to generate publicity.

They built up the right side of their body by exercising only that side, tanned that side, cut their hair short on the right, grew a half-beard, and wore jungle-style costumes to emphasize maleness. On the left side, they allowed their hair to grow and styled it, never exercised that side, and wore makeup, jewelry, and a false breast. They always wore women's clothing on that side, as well. The look was very convincing to the unsophisticated public of the day. One newspaper story about Josephine-Joseph was titled: "Seeing is Believing. Half of her can do a stevedore's work, the other half embroidery."

In 1928, The Josephine-Joseph Big Circus Sideshow toured America, bringing sideshow entertainment and a congress of freaks to the vaudeville stage. It's not clear if Josephine-Joseph was the promoter or manager of the show – although this is unlikely since they were only 15 years old at the time -- or if their act merely headlined it, but they always received top billing.

Other members of the show included a Fat Lady named Jolly Irene; Martha Morris, the "Armless Wonder;" Marie De Vere, a sword swallower; tattooed lady Mademoiselle Pictoria; Lionette, the "Lion-Faced Lady;" and Marie Howard, who allowed her husband to throw knives at her.

In 1930, Josephine-Joseph exhibited at Coney Island, and then in 1932, they played themselves in *Freaks*. They had a small speaking part as a passing love interest of the strongman. These small scenes were enough, though, to make them one of the most popular cast members among the cult following for the movie.

What happened to Josephine-Joseph after that remains unknown. It's possible that, as they got older, pulling off the feminine side of the act became harder, and they left show business. This was a common late career problem for many half-and-half acts, but if that's what happened, no record of it exists.

MARTHA MORRIS "THE ARMLESS WONDER"

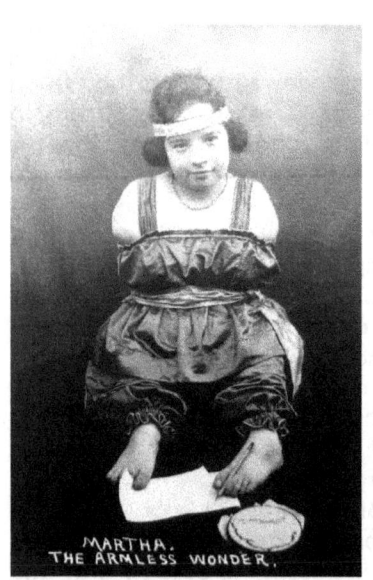

MARTHA MORRIS WAS BORN IN CHICAGO IN 1904 TO David and Jennie Morris, who were the parents of eight other children who'd been born without physical disabilities. Martha, though, was born without arms, plus her legs and torso were shortened and deformed. Her feet were attached to her body just below the hips, which meant she couldn't walk, dress, or feed herself and required a wheelchair and a nurse throughout her life.

Martha started her sideshow career in her early teens, billed as "The Armless Wonder." She made up for not having arms by becoming skilled at using her feet. She could write and type with her feet and even thread a needle. She appeared at Coney Island in the 1920s and traveled with a carnival. She also appeared at the Century of Progress exposition in Chicago.

Martha had a small part in *Freaks*, playing the wife of Angeleno, which must have been thrilling for her since, in one interview, her father said that Martha's favorite thing to do was to go to the movies.

He claimed she never got tired of going and could sit through the same film many times.

Martha never married and died in Chicago, suffering from pneumonia, in April 1937. She was only 33 years old.

OLGA RODERICK
"LADY OLGA, THE BEARDED LADY"

LONG BEFORE SHE WAS "LADY OLGA," SHE WAS JANE BANELL, and she was born in Wilmington, North Carolina, in January 1871. She had two siblings, but she was the only member of her family with a physical anomaly.

And her parents weren't very happy about it.

When Jane was only four years old – and her father was out of town for work -- her mother essentially sold her to a traveling circus that came through town. She ended up in Europe, where she became sick and was hospitalized, then quickly abandoned by the circus owners. Her father finally tracked her down in an orphanage in Berlin, where she'd been placed after being released from the hospital.

He took her back to North Carolina but pawned her off on his parents, where she was put to work on her grandfather's farm. Although she disliked the hard work, she stayed for several years until meeting a neighbor who worked as a strongman for a sideshow during the carnival season. He encouraged her to join the sideshow again, pointing out how much money she could make if she stopped shaving her beard. Jane was convinced and signed on with John Robinson's Circus in the 1890s, where she was billed as the lady with the 13-inch beard.

During this time, she gave birth to two children and was said to have been married twice before she turned 30, although no record of those marriages exists. It's believed that she may have invented the marriages to hide two illegitimate children, or it's also possible that, like other sideshow performers, she didn't worry about legal details when it came to weddings. Both children, though, died before 1906.

Jane went on tour with many of the major circuses of the time, including with Ringling Brothers and Barnum & Bailey Circus in the 1930s. She performed using several different stage names before finally settling on "Lady Olga." In the late 1930s and 1940s, Lady Olga exhibited at Hubert's Museum in Times Square and at the World Circus Side Show at Coney Island.

In 1931, Jane legally married Thomas O'Boyle, a veteran circus clown and talker. She was 60 years old, and the groom was 29, but they lived happily together until Jane died in Los Angeles in October 1951.

Jane also had a role in *Freaks*. She, of course, played the bearded lady, and in the film, she gives birth to a baby girl to the delight of the father, The Human Skeleton, and the other sideshow cast members. However, of all the cast members, she was the only one who criticized the movie and publicly stated that she regretted being cast in it.

PRINCE RANDIAN
"THE HUMAN TORSO"

THERE IS VERY LITTLE KNOWN ABOUT THE EARLY LIFE OF Prince Randian, including his real name. He appears to have been born in Demerara in British Guyana between 1870 and 1875. Ship manifests listed his race as African Black or East Indian, or a "Hindoo," and notes also were made that he could neither read nor write in 1917.

It was that year when he was traveling by ship with an attendant and was detained for two days in need of hospital care after arriving in the United States from St. Thomas, where he lived at the time. By

1923, he was living in Plainfield, New Jersey, and listed his occupation as "Theatrical Actor."

Prince Randian was born with Tetra-Amelia Syndrome, an extremely rare inherited condition that results in the absence of one or more limbs. There are only a few family lines in the world that are affected by this condition, and most children who have it are stillborn or die soon after birth because of other deformities that are caused by the condition. They include facial abnormalities, genital malformations, and heart, skeletal, and nervous system complications. In most cases, sufferers have trouble breathing because the lungs are usually deformed or not fully developed.

Someone in Prince Randian's life decided that he could overcome his difficulties, and he learned to be amazingly self-sufficient. During his act, he would shave himself, cut his hair, thread a needle, sharpen knives, roll cigarettes, and even fill and smoke a pipe. Sometimes, he was accompanied by a native South American orchestra that played upbeat background music while Prince Randian performed for a stunned audience.

When he was older, Prince Randian usually wore a knitted garment that wrapped around his body, visually defining his show name, "The Human Torso." Offstage, he was typically carried by a paid attendant, but onstage, he moved around by wiggling the upper and lower sections of his body like a snake or by simply rolling wherever he wanted to go. He was often photographed with a wooden box where he kept his show props, which he reportedly had constructed and painted himself.

His best-known show trick was rolling and lighting a cigarette using only his lips – an act that was captured on film in *Freaks*.

Prince Randian was a devoted family man. He married a fellow sideshow performer, Princess Sarah, who had been born around 1877 and played the parts of "harem girl" and "Native American squaw" during her brief sideshow career. The couple had four daughters and a son together and would eventually have eight grandchildren.

Prince Randian semi-retired to his home in Paterson, New Jersey, in his later years but continued to make occasional appearances at Coney Island. He'd tired of life on the road and the long days of travel.

His last public appearance was at Sam Wagner's 14th Street Museum in New York City on December 19, 1934. He collapsed and died shortly after the performance at the age of 63.

PETER ROBINSON
"THE HUMAN SKELETON"

PETER ROBINSON'S EARLY LIFE IS ALSO A MYSTERY. What little is known about his past comes from newspaper stories that may or may not be accurate. Reportedly, he was born in Springfield, Massachusetts, in April of 1877 or 1879. He was around 13 years old when he inexplicably started losing weight.

As an adult, Peter never weighed more than 60 pounds, and he was five feet, three inches tall. It's possible that he had a medical condition that prevented him from gaining weight, but more likely, he was a "created freak" who had starved himself into show business.

His career began in 1899 when he was in his early twenties, and he toured with P.T. Barnum and eventually with the Ringling Brothers and Barnum & Bailey Circus. He was also a Coney Island sideshow favorite. He was an accomplished harmonica player and loved nothing more than goading friends into political debates.

Beginning with one of the most famous "human skeletons," Isaac Sprague, publicity stunts often played out in the newspapers regarding marriages between the sideshow Fat Lady and the Human Skeleton. It was a favorite stunt of P.T. Barnum, and in 1924, the papers were buzzing about the marriage of Peter and Baby Bunny Smith, a sideshow Fat Lady who weighed 467 pounds. Bunny claimed that she'd won Peter away from Sweet Adeline, another Fat Lady, and quipped that her new husband had fallen in love with at least eight other Fat Ladies in the past.

Most of the stories about Petter and Bunny were reported in a "tongue-in-cheek" style that poked good-natured fun at the skinny groom and his blushing bride. Bunny was quoted saying things like, "I hope I don't roll over him in bed!" but the marriage was almost undoubtedly just a stunt.

In Freaks, Peter basically played himself, the "Human Skeleton," who was married to the Bearded Lady, played by Lady Olga.

The exact date and place of Peter's death are unknown, although most sources believe he died in 1947.

SCHLITZIE

SCHLITZIE IS PROBABLY THE MOST FAMOUS SIDESHOW PERFORMER that we know almost nothing about. His date of birth, where he was born, and his parents' names are all unknown, although it's commonly accepted that what is written on his death certificate and tombstone is at least somewhat correct. That's all we'll ever have because Schlitzie was never able to provide any information himself, and anyone who might have been able to shed some light on his background never did so. An educated guess – based on the times and the lives of other child stars in the sideshows – is that Schlitzie was either given or sold to a sideshow manager or that the showman found Schlitzie in an institution where his parents had abandoned him.

Schlitzie is believed to have been born in the Bronx, and his birth name was Simon Metz. He was born with microcephaly, a neurodevelopmental disorder characterized by an abnormally small brain, a pointed cranium, and unusually small stature. In the sideshows – and elsewhere in those days – anyone with this kind of disorder was labeled a "pinhead." The condition often caused intellectual disability, and, as an adult, Schlitzie only had the cognitive skills of a three-year-old.

In 1911, A.W. Mills, who was the owner of the sideshow that exhibited Schlitzie at the time, was fined $300 by a grand jury in Illinois for "exhibiting Schlitzie, the alleged idiot." At trial, three doctors testified that Schlitzie was nothing more than an idiot and that the manager and his wife, plus another manager, G.A. Johnson, should be jailed or fined for showing the idiot to the public. The good people in Sangamon County, where the complaint was filed, meant well, but Schlitzie was better off in the sideshow than in an institution somewhere or stuck in the life that he left behind. From every account, Schlitzie was loved and treated well by the sideshow community.

In the tradition of sideshow hype, he was originally billed as "Schlitzie, the Wild Girl," and promotion claimed he was a Mexican girl of 18, found among the Aztecs, and standing only 22 inches tall. It also claimed he had only three ounces of brain but was capable of understanding and speaking broken English and Spanish.

In this case – and in most cases -- Schlitzie was promoted as being female. This was largely because he couldn't master a zipper or buttons, so he wore a dress with bloomers underneath so that he could use the toilet by himself.

As an adult, Schlitzie only stood about four feet tall, so more likely, he was closer to eight years old when he started in the sideshow, not 18. He was also never able to speak more than a handful of words and form a few simple phrases. However, he could understand what others said to him, and he often mimicked them. He could also perform some basic tasks but always needed a caretaker.

Even though Schlitzie almost always had a smile on his face, he was often billed as "an untamable savage specimen of humanity from an age-old race" or an Aztec wild woman and sole survivor of an ancient race "who refuses to become pacified with the manners and customs of this section of the world." As late as 1921, Schlitzie was exhibited in a cage so "that she might not become ferocious at an inopportune moment." Promotional ads claimed that "years of patient training have failed to tame her occasional inclination to revert to savagery and run wild in a crowd."

All of this was far from the truth. Schlitzie was always described as being mild-mannered, affectionate, happy, and very sociable. *Freaks* director Tod Browning noted, "You forget the strange appearance of Schlitzie, the pinhead, because of his personality." Schlitzie especially loved to entertain children and to dance.

In addition to *Freaks*, Schlitzie appeared in several other films, like *The Sideshow, Island of Lost Souls, Meet Boston Blackie*, and others.

In 1965, Schlitzie's manager and legal guardian, George Surtees – who'd cared for Schlitzie since 1935 -- passed away, and with no family members willing to take on responsibility for his care, Schlitzie was placed in an institution. He might have remained there for the rest of his life if a former carnival worker hadn't recognized him.

Thanks to that, he spent his last years in Los Angeles, performing in a few sideshows and good-naturedly greeting people on the streets of Hollywood while his caretaker sold his trade cards. He also spent hours every day in the park, feeding the pigeons and talking to people who passed by. He soon became a local celebrity of sorts.

Schlitzie died on September 24, 1971, at Fountain View Convalescent Hospital in Los Angeles from pneumonia complicated by cancer. He was 70 years old and, by then, a ward of the state of California. No funeral was held, and his body was not embalmed. He was placed in an unmarked grave at Queen of Heaven Cemetery in Rowland Heights. In 2009, though, a kind-hearted fan purchased a tombstone for him after taking up a collection in his honor.

THE SNOW TWINS "PIP AND FLIP"

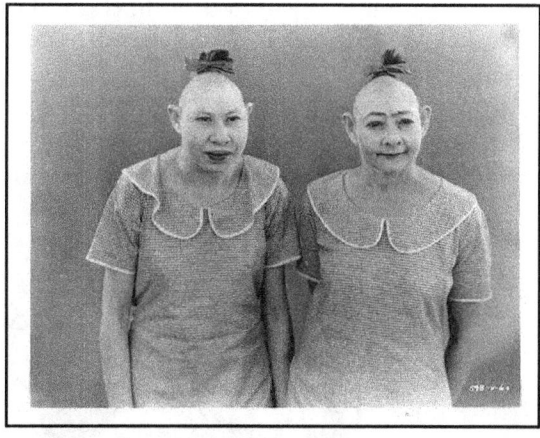

SO LITTLE IS KNOWN ABOUT THE SIDESHOW PERFORMERS DUBBED the "Snow Twins" that we don't even know where the name "Snow Twins" came from. A 1940 news article claimed they were the children of Dr. and Mrs. Winston Trimble of Athens, Georgia, and they were born in 1920, but there's no way to know if the story was accurate.

Worse, we don't even know if the Snow Twins were brother and sister or two sisters since they were advertised and dressed as both. Sometimes, it was said they were twins, and sometimes, they were not.

We do know they both suffered from microcephaly and were typically developed from the neck down, but each had a small cone-shaped skull with a small tuft of hair on top. They were also mentally challenged and small in stature, both conditions the result of their disorder.

The biographical details of the Snow Twins are all over the place. The information in their show brochure was very different from other printed sources, including newspaper stories of the day, so their true life story remains a mystery. Their manager, Cliff Snow, was rumored to be their brother, but again, it's unclear if this was true.

An interview article from 1932, when they appeared in *Freaks*, reported that "Elvira and Hattie Lee Snow were born in Hartwell, Georgia, 22 years ago." This would have made them sisters, born in 1912.

To confuse things even more, they used many different stage names during their sideshow careers – Zippo and Flippo; Zip and Pip; Pip and Flip; Zipo and Pipo; The Pin Head Twins; and possibly more. The name Elvira remains consistent, but the other Snow Twin was referred to as Clayton, Jennie, Hattie, Johnny, and Jenny.

See what I mean? No way we'll ever know the truth.

However, both twins were said to be friendly, happy, and very social. They loved entertaining the public, especially children. They were still performing in 1940, but not much is known about their life after that.

Hopefully, they ended up in a good place, perhaps with a family member who cared for them. And hopefully, they lived a long and happy life.

But, as you won't be surprised to hear, there's no way to know.

15. THE REST OF THE MIDWAY

THE FREAK SHOWS MAY HAVE BEEN THE MAIN ATTRACTION FOR many carnival sideshows, but they were not all that would shock and amaze you on the Midway. The 'Ten in One" was only part of the show. There were still a lot of other things to see, not to mention plenty of grab joints that offered every kind of grease-laden food imaginable that you could stuff into your face.

Before we go farther, though, you should probably know what you'll be getting yourself into. The grimy, dirty, sawdust-laden path ahead will eventually take you to the Ferris wheel, the roller coaster, the Scrambler, the Tilt-A-Whirl, and all the other rides that might make all that greasy food in your stomach think about coming back up again.

And, of course, there are the "dark rides" that lie ahead. The roller coaster allows the world to see its stomach-dropping slopes and twisting loops, but the dark rides keep their thrills hidden. As you're standing in like for the ride through the haunted house filled with ghosts and ghouls, a high-seas adventure with pirates, or take a trip through the Tunnel of Love, all you can see are the riders in front of you, who get into little cars before disappearing through swinging doors into the dark. You can hear the screams and shrieks coming from inside, and then an empty car arrives, stopping in front of you with a mechanical ka-chunk – you're next.

You'll also pass by the games of chance, trying to ignore the shouts of the carnies as they encourage you to lay down your hard-earned money and win a prize for your girl. You already know the games are rigged, making it almost impossible to win one of the

cheaply made stuffed animals that dangle overhead -- guaranteed to fall apart almost as soon as you leave the fairgrounds.

Or maybe you can toss a pin-pong ball into a fishbowl and take home a goldfish that likely won't survive the week.

But let's face it – they're hard to resist. There's the 3 In A Row, tossing softballs into a slotted box to get three in a row; the Penny Pitch, where you try and land your coins on a colored circle; the Punk Pitch, throwing bean bags at a face to knock it over; Coke Bottle Ring Toss; the stacked Milk Bottles; the Balloon Darts; the Wheel of Fortune; and so many others.

But if you can get past all the games with a little money left in your pocket, you'll find even more attractions ahead in the exhibit tents and trailers. There's no way to know in advance what might lie ahead, but sex and horror were always a staple of the midway shows – pickled punks, over-embalmed gangsters, opium dens, torture chambers, headless women, chickens that played tic-tac-toe – the options seemed endless. The "back-end showman," as the owners of these exhibits called themselves, was liable to have anything and everything waiting for the customer who was brave enough to pull aside the canvas tent flap and step into the shadows beyond.

So, once again, step right up, keep an open mind, and get ready to experience another part of American history that's been lost to time.

PART ONE:
BLOOD, SEX, DRUGS & TORTURE

ONE OF THE GREAT ATTRACTIONS FOR EARLY SHOWMAN WAS WAR. Prior to the 1860s, panorama shows (see the early section on P.T. Barnum) were starting to wane in popularity but it was the Civil War that saved the business. Even before the war was over, panorama showmen were displaying their battles on miles of canvas. Many of the audience knew men who fought on the front lines and were painfully interested in the colorful battlefield scenes that scrolled in front of them. After the war ended, photos and relics appeared in dime museums and the tents of touring showmen.

Most of the war shows that traveled with organized carnival companies after the 1893 World's Fair were either miniature mechanical shows, stereopticon views, or even short movies. The traveling exhibits consisted of views of Gettysburg and other battlefields, camps, prisons, wounded soldiers, and burials of the dead, mostly taken from 40-year-old War Department negatives. Fascination with the Civil War stuck around and remained popular at carnivals for years to come.

By the time of America's next big war, the carnival business had been firmly established. War shows on the midways depicted the horrors of the trenches, poison gases, rats, and "lifelike" actual-size reproductions of the German and Allied forces at war. In 1917, a war show with the Rutherford Carnival Company claimed to be the only fairgrounds attraction depicting terrible scenes of battles with zeppelins bombing cities and airplanes dumping poison gas.

Another show, exhibited by Lieutenant Colonel C.H. Ackerman, offered one of the first trench warfare exhibits on midways, allowing customers to experience trench mines, hand grenades, gas masks, dugouts, tunnels, and wounded soldiers.

Gee, that sounds like fun.

Inspired by Ackman's show, Sergeant G. Norman Shields started his own similar show, staffing it with soldiers who had returned from the battlefields of France. They brought along souvenirs from the battlefields – some of which turned out to be still lethal. Several incidents of live ammunition and gas canisters exploding on fairgrounds across the country prompted the government to issue rules on how artifacts and weapons could be secured and displayed. Helmets, uniforms, and guns could be shown, but no live shells or full gas canisters were allowed.

War shows lasted long enough for another conflict to come along and give fairgrounds showmen a new war to reenact. World War II had a whole new collection of horrors and villains. Midway war shows started to feature Hitler, Mussolini, and Tojo. Even the carnival game owners got in on the act, replacing clown targets with "Shrunken Jap soldiers" and Nazis for games like "Hit the Jap" and "Knock off Hitler's Head," which allowed patriots on the Homefront to vent their frustrations and win figurines of flag-carrying enlisted men and women. Carnival companies ran war bond drives and veteran showmen made good money pitching war booklets. After the war ended, showmen bought surplus searchlights, generators, and trucks, further enhancing the idea that the carnival shows were like an entire military force on the move.

Charles Buell, a showman who'd got his start making peep shows for the midway in 1922, turned out three or four new shows every season to keep pace with the wars. During World War II, he offered shows with titles like "The Great Atomic Bomb," "Jap and Nazi Atrocities," "Jap Atrocities in the March of Bataan," and the "Great Lightning War." An advertisement that ran for one show gave this description: "Nothing like it ever show since the beginning of time. Uncensored scenes direct from the front that wring people's hearts. Tanks, bombers, liquid fire, new weapons, all crashing down on humanity with men, women, and little children the fallen victims."

War shows hung around on the midways into the 1950s and then slowly faded away as America entered the "make love, not war" era of the 1960s. But the peace didn't last long. When the Vietnam War began, midway showmen jumped on that bandwagon, too, offering shows like the "Viet Cong Booby Trap" and a slew of others.

Americans just couldn't seem to slake their thirst for blood.

BUT THE TENT SHOWS WEREN'T THE ONLY WAY THAT WAR was embraced on the carnival midway. At the end of World War II, scores of Mercedes cars came over from Europe, several of which were billed as Hitler's personal cars, and all of them were exhibited on midways.

One Hitler car, owned by Christopher Janus of Winnetka, Illinois, was first exhibited in 1948. It drew big crowds while on display at the New York Museum of Science and Industry, so it was snapped up by

ONE OF THE MANY "HITLER'S CARS" THAT WERE EXHIBITED AT FAIRGROUNDS AFTER WORLD WAR II.

the Amusement Corporation of America, which started displaying it at fairs that summer, beginning in Springfield, Illinois, and publicity created crowds of more than 5,000 people each day. In April 1949, the car opened its exhibition tour in Little Rock, Arkansas, on the Hennies Brothers Shows midway. However, then it just sort of disappeared after that, not turning up again until 1972, when it went up for auction in Scottsdale, Arizona.

But Janus' Hitler Car wasn't the only one that was making the rounds in America at the time. Another one was also touring in 1949, and the owners boasted "Adolph Hitler's Genuine Personal Armored Limousine – Not Just the One He Rode In." Mounted in a semi-trailer, it attracted 220,000 admissions at one exhibition. While the car was on tour in Texas in 1957, the car was advertised for sale for $3,500, but I have no idea if anyone purchased it.

If they did, it's unlikely they went home with the real thing since there was yet another Hitler car also on tour with the World of Mirth shows at the same time.

And there was yet another one. Owned by Jack W. Burke of Baldwin, New York, his Hitler car went on tour in 1954, managed by Carl Hauptmann, who had been a field manager for units of the Ripley's Believe It of Not shows. Burke continued the show for several seasons, keeping it on the road as late as 1966. It was later purchased by Bill Hall, a carnival showman and collector, who traveled the country, showing it on carnival midways for years. Eventually, though, he discovered the car was a fraud and sold it for $30,000.

How many of Hitler's cars toured the country in the decades after World War II is unknown, but according to the Canadian War Museum, there were only two Mercedes vehicles in North America that Hitler actually used. One of them was used in various war bond drives to pay off war debt and then was sold to a Canadian man in 1956. The museum acquired it from him 14 years later.

In 1983, the only other authentic Hitler car was bought by Ralph Engelstad and became part of his "famed Imperial Palace Auto Collection" at the Imperial Palace Casino in Las Vegas. Five years later, he was fined $1.5 million for throwing a Nazi-themed party at the casino, which was found to have a secret room filled with Nazi artifacts. The Hitler car went up for auction in 2018 but received no bids. It's not clear what happened to it after that.

DURING CHRISTMAS WEEK OF 1888, A DIME MUSEUM in Boston offered a pair of opium eaters for exhibition. Even with an innocent wood-shopping contest on the same bill, newspapers reported it to be the "vilest act seem in Boston in a long time" and questioned if such an act was of any value.

The public responded with one sold-out show after another.

Drugs were nothing new to showmen, even in the nineteenth century. Newspapers offered frequent cures for various addictions. Drugs, "white slavery," and sinister foreigners, however, provided a combination that few showmen would pass up.

In 1899, a midway show was created that featured a Chinatown Opium Den, and after World War I, the New York Film Corps released a silent news film called Chinatown, which depicted Chinese opium dens and dope fiends at work. The lobby display that went with the film – which claimed to be approved by New York censors – was a realistic opium den with a mechanical moving figure of a girl and a Chinese man behind bars.

In 1917, the C. W. Parker Co. claimed to be the first to build a portable Underground Chinatown walkthrough show for midway showmen. Within a couple of years, they were barely able to keep up with orders, and at one point, they had five complete kits being churned out by their factories. One contained 22 wax figures, seven complete scenes, and a nine-section front that was sold for $1,500. A larger version featured an additional room and eight more characters, and it sold for $2,250. The figures were all costumed and had human glass eyes, planted hair, eyebrows, and eyelashes. All heads, hands, and visible feet were sculpted from reinforced wax.

In the 1920s, the Modern Show Building Company started offering Chinatown walkthrough shows that were promoted as a true reproduction of San Francisco's Chinatown, complete with shrines, opium dens, gambling parlors, secret tunnels, and slave girls.

For showmen who didn't want to drag around wax figures and huge sets, peep show man Charles Buell offered an enlarged photo display in 1926 that featured opium dens, white slave markets, opium dens, gambling joints, executions, poppy fields, and tong wars.

One thrill after another, right?

TORTURE DISPLAYS HAVE NOT ONLY BEEN THE BREAD AND butter of every wax museum that's ever opened, but they also drew big crowds on the midway.

One of the first major wax museum shows to tour the United States was Dr. Heidman's Great Museum of Anatomy, Ethnology, and Pathology in 1890. The most popular part of the show was the collection of wax and mechanical figures depicting scenes of torture during the Spanish Inquisition.

After that, torture chambers became part of just about every dime museum and wax storefront show that opened, but they didn't

WALK-THROUGH TORTURE SHOWS, USING REPLICA TORTURE IMPLEMENTSS AND WAX FIGURES, REMAINED A STAPLE ON MIDWAYS FOR DECADES.

make it onto the midways until the late 1930s. Showmen may have felt that Americans had been tortured enough by not being able to buy a drink during Prohibition, followed by the Great Depression.

A display and figure company called Messmore and Damon started a show in 1935 that would become the prototype for future midway torture shows.

George Messmore was born in Detroit and worked in his father's carpentry shop until he was 16 when he hopped a freight train to New York. When he arrived, he worked various jobs, including pasting posters on walls, building display floats, and selling beer at Coney Island.

He ended up getting into the display window business by putting little people out of work. At the time, midgets dressed in penguin suits were holding advertising signs in the hottest ad spaces. But they were hard to find and expensive, so Messmore invented a mechanical penguin that ran by clockwork. He then added a mechanical monkey and a seal. Department stores wanted them faster than he could build them, so in 1919, he partnered with artist Joe Damon. He built clay replicas for whatever figure they were making, and they worked together for the next two decades.

They got into show business when Messmore created the World a Million Years Ago walkthrough show, which scored big financially at the 1933 Century of Progress Fair in Chicago. He also built the Flash Gordon in the World of Tomorrow show for the 1939 World's Fair in New York. Messmore also invented a two-dimensional girlie show that consisted of life-size nudes that were blown up and given the illusion of movement by constantly changing lights – hot stuff for the 1930s.

Messmore and Damon's first foray into torture shows started in 1935 with a Coney Island horror show called the Torture Chamber. Six separate horror rooms with animated figures that talked and moved recreated gruesome things like the Iron Maiden, the Iron Boot, and

the Chinese Rat Torture. Another section offered a series of paintings highlighted by Marie Antoinette's death by guillotine.

Messmore took the show on the road, and to increase its drawing power, he added a live girl attraction he called the Crusader's Bride, in which a young woman wore nothing but a chastity belt. Fair officials told him that the girl's breasts had to be covered, or he'd be closed down. Messmore made a plaster cast of the girl's breasts, and when officials returned, they were shocked to see her breasts were still exposed. But Messmore pointed out that the young lady was actually wearing a thin, flesh-colored covering – she just looked nude under a spotlight. Since he wasn't technically breaking any rules, the show was allowed to go on.

The Lorrow brothers, a pair of sideshow and illusion showmen, were among the first to copy Messmore's formula. They put together a torture show that toured with the Hennies Brothers Shows in 1938. Others followed, like Ray and Mary Chambers, who had a similar show with World of Mirth in the 1950s and 1960s, and Bob Olson, who offered his own version around the same time. Inside the tent, there were nine complete torture displays with life-sized mechanical figures.

Eddie Keck, a former paymaster for the Ringling Brothers and Barnum & Bailey Circus, offered various back-end shows in the 1960s. One of them, his Graveyard Ridge torture show, was billed as the

"Greatest Scariest Show on Earth." It had the usual torture scenes and Hollywood monster figures inside, including a corpse that popped out of a coffin at customers.

BUT WAX FIGURES WEREN'T JUST USED FOR TORTURE shows on the midway. They offered an array of different kinds of shows that were designed to draw in paying customers.

In the late nineteenth century, most dime museums and storefront showmen had wax collections that ranged from anatomical specimens – usually naked wax female bodies – to figures of current subjects like President Lincoln, John Wilkes Booth, Napoleon, Queen Victoria, and others. Eventually, however, the "educational" shows would be discarded in favor of subjects that were more lurid and sensational.

By 1892, W.H.J. Shaw was offering showmen wax figures that included William Kemmler, the first man to be executed in the electric chair. He also advertised a mechanical sleeping-beauty wax figure without clothes, which proved to be especially popular with men on the fairgrounds.

In 1927, Shaw's son created the Missing Link, crafted half with wax and half with hair. Like his father, he also became a dependable supplier of two-headed wax babies (more about that later), and by the 1930s, his biggest sellers were John Dillinger, Baby Face Nelson, and Pretty Boy Floyd.

Starting in the 1920s and continuing for the next three decades, B.W. Christophel made wax figures and wax babies for showmen. A 1934 ad for his John Dillinger figure read: "Dillinger in wax. Lying in state. Same as the body left Chicago. Absolutely true to life and properly dressed." In the 1940s, he was offering a life-size "Caesarian operation" in a glass case, tiny shrunken heads, Indian mummies, and two-headed babies in jars.

In the late 1930s, Animated Displays Inc. in Hollywood and Leopold Schmidt in Jersey City, New Jersey, were Shaw's and Christophel's main competitors. Although there were only a handful of companies making wax figures for showmen and museums, there was a never-ending supply of subjects – presidents – living and dead, old-time outlaws, and contemporary killers and their victims.

Eventually, straight waxwork shows were far outnumbered by the more popular sex and crime shows, which had become the only way to cash in on wax shows on the midway. People had gotten "waxed out" since many cities had permanent wax museums, and mechanical figures were easily found in department store window displays at Christmas.

One short-lived trend for a handful of showmen was offering wax figures of some of the more famous freaks of the past. Many of them came from Schmidt and Sons, who started offering "Ubangi Disc-Lipped Savages" for wax shows in the early 1930s. Real-life Ubangi tribal members had been featured in several circuses at the time, as were "giraffe-necked women," who also began to be offered in wax. But it was Dave Rosen who began selling wax freaks in 1959. He described them as "life-sized reproductions in wax of the world's strangest and most sensational freaks," including a double-bodied, four-legged girl, Siamese twins joined at the head, and a Mexican two-headed man. The collection came with banners for each figure.

The showmen who bought these figures quickly found out they were nothing but "heat scores," which meant they generated nothing but complaints. The banners portrayed the famous freaks as if they were alive and inside the tent, which was the only way to sell the show. However, the dozen or so figures were a great disappointment to customers who'd expected to come inside and shake hands with General Tom Thumb.

Yes, people were actually that stupid. And then they showcased that stupidity by complaining about being scammed.

In the 1960s and 1970s, wax shows on the midway were grind shows on trailers and trucks, displaying celebrities, world figures, and music and movie stars. People would always pay 50 cents to see Elvis Presley or John F. Kennedy. Dead subjects were safe exhibits, but living celebrities could be a problem. One show, which had a Michael Jackson figure on display, quickly turned Jackson into Diana Ross when tabloids began labeling him as a pedophile.

In the late 1960s, showman Jimmy Dixon partnered with Royal American Shows to operate a wax show that was built into a semi-trailer. Their most popular display featured figures of all four of the Beatles.

By the 1990s, not only were the midways shows mostly gone, but so were the wax shows. One of the last closed in 1994 but still included 11 figures, including one of John Lennon. Newspaper headlines about his death had been blown up and framed around the figure to add a bit of pathos. The figures were sold at auction, and freak models of giraffe-neck women, Ubangi, pin heads, and the Chinese Man with the Horn Growing From the Back of Head sold quickly to collectors.

The wax shows had finally had their last hurrah.

PART TWO:
"WALL OF DEATH"
MOTORDROMES ON THE MIDWAY

NOTHING COULD STOP A CROWD WALKING ALONG THE MIDWAY like the sounds of motorcycles thundering around the wooden walls of the motordrome.

They were unique show venues. The customer bought a ticket, crossed the bally – usually a wagon or semi-trailer – and climbed steep steps to the top of the drome wall. A walkway circled the wooden bowl with a raised step behind it so two rows of onlookers could easily see inside. Down 18 feet below, on the middle of the wood floor, was a center pole that held up the round canvas roof. The crackle of the P.A. speakers wired to the pole could be heard over the voices of the excited onlookers.

In the wall closest to the bally platform was a heavy wooden door through which the riders entered the drome floor. Three or four

INDIAN MOTORCYCLES WERE THE GO-TO BIKES USED BY MOTORDROME PERFORMERS IN THE EARLY 1900S

motorcycles entered through the door, which closed behind them, becoming again part of the 50-foot circular wall.

The first attack on the senses of the crowd occurred when the first ride started on his motorcycle. Another of the riders picked up a microphone and warned the onlookers to stay behind the safety cable that jutted out about a foot or so around the top of the wall.

That would be the only protection that existed between the marks and the roaring bikes.

With those words of warning still hanging in the air, one of the riders gunned his engine and roared up onto the main wall, causing the entire place to shake. The heads of the crowd went from side to side as they tried to follow the rider's speeding progress as he circled the drome. They jumped backward as the bike came within inches of them – their eyes, ears, and body assaulted all at the same time.

The roots of the motordrome went back to the early 1900s when bike racing as a sport fueled the motorcycle craze on fairgrounds in large round tents. It was a bicycle dealer named George Hendee who was credited with developing the first practical motorcycle in America in 1901. By World War I, the round motordromes were beginning to appear on midways.

Before motorcycles, performers used bicycles to do a similar act on a wall of wooden slats. The act became popular in circuses, carnivals, and on vaudeville stages. It went from being one rider to two, with crisscrosses and other tricks worked into the routine. To make the act more exciting, the whole apparatus was lifted between vertical supports, and then the floor was removed. In circuses, the apparatus was often raised about a steel cage filled with lions.

One of the first to ride a bike on a fully perpendicular cycle whirl in America was a rider who called himself "Cyclo." He performed with the Barnum and Bailey Circus the first year the show returned from Europe.

A similar act followed in 1904, performed by Cane and Louisa McNutt, and then by Harry Cooper, who spent 24 weeks with the Ferrari Brothers Shows. His Bottomless Cycle Whirl was raised mechanically 50 feet into the air while four riders raced around inside it.

As the outdoor carnival business was coming into its own just before World War I, new portable rides were being invented and all kinds of new show ideas were being tried out on the public. One of the hottest was the motordrome. Swartz and Turpin, owners of the Joy Amusement Company, were the first to build a portable drome in 1912. Several other companies in Illinois and Michigan were soon producing their own dromes, and each claimed that theirs were the only portable ones on the market. By 1915, round canvas tents were commonly used to protect the riders and the walls from the elements.

The wooden tracks, echoing with the roar of the bike engines and the thud of the tires, became instant crowd-pleasers. The official bike was the eight-valve Indian motorcycle, from which the racers removed the mud guards and anything else that wasn't needed. Soon, the motordromes became more of a draw than even the most popular attractions, like the merry-go-round and the Ferris wheel.

J. Frank Hatch, who engineered portable water shows for carnival midways, worked out the physical aspects of the traveling motordromes. He started building them in a factory in Pittsburgh in 1914 and, within three months, had seven of them ready to go to various shows. His 50-foot-diameter drome – "the kind that gets the money," he said – sold for $650. He was also willing to build motordromes twice the size of the original for $2,000.

Hatch kept patent attorneys busy registering all his designs for the strengthening of the upright portable walls of his new "Autodrome" or "Devil's Tub," which was touted as the next midway sensation.

But they didn't come without problems. The early dromes took days to set up and tear down, limiting their operation to only a couple of days in each town. Some companies banned the dromes altogether because, although they made money, the noise could kill business for any shows or concessions that were near them.

Even so, motordromes became the hottest shows on the midways in the years leading into World War I. The first dromes had a small starting track for the bikes and then all-sloped walls. The trickier ones were developed with walls that went straight up and down with just a small, slanted jump board to help the rider get on.

As the dromes gained popularity, the danger increased because it drew bigger crowds. A rider named Brison Wickwire, with the Miller and Lachman Shows, began standing erect on the seat of his motorcycle while going full speed around the drome. More difficult tricks were added to the routines to lengthen the shows and, of course, to excite the public – which often resulted in accidents, injuries, and even deaths.

Eddie Hasha -- nicknamed the "Texas Cyclone" since he hailed from Waco – was racing in Newark, New Jersey, on September 8, 1912, against five other riders. Among them was Ray Seymour, who held the world record. As they roared around the walled track, Hasha held a slight lead until the third lap, when his motorcycle began to misfire.

EDDIE HASHA – THE "TEXAS CYCLONE"

447 | THE DEVIL'S CARNIVAL

Eddie reached down to make an adjustment and was overtaken by Seymour. A moment later, Eddie accelerated, catching up to Seymour, and then veered out of control. The bike rode up the wall and onto the rail, striking and killing a boy who stuck his head over the rail to watch the race. The bike then struck a post, sending Eddie flying. He was killed instantly, as were three other boys and a young man. The now riderless bike dropped back down onto the racing track and into the path of rider Johnny Albright. He was struck in the shoulder and slammed backward onto the wood track between the two machines. He died four hours later without regaining consciousness.

When spectators saw the spinning motorcycle coming their way, they panicked. As they fought and panicked, trying to get out of the way, many ended up with broken bones and injuries. It took more than an hour to clear the viewing area, and medics came from all over the city to care for the injured and those who had fainted.

Then, less than a year later, tragedy struck again in Ludlow, Kentucky. On July 30, 1913, rider Oden Johnson of Salt Lake City was running high up on the track when he hit a pole. The crash snapped off the pole, and the loose wires ignited Johnson's fuel tank. Johnson's lifeless body landed in the spectator area, along with what was left of his motorcycle, killing a spectator. Burning gasoline sprayed over a large crowd, which again set off a stampede of spectators trying to escape the burning fuel.

In the ensuing chaos, it took police almost an hour to get control of the scene and for rescue workers to reach all the victims. A total of eight people died in the next few days from injuries and burns incurred in the accident.

The deaths in New Jersey and Kentucky made front-page news in newspapers all over the country, reporting the injuries and fatalities in great detail. Soon, the press started calling the venues "murderdromes," and this led to many organizations banning them and some manufacturers ending production because of the negative publicity.

But that didn't last. The portable motordromes were just too popular – and made too much money for showmen – for them to be banished from carnival midways. Accidents continued, involving both riders and spectators. Even when accidents didn't occur, the dromes were still dangerous due to flying wood splinters and debris, as well as the primitive tire technology and head protection of the era.

Otto Kecker, known as the Flying Dutchman, was killed inside a drome in 1915, and later that same year, Pat and Johnny Dill, riders with the Heinz and Bechmann Shows, were badly hurt trying out a new

MIDWAY MOTORDROME IN THE LATE 1930S, WHEN THEY WERE STILL AT THE HEIGHT OF THEIR DEATH-DEFYING POPULARITY.

trick – a double criss-cross but with two riders going in opposite directions. The stunt ended in a head-on collision.

There would be more to come, but the dromes continued to do big business. In 1917, Margaret Gast became the first female rider and became famous for reaching speeds of up to 70 miles per hour. She'd been known as the "Mile-A-Minute Girl" throughout her career.

After risking death and crippling injuries while doing every kind of stunt imaginable inside wooden barrels that had been dubbed the "Wall of Death," showmen started looking for ways to make the shows even more dangerous. They came up with one beginning in 1923 when the Morris and Castle and the Benardi Greater shows came up with a new stunt. As three riders attained their maximum speed in the dromes, two male lions were placed inside with the motorcyclists. The lions tried to attack the riders, who tried to keep a safe distance from them.

The motordromes continued to be a midway staple for decades, reaching its highest point in the 1930s, when there were more than 100 "Walls of Death" in traveling shows across the country. Interest in them continued to rise and fall after World War II, depending on the popularity of motorcycle riding. The rise of biker gangs – as well as films and books about them – kept the dromes popular in the 1960s, and while interest remains high today, there are few of them left. Some of the dromes with the small truck carnivals were sold in the 1990s for the cost of lumber, while others just rotted away in the back lots of show winter quarters.

PART THREE:
THE ILLUSION SHOWS
GHOSTS, SPIDER LADIES
& HEADLESS GIRLS

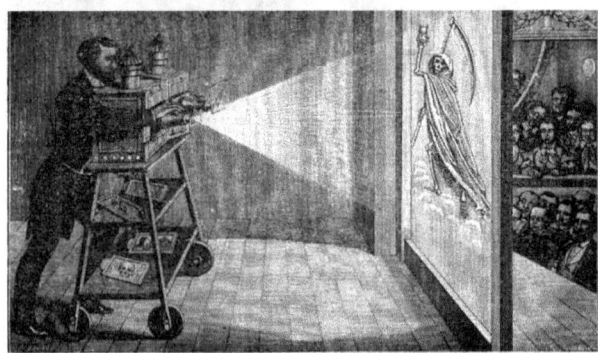

PHANTASMAGORIA IN 1901 USED THE SAME BASIC METHODS THAT WOULD BE PERFECTED IN YEARS TO COME AND BECOME A STANDARD ON MIDWAYS.

MAGIC AND ILLUSION WAS THE BASIS FOR MANY SHOWS that were presented by early traveling showmen, and it would eventually provide a lot of entertainment on carnival midways. Even today, the headless girl, the snake girl, and the girl that transforms into a gorilla remain as the last of the midway grind shows – still using some of the same tricks that were used back in the nineteenth century.

A Paris show called "Phantasmagoria" was first presented in London in 1901, using a magic lantern to create supernatural effects and horrify audiences. Etienne Gaspard Robert, a Belgian physics professor, invented the magic lantern, which became popular as home entertainment and was a popular form of early show business. Phantasmagoria terrified its audiences with images of snakes and floating ghosts, and its illusions depended on a magic lantern with adjustable lenses mounted on tracks behind a semi-transparent screen. The audience members seated in front of the screen were frightened as the ghosts rushed toward them and then disappeared.

The "ghosts" were created by placing an image of a specter on a black slide and then using light to cast the image on the screen. This is, by the way, almost exactly how Disney creates the ghosts inside the "Haunted Mansion" attraction inside their parks – more than 200 years after it was invented.

The frights of Phantasmagoria were enhanced by lights that mimicked thunder and lightning, as well as illusions created with skeletons. The skeletons were created with double slides, and they opened and closed their mouths. Their human faces turned into skulls, and clothed images became nothing but bones. The show closed with these figures advancing toward the audience and then sinking into the floor in front of them. This led many spectators to flee the theater in terror.

More advances to this kind of show followed. Henry Langdon Childe improved the dissolving views of the skeletons by inventing a metal shutter that closed on one side but quickly opened on another, so the audience saw just a brief moment of darkness during the switch. Then, Sir Goldsworthy Gurney invented "limelight," a gas made by applying a mixture of oxygen and hydrogen to a small ball of lime. The result was a light that was equivalent to a dozen lamps, letting showmen create sharper and brighter images from their slides. Shows with dissolving images quickly became popular, including one in 1833 called "Optikali Illusio," which had appearing and disappearing ghosts. It left its mark on history by coining the phrase, "Now you see it – now you don't."

In 1863, John Henry Pepper's design began to amaze people when he and Henry Dirks, a civil engineer, registered for a patent for an apparatus for exhibiting dramatic performances that involved the appearance and disappearance of a "ghost."

Pepper was a professor of chemistry and the honorary director of the British Royal Polytechnic Institute, and his invention was built to be able to put both an actor and a ghost on stage together. The set-up in the theater required – in addition to the main stage – a second lower stage that was hidden from the audience. The lower stage was strongly lit by artificial light and could be made dark instantly, while the main stage and the theater remained in normal light. A large glass screen was placed on the main stage and in front of the hidden one. This allowed the audience to see the actor behind it, not realizing that

THESE EARLY SHOWS PROJECTED THEIR IMAGES USING A DEVICE CALLED A "MAGIC LANTERN"

AN ILLUSTRATION SHOWING HOW PEPPER'S GHOST ILLUSION WORKED

person was behind glass. When the ghost character on the hidden stage was illuminated, the ghost's image was projected onto the main stage. When the hidden stage went dark, the ghost immediately vanished.

Pepper's ghost illusion was first shown at a small theater at the Royal Polytechnic. The scene took place in the room of a student who was hard at work with his studies. He looks up from his books and sees a ghost. Frightened, he jumps up, grabs a sword, and swings it at the ghost, which disappears and then keeps coming back and vanishing.

Pepper's assistant played the ghost, wearing a covering of black velvet while holding a skeleton with its lower half draped in white material. The assistant lifted his body up and down so the skeleton appeared to be coming up through the floor.

Although the show only lasted a few minutes, it attracted huge crowds with money in hand. The Polytechnic moved the show to a larger theater and continued to make money, even after allowing the method used to create the ghost to be leased out to other London theaters and music halls. By 1870, British inventors had managed to patent 16 addition mirror tricks that were inspired by Pepper's work.

And, of course, it wasn't long before Pepper's illusion arrived in the United States. With the rapid growth of carnival companies in the 1890s, "illusion shows" moved from theaters to fairground midways. One of the early American illusionist showmen was Professor E.E. Thornton, with his Palace of Illusions. Inside his tent, he presented Thauma, the Living Mermaid, and the Beautiful Rosebud Illusion. Professor G.W. Van had his own living mermaid, Galtea, and a showman named Slantino had his Temple of Illusions.

Ghost shows became a staple for theaters and vaudeville but soon showed up on the midway, too. The father of the fairground ghost show was Captain W.D. Ament, who introduced fairgoers to his shows in 1902, along with the Flying Maid of the Sea, the Statue Turning to Life, and Poses Plastiques, which was a way to offer nude girls in a "tasteful" way. The next season, Ament's was the top-grossing attraction for the Robinson Carnival Company. Other showmen hurried to copy what he was doing, although Ament warned them, "Not one in 50 can run a ghost show, even after being shown how."

But the illusion was not that tough to pull off – the hard part was getting that large sheet of glass safely from town to town. Illusions like the Statue Turning to Life were over in minutes, but the ghost shows were more elaborate, using scripted skits about hauntings and featuring other weird images. Ament's show with the Robinson carnival required ten performers, which included a piano player and a one-man band who played guitar and harmonica for a singer.

Other illusions became popular on the midway, but the ghost show hung on for years.

Henry Roltair became known as a genius at creating elaborate illusion shows at fairs and amusement parks. Born in London in 1853, he came to America as a teenager and began creating illusions for theaters that were unrivaled for decades. By 1894, he was designing shows for fairgrounds, like his new Pharoah's Daughter illusion, a 30-minute spectacle based on the biblical story of baby Moses. A male actor offered a dignified narration while two women performed, aided by lighting effects and mirrors. The show became a big hit at Coney Island from 1904 to 1906 and then was seen on many carnival midways for several seasons after that.

Another Roltair illusion became a permanent fixture on carnival shows as both a single-o show – a strong attraction that could stand on its own – and as part of sideshows was the Human Spider, also known as Spidora.

Roltair's designs inspired many other creators and showmen, like Fred Thompson and Skip Dundy, the founders of Dreamland at Coney Island, who built their own show called Trip to the Moon. This show, along with Roltair's Upside Down House, was the biggest attraction at the Pan-Am Exposition in Buffalo, New York, in 1901. Roltair's house was

ROLTAIR'S "CREATION" ILLUSION SHOW AT THE ST. LOUIS WORLD'S FAIR IN 1904

80 feet high, and it was literally an upside-down house standing on its roof. Customers entered through a dormer window in the attic. Once inside, they found themselves walking on the ceiling with everything reversed, including "live" views of the fairground that could be seen through the windows.

Through the early 1900s, Roltair's major show, "Creation," was worked by a large cast of performers, both human and animal. The show presented nearly every illusion known at the time, and it became the sensation of the 1904 St. Louis World's Fair. It took guests through rooms where special effects mimicked the biblical creation of the world. After the fair, it was moved to Dreamland, where it continued to operate for years until being destroyed by fire.

Roltair died in El Reno, California, while on tour in 1910. He was only 57 years old, which makes you wonder what other illusions he might have created if his career had continued.

ALSO AMONG THE MIDWAY ILLUSIONS WERE SUSPENSION shows, acts in which performers appeared to fly above the heads of audience members. They began in the early 1900s as Lunette the Flying Lady with pretty girls wearing invisible belt harnesses that were made with roller bearings so they'd run on silent lines.

One well-known suspension show operator was Fred "Happy" Holmes, who presented the Girl from Up There with the Gaskill-Munday shows in 1903. His crew was made up of a head electrician with one assistant, a lecturer, a ticket seller, a singer for the bally, and a piano player. The Girl from Up There was played by Etta Louise Blake, but she didn't stay in the air for long. By the 1920s, she was one of the top producers of "girl revues" on midways.

John Henry Shields started his show business career in 1875 as a purchasing agent with the Barnum and Bailey Circus. He later became ringmaster for the Dan Rice Circus for five seasons. He later managed the sideshow for several circuses before putting on the first Lunette show for midways. In 1912, his show with the Barkfoot Carnival featured Lunette flying out over the heads of the audience and shaking hands with members of the crowd.

It wouldn't be long, though,

THE ENTRANCE TO HAPPY HOLMES' "GIRL FROM UP THERE" SHOW, WHICH BEGAN IN 1903.

before illusion shows – encouraged by customer demand -- would become even more thrilling.

THANKS TO SUCCESS THROUGH THE 1910S AND 1920S WITH various kinds of illusions, midway showmen had proven these kinds of attractions were ideal for traveling carnivals. The mystery of each show was the main draw, followed closely by the lovely female subjects, and they were flexible in timing, too. A show could last anywhere from 10 to 20 minutes, depending on the business.

In the early part of the twentieth century, when carnival companies were just developing, illusions were easily crated and shipped by baggage car and moved to and from the fairgrounds. This made them extremely popular for showmen, as well as their customers. For instance, out of the 12 shows the Robinson Carnival Company presented in 1902, one-third of them were illusion shows – Lunette, the Flying Lady; Galtea, the Statue Turning to Life; The Girl from Up There, and She, a show based on the H. Rider Haggard novel of the same name, in which the heroine suffers a horrible death by fire.

Illusion shows changed and updated in the years that followed. By World War I, they were competing with the new Ten-In-Ones and were holding their own. Zelma the Human Butterfly was big, along with Spider-Girl.

F.B. Kellar, who operated out of Columbus, Ohio, became a well-known provider of illusion shows for the midway, advertising "new startling scenic and illusionary effects for the coming season." He

ENTRANCE TO THE SPIDER GIRL SHOW IN THE EARLY 1920S. AS YOU CAN IMAGINE, THE "SPIDER GIRL" INSIDE LOOKED NOTHING LIKE THE AMAZING AND COLORFUL BANNERS OUTSIDE.

offered Phantasmagoria, Birth of Venus, Revolving Statuary, and Down Among the Sea Nymphs. The details of some of these shows have been lost to time, but you can probably imagine what they must have been like based on their names.

The Sea Nymphs show, by the way, was one of the earliest nude lady shows in carnivals. The platform show had higher-than-usual staging and steps so that customers peered down into a deep well – and were glad they did. It was one of the earliest fairground shows to be shut down by local authorities.

In addition to illusions, Kellar also designed elaborate fronts for shows and sold more than 20 different scripts for ghost shows, which remained popular – mostly because so many showmen were using an extension of John Pepper's ghost illusion and calling it Galatea, The Statue Turning to Life.

The illusion began with a stone statue that slowly changed into a living woman, using lights and mirrors. Over the next three minutes or so, she began to age, turn into a corpse, and then become a skeleton before the eyes of the audience. Charles Weston of Lawrence, Massachusetts, offered the illusion for sale, noting that it could be set

"MYRNA THE MERMAID" AND ALL THE ASSORTED "SEA NYMPH" SHOWS WERE ALL DESIGNED WITH THE SAME BASIC PREMISE OF ALL THE ILLUSION SHOWS.

up in an hour, ran on kerosene, and was secured in three boxes for the price of $150.

The show was presented under various names on midways across the country, and there were many variations. The show was basic, with the main thing needed being a black tent. The statue was generally made of papier-mâché and could be a full figure or just a bust. Sometimes, it wasn't a statue at all. One show that ran in the 1920s was called "Anastasia," and it featured a mummy that was brought to life, cashing in on the "Egypt-mania" that followed the discovery of King Tut's tomb.

The living statue version of the show was still going strong into the 1960s. The Ross Manning shows during that time were offering it as part illusion and part cooch show. After the statue came to life, she'd step out and perform a suggestive dance that showman Ken Greenlaw described as "No smut, but a tent full of marks walked out with their hands in their pockets!"

It was also in the 1960s that the premise of the show changed again, and it was revived as the Girl to Gorilla Show, dazzling a new generation of fairgoers. The production was a simple one, despite the promises that ticket-buyers would see a living girl turn into a live terrifying gorilla "right before their eyes."

ENTRANCE TO THE "GIRL TO GORILLA" SHOW

The gorilla woman started out on the bally, inside a steel cage, as a bikini-clad beauty. The talker warned the crowd that "those with a weak heart shouldn't go inside the tent." Onstage, under the dim lights, the girl the audience had seen outside was still in her cage. She was a knock-out, no doubt about it, but then she started to grow dark hair all over her body, her arms and teeth grew long, and she turned into a gorilla – as promised – before the eyes of the guests. The gorilla, with a roar, grabbed the bars of the cage, flung the door open, and charged toward the audience – or what was left of it. Most of them had already run toward the exit as soon as they saw the cage door open.

One thing you had to be sure of about the Girl to Gorilla Show was that you had to have the audience standing and the exit clear. When the transformation took place, and the rubes saw the gorilla in the cage, only a second or two passed before there was a loud ringing noise and a siren; the cage flew open, and the gorilla jumped out toward the audience. They might have been skeptical, but when the gorilla charged them, they ran. That was why the main person in the show wasn't the girl or the gorilla, but the guy who yanked the curtain at the exit at just the right time. No one wanted a crowd running out through a side wall and falling on stakes or being cut by the guy ropes.

No matter how many times the talkers assured the crowd coming in that was an illusion, once the gorilla escaped, people forgot about everything they'd heard. A wild stampeded for the exit always occurred at the end of the eight- or nine-minute show – which was the best advertising possible. A crowd running out of the tent onto the midway was guaranteed to sell the next show.

When I was around the carnival – in the fading days of the sideshows – this was one of my favorites. I knew how it was done, but it was so fun to watch and to see the reaction of the crowd. The illusion really did happen right in front of your eyes – using a sliding glass patio door (no kidding!) for the glass that Pepper had used to create his ghosts. In this case, the glass was situated at a 45-degree angle.

The show began with a live bally show in which the talker brought out an "exotic" girl in a leopard skin bikini. He explained that she was found living wild in the jungle and that when hypnotized, she would revert to her primitive gorilla state before the eyes of the audience. This got the crowd moving into the tent, and the admission price at that time was $2.

Inside, the lecturer took over. The girl was in her cage, and he told the crowd that she was being put into a trance. As he urged her deeper and deeper into her trance, the transformation began, and before we knew it, she'd become a hairy ape. The marks were warned about making any sudden moves, but suddenly, the gorilla broke out of its cage and charged toward us. The lecturer then fired off a gun loaded with blanks to try and stop the panic – or really, to cause more panic – and a show hand whipped open the canvas at the entrance to allow everyone to make an easy escape.

To a kid like me, who'd seen the show a couple of dozen times, the whole thing was a hoot, but I found out later that while the show was a big moneymaker – sometimes $2,000 a day on a big weekend – it could also be a headache for showmen. The Girl to Gorilla Show required more liability insurance than most other shows because of the accidents that occurred while people were running out of the tent.

"I remember one time when the gorilla jumped out of the cage, and this old guy turns around to run and he went smack into the center pole," a former showman recalled one incident for me. "He's knocked out cold. The guy in the gorilla suit bends down to try and wake him up and when the old man comes to, he sees the gorilla on top of him, panics, gets up, and runs into another pole. Yeah, it was bad."

And that wasn't the only problem with running this kind of show. Apparently, the gorilla suit often picked up lice from the fairgrounds where they performed. The only way to get rid of the bugs was to wash the suit in gasoline and hang it in the shade to dry – not the sun. In fact, drying the suits at night was best. If they were hung in the hot sun, the gasoline would eat through the rubber in the suit.

AT LEAST ONE ILLUSION SEEMED TO DEFINE EVERY DECADE on the midway. In the 1920s, it was the Sawing a Lady in Half show, which was big on the vaudeville circuit, too. In this well-known act, a woman was placed in a coffin-like box and sawed in half. The halves of the box are pushed apart, and the woman inside not only wiggles her feet but also waves her hands. There were a LOT of showmen who claimed to have created this illusion, but there's no clear record of who actually did.

In the 1930s, one of the best shows on the midway was the Death by Guillotine illusion. One newspaper described the show: "Youngsters' eyes almost popped out of their heads as they watched this alarming feat. The girl's head is neatly placed under the evil-looking machine. Down comes the blade, and off comes her head into a box held by the assistant. He takes the head and places it on a chair several feet from the guillotine, where the hands are still seen. While apparently decapitated, the girl talks, winks, and answers questions freely."

While the guillotine part of the act didn't stick around, the Headless Girl certainly did, and in fact, she became a staple of late 1930s sideshows, took a break, and then returned bigger and better from the 1960s through the 1980s. This has always been another one of my favorite illusion shows.

The illusion as allegedly brought to America from Germany by Dr. Egon "Dutch" Heinemann, who had been exhibiting a headless girl in an amusement park before crossing the Atlantic and hooking up with the Good man Wonder Shows in 1937. Heinemann gave his headless lady the name Olga, and she soon started popping up as a 10-cent grind show on dozens of midways two years later. This was thanks largely to Edward Murphy of San Francisco, who sold plans for the illusion for $100 a set.

Olga was used by many showmen as a blow-off. Once the rubes were inside the tent, the lecturer, dressed as a doctor or a nurse, would select a volunteer from the audience to come up and feel Olga's pulse and her chest movement, confirming that she was "alive."

Of course, she was. It was the same illusion that could be traced back to Pepper's Ghost Show and Spidora, the living girl with a spider's body. The illusion was easy to construct, but the drawback was that a living girl with a good figure was required to sit in the illusion for hours while patrons passed by. Sometimes, two girls were employed, one playing the "nurse" while the other plays the headless girl and later switching roles for a break.

Where the Headless Girl illusion had the advantage over something like Spidora, while both required a living girl to always be present in order for it to grind, the spider girl show left the hapless young woman's face on display to be subjected to the taunts and comments of the marks. No one bothered to talk to the girl with no head, but a girl whose head is out in the open was a target for abuse from "fun seekers" on the midway. A phony nurse or doctor was usually on hand to keep this kind of "fun" from getting out of hand.

In the 1960s, Olga was revived by showmen. The story was the same – for 50 cents, the public went into a trailer and started at a headless lady, usually wearing a low-cut blouse or dress.

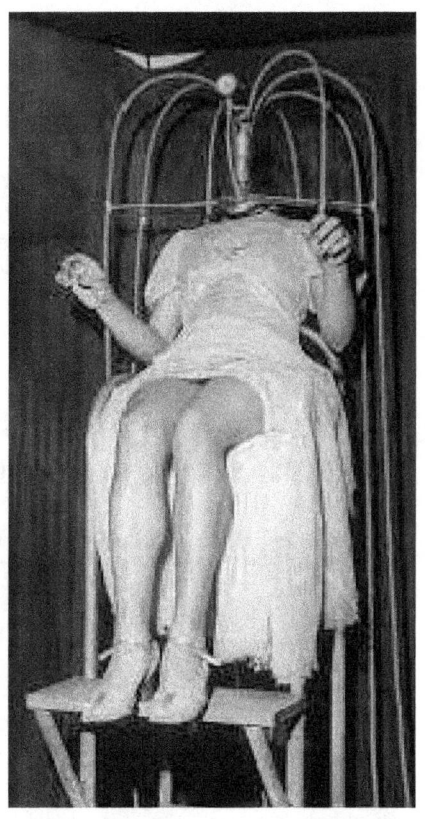

THE HEADLESS GIRL ILLUSION WAS ALWAYS A WINNER. ON RARE OCCASIONS, YOU'LL STILL FIND IT ON A MIDWAY TODAY.

By the '60s, it was often displayed as the Headless Centerfold with gaffed newspaper articles displayed outside mimicking the Jayne Mansfield automobile tragedy in which rumor had it that the movie star lost her head for real. She didn't – what passing motorists thought was Jayne's head was actually one of her blond wigs lying in the grass.

But who says a sideshow story needs to be true? Literally, no one.

In the 1970s, she was the Headless Bikini Girl who had unfortunately lost her head in a shark attack – cashing in, of course, on the popularity of the film *Jaws*.

By the 1980s -- when I first saw this illusion -- showmen wanted to push the envelope a little more and came up with some kind of amazing equipment that was credited for keeping the headless girl alive and breathing. The apparatus usually amounted to gaff tubes of liquid flowing in and out of the girl's neck. Occasionally, there were monitors, control boards, spark-makers, and motors that looked like something out of Dr. Frankenstein's laboratory.

It was laughable, but there's no question that it added a little fun and a lot of charm to the show.

PART FOUR:
PICKLED PUNKS
THE BABY SHOW ON THE MIDWAY

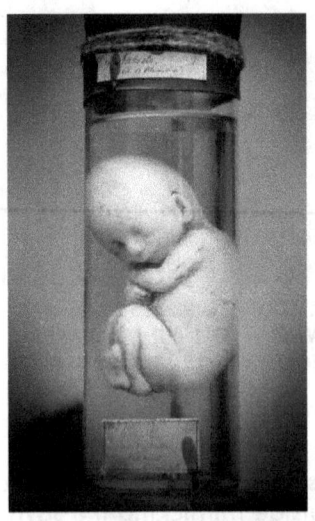

I'M ALWAYS GOING TO HAVE A SOFT SPOT FOR THE "PICKLED Punk." They were my entry into the sideshow world, or at least the thing that convinced me that it was okay to be weird and to love strange things like two-headed babies that are kept on display in jars.

If you'll recall from the opening pages of this book, a Pickled Punk was a carnie term for a human fetus in a jar -- usually one with a big head, an attached twin, or some other kind of deformity. They were a midway staple, dating back to the earliest days of the traveling shows, but they were placed in jars and preserved for one simple reason -- it was too hard to take live babies on the road.

Live babies had been on display as far back as 1902 when they became a big attraction at Coney Island with an exhibit called the Baby Incubator. Dr. Martin Arthur Couney had specialized in pediatrics in Paris in the 1890s at a time when premature babies were left to die or placed under a blanket surrounded by hot bricks in a kitchen in a feeble attempt to keep them alive. In 1896, he invented an incubator and put it on display at an exhibition in Berlin as a way of embarrassing the French government into giving him more money for research. It didn't work – in fact, he became the butt of jokes at the fair, but his display of incubators with premature babies inside also became one of the best-attended attractions there.

In 1903, amusement park builder Frederic Thompson invited the doctor to place his incubators on display at Coney Island. Babies were brought to the exhibit from all over New York and from cities that didn't have adequate facilities for premature babies. The public was led into the incubator room, given a lecture, and then moved on to the nursery, where four or five nurses were always on hand to feed the babies milk.

LIVE BABIES – PREMATURE BIRTHS – ON DISPLAY IN INCUBATORS ON THE PIKE AT THE ST. LOUIS WORLD'S FAIR IN 1904.

The incubators were such a hit that a Baby Show was also a year-long exhibit at the 1904 World's Fair in St. Louis. On the Pike – which was the St. Louis Fair's answer to the 1893 Chicago Fair's Midway – was a premature baby incubator attraction where hot air was pumped under the floorboards to keep the room's temperature constant. Trained nurses cared for the infants, who were separated from curious fairgoers by a wall of plate glass. About 25 babies were on display each day while lecturers informed the crowd about the machines that kept them alive. After viewing the babies, visitors could buy a souvenir soap baby or have lunch at the Incubator Café.

Live babies continued to be popular for years, all the way into the 1920s, when exhibits appeared on the Atlantic City Boardwalk and in amusement parks around the nation.

However, living babies didn't really have a place on the midway, which is why the embalmed and preserved kind had to do. But they didn't start there – showman Lou Dufour legitimized embryo and pickled baby exhibits in the 1930s by displaying them at several World's Fair shows.

In 1927, Lou had been running auction stores with carnivals, and while he was at a fair in Louisiana, he watched crowds line up to see 20 specimens displayed in a tent by a local doctor. He also remembered a visit he'd made to the Smithsonian Institution, where he'd seen people stand amazed in front of displays of human embryos. Lou convinced the doctor to sell him his show – he was a doctor, so there were more where those came from – and he started exhibiting it with the name UNBORN. He opened the exhibit the next season on the Johnny J. Jones midways and soon had dozens of shows traveling around the country.

In 1933, Lou teamed up with Joe Rogers, another carnival showman, to put two shows on the midway at the Century of Progress Exhibition in Chicago. One was the Life Museum, and the other was a Live Two-Headed Baby. Felix Blei, the agent of magician Carter the Great, had discovered a lady in Hong Kong who had given birth to a two-headed infant that lived. Contracts were signed, but the baby died just a few weeks before the fair opened. Rogers and Dufour scrambled and managed to purchase a two-headed baby that had been on display in a doctor's office for a few years. For $1,500, they were back in business with their star attraction, although it was floating in a three-foot jar of formaldehyde.

The artwork at the entrance was changed from "LIVE TWO-HEADED BABY" to "REAL TWO-HEADED BABY."

The show may not have made quite as much money as it would have with a baby that had two heads, but the "pickled punk" version was still a great success.

Patrons who entered the Life Museum show were met by a lecturer dressed in a white hospital smock, who lectured on the contents of the medical jars, describing life from conception to birth. There were signs and explanations everywhere among the punks, and then, as the crowd entered an open area, a recorded voice announced, "Now, look at the nude woman." A curtain opened, and there was a plastic model of a woman, and in her belly was a screen. There was a projector in the back that started a movie, about which the voice said: "You are going to see a natural birth and a Caesarean birth, or birth by surgery."

Often, a couple of the marks would pass out when they saw the film, even though it was black and white. As soon the first scalpel shot came on the screen, and blood started coming out, young men watching the film dropped like flies.

At the end of the show, the "doctor" in the white smock pitched a booklet that dealt with sexual problems and pregnancy for the steep price of 50 cents – even though it had information in it that was freely given out at clinics and hospitals.

MANY OF THE MIDWAY BABY SHOWS LURED IN PEOPLE BY OFFERING A FILM OF A LIVE BIRTH – WHICH OFTEN CAUSED MEN TO FAINT IN THOSE DAYS – AND MADE THEIR MONEY WITH CHEAP PITCH BOOKS.

The pitch, though, was what really sold the booklets – one for men and one for women. The doctor/talker told the crowd that the booklets were so important that they should be in every home in America, selling for a much higher price. However, they were offering them at a discount in hopes that they might save at least one young girl from the shame of unwed motherhood or one young boy from the horrors of venereal disease.

Showman Dave Friedman, who worked with Lou on the show, later said, "We probably got more poor girls pregnant with that phony crap, but it was the strongest joint ever set down."

BY THE 1970S, THINGS HAD GOTTEN A LITTLE TRICKY when it came to what you could and couldn't exhibit on midways. The punk business got into trouble at a small fair just north of Chicago. Chris Christ and Ward Hall had their World's Strangest Babies show booked at the Lake County Fair in Grayslake, Illinois, but shortly after opening, they were arrested by detectives sent by Coroner Robert Bobcox, acting on a complaint from someone whose daughter had seen the show.

Coroner Bobcox was quoted in the newspaper: "When we first saw the exhibits, we thought they were plastic or rubber. But assistant pathologist Dr. Vernon Zech examined them and found them to be human monstrosities. It was absolutely ghoulish."

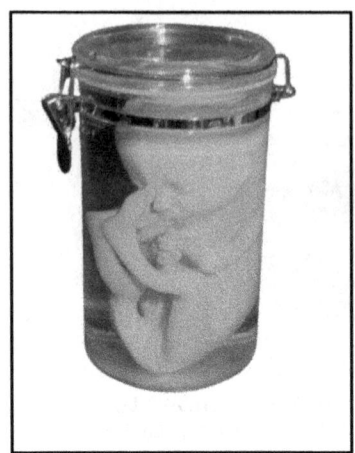

BY THE 1970S, THINGS HAD GOTTEN TRICKY WHEN IT CAME TO DISPLAYING REAL BABIES IN JARS, SO MOST SHOWMEN PLAYED IT SAFE BY SWITCHING TO "BOUNCERS," WHICH LOOKED LIKE THE REAL THING.

The showmen were charged with transporting dead bodies without permits, and their 20 fetuses and embryos were confiscated, along with their signs and other parts of the show. An attorney named Raymond Carlson was hired to defend them and get their show back.

But Bobcox was adamant that there was no way the babies were ever leaving his morgue unless it was for a proper burial. He told reporters, "The only way anyone could obtain malformed fetuses and babies would be to buy them from either a morgue in a large city, a second-rate abortionist, or medical schools. I will not let this practice go on."

However, it soon became clear that the babies may have been inside those jars for 40 years, which made them impossible to trace. With Bobcox's case falling apart, he called the police in Hillsborough County, Florida, to get the records of the two showmen, only to find they were clean. However, at their property in Gibsonton, the cops found 13 other babies stored in jars inside metal containers. Some of them were wrapped in newspapers that dated back a decade or more. Florida police charged the pair with "failure to register fetal death," which was never going to stick.

And they didn't – and neither did the charges in Illinois. To avoid further harassment, both men agreed to give the babies a proper burial. And yes, they tried to sell tickets to that, too, but the cemetery protested.

On November 17, 1977, minsters of Protestant and Catholic faiths, plus a Jewish rabbi, attended a graveside ceremony for 14 of the babies in Highland Park, Illinois. The burial of the babies in a single grave was accompanied by a four-minute ceremony at which Reverend Richard Hunt commented: "We also bury the idea that human life can be a grotesque spectacle, cheap and exploited."

Now, there's a guy who's never spent any time on the midway.

Once the dust settled, Christ and Hall re-started the show, using "bouncers" in place of the real babies they'd surrendered. The word "replica" was painted in small letters on the entrance banner.

Every showman in the punk business panicked in the wake of those legal problems. Across the country, dozens of babies were buried and replaced by rubber replicas by showmen who feared trouble of their own. Though it would be very hard to make any charges stick, if prosecuted, showmen would lose their attractions and spend thousands in legal fees. No one wanted to risk it, and before long, the showing of pickled punks slowed down until there were only a handful of small shows that were displaying the real thing – and most of them didn't last.

In more recent years, the biggest market for punks – both real and man-made – has been collectors fascinated with sideshows or people like me who display them as a nod to carnival history.

In the early 1990s, showman Bobby Reynolds took a big chance and exhibited his real two-headed baby show at Coney Island. He was soon arrested, but he won his court case.

In 1999, Jack Constantine had a three-banner baby show that he'd bought from Ward and Christ a few years earlier. All the babies were bouncers and were displayed in individual cases inside a single glass case.

Constantine only played for one season, but Bobby Reynolds returned with his two-headed baby show in 2000 and did a brisk business on the midway. "The boys," as he referred to his punk, rotated in a medical jar on a turntable. He later described how each revolution of the jar brought new expressions to the faces of the marks. "People were fascinated," Reyolds recalled. "No one seemed disgusted."

He found a clever way to slip past the critics and make his show a "public service." The spiel on the grind tape said it was a medical presentation – a warning to young mothers about drugs and alcohol consumption during pregnancy.

Everyone seemed to buy it.

PART FIVE:
"NO TICKET NEEDED"
MIDWAY MARKS AND THE DING SHOWS

SHOWMEN ALWAYS LOVED THE DING SHOWS – WHAT MANY called the "donation" or "needle" shows. These were the shows advertised as being free, but when a mark reached the end of the exhibit, they were faced with a narrow exit and a large box with a sign suggesting they put something in it – preferably money.

Incubators, unborn shows, iron lungs, war exhibits, and wildlife shows were some of the attractions that were operated as ding shows. Dings could be found at the circus, but they were mainly on carnival midways.

During the World War II years and after, many dings were walk-through shows. The midway show Hitler and His Henchmen After Death – comprised of wax figures of Hitler, Eva Braun, Mussolini, and a lot of war relics – was operated as a ding show during the mid-1950s. The panel and banner front had a sign over the entrance that read ENTRANCE – WALK IN. Another sign below it on the ground noted NO TICKETS SOLD. Like most small ding shows, it was located inside a tent with exhibits on both sides. A guest walked toward the back of the tent and made a U-turn, walking back up toward the front before leaving through a side exit – where, of course, the donation box was waiting.

Carnival ding shows were often run by part of the grift mob who ran the controlled games with the show – the three card monte and shell game scams and the old machine games into which you dropped quarters in hopes the moving arm inside would dump more quarters into the tray.

The dings often took place before the marks even got into the tent. If the town was securely "patched" – in other words, the authorities had been paid off – the grifters might work right out in the open on the lot. Usually, though, they worked the parking lots and the streets approaching the circus ground.

Characters who worked for ding shows approached the patrons as they walked up to the lot. They offered them flowers, cards, or flag pins, but if they didn't ante up a donation, the items were taken away. Today, ding mobs still work parades, gatherings, and tourist destinations, like the "monks" who put bracelets on the wrists of

THE MOST EFFECTIVE DING SHOWS IN THE 1930S AND 1940S WERE THE IRON LUNG SHOWS, WHICH WERE SET UP AS INFORMATIVE EXHIBITS THAT WERE ARRANGED FOR CHARITY.

inebriated folks on the streets of New Orleans before demanding payment.

One of the most effective carnival dings of the 1930s through the 1950s was the iron lung exhibit. Medical science came up with these machines to do the breathing for polio patients. However, because the equipment was very expensive, fraternal groups and clubs held drives to raise money to purchase iron lungs for local hospitals. Several companies made the machines and were eager to get their product advertised, having no qualms about putting them in exhibitions operated by midway showmen.

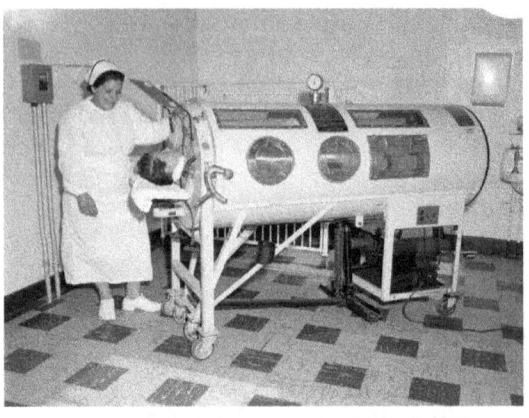

AN IRON LUNG FOR POLIO PATIENTS

The key to the operation – or rather, to stay out of trouble – was the word EXHIBIT, which appeared on every lung show. It didn't stop the public from attending and donating, though. If questioned, the operator could point to the word and say that it was a demonstration to promote awareness of the disease and show how iron lungs helped those who suffered from it.

The lung shows were some of the best ding shows – the eerie noise of the respirators alone drew people into the tent. The best dings were those that left the viewers feeling guilty when they passed by the donation box. What could be better than a pretty young woman trapped inside a humming iron medical contraption to make you feel lucky enough to help out with a little spare change or a dollar or two? Staff in medical uniforms and the spotless exhibition area made the mark feel like they were in a hospital setting.

Well, as long as they weren't still around when the show closed at night to see the "unfortunate" young woman climb out of the machine and go back to her trailer.

THERE WERE OTHER POPULAR DING SHOWS THAT APPEARED on carnival midways for years, including religious shows that offered a "guaranteed trip to Heaven" for a small donation or let people into a tent to see a life-sized "Last Supper" or some other biblical scene.

WILDLIFE DING SHOW IN THE 1950S

There were also "unborn shows" that displayed pickled punks and bouncers and medical shows that sold patent medicines to the marks.

One very popular ding show was the wildlife show, which consisted of a display of wild animals in cages. Most of them were smaller animals who could handle small cages, and many were easily found on farms or in local woods and lakes, like foxes, raccoons, otters, cows, pigs, and sheep. Some shows were a little more exotic, offering monkeys, coatimundis, and other tiny jungle creatures.

A few shows did carry one or two big animals as a drawing card, like a camel or a single elephant. For several seasons, the wildlife show that toured with the World of Mirth featured two lions. Some showmen exhibited bears, and one even advertised a gorilla.

Many wildlife shows were framed and painted to look like displays the National Park Service, Fish and Wildlife, or Bureau of Land Management might have at a county or state fair. Showmen found that anything that looked official made the marks much quicker to donate.

But the wildlife ding shows did have their drawbacks. Veteran showmen often said they'd never own anything that needed to eat. Once they bought that kind of show, they had to keep working all the

time to make sure they had the money to feed the attractions. This led to many wildlife showmen being forced to work in the off-season to make sure they always had cash coming in for animal feed.

But the more animals you had, the bigger the show and the more money you could make. The real trick to running a wildlife show was making it look inviting and appealing to the families on the fairgrounds. Kids could never pass up the chance to see animals up close and often dragged their parents into the show. Of course, any reluctance mom and dad might have had disappeared when they discovered it was "free."

Wildlife showman Don Prevost, whose parents had started in the business in the 1920s, noted, "On the ding, you had to flash the ding table with money – ones and fives. You had to ask everybody! We tried to make it look like those exhibits the conservation officials put out at fairs. We had green-painted cages, and all the staff wore green pants and white shirts."

But Don, along with most of the other wildlife showmen, left the business in the 1970s. He explained, "The animal activists started coming in and asking how big the cages were, how much water does that animal drink? They were never satisfied, raising the requirements another step once you met their last one. No matter what you did, it was never good enough." He left the wildlife business in 1974 and bought a string of concession stands.

Animals or no animals, ding shows were the life's blood of a lot of midways during the mid-twentieth century. They were always about the money, of course, as proven by one of my favorite stories, told by ding show operator Frank Hansen.

He would set up his shows so there were one-way gates at the beginning and end of the exhibit. They couldn't go back out of the entrance, so they had to leave by the exit, where the donation box was located. Frank recalled, "If people forgot to leave a little something to show their appreciation on exiting, I wouldn't press the lever to make the turnstile work. People would look at me, and I would say, 'Maybe you forgot something?'"

PART SIX:
"CRIMES DOESN'T PAY!" OR DOES IT?
DEATH CARS, ELECTRIC CHAIRS & CRIME SHOWS

CRIME SHOWS WERE PART OF THE EARLIEST EXHIBITIONS shown to the public in peep shows and dime museums. The shows often included battles, war carnage, and grisly crime scenes. As far back as the 1880s, links had been made between American show business and the exploitation of crime.

It was in 1889 when showman Fred Wilson surprised the entertainment world with a patented electric act intended to portray an execution onstage. It was supposed to emulate an invention that had been promoted by Thomas Edison and accepted by state legislatures as a new way to execute criminals. Soon, the electric chair became a permanent prop in both crime shows and sideshows.

THE JAMES GANG

AMERICANS HAVE ALWAYS BEEN FASCINATED BY TALES OF bandits, shootouts, stagecoach robberies, and Indian massacres. In the late nineteenth century, there were no outlaws more publicized than Jesse and Frank James and their cousins, Cole and Jim Younger. The Bonheur Brothers were some of the first showmen to cash in on the notoriety of the James gang. Starting in 1880, the Bonheurs began offering a lantern show that portrayed Western life. The brothers carried their own cameras and traveled extensively in Missouri, often meeting with actual members of the gang. As the infamy of the outlaws increased, the Bonheurs added photos to the show, and when Jesse James was killed, the shows became even more popular. In just one season in Ohio and Indiana only, the Bonheurs made more than $10,000.

In 1903, Frank James and Cole Younger began fronting a Wild West show that had formerly belonged to a showman named Buckskin Bill. One of the backers, Senator Stephen Benton Elkins of West Virginia,

THE COLE YOUNGER AND FRANK JAMES WILD WEST SHOW IN 1903

had put up $20,000 to get Cole out of prison. Their friendship went back to the Civil War when Cole saved his life.

During the show, only Frank performed. He "rescued" a stagecoach from an Indian attack and engaged in some shooting demonstrations. They claimed that at no time during the show would the public witness any unlawful acts. One stipulation of Cole's release was that he would take part in any public exhibitions, so he limited himself to being the show's treasurer. But Cole did have a book that he's written about their outlaw exploits, which sold well to those who attended the show.

But things didn't always go smoothly when the show rolled into town. Ministers and newspaper editors were outraged about the former bandits traveling the country and capitalizing on their crimes. Over 100 people had been killed during robberies by the James and Younger gang, and there were a lot of relatives still looking for revenge. Both men were suspicious of people and were paranoid about something shooting them.

But is it really paranoia when someone is actually out to get you?

While Frank may have been an outlaw, he really wanted to be an actor. He had appeared in a dramatic program before the Wild West show, and when it ended in 1904, he went back to the stage in a play called *The Fatal Star*. Four years later, though, Cole opened another Wild West show and brought Frank on board, but it only lasted one season. After that, Cole and partner Lew Nichols ran a theater and amusement company in Lee's Summit, Missouri, where Cole died in March of 1916.

Frank James died in 1915, but an incident from 1911 still happened around the sideshow circuit at the time. Tom L. Wilson recalled that incident, which took place while Tom was with the Dan B. Robinson Carnival Co. at a fair in Miles, Ohio. Tom recounted:

FRANK JAMES

On the midway, we had as a feature a show called The James Brothers in Missouri. *Word got to the carnival office that Frank James himself was the official starter of the horse races and that he was coming onto the midway as well. The Robinsons were afraid Frank might object, since the show depicted the James Brothers in a negative way because of their crime sprees. They wondered if Frank, angered by the show, might shoot up the place.*

"At 4:00, Frank showed up at the ticket box of the show. He was short in stature, then middle-aged and graying, quiet and unassuming. He went in and sat down and watched the movie. When he came out, he asked permission of the talker to say a few words to the crowd that had gathered. He said: 'My friends, inside this top is a representation of myself, my brother Jesse, the Youngers, and our former gang of bad men, depicted true to life and nature. The pictures, the scenes are correct, and while looking at them I found food for thought and saddened reminiscences. I advise you all to go in and see them.'

He turned and thanked the announcer and then quietly walked back to the judges' stand and the racetrack.

Those early bandits also inspired midway showmen to put on crime shows called "Law and Outlaw" shows. Showmen liked them because the wax or paper-mâché figures were light and easy to load for travel. The show could be exhibited at carnivals and in storefronts year-round.

Best of all, the cast didn't eat or draw a salary.

And they were fairly easy to get. St. Louis wax sculptor W.H.J. Shaw, who started specializing in making and selling wax outlaw shows in the early 1890s, called Jesse James the "King of the American Bandits." Jesse was Shaw's best seller, but he also offered a list of other bandits that were always ready to ship.

In 1915, he also started offering crime showmen the life-size wax figure of murderous cop Charles Becker, which came with an electric chair, death cap, battery, and wires for only $50. If the buyer threw in another $20, they'd also get a painted banner to go along with it.

Although largely forgotten today, Charles Becker was one of the most notorious criminals of the day. He had been a lieutenant in the New York Police Department who was convicted of first-degree murder because he was the "only police officer executed for crimes connected to his official performance" and was part of a scandal that rocked New York City politics to its core.

CHARLES BECKER

CHARLES BECKER'S SENSATIONAL MURDER CASE MANAGED TO DRAW BIG CROWDS TO SHOWS ABOUT HIM IN THE EARLY 1900S

CHARLES BECKER WAS BORN IN 1870 IN THE VILLAGE OF Callicoon Center, in Sullivan County, New York. His parents were German American immigrants, and Charles worked on their farm while he was growing up. But the lure of the big city began calling to him as a young man, and he moved to New York City in 1890. The burly former farmer went to work as a bouncer in a German beer hall in the Bowery.

Three years later, he joined the New York Police Department, and, in the fall of 1896, Becker gained a lot of attention when he arrested Ruby Young -- alias Dora Clark – for prostitution. The arrest got the attention of the papers and the public because Ruby was arrested in the company of popular writer Stephen Crane.

The next day, at Ruby's hearing, Crane stepped forward and defended her. His popularity helped to get the case against the young woman dismissed. Afterward, Crane told the press, "If the girl wants to have the officer prosecuted for perjury, I will gladly support her."

Three weeks later, Ruby filed formal charges against Charles Becker. Trying to defend himself, Charles gathered evidence, hired experienced lawyer Louis Grant, and rallied the support of his law enforcement colleagues. On October 15, 1896, Charles entered the courtroom surrounded by a dozen uniformed policemen. Commissioner Frederick Dent Grant – son of Ulysses S. Grant – oversaw the proceedings. After almost five hours of examination, Charles was acquitted and earned an important lesson – the power of the badge could get him out of almost anything.

Soon after he was cleared of wrongdoing, Charles got married for the first time. His wife, Letitia Stenson, was a new arrival from Canada, and the couple had one child, a son named Howard, in 1899. Six years later, they were divorced, and Charles married again in 1905. His second wife, Helen, was a schoolteacher and, later, assistant principal. They had one daughter, Charlotte, but she died less than one day after her birth in 1913.

Helen would always believe her husband was wrongfully convicted of murder.

Before Charles ended up behind bars, he was one of the leaders of a patrolman's reform movement, agitating for a new system that would significantly reduce the number of hours that police officers were expected to work. He also became part of a special unit that investigated alleged corruption by Police Inspector Max F. Schmittberger, who was subsequently prosecuted for it. As a result, Police Commissioner Rhinelander Waldo was so impressed with Becker's work that he appointed Charles, who was now a lieutenant, as head of one of the city's three anti-vice squads.

It was then, in this new position of power, that Charles Becker found himself neck-deep in corruption of his own.

Charles used his position to extort substantial sums – later shown to be over $100,000 – from Manhattan brothers and illegal gambling parlors in exchange for protection from interference by the police. Percentages of Becker's take were regularly delivered to politicians and other cops. The operation was kept running smoothly by politicians like Timothy "Big Tim" Sullivan, who was the leader of New York's political machine, Tammany Hall.

Occasionally, though, the police needed to carry out a raid or two for show. In early 1912, Herman Rosenthal, a flamboyant Estonian immigrant who ran several illegal casinos in the Tenderloin district, drew the unlucky straw. After the raid, Rosenthal was irritated by the damage the cops left in their wake, so he complained about Becker to the press, telling reporters that Becker "collected 20 percent of the take there."

The complaints got the attention of the *New York World*, who began investigating. In July 1912, editors announced they'd collected evidence against three senior police officials who'd been extorting money from Rosenthal's casinos.

Charles Becker was one of them.

A grand jury was convened to investigate the claims. On the day that Rosenthal was supposed to testify, he was murdered as he left the Hotel Metropole, just off Times Square, at 2:00 A.M. Four men – Louis "Lefty Louie" Rosenberg, Jacob "Whitey Lewis" Seidenscher, Frank "Dago Frank" Cirofici, and Harry "Gyp the Blood" Horowitz – were witnessed shooting Rosenthal from a passing car. All were separately tried, convicted, sentenced to death, and executed.

But there was more to the story of the murder.

Manhattan District Attorney Charles S. Whitman – who was supposed to meet with Rosenthal before he was murdered – alleged that the four gangsters had committed the murder on orders from Charles Becker. A major public outcry and extensive press coverage followed, and Becker was quietly transferred to the Bronx and put on desk duty in hopes that things would die down.

They didn't, and Whitman's office continued to investigate the murder. Finally, on July 29, 1912, Charles was arrested by special detectives from the District Attorney's office. He was tried and convicted of first-degree murder that fall after a trial that was presided over by John Goff, a judge who was immediately accused of being "intensely biased against Becker" and whose charge to the jury was "slanted toward conviction." The verdict was overturned on appeal, and in 1914, Becker was tried again. He was convicted once again and sentenced to death – the first NYPD officer to ever receive such a sentence.

Becker, though, continued to profess his innocence – sort of. On the day before he was executed, he told the warden: "Sure, I told them to put Rosenthal out of the way, but I didn't mean they should kill him. I wanted them to get him out of town so he wouldn't blab. Killing him was Rose's idea and the others. They wanted to save their own skins."

The Rose he was referring to was Jack Rose, who served as a prosecution witness along with other underworld characters, including Harry Vallon, Sam Schepps, and Bridgey Webber. They were also involved in the crime but had been offered immunity by the D.A. if they testified against Becker.

Charles went to the electric chair at Sing Sing on July 30, 1915. It didn't go well. The execution took nine minutes, and Becker seemed to be in agony the entire time. For years after, it was recalled as "the clumsiest execution in the history of Sing Sing."

And it was one that carnival-goers could experience for themselves every time they walked into a crime show tent – at least until the notoriety of Charles Becker faded away and another American lawbreaker replaced his wax figure, that is.

CRIME ALWAYS PAYS

ANOTHER ST. LOUIS WAX FIGURE MAKER WHO STARTED IN the 1920s was B.W. Christophel, who offered Wild West bandits for years before switching over almost exclusively to Public Enemy shows around 1935. By then, the Wild West bandits had been replaced by the bank robbers of the Depression era. The characters on his roster included John Dillinger, Pretty Boy Floyd, Baby Face Nelson, and Bonnie and Clyde.

In 1932, showman R.E. Norman wrote Christophel and requested a seated wax figure in an electric chair that he could mount on the front of his crime display truck. Christophel wrote back but stated that the figure would have to be made from papier-mâché because the wax would melt in the sun.

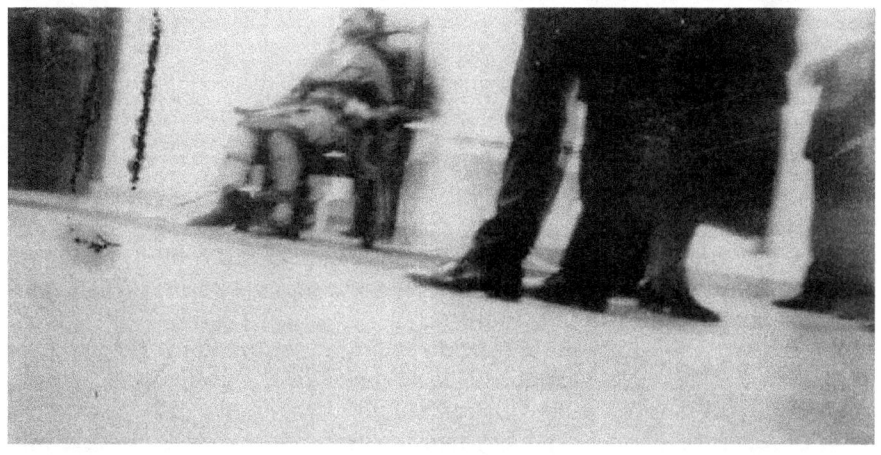

THE PHOTOGRAPH OF RUTH SNYDER IN THE ELECTRIC CHAIR APPEARED ON NEWSPAPER FRONT PAGES AROUND THE COUNTRY – AND IN CARNIVAL CRIME SHOWS WITH A WAX DUMMY RECREATING THE MOMENT.

Unlike most showmen who wanted outlaw figures, Norman wanted to purchase a female character – a killer named Ruth Snyder, whose recent execution had marked the first time that a woman had been captured in a photograph as she went to the electric chair.

Ruth Snyder had been a Long Island housewife in 1925 when she and her lover, Henry Judd Gray, murdered Ruth's husband, Albert. After several attempts with a variety of weapons, including picture-hanging wire, they were finally able to finish him off with a window weight. With Albert dead, the pair tried to make the murder look like a robbery gone wrong by hiding some valuables, messing up the house, and tying Ruth's hands and feet. But the police weren't fooled for long, especially after some of the "stolen" valuables were found hidden in the house.

Celebrated newsman Damon Runyon later wrote that the lovers were "inept idiots" and dubbed the affair the "Dumb-Bell Murder."

Ruth and Henry were both convicted at trial and sentenced to death. Henry died first, but when it was Ruth's turn in the electric chair, a reporter from Chicago managed to snap a photo of her with a hidden camera just as the switch was thrown.

The photograph became front-page news all on its own and created a sensation across the country, especially for those who had been following the soap opera-like trial from its start.

The figure of Ruth Snyder in the electric chair was the perfect decoration for a truck used to transport a "crime never pays" show around the sideshow circuit.

THE OUTLAW TRAIL

BUT NOT EVERY SHOWMAN COULD AFFORD THE COSTS of wax figure crime shows. For those a little more cash-strapped, Charles Buell from Newark, Ohio, offered walk-through peep shows starting in 1929. His Underworld, Great Chicago Gang War, and Prohibition Killing shows came with 20 viewing boxes, 52 enlarged views on panels, plus a script for an entertaining lecture.

During the 1930s, Buell produced a constant line of gangster shows with titles like Gangland: Its Crimes and Punishments. It was elaborate for one of Buell's usual bargain basement shows. It came with an electric chair and a big five-banner front, plus 18 viewers into which customers could peer to look at the violent scenes. For those who coughed up the $285 to own it, he also threw in 26 glass frames that came with an additional 100 crime scene photos.

The top Law and Outlaw showman of the 1920s and 1920s was Scout Younger - a former member of the outlaw gang. He put together a wildly popular show with help from the Chicago wax figure studio of Gustus Schmidt and Sons. He obtained a half-dozen contracts from different carnivals and ran storefront shows in several cities.

His shows - whether storefront operations or carnival set-ups - had between 25 and 40 figures of famous outlaws, including Wild Bill Hickok, Allen Pinkerton, Belle Starr, the Dalton gang, Bill Doolin, and, of course, the Dalton gang - Cole, Bob, John, Jim, and Scout.

Yes, he had a wax figure of himself in his outlaw shows.

In 1929, Scout retired and sold off his wax attractions to Dodson's World's Fair Shows. He died in Tulsa, Oklahoma, in 1938.

Scout Younger inadvertently started a trend that took off in the 1930s - having the family members of outlaws, and even criminals themselves, on tour with "Crime Doesn't Pay" shows.

PUBLIC ENEMIES

In the summer of 1934, John Castle, who was part owner of the United Shows of America, hired the mothers of both Clyde Barrow and Bonnie Parker for his shows. The outlaw couple had been shot to death on a country road in Louisiana just a few months before. However, harassment by lawmen and prosecutors forced their families to look for a way to pay their mounting legal bills after they were charged with sheltering their children from the law.

During the Great Depression, Bonnie and Clyde's love story captured the attention of a nation that was sick of banks and the U.S. government. Their exploits captured the attention of the American press and its readership because they were anti-heroes like Dillinger, Baby Face Nelson, Pretty Boy Floyd, and others.

Bonnie and Clyde became known for robberies and murders, killing at least nine police officers and four civilians during a three-year crime spree. But in May 1934, the couple was ambushed and killed by lawmen, and their deaths became as sensational as their lives. Thousands demanded to see the bodies of

481 | THE DEVIL'S CARNIVAL

JOHN DILLINGER, SR. – FATHER OF THE BANK ROBBER AND OUTLAW (LEFT) WHO WAS ALLEGEDLY GUNNED DOWN OUTSIDE THE BIOGRAPH THEATER IN CHICAGO IN 1934.

the slain outlaws – a demand that would extend to the guns, clothing, and belongings they'd left behind.

And that's when the carnival showmen cashed in.

With the mothers of Bonnie and Clyde already thrilling audiences, Castle had the cash to win over the father of John Dillinger, too. The senior Dillinger appeared in the show dressed in his son's clothing and holding what was alleged to be the real wooden gun that his son had used to escape from the old Lake County Jail in Crown Point, Indiana.

Dillinger was another of the American public's fascination during the Depression years. Over just a handful of years, he was accused of robbing 24 banks and four police stations. He was imprisoned several times and escaped twice, which only added to his legend. He loved publicity, and the media was more than happy to write stories about his bravado and colorful personality, describing him as a "Robin Hood-type" character.

One of his most famous Dillinger escapes involved the wooden gun his father liked to display during the Crime Doesn't Pay shows.

On January 25, 1934, Dillinger and his gang were captured in Tucson, Arizona, and Dillinger was extradited to Indiana for the murder of a policeman who'd been killed during a bank robbery that occurred in East Chicago, Indiana, just 10 days earlier. Dillinger had been in Florida at the time, so that he couldn't have been involved in the robbery or murder, but there were plenty of other things that he had done that more than justified his arrest.

After arriving at the county jail in Crown Point, the local police boasted to reporters that while they had recruited extra guards from the Indiana National Guard as a precaution, their jail was escape-proof – Dillinger wasn't going to escape this time.

They were wrong.

On Saturday, March 3, 1934, Dillinger easily escaped from the jail by producing a pistol and catching deputies and guards by surprise. He walked out the jail's kitchen door without firing a shot.

THE LAKE COUNTY JAIL IN CROWN POINT, INDIANA, FROM WHICH DILLINGER ESCAPED IN MARCH 1934.

Almost immediately, the conjecture began about whether the gun Dillinger displayed was real or not. According to Deputy Ernest Blunk, Dillinger had escaped using a real pistol. FBI files, on the other hand, indicate that Dillinger used a carved fake pistol. Sam Cahoon, a trustee whom Dillinger took hostage in the jail, also believed

Dillinger had carved the gun using a razor and some shelving in his cell.

Allegedly, the carved gun that John Dillinger, Sr. displayed during this midway show was the gun that his son used to bluff his way out of jail – but there have been several other guns that have appeared since that time that also claim to be the "authentic" carved pistol. It's probably no surprise to anyone that the Crime Doesn't Pay show pistol was probably a fake.

Less than four months after Dillinger's escape in Crown Point, he was purportedly shot to death by local and federal law enforcement officers at the Biograph Theater in Chicago.

IN 1936, DILLINGER'S GIRLFRIEND, EVELYN "BILLIE" FRECHETTE, JOINED THE DILLINGER SHOW WITH HER FORMER LOVER'S FATHER. SHE CONTINUED TO TOUR WITH CRIME SHOWS INTO THE 1950S.

In 1936, Dillinger's girlfriend, Evelyn "Billie" Frechette, also joined the show after being released from the Michigan State Penitentiary, where she'd served time after being convicted for aiding and abetting Dillinger's crimes. The pretty brunette turned out to be an entertaining and well-spoken storyteller and, together with the elder Dillinger, drew big crowds on the midway.

C.R. Dent and his wife bought out Scout Younger when he retired, and they toured with Billie Frechette, a wax figure show and a gangster film that continued to bring in large audiences. The Dents described Billie as "a real trouper." During the 1936 season, she worked for four months straight without a day off.

She remained their star attraction the following year, and press releases described her as "a black-eyed beauty with Indian bloodlines." The talker on the show introduced her by saying, "She didn't talk out of the side of her mouth or tote guns. All she ever did, really, was love a rascal."

Billie and John Dillinger, Sr. made a good living on the midways after the death of a lover and a son. They continued to work in carnival crime shows and on lecture tours into the 1950s.

Sometimes, I guess, crime does pay, after all.

THE LAWSON TRAGEDY

MOST CRIME SHOWS THAT APPEARED ON MIDWAYS IN THE late 1920s and 1930s couldn't bring along criminals and family members. Many couldn't afford it, but in other cases, they weren't able to do it because the crimes that attracted the carnival crowds had left no survivors behind.

THE LAWSON FAMILY IN 1929

In those cases, the promoters had to show off the items that belonged to the victims and killers, the murder weapons used, and clothing and personal items, which were sometimes still covered in blood. Sometimes, these shows seemed anticlimactic when compared to the sensational crimes that spawned them, but in other cases, the shows were as lurid and gruesome as the murders themselves.

One crime that was turned into a midway show occurred after an unassuming farmwife and six of her seven children were murdered on Christmas Day in 1929. And if that wasn't bad enough – the killer was the husband of that farm wife and the father of those six children. Worse, he took his own life just after slaughtering his family.

What became known as the "Lawson Family Massacre" took place near Germanton, North Carolina, where a husband, father, and tobacco farmer named Charlie Lawson worked hard, kept his family fed, made sure his debts were paid, and kept a roof over everyone's head. Everything seemed right in the world for Charlie Lawson, but as they say, looks can often be deceiving.

As Christmas approached in 1929, the Lawson children grew more excited. They didn't expect many gifts since they had just received new clothing a short time before, but there would be lots of food to eat and lots of fun to have with friends and relatives who lived nearby.

THE LAWSON FAMILY HOME

(BELOW) A CRIME SCENE PHOTOGRAPH TAKEN INSIDE THE KITCHEN OF THE HOME, WHERE CHARLIE KILLED SEVERAL OF THE CHILDREN.

They had no way of knowing that the day would be anything but happy – it would end in a terrible murder.

The victims included six of the children and Charlie's wife of 20 years, Fanny. The youngest child was Mary Lou, who was only four months old at the time of her death. The only child not slain that horrific day was Arthur, a 16-year-old that everyone called Buck. He only survived because he was sent on an errand by his father that Christmas afternoon. Buck and his cousin were sent trudging through the snow to Germanton to buy more shotgun shells for Charlie.

But Charlie hadn't needed more shells – he just needed his oldest son – as tall and strong as Charlie himself -- to be out of the way when he carried out his terrible deeds.

Buck was, of course, stunned when he found out that his mother, sisters Marie, Carrie, Maybell, and baby Mary Lou, and brothers James and Raymond were all dead.

They had been killed one by one by his father.

Charlie had killed Carrie and Maybell first while they were walking to their uncle's house for Christmas lunch. He waited for them by the barn and shot them as they walked by. He finished them off by beating their heads with a board, and then he took them into the barn, laid them on the floor, crossed their arms, and closed their eyes – as if they had died peacefully.

Charlie then went to the house and shot his wife to death on the porch where she'd gone to get firewood for the stove. Inside the house, he killed his oldest daughter, Marie, and then his sons, James and Raymond, who were 2 and 4. He chased them around the house until he caught them and then beat them to death with the butt of his shotgun. He killed baby Mary Lou in her crib.

Charlie had annihilated his entire family. The interior of the house looked as though it had been drenched with buckets of blood.

The crime scene was later discovered by his brother and nephews, who had stopped to wish the family a Merry Christmas. When they saw the carnage, they ran to a neighbor's house to ask the man to call the sheriff. They were sure that intruders had broken in and killed the family. As lawmen arrived on the scene, though, they came to a grim realization about what had occurred – Charlie Lawson had been the one who did the killing.

A search began for Charlie. Hours passed before he was found dead in the woods. He'd apparently fled to the site right after the murders, and he'd walked and walked in a circle around a tree for so long that the snow had melted in his path. Eventually, he sat down at the base of the tree, leaned back, put the gun barrel in his mouth, and pulled the trigger.

Newspapers in at least 19 states printed stories were massive headlines about the murders the next day. There was no apparent motive. The Lawsons weren't rich, but they weren't having any financial problems. Charlie Lawson was a likable man. He was a hard worker. No one knew him to have any strange habits, and he'd always been a religious man. Most people in the community liked and respected him. They couldn't imagine why he would have done such a terrible thing.

Soon, though, two theories emerged. The first was that Charlie had a medical condition that affected his mind and made him snap that day. Earlier that summer, while breaking up some new fields, Charlie had been hit in the head with a tool. He didn't seem severely injured by it, but a few weeks later, after experiencing trouble sleeping, he started seeing a local doctor for what he described as blinding headaches. A few friends belatedly admitted that Charlie had never been the same after the injury.

The second theory that emerged was much more scandalous. There were rumors that Charlie had impregnated his teenage daughter, Marie, and had killed his family to prevent the incestuous scandal from being known.

Whatever the truth was, though, Charlie took it to his grave.

The murders attracted so much attention that at least 5,000 curiosity-seekers showed up for the funeral of the Lawsons, who were buried in a single plot at the Browder Family Cemetery. The funeral drew a lot of onlookers, but what happened next shocked many in the community.

To protect the Lawson murder house, Marion Lawson, one of Charlie's younger brothers, planted posts around the farm and strung up a wire fence around the site. Townspeople assumed that Marion was trying to keep away the morbidly curious, but that was not the case – he was turning the house into a tourist attraction.

In the spring of 1930, hundreds of travelers came to see the place where the murders occurred. They handled the family's belongings, gaped at the bloodstains on the floors and walls, and stood on the spot where the Lawson children breathed their last.

The locals grumbled about the "shameful" attraction for a time, but only until they realized that the tourists were stopping in town to eat, buy gas, and stay in the new hotel. With the money the town was making from the tourists, the little town began to thrive during an era when most of America was suffering. As morbid as it may sound, it's believed that Charlie Lawson saved Germanton from the Great Depression.

There were plenty of others who also got in on the act – publishing lurid booklets and even writing songs about the murders. One song about the massacre was recorded and released by a group called the Carolina Buddies in 1930, and it became a regional hit.

As the depression deepened in the mid-1930s and tourist traffic at the farm slowed down, the blood-stained furniture, photographs, clothing, and even Charlie's shotguns were packed up and taken on the road. A "Lawson Family Massacre" show began playing on carnival midways for the next few seasons, especially in the South and Midwest.

One of the biggest draws at the show was a two-layer Christmas cake that Marie made on the morning of the murders as a surprise for her family. The cake was still sitting on a counter, untouched, after the murders were discovered. It remained there for the next few years while the house was operated as a tourist attraction. However, it eventually had to be covered with a glass dome because visitors kept taking the raisins Marie had decorated the cake with as souvenirs. The cake remained a curiosity on the sideshow circuit, but after the show closed and the family items were returned home, a relative buried the cake on the Lawson farm.

After the Lawson sideshow closed, most of the family items were returned to the house, but as the decades passed, they fell into disrepair. Children and adults wandered the property, exploring and sometimes looking for ghosts. Many who ventured onto Charlie's old farm claimed to leave the place with a feeling of deep sadness. Many inexplicably burst into tears. Photographs taken there were often found to be blank when developed.

By 1980, the Lawson house was gone. But, even so, it was said that the ghosts remained. A neighbor claimed to see two children on her adjoining property that she claimed were two of the murdered children – Maybell and James.

There is also a lingering haunting in the nearby town of Madison. Long before it was the dry goods store that it is today, it was the local undertaker's parlor, and it was here that the bodies of the Lawson family were prepared for burial. The owners believe that Charlie's ghost haunts the place. Footsteps have frequently been heard in the empty back room, and the owners – and customers – have seen Charlie as he wanders about the place.

There are also said to be ghosts that linger at the Browder Family Cemetery, where the entire Lawson family was buried in a single mass grave. Voices and the sound of weeping has been heard in the graveyard, and local legend has it that if you drive out to the cemetery at night, park outside, sprinkle baby powder on the back of your car, and wait – the handprints of the Lawson family children will appear in the powder.

ELMER McCURDY

SOMETIMES, THE CRIME SHOWS THAT THRIVED ON CARNIVAL midways managed to surprise more than just the marks and rubes who coughed up their cash to look at the gruesome exhibits on display.

In 1976, a crew for a television show was filming a scene inside a dark ride in Long Beach, California, and accidentally knocked one of the funhouse figures from its hook. When the crew went to hang it back up, they saw what looked like a human bone protruding from the arm. A coroner who examined it announced that it was no dummy – it was an actual corpse.

And when the identity of the corpse was eventually learned, it revealed a history that was so strange and unusual that it could only be a take that involved the carnival sideshows.

THE CORPSE FOUND HANGING IN THAT FUNHOUSE in 1976 turned out to be the body of a failed and unlucky outlaw named Elmer McCurdy. He'd been born in Maine in 1880, the son of an unmarried 17-year-old named Sadie McCurdy.

In hopes of saving Sadie from the social stigma of raising an illegitimate child, her brother, George, and his wife, Helen, legally adopted Elmer. However, Sadie lived with the family and cared for her son. After George died of tuberculosis in 1890, Helen, Sadie, and Elmer moved to Bango, Maine. Sadie eventually told Elmer the truth, revealing she was his mother, and this caused Elmer to become "unruly and rebellious" during his teenage years. He began drinking heavily around this time, a habit that would continue throughout his life.

Elmer eventually went to live with his grandfather and became an apprentice plumber. He was a skilled worker and lived comfortably until an economic downturn in 1898. Elmer lost his job, and in 1900, his mother died from a ruptured ulcer, and his grandfather died from Bright's Disease in a span of just two months. Soon after his grandfather died, Elmer left Maine and started drifting around the eastern United States, working as a plumber and a miner.

ELMER MCCURDY – AND YES, HE WAS ALREADY DEAD WHEN THIS PHOTO WAS TAKEN. THE ONLY PHOTO OF HIM THAT EXISTS WAS TAKEN WHEN THE BODY WAS ALREADY IN A CASKET.

Unfortunately, thanks to his drinking, he was unable to hold onto a job for long, and he eventually drifted west to Kansas. He settled in Cherryvale for a while, working as a plumber again, and then moved to Iola, Kansas, where he was arrested for public intoxication in 1905.

Two years later, Elmer joined the U.S. Army. Assigned to Fort Leavenworth, he was trained to operate a machine gun and to use nitroglycerin for demolition purposes. He was honorably discharged in 1910.

After his stint in the military, Elmer made his way to St. Joseph, Kansas, where he met a friend from the army. On November 19, both men were arrested for possessing burglary tools – chisels, hacksaws, funnels for nitroglycerin, gunpowder, and money sacks. During his arraignment, Elmer told the judge they'd needed the tools to work on a foot-operated machine gun they were inventing. Two months later, a jury believed the story, and Elmer was acquitted – but his robbery career was just getting started.

Soon, Elmer put his training with explosives to good use. He began targeting banks and trains, but he turned out to be a lousy bandit. He usually failed to determine the correct amount of explosive to use, and his robberies turned into bungled affairs.

After moving to Lenapah, Oklahoma, in March 1911, Elmer and three other men decided to rob the Iron Mountain-Missouri Pacific Railroad train No. 104. Elmer had heard a rumor that one of the cars had a safe with $4,000 in it. They successfully stopped the train and located the safe, but then it was Elmer's turn. He measured out the nitroglycerin to blow the door but, of course, used too much. When the safe exploded, it was completely destroyed – and so was the cash inside. Elmer managed to grab a bag of silver coins worth about $500, although most of them had been melted in the blast.

On September 21, 1911, Elmer and two other men attempted to rob the Citizens Back in Chautauqua, Kansas. After spending two hours breaking through the bank wall with a hammer, Elmer placed a nitroglycerin charge around the door of the bank's outer vault. The massive blast that followed caused the vault door to launch outward into the bank, destroying everything in its past – but the indoor door to the vault remained locked. Elmer tried to blow that door open, too, but the charge wouldn't go off. After the lookout man got scared and ran off, Elmer and his partners stole about $150 in coins from the teller's windows and fled.

Later that night, the men hopped on a train that took them to the Kansas border. They split up from there, and Elmer made his way to a ranch owned by a friend outside Bartlesville, Oklahoma, where he camped out in the barn for a few days and drank away his troubles.

Elmer's final robbery took place on October 4, 1911, near Okesa, Oklahoma. He and two accomplices were after a train that was transporting $400,000 in cash that was intended to be a royalty payment to the Osage Nation. However, the bandits stopped a passenger train instead and were only about to steal $46 from the mail clerk, two bottles of whiskey, a revolver, a coat, and the conductor's watch. A newspaper account of the disaster later called it "one of the smallest in the history of train robbery."

Elmer, disappointed by another failed heist, returned to his friend's ranch on October 6, where he drank the two bottles of whiskey he had stolen. By this time, he was sick with tuberculosis – developed after working in the mines – and had a mild case of pneumonia. After getting drunk that night with some of the ranch hands, he went to sleep in the barn – not knowing that he'd been implicated in the failed train robbery and a $2,000 reward had been posted for his capture.

In the early morning hours of October 7, a posse of three deputy sheriffs, brothers Bob and Stringer Fenton and Dick Wallace, tracked Elmer to the ranch with bloodhounds. They surrounded the barn and wanted for daylight.

Around 7:00 A.M., Elmer stirred and realized he was surrounded – and his escape went about as well as his robberies did. After exchanging gunfire with the lawmen outside for nearly an hour – Elmer missing every shot, of course -- the gunshots from inside stopped, and the deputies crept into the barn.

They discovered that Elmer had been killed by a single bullet wound to the chest. And after that, things started to get weird.

ELMER'S BODY WAS TAKEN TO THE UNDERTAKER IN Pawhuska, Oklahoma, where it went unclaimed. After a few days of waiting for someone to show up and pay for a burial, owner, and undertaker Joseph L. Johnson embalmed the body with an arsenic-based preservative, typically used to preserve a body for a long period of time. He then shaved Elmer's face, dressed the body in a suit, and stored it in the back of the funeral home.

As the weeks dragged on without Elmer's corpse being claimed, Johnson refused to release the body until he was paid for his services. Finally, he decided to exhibit the body to make some money. He dressed the body in work clothes, placed a rifle in its hands, and propped it up in the corner of the funeral home. For a nickel, Johnson allowed visitors to see the "Bandit Who Wouldn't Give Up," The corpse became a popular attraction at the funeral home and later drew the attention of carnival promoters. Johnson received dozens of offers from showmen trying to buy the embalmed bandit, but Johnson always refused.

Then, on October 6, 1916, a man named Aver contacted the undertaker, claiming to be Elmer's long-lost brother from California. Aver had already spoken with the Osage County sheriff and a local attorney and obtained permission to take custody of the body and have it shipped to California for a proper burial.

The following day, Aver arrived at the funeral home with a man named Wayne, who also claimed to be Elmer's brother. Johnson released the body to the men, who then loaded it on a train, presumably bound for San Francisco.

It wasn't. The body was instead taken to Arkansas City, Kansas, because the men who claimed to be Elmer's brothers were, in fact, James and Charles Patterson, owners of the Great Patterson Carnival Shows. After hearing about the popular "Embalmed Bandit," the two concocted a scheme to get the corpse and feature it in the carnival's sideshow. The body continued to be featured in the carnival as "The Outlaw Who Would Never Be Captured Alive" until 1922 when the operation was sold to another showman, Louis Sonney.

Sonney used Elmer's corpse in his traveling Museum of Crime, which featured wax figures of famous outlaws like the Dalton gang, Jesse James, and others. Sonney continued touring with the body for years. In 1933, it was loaned out to director Dwain Esper to promote his exploitation film *Narcotic*. Elmer's corpse was placed in the lobby of the theaters as a "dead dope fiend," whom Esper claimed had committed suicide while surrounded by the police after robbing a drug store to support his habit.

By then, Elmer's body was in pretty bad shape. It had become mummified, and the skin had become hard and shriveled, causing the body to shrink. Esper, however, claimed that the body's deterioration was proof of the supposed drug fiend's drug abuse.

After Sonney died in 1949, Elmer's corpse was placed in storage in a Los Angeles warehouse. In 1964, Sonney's son, Dan, loaned out the body to filmmaker David F. Friedman, resulting in a brief appearance in Friedman's film *She Freak* (1967).

The following year, Dan sold the body with the other wax figures for $10,000 to Spoony Singh, the owner of the Hollywood Wax Museum. They were not for his museum but to be loaned out for two showmen from Canada, who'd arranged an exhibit at Mount Rushmore in South Dakota. While on display there, Elmer's corpse sustained some damage during a windstorm, which damaged the tips of the ears, as well as the fingers and toes. When the corpse was eventually returned to Singh, he decided that it looked "too gruesome" and no longer lifelike, so he sold it to Ed Liersch, co-owner of The Pike, an amusement area

THE LAFF IN THE DARK FUNHOUSE IN LONG BEACH, WHERE THE BODY OF ELMER MCCURDY HAD BEEN USED AS A PROP FOR SEVERAL YEARS.

in Long Beach, California. Elmer's body was moved into the Laff in the Dark funhouse, where it hung from a gallows as a prop for several years.

Then, on December 8, 1976, the production crew of the television series *The Six Million Dollar Man* was filming scenes at The Pike for an episode called "Carnival of Spies." During the shoot, a prop man moved what was thought to be a wax mannequin hanging from a rope, but when its arm broke off, the prop man was stunned to see human bone and muscle tissue in the "fake" arm.

It wasn't a mannequin – it was an embalmed human corpse.

The police were notified of the discovery, and the corpse was taken to the Los Angeles coroner's office. On December 9, Dr. Joseph Choi conducted an autopsy and determined that the body was that of a human male who had died of a gunshot wound to the chest. The body was nearly petrified, covered in wax and layers of phosphorus paint. It weighed approximately 50 pounds and was five feet, three inches in length. A small amount of hair was still visible on the sides and back of the head, while the ears, big toes, and fingers were missing.

The examination revealed incisions from the original embalming, and tests conducted on the tissue showed the presence of arsenic, which had been used in most embalming fluids until the late 1920s. The corpse also showed damage from tuberculosis in the lungs, as well as bunions and scars that were later matched to Elmer McCurdy. While the bullet that caused the fatal wound was presumably removed during the original autopsy, the bullet jacket was found. It was a type that was used between 1905 and 1940, which helped investigators narrow down the years when the man had been killed.

More clues were found when the jawbone was removed from the body for dental analysis. Inside the mouth was a 1924 penny and a ticket stub for Louis Sonney's Museum of Crime, likely placed there by a prankster who'd toured the show at a carnival. The police traced Louis Sonney, which led them to Dan Sonney, who told them that the body belonged to Elmer McCurdy. A forensic anthropologist named Dr. Clyde Snow confirmed the identification using radiographs of the skull, which he compared to photographs of Elmer.

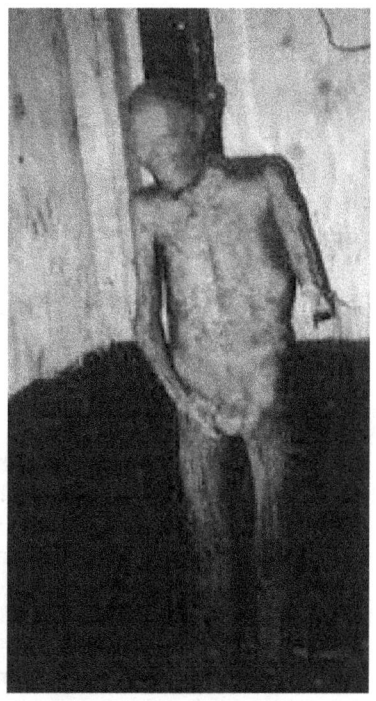

MCCURDY'S BODY IN 1976, AFTER IT WAS DISCOVERED THAT THE FUNHOUSE "PROP" WAS ACTUALLY THE BODY OF WHAT HAD APPEARED IN SIDESHOWS AS "THE EMBALMED OUTLAW."

By December 11, Elmer's story had been featured in newspapers, on television, and the radio. Several funeral homes called the coroner's office and offered to bury McCurdy free of charge, but officials decided to wait and see if any living relatives – real relatives, this time – could come forward and claim the body.

None were found, but Fred Olds, who represented the Indian Territory Posse of Oklahoma Westerns, eventually convinced the authorities to allow him to bury the body in Oklahoma. After a few more tests to ensure the body really did belong to Elmer McCurdy, Olds was allowed to take custody of the body.

On April 22, 1977, the remains of Elmer McCurdy were taken to the Boot Hill section of the Summit View Cemetery in Guthrie, Oklahoma. Around 300 people attended a graveside service, and Elmer was buried next to Bill Doolin. To make sure the body stayed where it was supposed to be, two feet of concrete was poured over the casket.

Elmer's body had traveled far enough. After 66 years, "The Outlaw Who Would Never Be Captured Alive" certainly earned the right to rest in peace.

"THE ASSASSIN WHO KILLED PRESIDENT LINCOLN"

ELMER MCCURDY'S BODY WASN'T THE ONLY ONE DISPLAYED in sideshows across the country – not by a long shot – but there was another that had a mystery connected to it that was so baffling it remains unsolved today.

Maybe.

This is a story about a man named Finis L. Bates and his search for the truth of what really happened to one of the most infamous men in American history – John Wilkes Booth, the actor who assassinated Abraham Lincoln.

IN THE EARLY 1870S, FINIS BATES WAS A YOUNG ATTORNEY living in Granbury, Texas. His practice was struggling, so he must have been happy when a new client named John St. Helen walked into his office one day and asked for help defending him against a charge of operating a saloon without a license in the nearby town of Glen Rose. St. Helen admitted that he was guilty of the offense but did not want to appear in federal court over it. John St. Helen was not his real name, he confessed, and feared that his true identity might be exposed in court.

Bates took the case and resolved the issue for him. St. Helen became a regular client, and he got to know the man fairly well. He later recalled that St. Helen seemed to have more money than his status should have allowed and that he had an intimate knowledge of the theater and the works of Shakespeare, most of which he could recite from memory.

Then, late one night in 1877, Bates was summoned to the sickbed of his client. St. Helen was seriously ill, and he told Bates that he did not expect to live much longer. He directed Bates to reach under his pillow, and the attorney pulled out an old tintype that showed the face of a much younger St. Helen. The sick man told the attorney that if he died, he was to send the photograph to a man named Edwin

FINIS L. BATES – MUCH OLDER THAN WHEN THE STORY BEGAN – AND THE BOOK HE WROTE ABOUT WHAT HE BELIEVED WAS THE TRUE STORY OF JOHN WILKES BOOTH AND HIS ESCAPE FROM THE LAW.

Booth in Baltimore with a note that said the subject of the tintype had passed away. In between coughing fits, St. Helen explained to the stunned attorney that his real name was John Wilkes Booth and that he had assassinated former President Abraham Lincoln.

Bates was shocked and dismayed at the revelation, but he knew that he could not betray his client's confidence. He replied that he would send the photograph if needed, and he sat next to St. Helen's bed throughout the rest of the night, waiting for the man to die. His mind whirled throughout the night, stunned by the secret that he learned. He wondered what he would have done about it had his client not been dying.

But John St. Helen didn't die.

He was sick for several weeks, but then he began to recover. Once he recovered, he met with Bates and again confessed to being John Wilkes Booth. He begged for the attorney to keep the secret, and Bates was bound by attorney-client privilege – he had to agree. He did demand some answers, though, knowing full well that John Wilkes Booth was reportedly dead.

JOHN WILKES BOOTH – ONE THING WE DO KNOW ABOUT THIS STORY IS THAT HE ASSASSINATED PRESIDENT ABRAHAM LINCOLN. BEYOND THAT? IT'S A WILD AND CONFUSING MESS.

Booth explained that Andrew Johnson, the vice president, was the principal conspirator behind the assassination. St. Helen said that he had met with Johnson just hours before Lincoln was killed, and Johnson told him that with General Grant away from Washington, Booth would have an easy escape route into Maryland. St. Helen then went on to provide details of the assassination plot, the actual event, his escape from Ford's Theater, and his flight into the countryside.

His descriptions were detailed, and to Bates, who initially believed none of the far-fetched story, they seemed to have intricacies that only someone intimately involved with the assassination plot would have known. Most of all, they were different enough from the published accounts of the events that Bates reluctantly began to think St. Helen's story might be true.

St. Helens told the attorney that he had escaped into Kentucky in late April and eventually made his way west of the Mississippi and into the Indian Territory. After spending some time there, he disguised himself as a priest and entered Mexico. In 1867, he traveled to California and met with his mother and older brother, Junius, in San Francisco. Later, he drifted to New Orleans, where he taught school, and then moved to Texas, where he assumed the name John St. Helen and opened a tavern.

Bates was never entirely convinced by the story – it was just too much to believe -- and the two eventually parted ways. Several months after he heard the confession, Bates moved to Memphis, where he established a new law practice. He became very successful, and as the years passed, he developed a deep interest in Abraham Lincoln, especially in the events surrounding his death. In his spare time, he read everything that he could get his hands on about Lincoln and

Booth, and the more he studied, the more convinced he became that his old client had been telling the truth.

John St. Helen, he believed, really had been John Wilkes Booth.

ON JANUARY 13, 1903, THE STORY TOOK ANOTHER TURN.

The corpse of a man named David E. George arrived at the undertaking parlor of W.B. Penniman in Enid, Oklahoma. George, who had been working in Enid as a handyman and house painter, had apparently committed suicide by ingesting a large dose of strychnine. He was known about town as a heavy drinker and was frequently depressed. No one was terribly surprised that he had ended his life.

As Penniman's assistant, W.H. Ryan, was embalming George's body, the Reverend E.C. Harper stopped in at the funeral parlor. Harper urgently needed to talk to the undertaker. He had a stunning story to tell – the dead man on the embalming table, he explained, was none other than John Wilkes Booth!

He had confessed his identity to the minister's wife in 1900. Mrs. Harper was summoned, and she identified the corpse of David E. George as the man who had told her that he was Booth. She later wrote and signed a statement, swearing that the confession had taken place.

Over the course of the next few days, several newspapers carried the story that a man believed to be Booth had died in Oklahoma. One of the newspaper stories caught the attention of Finis Bates in Memphis, and he wondered if the late David E. George might be the man he once knew as John St. Helen. Curious, he decided to go to Enid and see.

Bates arrived in Oklahoma on January 23 and, the next morning, went to the undertaker's parlor to compare the face of the dead man with the tintype photograph that he still possessed. He placed it next to the face of the corpse and compared them. It was, Bates stated without a doubt, the same man.

The body remained on display at Penniman's parlor, and after months had passed without it being claimed, it was moved into storage in a back room, where visitors were still allowed to see it for a small admission fee.

Years later, Finis Bates, still interested in the mystery of the body, made Penniman an offer and purchased the remains of David George, who he was still convinced had been John Wilkes Booth. By this time, the body had turned brown and had shriveled. The undertaker had used a strong, arsenic-based preservative on the body, and over time, it appeared as though it had been mummified.

In October 1931, the corpse was examined by a group of seven doctors at Chicago's Northwestern University. It was studied, x-rayed, and dissected, and the team found evidence of a healed broken leg, although the report did not state whether it was on the right or the left. Booth had broken a leg jumping from the president's box at Ford's Theatre on the night of the assassination.

The most compelling discovery, though, was that of a ring that had somehow become embedded in the flesh of the body cavity. Digestive juices had damaged it over time, but the researchers present believed that the initials "JWB" could be discerned on the surface of it. Dr. Otto L. Schmidt, president of the Chicago Historical Society at that time, subsequently wrote, "I can say safely that we believe Booth's body is here in my office."

THE EMBALMED BODY OF DAVID E. GEORGE AT PENNIMAN'S FUNERAL PARLOR IN ENID, OKLAHOMA, WHILE STILL ON DISPLAY THERE. MANY MAINTAINED THAT GEORGE WAS ACTUALLY JOHN WILKES BOOTH.

Finis Bates eventually sold the body, and by the late 1920s, it was making regular appearances on carnival midways across the country, where a promoter named J.W. Wilkerson was charging 25 cents for customers to view "The Assassin of President Abraham Lincoln."

He continued to exhibit the Booth mummy into the 1940s, but after he went bankrupt and moved to Idaho, he resorted to placing the corpse in a chair on his front porch and charging visitors a dime to look at it.

Eventually, the mummy disappeared, and to this day, no one knows what became of it. It is rumored to be in a private collection somewhere, but no one knows for sure.

The question of where this carnival show attraction finally ended up is just as mysterious as the questions that linger today about John Wilkes Booth. Was the man that Finis Bates as John St. Helen and David George actually John Wilkes Booth?

Some think it's possible.

The two men had many of the same character traits. They were both heavy drinkers with a flair for the dramatic. Both had an intimate knowledge of Shakespeare and an extensive education, and they favored the same style of clothing. In addition, there were many striking physical similarities between the two men, including the shapes of their heads, jaw lines, and the bridges of their noses. And while this isn't positive proof of anything, it is intriguing.

THE JOHN WILKES BOOTH (?) MUMMY IN 1931, WHEN IT WAS EXAMINED AT NORTHWESTERN UNIVERSITY. IT WAS ALSO ON TOUR WITH CARNIVAL SIDESHOWS AT THIS SAME TIME.

However, there are also problems with the theory.

According to the undertaker in Enid, George had blue-gray eyes, while government documents say Booth's eyes were black. On the other hand, Asia Booth, the actor's sister, wrote that they were hazel.

Finis Bates wrote that David George had a broken right leg, not the left leg that Booth broke jumping from the theater box. Of course, the government's own records stated that the body that was dug up from beneath the floor of the Old Penitentiary had a broken right leg, but that was just one notation. Everyone else agreed that Booth's left leg was broken.

Bates showed photographs of David George to a number of people who had known Booth, including those who had seen him perform many times. All of them stated that the man in both photos was John Wilkes Booth.

Another mysterious piece of evidence involved the signet ring worn by Booth. The actor was seldom seen without the ring, which was inscribed with his initials, and he was photographed wearing it many times. The ring was not on the finger of the man who was killed by Union troops in Virginia, even though everyone agreed it was Booth.

Many recalled that David George wore a similar ring. Some weeks before his death, George told one of his neighbors that he was being followed. That same neighbor told Finis Bates that when George saw two sheriff's deputies walking toward him one afternoon, his paranoia got the better of him, and he removed the ring from his finger and swallowed it. As we know, when the David George mummy was autopsied in 1931, a ring was discovered in its stomach with the initials "JWB" on it.

Even though the chances of Booth escaping death in Virginia, only to die almost 40 years later, are somewhere between slim and none, there are enough odd bits of evidence mixed into the whole thing that the story stayed alive for decades – and brought a lot of people into sideshow tents for a look at the mummy of the man who may have killed the president.

CRIME ON WHEELS

BY THE LATE 1930S, SHOWMEN HAD STARTED ADDING CRIME CARS to their shows. A crime show that toured with Hennies Brothers in 1941 had a bullet-riddled gangster car parked behind the bally platform. Although the guy on the bally wore a prison uniform and leg irons, the show inside was on film. Continuous news clips and stock footage showed the execution of Bruno Hauptmann – kidnapper of the Lindbergh Baby – the ambush of Bonnie and Clyde, and the killing of John Dillinger. An expose of sex maniacs of the underworld was the blow-off feature.

In that show, the gangster car was the bally, but most showmen were using crime cars as the main attraction, just as so many showmen had done with Hiter's (many) cars after World War II. Crime cars became a lucrative draw for savvy promoters. However, establishing the authenticity of the cars and tracking down their owners was another story, as was shown by what happened with Al Capone's "original" car.

Harry La Breque, the secretary of the New Jersey State Fair, owned several attractions at amusement parks on the east coast. In 1933, he bought Al Capone's 1931 Lincoln, which Jersey gangster Dutch Schultz had built. Cashing in on a European fascination with American mobsters, he sent the car to England for a tour of fairs and carnivals. In 1956, though, the car was suddenly placed into storage, and a rumor circulated that it had been removed from an exhibition at the suggestion of the U.S. State Department, which wanted to play down

ONE OF THE MANY "REAL" AL CAPONE CARS ON ONE OF THE MANY CARNIVAL MIDWAYS WHERE IT WAS DISPLAYED FOR YEARS.

the image that America had gained as a place of crime and gangsters. Two years later, the car was purchased by Tony Stuart, who returned it to the United States.

At the same time, though, Frank Platten of Sacramento, California, listed a car that he had for sale --- Dutch Schultz's 1931 Lincoln, which Al Capone had also owned. And no, it was not the same car that had been in England for two decades.

And that wasn't the only one. The Mighty Sheesley Shows had been exhibiting Al Capone's car since 1936, and Carl Sedlmayr, Jr. started showing a Capone car with the Royal American Midways in 1938.

Visitors to the Minnesota State Fair in 1975 not only got to see Al Capone's car but also met one of his drivers, 76-year-old Morris "Red" Rudensky. Red, who had known Capone for years, had spent most of his life in jail and

A YOUNG MORRIS "RED" EUDENSKY WHEN HE WORKED FOR CAPONE.

had even shared a cell with the boss at the federal penitentiary in Atlanta after Capone was convicted of tax evasion. The car belonged to a man named Paul Elkins, who owned the Gay '90s Village in Sikeston, Missouri, and had bought Capone's 1931 Cadillac from a millionaire in Arizona. He'd found Red working in a factory in St. Paul, and he attested to the authenticity of the car, claiming that only 43 Cadillacs with that particular body shape had been made. Not only that, but Capone had spent $50,000 to have this one customized with armored plates and window slots for machine guns.

So, that's at least five cars that claimed to be Al Capone's "original" ride, but who owned the real one remains a mystery.

A CAR ALLEGED TO HAVE BEEN USED FOR A SUCCESSFUL ESCAPE BY JOHN DILLINGER MADE THE ROUNDS OF SIDESHOWS BEFORE LATER ENDING UP IN A AUTO MUSEUM.

IT'S PROBABLY NO SURPRISE THAT A "JOHN DILLINGER CAR" joined others on the midways in the 1940s. Tom Hughes had switched from owning rides to operating grind shows when he bought a crime car in 1948 and started touring it as one once driven by John Dillinger. The 1931 V-8 Lincoln was completely armored, including the roof, and was custom-built with one-inch bullet-proof glass windows and a secret machine gun compartment. The windows had slots from which to fire guns.

I've found no information about where Hughes' car came from, where he acquired it, or where he found the information that linked it to Dillinger, but this was the kind of car the bank robber preferred. Dillinger didn't actually own any vehicles during his 1933-1934 crime spree, but he frequently stole them, and when he did, he always looked for new, powerful cars with large engines. It was easy for him to escape from pursuing police officers, who normally had older, outdated vehicles that Dillinger and his gang easily left in the dust.

But that's not the only thing that suggests this might have been a Dillinger car. He frequently used a garage located on Broadway in Chicago that would bulletproof a car with steel plates behind the backseat, which prevented bullets from pursuing vehicles, getting through to hit the occupants of the car.

Hughes continued to exhibit the car until 1916 when he put it up for sale for $1,000. What happened to it after that is unknown.

THERE IS NO CRIME CAR. HOWEVER, THAT IS AS FAMOUS as the "Bonnie and Clyde Death Car" that the bandit couple were killed in back in May 1934.

The "Death Car" – or perhaps I should say "cars" plural – have a colorful history on American midways, starting back in 1939. That was the year that Charles W. Stanley, a crime expert known for the "blood operas" he staged for the midway, began showing the "real" Bonnie and Clyde car. Stanley used the vehicle outside for bally purposes because inside the tent was a film that showed the actual ambush.

He continued touring with the car at carnivals, state fairs, and Coney Island until 1952 when he posted an ad offering the "Bonnie Parker and Clyde Barrow world-famous bullet-riddled death car" for sale. Apparently, though, it didn't sell, and he retired from the road that season to manage the Coney Island amusement park in Cincinnati. He was still exhibiting his car there in 1960.

But like the "original" Al Capone car, Stanley's Bonnie and Clyde Death Car wasn't the only one making the rounds on American midways.

In 1949, showman Charlie Hodges exhibited a Bonnie and Clyde car with his Ten-In-One show. In 1968, veteran promoter Frank Siro also had a Bonnie and Clyde car on midways.

And so did showman Ted Toddy, who not only claimed to have the original car but was willing to defend it against all the fakes and frauds that were out there. In fact, he won a suit for an injunction over the use of the Bonnie and Clyde name in 1969. He had sued Johnny and Marilyn Portemont – owners of Johnny's United Shows – who also claimed to have the "real" death car. Showmen were warned to avoid using that name, especially around Toddy's home base of Atlanta.

In 1971, Toddy leased his car to Royal American Shows, who promised to build a $50,000 trailer and front for it. The car and a short clip from the Bonnie and Clyde ambush film were shown that season. In 1972, the bookkeeper for Royal American shows, Guy Gardiner, leased the car and exhibited it during that season – which would be its last on the midway. In early 1973, it was announced that the trailer and exhibition equipment would be sold off that spring, and the car would be returned to Toddy.

After that, the story took another turn, but we'll come back to that in a moment. First, we're going to go back to 1934 and trace the journey of the authentic Bonnie and Clyde death car and see where it ended up – and who actually had the right to defend the use of the name.

BONNIE AND CLYDE DROVE TO THEIR DEATH ON THE morning of May 23, 1934. They were lured to the family farm of a young gunman named Henry Methvin, who'd been on the road with them. But the couple had no idea that Henry's father, Ivy, had arranged for them to be captured by a group of lawmen led by former Texas Ranger Frank Hamer.

They also had no idea that the lawmen had no interest in capturing them. The six of them had parked and hiked to the ambush site with an arsenal of weapons, where they settled down to wait. When Bonnie and Clyde drove down that isolated country road, the lawmen planned to open fire.

Around sunrise, a nervous Ivy Methvin joined them at the site. He parked an old truck on the side of the road, jacked it up, and removed a tire. The cops figured that Clyde might pass the ambush spot, but if he saw Henry's father next to a broken-down truck, he'd likely stop to see if he needed help.

Hamer and the other lawmen waited for hours, swatting mosquitoes while Bonnie and Clyde were getting breakfast from a local café. They were eating sandwiches as they drove toward the Methvin house.

The lawmen heard the Ford V-8 before they saw it, and then there it was, flying along the road. As they got closer, Clyde saw Henry standing next to his truck and saw the tire lying on the road next to it. He slowed down, coming almost to a stop.

The men hiding in the woods carefully aimed their guns.

Just then, a logging truck appeared, coming from the other direction. Clyde rolled forward to make room for it to pass.

In the brush, Deputy Prentiss Oakley tensed up. Maybe he believed that Clyde was driving off, or perhaps he was overcome with nerves, or, more likely, Frank Hamer had made it clear that Bonnie and Clyde didn't need to be taken alive. There was no need to give them a chance to surrender.

Oakley fired two times. One of his bullets hit Clyde just in front of his left ear, probably killing him instantly.

The only sound for a moment was Bonnie's scream.

Then, the other lawmen opened fire. Bullets rained down on the Ford, shattering glass, punching holes in steel, and ripping apart the bodies of the couple inside. It was a continuous roar that went on for several minutes. Hundreds of bullets pounded into the car and made Bonnie and Clyde shake and jerk back and forth across the front seat. The screaming had since stopped, but the gunfire continued long after the outlaws were dead.

THE CAR THAT CLYDE AND BONNIE HAD BEEN DRIVING ON THAT MAY MORNING WAS FILLED WITH BULLET HOLES AFTER THE AMBUSH BY THE POSSEE LED BY FORMER TEXAS RANGER, FRANK HAMER.

(BELOW) THE BODIES OF BONNIE AND CLYDE AFTER THE AMBUSH

When it finally stopped, Clyde slumped sideways, and his foot came off the brake pedal. The car rolled forward a short distance and slid into a ditch.

Deputy Sheriff Bob Alcorn worried they were still alive – or so he later claimed – came down the hill and fired more shots through the broken back window of the car. The bullets punched into the backs of the lifeless outlaws' heads.

THE BONNIE AND CLYDE "DEATH CAR" WAS SEEN BY THOUSANDS OF PEOPLE AFTER IT WAS TOWED FROM THE AMBUSH SITE.

    The inside of the car looked like a slaughterhouse. Part of Clyde's skull was now missing. Bonnie's right hand was gone. Blood and tissue covered the car's interior. Clyde's head was hanging out the window. After Alcorn's last shots, Bonnie had fallen forward against the dash.
    There were guns near them in the car, but neither had time to raise them or to return fire. There had been no threat to the lives of the lawmen. In interviews after the ambush, some of the lawmen claimed they had yelled for them to stop or had told them to surrender, but those stories were outright lies.
    After the smoke cleared, Ivy Methvin took off. Hamer and two others went to the closest towns to find a coroner, get a tow truck, and make telephone calls to take credit for killing Bonnie and Clyde.
    By the time the lawmen returned to the ambush site, locals who'd heard the gunfire were already converging on the scene. When they found out what happened – and who was killed -- they grabbed any kind of souvenir they could. They pried loose pieces of broken glass

and stole snippets of hair and clothing. Others picked up bullets and shotgun shells.

A tow truck took the bullet-riddled car – with its bloody occupants still inside – to Arcadia, Louisiana, roughly 10 miles away. A caravan of at least 150 vehicles followed behind it. Thousands more gathered in Arcadia, hoping for a glimpse of the car and the bodies.

In town, the bodies were placed on stretchers and taken in through the back doors of Conger's Furniture store, which doubled as a funeral home.

The coroner announced that Bonnie and Clyde had both been hit more than two dozen times. He recorded their many wounds, cuts, scars, and tattoos in the small, hot, crowded room while the mob grew outside. Eager to see the dead bandits, more than 500 people had jammed into the furniture store, ripping a door off its hinges, climbing on new furniture, and causing about $1,000 in damages. The streets outside were full.

Once the paperwork was completed, the bodies were covered by white sheets up to the necks and moved out into the store's showroom. Just out of reach of the crowd, they were put on display, and once a semblance of order was restored, the curiosity-seekers filed past for a look over the next several hours.

Just as people would continue to do with the car, the couple died in over the decades to come.

AFTER THE AMBUSH, THE FORD V-8 THAT CLYDE HAD BEEN driving was towed to Arcadia with the bodies of the slain couple still inside. It ended up at the local funeral parlor and then ended up in the possession of Bienville Parish Sheriff Henderson Jordan, who had been a member of the ambush party.

Jordan fully intended to keep the car, I guess believing he'd earned it for setting up the outlaw pair to be killed. But Jordan hadn't counted on the tenacity of Ruth Warren, the owner of the car. Clyde had stolen the Ford from her garage in Topeka, Kansas, and she wanted it back. When she contacted Jordan, he told her that she'd have to pay $15,000 to claim it – so she took him to court. She won the case and, in August 1934, had the Ford back in her possession. It had been untouched since Bonnie and Clyde had died in it, so it was still covered in blood and tissue.

She was smart enough not to clean it.

Instead, she sold the car to John Castle, who began exhibiting it the following season. Unfortunately, though, he didn't make the payments on time, and attorneys for Ruth Warren had it repossessed.

THE BONNIE AND CLYDE "DEATH CAR" IS ON DISPLAY TODAY AT BUFFALO BILL'S CASINO IN PRIMM, NEVADA, JUST WEST OF LAS VEGAS.

Finally, she sold the bullet-riddled car to Charles Stanley, whose claims of having the "real" Bonnie and Clyde Death Car turned out to be true. After he retired, he continued to show the car at the amusement park in Cincinnati until selling it to Ted Toddy in the early 1960s.

Toddy exhibited the car until 1971 when he leased it out for the next few seasons. It was during that decade or so that it gained an unusual reputation.

Hugely popular on carnival midways, it attracted thousands of people who wanted to see the car the famous couple died in. After a movie about their exploits was released, starring Warren Beatty and Faye Dunaway, in 1967, there was an even bigger demand for tickets. During this time, visitors were even allowed to sit inside the car and have their photos taken – for an extra fee, of course.

But many who paid to see the Ford during those years claimed to be overwhelmed by creepy, unnatural feelings while standing near the car. Many burst into tears or became so frightened after being touched by unseen hands that they ran away screaming.

After the Death Car was returned to him, Toddy sold it to Peter A. Simon, owner of the Oasis Casino in Jean, Nevada, for $175,000 – a price tag that set a new record for the sale of an antique automobile. It sold again in 1988 to Primm Valley Casino Resorts for $250,000. Over the next decade or so, the car was on and off display and was even loaned out for a while to the FBI.

When the car was returned, it was placed on display at Whiskey Pete's Casino in Primm, Nevada, about a half-hour west of Las Vegas on Interstate 15. It remained there for years before being moved to the other side of the highway to Buffalo Bill's, another casino owned by Primm Valley Casino Resorts.

I WAS LUCKY ENOUGH TO GET TO SIT IN THE BONNIE AND CLYDE CAR WHEN I WAS IN LAS VEGAS IN 2024.

Visitors to Buffalo Bill's can see not only the car with its 112 bullet holes but also a display that features a timeline of Bonnie and Clyde's exploits, artifacts owned by them, and even the bloody, bullet-torn shirt that Clyde was wearing on the day of the ambush.

It's behind glass today, but before it was, the feelings of dread once reported on carnival midways continued to be experienced by visitors – as were the sensations of being touched. Some reported hearing a whisper in their ear as they stood next to the car. The whispers, they claimed, told them to "go away" – and they usually did.

ED GEIN'S "DEATH CAR"

THERE IS ONE MORE DEATH CAR THAT IS WORTHY OF MENTION, although its time on carnival midways was short and ended with the car disappearing and never being seen again. This car once belonged to the infamous Wisconsin killer and graverobber, Ed Gein.

WISCONSIN GHOUL ED GEIN

Edward Theodore Gein grew up on a farm a few miles outside of the small town of Plainfield, Wisconsin. His father, George, was a hard-luck farmer with little talent for working the soil and a taste for alcohol. He was a drunk and a bully, but he was no match for his wife, Augusta.

Augusta was a terrifying woman who hated alcohol, men, and anything to do with sex. How she managed to become pregnant with her two sons, Eddie and Henry, remains a mystery. She considered the small town where they lived a terrible place and kept her sons on the farm away from the sinful influences of women and carnal love.

In 1940, George Gein dropped dead from a heart attack. Most likely, he was not sorry to go. The years spent with Augusta had undoubtedly taken their toll on him.

The two boys were left alone with their mother, and soon Ed was even deeper under her terrible spell. Henry attempted to break away and have a normal life, but his rebelliousness came with a price. In 1944, he was found dead on the Gein property. The young man had allegedly died from a heart attack. Apparently, when he had fallen over, he was bashed in the back of his head.

Ed finally had his mother all to himself, but that also came with a price. In 1945, Augusta had a stroke and was confined to bed. Ed waited on her night and day when she screamed at him and criticized him for hours at a time. Then she grew quiet and told Ed to crawl into bed with her while she whispered to him as he slept. Ed prayed that she'd never die and leave him alone.

Because, you know, a boy's best friend is his mother.

Ed's prayers failed him, though, and Augusta died in December 1945. Ed was now 39 and alone to fend for himself. It was at this point that he began to descend into madness.

For a while, no one seemed to notice. Even in a town as small as Plainfield, Ed was a loner and rarely ventured off the farm. He only showed up in town when he needed to run an errand, perform some handyman chores, or stop in for an occasional beer at Mary Hogan's tavern. No one seemed to think that he was any stranger than before. He had always been an odd little man in need of a bath, but he seemed no different than he had been before his mother's death.

AUGUSTA GEIN – A BOY'S BEST FRIEND IS HIS MOTHER

It would be later – after the horrors of his farmhouse were revealed – that Gein's peculiarities seemed to stand out. Local folks would later recall his barroom discussions of articles that he had read in men's magazines -- stories of Nazi atrocities, island headhunters, and sex-change operations.

His sense of humor was a little odd, too. When Mary Hogan, the tavern owner, suddenly disappeared, Ed began joking that she was staying overnight at his house. Mary had vanished from the roadhouse, leaving nothing but a puddle of blood behind, and many thought Gein's jokes about the poor woman were tasteless but nothing more.

Ed would never hurt anybody, the townspeople thought. He was a strange little guy who disliked the sight of blood. He wouldn't even go deer hunting with the other fellows in town.

That's what everyone in Plainfield said – until Bernice Worden disappeared.

She vanished on November 16, 1957. That afternoon, her son, Frank, returned to town after an unsuccessful day of deer hunting and stopped by the hardware store that his mother owned and operated.

Strangely, Bernice wasn't there. She had apparently just walked out, leaving the front door unlocked and the back door standing open. Frank then discovered something terrifying -- a trail of blood leading from the storefront to the back door. A quick search revealed a receipt

THE GEIN FARMHOUSE, LOCATED OUTSIDE OF PLAINFIELD, WISCONSIN.

(BELOW) ONLY ONE OF THE MANY VIEWS OF THE HORRIFIC CONDITIONS INSIDE OF GEIN'S HOME

that had been left behind. The receipt was for a half gallon of antifreeze. It had been made out to Ed Gein.

Frank notified the police, and sheriff's deputies went to Gein's farmhouse to question him about Mrs. Worden's whereabouts. Ed had not been expecting company, as was evidenced by what they found in the summer kitchen behind the house.

In the broken-down little building, they discovered the body of the missing Bernice Worden. She was naked and hanging by her heels from an overhead pulley. She had been beheaded and disemboweled and was dressed out like a butchered deer.

Ed had been in the process of tanning her hide and had used the skin of her face to create what appeared to be a mask. No one knew what he planned to do with them – not yet, anyway.

The stunned and sickened officers immediately called for reinforcements. A short time later, more than a dozen lawmen were combing the farm and exploring the contents of what would become known as Ed Gein's "house of horrors." What they found that night was like nothing that had ever been seen before by American law enforcement.

The state of the dilapidated house was beyond anything the lawmen could imagine. The only room that was clean and orderly was

ED GEIN SOUP BOWL MADE FROM A HUMAN SKULL. (RIGHT) AN INVESTIGATOR REMOVES A CHAIR WITH A SEAT MADE FROM HUMAN SKIN.

his mother's former bedroom. Ed had left it just as it was when she died. It was sealed off from the squalor of the rest of the house.

The rest of the house was a nightmare.

The police found chairs that had been upholstered in human skin. Lamp shades had been fashioned from flesh, giving off an eerie and yellow glow. A box that contained nothing but human noses was discovered. A belt had been made from female nipples. A shoe box found under a bed contained a collection of dried female genitalia. Soup bowls were made from the sawed-off tops of human skulls. A human head was found in a box.

The faces of nine women, carefully mounted, were hanging on one wall,

A HUMAN HEAD FOUND INSIDE OF A BOX IN GEIN'S HOME (BELOW) A TANNED BELT MADE FROM WOMEN'S NIPPLES

peering down at furniture that had been constructed out of human bones. On a table was a bracelet of skin, a drum made from a coffee can and human flesh, scattered pieces of human remains, and more.

One of the most disturbing discoveries was the vest that had been fashioned and sewn from a female torso, complete with breasts. The skin had been taken from a middle-aged woman and tanned like deerskin. Ed later confessed that he often put the shirt on at night and pretended to be his mother.

During the many hours of confession that followed, Ed admitted to the murders of two women: Bernice Worden and tavern owner Mary Hogan. The rest of the gruesome remains in the house had been scavenged from the local cemetery. For years following the death of his mother, Gein had been slipping into the Plainfield cemetery at night and robbing graves.

THE RUINS OF ED GEIN'S HOME AFTER THE FIRE ON MARCH 20, 1958.

For months after Ed was taken away, neighbor boys threw rocks, and locals peered into the windows of his abandoned farmhouse. Eventually, notice was posted that the contents of the house and the farm itself would be auctioned off. The townspeople were in an uproar about the bad publicity, but there was nothing to be done about it – or so some people thought.

Then, on the night of March 20, 1958, Ed's home mysteriously caught fire and burned to the ground. Arson was suspected, but no one cared. The people of Plainfield were just delighted to see it gone.

By the time Ed Gein died in July 1984, he had become a ghoulish legend. He was buried in the Plainfield Cemetery – the same place where he'd done his nocturnal grave robbing for years – and not surprisingly, souvenir-seekers chipped away pieces of his gravestone. What was left was stolen in 2000, and while the stone was eventually recovered, his grave has been unmarked ever since.

But Ed's story didn't end there.

THE 1974 FILM, *THE TEXAS CHAINSAW MASSACRE*, WAS LOOSELY BASED ON SOME OF GEIN'S CRIMES – AS WAS THE 1960 FILM, *PSYCHO*

In 1957, author Robert Bloch read about the discoveries at the Gein family farm when they hit the newspapers. He was living a short distance from Plainfield at the time. Using the little detail that he gleaned from the news stories, Bloch wrote his seventh book in only six weeks.

It told the story of a young man named Norman Bates who, like Ed Gein, was obsessed with his mother and lived in a small town where he seemed normal enough not to raise too much suspicion.

Left out of Bloch's story were the gruesome souvenirs and furniture that were found in the farmhouse and Ed's woman suit – which would have never been acceptable in a novel of the time.

Those things were also left out of the movie version of the book when *Psycho* was made into a film by Alfred Hitchcock in 1960. The film starred Anthony Perkins as Norman and changed movie history with its depiction of the seemingly normal man with a terrible secret.

Since that time, the story of Ed Gein has inspired books, songs, documentaries, plays, comic books, and even a musical. It has also inspired two other horror films, although in very different ways.

In 1974, Tobe Hooper wrote, produced, and directed *The Texas Chainsaw Massacre* – a film that follows a group of friends who fall victim to a family of cannibals while on their way to visit an old homestead. The film was marketed as "based on a true story" to attract a bigger audience and to act as a social commentary on the political climate of the day. However, the character of Leatherface and the gruesome décor of the Sawyer farmhouse was pure Ed Gein -- including the skin mask, the lamp shades, furniture from human bones, and more.

The suit made from a woman's skin appeared as a major plot point in 1991's *Silence of the Lambs*. Adapted from a novel by Thomas Harris, it stars Jodie Foster as Clarice Starling, a young FBI trainee who is hunting a serial killer dubbed "Buffalo Bill" because he skins his female victims to create a new body for himself as a woman. Of course, she seeks the advice of Dr. Hannibal Lecter -- played by Anthony Hopkins -- a brilliant psychiatrist and cannibalistic serial killer, which overshadows the Ed Gein stuff in the plot, even though it's definitely still there.

The story of Ed Gein seems to be here to stay, but the same can't really be said for the notorious "Ed Gein Death Car."

THE AUCTION AT THE GEIN FARM BROUGHT OUT SEVERAL THOUSAND PEOPLE WHO WANTED TO SEE THE ITEMS BEING OFFERED. HOWEVER, FEW OF THOSE WHO CAME WERE THERE TO BID ON ANYTHING.

THE SUSPICIOUS FIRE THAT DESTROYED ED GEIN'S FARMHOUSE didn't put a stop to the auction that was scheduled for March 30 – or the bad publicity that his crimes brought to Plainfield.

On the day of the auction, thousands of people showed up, although only a few of them were there to enter bids. Most were the morbid curious, just there to watch the show.

On the dirt roads leading to the farm, the local sheriff and his deputies did their best to keep cars moving. One of Ed's neighbors posted a sign on his property offering parking for 25 cents per car, but most of the tourists just parked wherever they wanted on Eddie's land.

Deputies put up a snow fence around the ruins of the burned house, but that didn't stop people from pressing up to it so they could get a closer look or from walking off with dirt, bricks, and ashes as souvenirs.

A company named Farm Sales Service from Reedsburg handled the auction. They had printed inventory lists and distributed them all over the state. Without all of Eddie's gruesome souvenirs, the contents of his household seemed unexceptional – the kind of stuff offered for sale at any country auction. There were stoves, cupboards, pots and pans, dishes, beds, couches, a sewing machine, lamps, radios, family albums, rugs, a carpet sweeper, and several antique pieces of furniture from Augusta's room.

There were also various pieces of farm equipment and machinery – several plows, a rake, a manure spreader, a mower, and more. Eddie's 1940 Chevrolet pickup truck and his 1949 Ford Sedan were also being offered for sale.

The farm itself was being offered in either one or two separate parcels, including the nine-room house, barn, granary, chicken coop, corn crib, machine shed, and 40 acres of farmland. The second parcel was the remaining 155 acres of land, which had no buildings on them.

On the surface, it seemed like an ordinary farm auction – and it would have been if it wasn't offering items for sale that belonged to Wisconsin's most infamous ghoul, Eddie Gein.

Plainfield junk dealer Walter Golla bought most of Eddie's rusted old farm equipment, including a plow for $14, a disk and a mower for $9 each, and a manure spreader for $35 bucks.

The remaining pieces of scrap iron went to Chet Scales of Chet's Auto Wreckers, who hauled them away with his other major purchase – Eddie's 1940 pickup truck, which he'd bought for $215. Other bidders left with piles of lumber, old plowshares, wagon wheels, the iron stove, and more.

The farm itself – all 195 acres of scrub pine and sandy soil, plus the burned house and the five rundown outbuildings – was sold to Sun Prairie real estate developer Emden Schley for just over $3,800.

Within months, he demolished the outbuildings, planted more than 60,000 trees on the land, and effectively erased all traces that the farm had ever existed. The locals couldn't have been happier.

The only surprise of the afternoon – which would prove to be an unwelcome surprise – was the sale of Eddie's maroon Ford sedan. It was the car he'd been driving on the afternoon of Bernice Worden's murder.

When it came up in the auction, it set off a bidding war with 14 people competing for it. In the end, it sold for the remarkable sum of $760 to a mysterious buyer who was identified variously as "Coke Brothers," "Cook Brothers," and "Kook Brothers," from Rothschild, Wisconsin. Why anyone would pay that much money for a beat-up, nine-year-old car was both troubling and puzzling to Plainfield residents.

But the mystery was quickly solved – much to their dismay.

THE TENT FOR ED GEIN'S DEATH CAR ON DISPLAY AT CARNIVALS

The mysterious buyer turned out to be a fictional identity used by a sideshow exhibitor named Bunny Gibbons of Rockford, Illinois. Bunny had already done well on carnival midways with a car allegedly

A 1949 FORD SEDAN – THE SAME MAKE AND MODEL AS THE CAR THAT WAS DRIVEN BY ED GEIN BUT THIS IS **NOT** GEIN'S CAR. NO KNOWN PHOTOGRAPHS OF THE CAR THAT WAS PURCHASED BY BUNNY GIBBONS EXIST.

once used by bank robber John Dillinger, so when he saw the Gein car being advertised for sale, he took a chance.

After winning the auction, he spruced up the car and added a couple of wax dummies to the exhibit – one of Eddie in the front seat behind the wheel and a mutilated and bloody woman in the back.

The "Ed Gein Death Car" made its first public appearance at a county fair in Seymour, Wisconsin, in July 1968. It was displayed there for three days inside a canvas tent that was covered with signs that read:

- SEE THE CAR THAT HAULED THE DEAD FROM THEIR GRAVES!
- YOU CAN READ ABOUT IT IN LIFE MAGAZINE – IT'S HERE!
- ED GEIN'S CRIME CAR! $1,000 REWARD IF IT'S NOT TRUE!

There were also signs showing a man dragging a casket out of a grave, another depicting a woman about to be hit in the head with a board, and at the top of the tent, three skull and crossbones flags waved in the breeze.

More than 2,000 people paid a quarter each that weekend for a peek at the death car. Within days, though, news of the exhibit had spread across the state, setting off a major controversy. Plainfield people were mad. Local parents were angry, claiming the car was emotionally damaging their kids. Representatives from the Wisconsin Association for Mental Health protested the car display, saying that it presented a negative view of mental health issues.

Bunny Gibbons was, of course, thrilled by the outrage. He laughed it off and told a reporter, "People want to see this kind of thing." He even promised that one day he was going to play Plainfield. He didn't, and in fact, even skipped the county fair in the neighboring county because he didn't want to stir up the locals.

But even in other parts of the state, he ran into trouble. At the Washington County 4-H Club Fair in Slinger, the car had only been on display for a few hours before the sheriff arrived and ordered Bunny to pack up his tent. Soon, fairs across the state were banning the show. Bunny, grumbling about this turn of events, had no choice but to head south for the fairgrounds in Illinois, where he hoped people would be a little less touchy about the subject of Eddie Gein.

Soon after that, however, both Bunny Gibbons and the death car disappeared from history. What happened to the car remains a mystery today.

THE END
THE FAT LADY IS SINGING NOW

A LOT HAS CHANGED ON THE CARNIVAL MIDWAY IN THE LAST 100 years. I'm not sure that I'd say those changes were good, but time marches on, and there isn't much we can do to turn back the clock.

I probably feel about those changes the same way that some people did back when Americans started to have a new attitude toward entertainment in the wake of the 1893 World's Fair. Some people probably hated the new ideas that emerged in those days, but for the rest of us, we were thrilled when entertainment no longer had to be "educational" – it could be enjoyed just for the fun of it. By the end of World War I, going to fairs, carnivals, amusement parks, tent circuses, and hundreds of other distractions had become part of normal life in America.

But it couldn't last forever. Nothing good ever does.

In those days, carnival visitors viewed the shows and attractions with a healthy curiosity. These days – if the midways were still around – we'd run across a two-headed baby and no longer wonder if the baby was alive but wonder if seeing a fake was worth spending 50 cents.

Midway shows, and circuses became so besieged with "political correctness" and false images thrown at us by politicians, well-meaning do-gooders, and animal activists that the sheer fun of the fairgrounds was erased. Audiences began to consider themselves so sophisticated that a sideshow was beneath them. No one would stand in a line in front of a bally stage and get herded into a tent anymore. They'd be too concerned with being seen themselves than being just an observer.

Shows on midway back ends started to thin out in the late 1960s when fairs began demanding higher percentages from carnival owners. The owners passed on the cost to the showmen, who were now paying more than 50 percent of their gross for an exhibit, as well as fees for parking, electricity, garbage pickup, and more.

Today, at most fairs, there are no shows among the rides, games, and food stands – and fairs are much worse because of that. There may be less than two dozen back-end shows still touring the country, even though there are hundreds of fairs and midway dates on the calendar. Of those shows, two or three are tented museums, while the rest are small grind shows with either a single animal or a single human attraction inside. There are a couple of "girl to gorilla" type shows still out there, along with some live magic shows or "sideshows" of people performing strange feats.

After a search, I discovered a handful of grind shows, too – the world's largest and smallest horses, alien bodies, a home in a big tree, and a few other only mildly exciting ones.

Aside from the occasional little person, though, there are no freaks on exhibition anywhere. At some point in the 1960s, staring at freaks became something to be ashamed of. Parents dragged their kids past the last of the freak shows on their way to the fair grandstand to watch the tractor pull or the demolition derby. Girl shows were disappearing from midways at a time when strip clubs and topless bars were flourishing in the "straight" world. Displays of torture items -- and depictions of their use on wax victims – were viewed with the same disgust as gawking at the girl with three legs and the alligator-skinned man.

But political correctness – as it would eventually be called – was not the only thing that killed off the Ten-In-One shows. Even though many people preferred not to stare at freaks anymore, those who still wanted to do so found there wasn't much left to stare at. By the 1970s, all the famous freaks had either retired or passed away – and there just weren't many to take their place.

Infant deformities began to be corrected shortly after birth. The freaks that medical science somehow missed survived on government assistance, which hadn't existed during the heyday of the freak shows. Back then, freak show performers took pride in not being a burden to anyone – the sideshows allowed them to escape from being placed in an institution or a home. The sideshows gave them independence, friends, family, and a way to have a "normal" life.

Just as there were no more freaks to choose from, showmen also found a shortage of working acts. There had once been hundreds of knife-throwers, sword swallowers, and fire eaters, but they soon dwindled to only a few. The talkers disappeared, too. By the 1960s, they had been replaced by tape-recorded spiels, and today, there's no need for them at all.

By the late 1980s, sideshows disappeared almost completely from the circus and carnival midways. A few held on into the 1990s, but as the shows faded, some of us began to realize that we were seeing the last of not only a unique form of show business but also all physical evidence of it. As time has gone by, the signs, banners, and exhibits have found new homes in collections and museum displays.

So, while gone, the circuses and carnivals are gone but not forgotten. I've tried to do my part to keep their memory alive, so I hope that I've succeeded in some small way.

As mentioned at the start of this section of the book, the talkers on the bally during the final days of the sideshows started using the line, "See it now or miss it forever."

Luckily, some of us got to do both. We saw it while we still could, but we're never going to stop missing it.

CARNY GLOSSARY

BABY SHOW
A show that displays preserved babies – usually deformed in some way – in jars filled with formaldehyde.

BACK END
The back section of the standard midway, where all the shows were located.

BALLY
The free show in front of a carnival attraction, meant to hold the crowd while the talker introduces the attraction and urges the crowd to buy tickets.

BANNER
Large canvas painting depicting the various sights to be seen inside the show. Created in various sizes, they were erected on what was called the "banner line" – a series of poles that reached heights of 14 feet or more, making the banners visible from a distance.

BEEF
Customer complaint

BLANK
A place or date where no real money is made, resulting in bad business.

BLOW-OFF
An extra attraction inside a show, usually hidden behind a canvas curtain, for which separate admission is charged.

BOUNCER
A fake rubber baby in a jar.

BULLET
Buzz words like ALIVE or ADULTS ONLY that were painted in brilliant colors on banners and meant to draw customers into the tent.

CONTROLLED GAMES
Games at carnivals where the operators determine the winners and losers. Customer complaints about cheating eventually led to them being banned on most midways – allegedly.

COOCH SHOW
A type of girl show that featured nudity, although most large revue shows featured strippers but not complete nudity.

DING
Any extra charge or additional request for money inside the show.

FIXER
The guy who "fixes" things with the local authorities, usually beforehand, or after when there have been complaints about shady game operations.

FRAME UP
The term used to describe building up a new show.

GAFF
A fake, rigged show attraction. Barnum's Feejee Mermaid is an example of a famous gaff.

GEEK
A performer who worked in pit shows, handling snakes and such. Often portrayed as a wild man, the act was rumored to use old drunks who worked for booze. A variation of the GEEK was the GLOMMER, who bit the heads off snakes, live chickens, and other animals.

GRAB JOINT
A quick food stand on the carnival lot.

GRIFTERS
Name given to pickpockets, short-change artists, and operators of controlled gaming devices. Their operations were referred to as "grifts."

GRIND SHOW
A smaller show that bypassed the usual bally stage approach and operated continuously. Customers didn't stay long, and the TIP was turned over repetitively all day long.

HEAT
Trouble with the law or complaints from disgruntled customers.

HEY RUBE
A physical confrontation between locals and carnies. A call of "Hey Rube!" meant trouble was brewing and that assistance was needed in a hurry.

ILLUSION SHOW
A show that presented an illusion, like the Spider Girl, Headless Girl, or Girl to Gorilla show.

INSIDE MONEY
The money the showman got from sales items, pitches, dings, and blow-offs inside his show, as opposed to the ticket box money that he had to share with a fair or carnival owner.

LOT
The grounds where the carnival sets up.

LOT LICE
People who hang around the midway but never seem to spend any money.

MARK
The customer or the patron who spends his money on the midway. It was also a term for "sucker," but you have to remember that carnies see themselves as separate from the people who frequent the shows.

MITT CAMP
Carnival fortune teller.

MOOCH BOX
To "mooch" on a show means to beg. This is a term for the donation box at the ding show.

NUT
The amount of cash that it takes to break even each day.

PICKLED PUNKS
A preserved human fetus in a jar.

PIG IRON
A ride attraction, like a Tilt-A-Whirl or Scrambler.

PIT
A sectioned off low canvas divider in which an act or attraction is displayed inside the tent. Often used for a SINGLE-O small animal, geek or illusion show.

PITCH BOOK
A small booklet sold by various freaks and sideshow performers. Early ones were multi-page biographies. The term also referred to any booklet sold – or pitched – inside a show.

PRIVILEGE
The money paid to the carnival owner for the opportunity to play on his lot.

RIGHT HAND SIDE
Since it's believed that most people will naturally gravitate to the right side of the midway, this became a desirable location for independent operators.

ROUTE
The lineup of dates and locations played by a carnival.

SINGLE-O SHOW
A show on the midway with just one exhibit of attraction inside.

SPOT
A date or location played.

TALKER
The person who did the talking or the spiel outside of a show. They were never referred to as a TALKER, except by people who didn't know any better.

TEAR DOWN
Breaking down a show for travel to the next spot.

Ten-In-One SHOW
A sideshow presentation with 10 acts in one tent. It was a basic sideshow operation for many years.

TIP
The crowd that gathers in front of the bally to see the free show – a show, by the way, during which nothing really happens – to entice paying customers into the tent.

WALK THROUGH
A show in which the customers "walk through" and look at the exhibit as opposed to sitting or standing and having a show performed for them.

BIBLIOGRAPHY

Adams, Rachel - *Sideshow USA*, Chicago, IL, University of Chicago Press, 2009

Albracht, Ernest - *The New American Circus*, Gainesville, FL, University of Florida Press, 1995

Axelrod, Alan - *The Gilded Age*, New York, NY, Sterling, 2017

Badger, R. Reid - *The Great American Fair: The World's Columbia Exposition and American Culture*, Chicago, IL, Nelson Hall, 1977

Barnum, P.T. - *Barnum's Own Story: The Autobiography of P.T. Barnum*, Mineola, NY, Dover Publications, 2017

Barth, Tack, Doug Kirby, Ken Smith, and Mike Wilkins - *Roadside America*, New York, NY, Fireside, 1986

Bogdan, Robert - *Freak Show: Presenting Human Oddities for Amusement and Profit*, Chicago, IL, University of Chicago Press, 1990

Bondeson, Jan - *A Cabinet of Medical Curiosities*, New York, NY, W.W. Norton, 1997
------------------ - *The Lion Boy and Other Medical Curiosities*, Stroud, Gloucestershire, UK, Amberly Books, 2018

Bradna, Fred A. - *The Big Top: My Forty Years with the Greatest Show on Earth*, New York, NY, Simon and Schuster, 1952

Brett, Mary and Stevan Gould - *Freaks of Sideshows and Film*, Atglen, PA, Schiffer Books, 2015

Castner, James L. – *Shrunken Heads: Tsanta Trophies and Human Exotica*, Gainesville, FL, Feline Press, 2002

Chindahl, George L. – *A History of the Circus in America*, Caldwell, ID, Caxton Press, 1959

Christopher, Milbourne – *The Illustrated History of Magic*, New York, NY, Thomas Y. Crowell, 1973

Comerford, Michael Sean – *American Oz: An Astonishing Year Inside Traveling Carnivals at State Fairs and Festivals*, U.S., Comerford Publishing, 2020

Cross, Gary S. – *Freak Show Legacies*, New York, Ny, Bloomsbury, 2021

Crowe, Richard and Carol Mercado – *Chicago's Street Guide to the Supernatural*, Oak Park, IL, Carolando Press, Inc., 2000

Culhane, John – *The American Circus*, New York, NY, Holt, 1990

Dadswell, Jack – *Hey There, Sucker*, Boston, MA, Bruce Humphries, 1946

Daly, Michael – *Topsy*, New York, NY, Atlantic Monthly Press, 2013

Davis, Janet M. – *The Circus Age: Culture and Society Under the American Big Top*, Chapel Hill, NC, University of North Carolina Press, 2002

Demaris, Kirk – *Mail-Order Mysteries*, San Rafael, CA, Insight Editions, 2011

Dennet, Andrea Stulman – *Weird and Wonderful: The Dime Museum in America*, New York, NY, University Press, 1997

Drimmer, Frederick – *Very Special People*, New York, NY, Amjon Publishers Inc., 1973

Fadner, Frederick – *The Gentle Giant: The Biography of Robert Pershing Wadlow*, Roswell, GA, Whipporwill Publication, 1981

Feiler, Bruce – *Under the Big Top: A Season with the Circus*, New York, NY, Scribner, 1995

Fiedler, Leslie – *Freaks: Myths and Images of the Secret Self*, New York, NY, Simon and Schuster, 1978

Fleming, Candace – *The Great and Only Barnum*, New York, NY, Schwartz and Wade, 2009

Funnell, Charles E. – *By The Beautiful Sea: The Rise and High Times of That Great American Resort Atlantic City*, New York, Ny, Knopf, 1975

Geyer, Celesta and Samuel Roen – *Diet or Die: The Dolly Dimples Weight Reducing Plan*, New York, NY, Frederick Fell Publishers, 1968

Gresham, William Lindsay – *Monster Midway*, New York, BY, Rinehart, 1948

Hammer, Carl and Gideon Rosker – *Freak Show*, San Francisco, CA, Chronicle, 1996

Hartzman, Marc – *American Sideshow*, New York, NY, Penguin, 2005

Hornberger, Francine – *Carny Folk: The World's Weirdest Sideshow Acts*, New York, NY, Citadel Press, 2005

Huang, Yunte – *Inseparable: The Original Siamese Twins and their Rendezvous with American History*, New York, NY, Norton, 2018

Hunter, Jack – *Freak Babylon: An Illustrated History of Teratology and Freak Shows*, New York, NY, Creation Books, 2010

Jay, Ricky – *Learned Pigs and Fireproof Women*, New York, NY, Warner Books, 1986

Johnson, Randy, Jim Secreto, and Teddy Varndell – *Freaks, Geeks & Strange Girls: Sideshow Banners of the Great American Midway*, Honolulu, HI, Hardy Marks, 1995

Joys, Joanne Carol – *The Wild Animal Trainer in America*, Boulder, Co, Pruett, 1983

Kasson, John F. – *Amusing the Millions: Coney Island at the Turn of the Century*, New York, NY, Hill & Wang, 1978

Kirby, Irwin, with Lou Dufour – *Fabulous Years: A Showman's Tale of Carnivals*, World's Fairs, and Broadway, New York, NY, Vantage, 1977

Kunhardt, Jr., Phillip B., Phillip B. Kunhardt III, and Peter Kunhardt – *P.T. Barnum, America's Greatest Showman: An Illustrated Biography*, New York, NY, Knopf, 1995

Leonard, Maurice – *People From the Other Side: The Enigmatic Fox Sisters and the History of Victorian Spiritualism*, Stroud, Gloucestershire, UK, History Press, 2008

Levenson, Randal – *In Search of the Monkey Girl*, New York, NY, Apeture, 1982

Lewis, Arthur – *Carnival*, New York, NY, Trident, 1970

Lilliefors, James – *America's Boardwalks: From Coney Island to California*, Brunswick, NY, Rutgers University Press, 2006

Lytle, Richard M. – *The Great Circus Train Wreck of 1918*, Charleston, SC, History Press, 2010

MacDougall, Curtis D. – *Hoaxes*, New York, NY, Dover, 1940

Mannix, Daniel – *We Who Are Not As Others*, New York, NY, Simon & Schuster, 1976
-------------------- - *Step Right Up!* New York, NY, Harper Brothers, 1950

Martin, Howard – *Victorian Grotesque*, London, UK, Jupiter, 1977

Meislas, Susan – *Carnival Strippers*, New York, NY, Farrar, Straus and Giroux, 1976

Mifflin, Margot – *Bodies of Subversion: A Secret History of Women and Tattoo*, Brooklyn, NY, Powerhouse Books, 2013

Miller, Sarah – *Violet and Daisy: The Story of Vaudeville's Famous Cojoined Twins*, New York, NY, Schwartz and Wade Books, 2021

Nassaw, David – *Going Out: The Rise and Fall of Public Amusements*, New York, NY, Basic Books, 1993

O'Nan, Stewart – *The Circus Fire: A True Story*, New York, NY, Doubleday, 2000

Osterud, Amelia Klem – *The Tattooed Lady: A History*, Golden, Co, Speck Press, 2009

Pilat, Oliver and Jo Ransom – *Sodom by the Sea: An Affectionate History of Coney Island*, New York, NY, Doubleday, 1941

Ray, Fred Olen – *Grind Show*, Hollywood, CA, American Independent Press, 1993

Register, Woody – *The Kid of Coney Island: Fred Thompson and the Rise of American Amusements*, New York, NY, Oxford University Press, 2001

Rosen, Fred - *Lobster Boy: The Bizarre Life and Brutal Death of Grady Stiles Jr.*, New York, NY, Open Road Media, 2015

Silverman, Stephen M – *The Amusement Park*, New York, NY, Black Dog and Leventhal, 2019

Skidgell, Michael – *The Hartford Circus Fire: Tragedy Under the Big Top*, Charleston, SC, History Press, 2014

Sloan, Mark, Roger Manley, and Michelle Van Parys – *Dear Mr. Ripley: A Compendium of Curiosities from Believe It or Not! Archives*, Boston, Ma, Little Brown, 1993

Standiford, Les – *Battle for the Big Top*, New York, NY, PublicAffairs, 2021

Stencell, A.W. – *Circus and Carnival Ballyhoo*, Toronto, ON, Canada, ECW Press, 2010
---------------- - *Girl Show: Into the Canvas World of the Bump and Grind*, Toronto, ON, Canada, ECW Press, 1999
---------------- - *Seeing is Believing*, Toronto, ON, Canada, ECW Press, 2002

Tattersall, Ian and Peter Nevraumont – *Hoax: A History of Deception*, New York, NY, Black Dog and Leventhal, 2018

Taylor, James and Kathleen Kotcher – *James Taylor's Shocked and Amazed: On and Off the Midway*, Guilford, CT, Globe Pequot, 2002

Thompson, C.J.S. – *Giants, Dwarves, and Other Oddities*, New York, Citadel, 1968

Wakefield, Nathan – *The Rise and Fall of the Sideshow Geek: Snake Eaters, Human Ostriches, and Other Extreme Entertainments*, Outside Talker Press, 2023

Wallace, Irving – *The Fabulous Showman: The Life and Times of P.T. Barnum*, New York, NY, Knopf, 1959

Watkins, T.H. – *The Great Depression: America in the 1930s*, New York, NY, Little Brown, 1993

West, Rick – *Pickled Punks and Girlie Shows: A Life Spent on the Midways of America*, Atglen, PA, Schiffer Books, 2011

Wilson, Robert – *Barnum: An American Life*, New York, NY, Simon and Schuster, 2019

Woolf, John – *The Wonders: The Extraordinary Performers Who Transformed the Victorian Age*, New York, NY, Pegasus Books, 2019

SPECIAL THANKS TO

April Slaughter: Cover Design
Becky Ray: Editing
Samantha Smith
Athena & the "Aunts" - Sue, Carmen & Rocky
Orrin and Rachel Taylor
Rene Kruse
Rachael Horath
Bethany Horath
Elyse and Thomas Reihner
John Winterbauer
Cody Beck
Trey Schrader
Tom and Michelle Bonadurer

Lydia Rhoades
Cheryl Stamp and Sheryel Williams-Staab
Joelle Leitschuh and Tonya Leitschuh
Scott and Hannah Rob
Victoria & Reese Welch
Dave and Donna Nunnally
And the entire crew of American Hauntings

ABOUT THE AUTHOR

Troy Taylor is the author of books on ghosts, hauntings, true crime, the unexplained, and the supernatural in America. He is the founder of American Hauntings Ink, which offers books, ghost tours, events, and the Haunted America Conference, as well as the creator of the American Oddities Museum in Alton, Illinois.

He was born and raised in the Midwest and divides his time between Alton, Illinois and wherever the wind decides to take him. See Troy's other titles at: www.americanhauntingsink.

www.ingramcontent.com/pod-product-compliance
Lightning Source LLC
Chambersburg PA
CBHW070945160426
43193CB00012B/1805